Business Analysis with QuickBooks®

Business Analysis with QuickBooks®

Conrad Carlberg

WILEY

Wiley Publishing, Inc.

Business Analysis with QuickBooks®

Published by
Wiley Publishing, Inc.
111 River Street
Hoboken, N.J. 07030
www.wiley.com

Copyright © 2010 by Wiley Publishing.

Published by Wiley Publishing, Inc., Indianapolis, Indiana

Published simultaneously in Canada

ISBN: 978-0-470-54314-6

Manufactured in the United States of America

10 9 8 7 6 5 4 3 2 1

For general information on our other products and services or to obtain technical support, please contact our Customer Care Department within the U.S. at (800) 762-2974, outside the U.S. at (317) 572-3993 or fax (317) 572-4002.

Wiley also publishes its books in a variety of electronic formats. Some content that appears in print may not be available in electronic books.

Library of Congress Control Number: 2009937272

Trademarks: Wiley, the Wiley logo, and related trade dress are trademarks or registered trademarks of John Wiley & Sons, Inc. and/or its affiliates in the United States and other countries, and may not be used without written permission. All trademarks are the property of their respective owners. Wiley Publishing, Inc. is not associated with any product or vendor mentioned in this book.

Colophon: This book was produced using the Berkeley Oldstyle typeface for the body copy and titles, and using Optima for the caption text.

For Tabben

Credits

Acquisitions Editor
Stephanie McComb

Editorial Manager
Robyn B. Siesky

Vice President &
Executive Group Publisher
Richard Swadley

Vice President and
Executive Publisher
Barry Pruett

Business Manager
Amy Knies

Marketing Manager
Sandy Smith

Technical Editor
William H.B. Murphy

Cover Design
Michael Trent

About the Author

Conrad Carlberg has authored, coauthored, and contributed to more than 15 books about business analysis, quantitative forecasting, and database management. For several years, Carlberg has developed applications for use with QuickBooks in concert with Microsoft Excel, Word, and SQL Server.

He received a PhD from the University of Colorado, where he specialized in inferential statistics. Carlberg lives near San Diego, where he shares a home with two female cats, one of them well over five feet tall.

Acknowledgments

I would like to thank Stephanie McComb, senior acquisitions editor at Wiley Publishing, for taking control of this project and seeing it through from early concept to publication. And this book's technical editor, an MBA and Certified QuickBooks ProAdvisor who I was very fortunate to find — people, give it up for Bill Murphy.

Contents

Contents

Contents

Introduction

Business Analysis with QuickBooks is all about getting more bang for your QuickBooks buck. Now, I grant you: The QuickBooks software itself is a bargain. Although QuickBooks has some real drawbacks (such as letting the user sell more inventory than is apparently on hand), when you buy QuickBooks you get a functional accounting package with a friendly user interface at a remarkably low price. So how much buck is there to get bang from?

Well, consider how much time you spend putting data into QuickBooks. You often need to record a sales receipt for a cash or credit card sale. You should prepare an invoice for every sale in which you extend credit terms. You need to record your accounts payable, all your payroll expenses, and the payments you make to vendors. You need to keep your item lists up to date. You may need to do periodic physical inventories and record adjustments as required. You need to record customers' payments in Undeposited Funds and then make the necessary deposit transactions.

In fact, if you use QuickBooks conscientiously to record the company's transactions and to obtain routine reports of business activity, it's likely that you spend an appreciable amount of time navigating its windows, forms, and user interface generally. Why not spend just a little more time to arrange extra payback for that investment? One great way to claim that payback is by analyzing all that very specific data — the sales receipts and invoices and payments and investments and cost of goods sold and so on — in the aggregate. Doing so can tell you a lot about the business that might not have been apparent.

You've probably already explored some of the built-in reports that come with your QuickBooks software, and you already know the categories: Company & Financial, Customers & Receivables, Sales, and so on. Many of these reports are indispensable for managing the business and for providing accurate data to the IRS, to your lenders, and to your investors.

The balance sheet reports may tell you that you have $50,000 in total current assets. The P&L reports may tell you that you incurred $25,000 in payroll expenses during the prior accounting period. You need to report those figures to people and agencies that have a legitimate interest in the company's finances. But by themselves they're just numbers. Without a context to interpret them, they do not help you understand whether the company is profitable, whether it is likely to continue to be profitable, and how it goes about creating profit.

If you delve into the mysteries of modifying QuickBooks reports, you find that you can get some of that context. You can compare the company's accounts with those from an earlier period. You can compare one product line with another: how they stack up as measured by both their revenues and their costs.

Introduction

You can combine a report's numbers in ways that give you insight into a company's current financial status and its management's priorities. The methods a company uses to create and spend working capital can tell you about management's tolerance for financial and operational risk, and whether or not the results justify the management's strategies.

You can even compare a small business's pattern of sales and expenses to those of a Fortune 500 company. You do need to know where to look, and how to make the numbers commensurate; after all, you don't learn much by comparing apples to bowling balls.

Not all of these capabilities are evident when you scan the list of reports that the QuickBooks menu shows you. You can find out much more about how to use those reports in this book. Part I, "Exploiting Your QuickBooks Data," covers both the basics and the finer points of getting data out of QuickBooks and into an analysis package such as Microsoft Excel.

QuickBooks is an accounting and bookkeeping application. It's not a financial analysis package, and it was never designed to be one. There are some valuable analyses that you can carry out without leaving the comfortable surroundings of the QuickBooks user interface, but if you want to use tools such as ratio analysis, quality control, and true quantitative forecasting, you have to give yourself some elbow room. You have to go outside.

The one numeric analysis application that's almost certain to be found on the same local drives or servers as QuickBooks is Microsoft Excel. If you have a way to get your carefully entered revenue and expense data out of QuickBooks and into Excel, then you're perfectly positioned to take advantage of all Excel's analysis functions, from data-driven sales forecasts to working capital analysis to contribution costing.

Fortunately, QuickBooks' reports, when exported, do an excellent job of laying out your data for analysis by other applications. If you set up the reports right, perhaps even if you prepare custom reports, the QuickBooks output conforms beautifully to the data layouts required for more informative analysis. You do need to know the best methods for getting the data out of QuickBooks, and how to manage it properly once it's been exported. Again, you'll find all that covered in Part II, "Analyzing Financial Statements," and Part III, "Controlling Costs and Planning Profits."

The QuickBooks Software Development Kit, or SDK, is a freebie from Intuit. You do need to download it from an Intuit site, but once you have your hands on it, you can bend QuickBooks to your will. Change the way QuickBooks calculates the average cost of inventory items. Base an item's default sales price on its average cost rather than some arbitrary figure, possibly one that's out of date, on the item record. Have QuickBooks run a whole series of reports for you every month, just by clicking a button in an Excel worksheet or a Word document.

The best part is that most of the work required has already been done for you. The SDK has 200 collections of procedures, all of them precoded for you, that extract data from QuickBooks, that add or delete or modify existing records, that customize and modify reports, and so on. Those procedures put the data in your hands; all you have to do is decide what you want to do with it, and provide a little Basic code to complete what you have in mind.

Much has been written about the QuickBooks SDK, but very little light has been shed. The final two chapters of this book remedy that. See Part IV, "Designing Your Own Analysis with the Development Kit."

Who This Book Is For

Suppose you use QuickBooks to record information about income and about the costs you incur to produce income. Periodically, you send your company file to your accountant or enrolled agent, who sends it back to you with the required adjusting journal entries, and sometimes with the required tax forms. If that's all you want QuickBooks to do, you don't want this book. Save your money and use it to pay your accountant.

But if you own or help operate a small business and you want to get more value from the time you spend entering data into QuickBooks, know that I wrote this book largely for you. You don't need to be a programmer (although towards the end of the book you'll find that a little programming experience can help). You don't need a CPA or an MBA to interpret the results of the analyses you find in this book. You'll see how to do very basic, standard financial and management analysis of the data in your QuickBooks file — analysis that will help you better understand your company's financial status today, and where your company's history says it's going.

If you're an accountant or an enrolled agent with clients who use QuickBooks, much of the material in this book is probably old hat to you. (Although I do know a very fine enrolled agent who until recently had never heard of a common-sized income statement.) But some of your clients could benefit from the information. You don't want them phoning to ask you how to calculate a quick ratio. Give them this book and then go spend your time on the high-margin jobs.

Conventions Used in This Book

Before I begin showing you the ins and outs of using QuickBooks for analysis, I need to briefly review the terms and conventions used in this book for working with software programs.

The commands that you select by using the program menus appear in this book in normal typeface. When you choose some menu commands, a related dropdown appears. If this book describes a situation in which you need to select one menu, and then choose a command from a secondary menu or list box, it uses an arrow symbol. For example, "Choose Edit ▶ Preferences" means that you should choose the Preferences command from the Edit menu.

Some QuickBooks capabilities are accessed through keyboard shortcuts comprised of two keystrokes. If you're supposed to press two keys at the same time, I indicate that by placing a plus sign (+) between them. So, Ctrl+Q means press and hold the Ctrl key as you press the Q key. Then release them.

Part I

Exploiting Your QuickBooks Data

Using QuickBooks to Analyze Business Data

How did you happen to start using QuickBooks? If you're like most of us, you picked it up because you needed an inexpensive way to do bookkeeping. Maybe you saw an ad on TV or some Web site, or a friend told you about it, or your accountant recommended it.

However QuickBooks first appeared on your computer screen, you probably noticed a few of its characteristics before you bought:

■ And QuickBooks is not merely a bookkeeping application with some T-accounts and a P&L thrown into the mix. It really is an accounting package. Maybe it's not MAS 90, but you do get actual income statements, balance sheets, inventory histories, and so on: the records needed to back up tax returns and loan applications.

But does QuickBooks provide enough tools? That depends on how much you want to get from the application. If all you want or need is to record your revenues and costs so that your accountant can complete your company's tax filings, you're probably all set. There's not much else you need, and my first and only suggestion for you would be to put this book back on the bookstore shelf. (The top shelf would be nice. Thank you.) On the other hand …

The first textbook on accounting I ever saw was Meigs and Meigs' *Accounting*. What really struck me about it was its subtitle: *The Basis for Business Decisions*. For me, that subtitle suddenly took the whole notion of accounting out of the realm of sleeve garters and green eyeshades, columns of boring numbers, and stultifying trial balances. The idea that you could actually *use* those numbers to make better decisions about a business was more than just a pleasant surprise. I won't say it was an epiphany, but it was pretty cool.

That book went on to show how a business owner or manager could make some very smart moves based on the numbers just sitting there in the journals and statements prepared by the accountant. Those numbers are available to you, too. You just need to know how to get at them and, once you have your hands on them, what to do with them.

It's a little ironic that a software package that makes it easy to enter data makes it kind of tough to get information out, but that's the case with QuickBooks. Thus, it's the purpose of this book to show you how you can get your hands on the informantion that you might have already broken your fingers typing in.

Advantages and Drawbacks to QuickBooks Reports

If you can arrange to get QuickBooks to handle all your financial analysis for you, you're ahead of the game. After all, analyzing the data using other software means that either you have to enter the data twice, or you have to arrange to get the numbers out of QuickBooks and into the other package.

Either task can be error-prone or time-consuming, and sometimes both. There are ways — ways that this book explains — to minimize the errors and the time involved, but you can't eliminate them completely. That's why predesigned reports, as well as reports that you create and tell QuickBooks to memorize, can be so useful. The numbers never have to leave the program.

This book, and its first two chapters in particular, go into the topic of reports in QuickBooks in detail. The reason is not that the structure and function of QuickBooks reports are intrinsically interesting. Quite the opposite.

Nevertheless there are several reasons to become familiar with QuickBooks reports:

So QuickBooks reports have great value for business analysis. It pays to understand the tools QuickBooks gives you to fine-tune the 225 canned reports you see in the Reports menu of the Accountants Edition — and the 138 reports in the Pro Edition.

After all this coverage of the advantages to using QuickBooks reports to get at your data, I need to point out the disadvantages — if only to maintain some credibility:

Most quantitative reports in QuickBooks (that is, reports that do something more than just listing customer names) are simple totals meant to answer typical, everyday, important questions: What's today's balance in current assets? How many cabinet pulls did we sell last month? What was third quarter's net income? You can also dig up a relatively sophisticated average if you look hard. (Hint: Check the inventory valuation reports.)

But just try to find a current ratio in the Reports menu. An inventory turns ratio. The available working capital. Any one of scores of indicators accountants and other business analysts use to gauge the financial health of a company. They aren't in the reports. Oh, every so often Intuit brings out something such as the Financial Statement Designer or the Intuit Statement Writer, tools that will calculate that kind of quantitative analysis. But it's only the high-end editions that come with those tools — and they don't seem to stick around long anyway.

So if you want to get your hands on that kind of analysis, you won't find it in a QuickBooks report. The raw material is there, though, so the answer for most of us is to export the reports to an analysis package such as Excel or a database that acts as a front end to other analytic engines. QuickBooks provides tools to support that export, and Chapter 2 goes into the mechanics of exports in some detail. Still, most people would consider it a drawback that you might find it necessary to export a report to Excel to get an inventory turns ratio, instead of finding it right in a QuickBooks report.

There are other problems involved in exporting QuickBooks reports. Again, Chapter 2 covers these problems at greater length. Briefly, though, if you want to use an application such as Excel to do more sophisticated analysis than QuickBooks supports, you need to be working with individual records: for example, a list of all the sales receipts the company created last quarter. You don't want subtotals and totals interspersed among the underlying transactions. But that's what you get with most QuickBooks reports, and so there's inevitably some pruning to do before you can get down to the business of quantitative analysis.

On balance, the advantages to QuickBooks reports well outweigh their drawbacks. The next section gives you a leg up in understanding some of the reports' finer points.

Understanding QuickBooks reports

If you seldom work with QuickBooks reports other than looking over an income statement or balance sheet from time to time, you might be surprised at how much good information you can find in them.

It's true that, unless you've spent years as an accountant, numbers in a financial statement are not going to jump off the page and compel you to run a complete physical inventory before you create even one more invoice. You need to know what to look for and where to look for it — and that's information you'll find in subsequent chapters.

Still, you should also know about some of the tools you can bring to bear in built-in QuickBooks reports. You need the tools to answer questions that are important to you, but might not have occurred to the report designers at Intuit. There are standard types of financial analysis covered in depth in later chapters in this book, such as ratio analysis and working capital analysis.

But there are nonstandard kinds of questions that every business owner and accountant asks, which no built-in QuickBooks report is designed to answer. For that, you need to know some basics regarding QuickBooks reports. In particular:

Types of QuickBooks reports

Most reports in QuickBooks are either summary reports or detail reports. As the terms suggest, a detail report provides very specific information and allows you to see that you sold 50 linear feet of PVC to Kay Evans on 9/28/2010 for $19.48 in cash.

By contrast, a summary report rolls that specific information into categories that tell you, for example, that you sold $556.23 worth of PVC in September. A record in a summary report totals across customer names, method of payment, cash or credit, and other bits of data that, taken together, distinguish one detail record from another.

From the perspective of business analysis, the summary and the detail are the most useful reports available in QuickBooks, and this book has much more to say about using them to help figure out where a business has been and where it should go. For clarity, though, I mention a third type of report, which calls out the members of different lists.

The term *list* is overworked in QuickBooks, because it can mean a set of data consisting of, for example, customer names, customer addresses, phone numbers, jobs, and so on. In this way it acts like what a database user would think of as a table. Or a list can be a simple enumeration of categories, such as types of transaction (invoices, sales receipts, bill payments, paychecks, and so on).

QuickBooks has a variety of reports whose purpose is not to associate dollar amounts with a particular transaction or customer or inventory item, but to show you the current contents of a given list. So the customer phone-number list report by default shows you two fields in the customer list, name and phone number. The Account Listing shows you the names, numbers (if used), type, description, balance, and tax line for each defined account. No transaction information, whether summarized or detailed, is in the listing reports.

Bear in mind that QuickBooks uses the terms *summary report*, *detail report*, and *list report* somewhat loosely. There are several summary reports that don't include the word summary in their name, and the same is true for detail and list reports. And some reports that have the word *List* in their name are actually detail reports (for example, Transaction List by Date). You can generally tell a true list report by double-clicking a line in the report. If you get an Edit Item dialog box, it's a true list report. If you get something such as a Sales Receipt dialog box that enables you to edit a specific transaction, it's a detail report. And if double-clicking a line in the report opens a detail or transaction report, you're working with a summary report.

Because this book is primarily about using QuickBooks data for quantitative analysis, it has little to say about true list reports.

Deciding between using a summary report and a detail report

Quite a few QuickBooks reports come in two flavors: Summary and Detail. There are several differences between a summary and a detail report. This section gives you a brief overview of those differences, using QuickBooks' Rock Castle Construction sample file as a basis.

Showing transactions

If you open, say, the Sales by Customer Summary report, you see information about each of your customers and, if present, separate jobs within each customer. For example, you'll see the total sales dollars for Kristy Abercrombie's Family Room job, Remodel Bathroom job, and Other job. The customers and jobs may or may not appear depending on whether they experienced any sales activity during the period covered by that report.

But if you open the Sales by Customer Detail report, you'll see not only customer and job records in the summary report but also the individual transactions: every invoice, sales receipt, and credit memo transaction for that job, within that customer, within the date range used in the report.

Accounting basis

All summary and detail reports can be based either on the accrual method or the cash method. The difference is in the applicable dates. Under the accrual method, a transaction's date is defined by the date that a sale was made or an expense incurred. Under the cash method, the transaction date depends on the date that the revenue was received or the payment made.

You can specify the method you want to use in any individual summary or detail report. Click the report's Modify Report button and select Accrual or Cash on the Display tab.

For summary reports *only*, you can set a default basis. Choose Edit Preferences Reports & Graphs and click the Company Preferences tab. Choose your preference in the Summary Reports Basis area and click OK. Whichever option you chose will now be the default for summary reports. You can of course override that default in summary reports that you create later.

This option is not available for detail reports. If you want to change the basis of a detail report you have to do so after it is created, by way of the Modify Report button.

Collapsing a report

Some detail reports enable you to partially suppress details. This is called *collapsing* the report and you do that using the Collapse button at the top of the report. That button is a toggle, so a collapsed report has an Expand button instead of a Collapse button.

The detail reports that can be collapsed and expanded include the general ledger, profit-and-loss detail, balance sheet detail, journal, and transaction detail by account.

For example, if Timberloft Lumber sends you a bill for both rough and trim lumber, each item occupying a different line on the bill, both lines (and their amounts) appear in an expanded Profit & Loss Detail report. They would be combined on one line with the total amount in a collapsed report. When two or more lines are collapsed into one, text fields that have different values (such as the Memo field) show "MULTIPLE."

Even in collapsed mode a detail report shows you each transaction. Because most summary reports don't show individual transactions, they have no Expand or Collapse capability. A limited number of summary reports, such as the Profit & Loss Standard and Balance Sheet Standard can be collapsed to condense subtotals.

Selecting columns

The QuickBooks Help documents say that you can add or delete columns in a detail report, implying that you cannot do so in a summary report. It is true there can be more than seventy columns to choose from and show in a detail report.

But there are columns you can choose to display or suppress in a summary report. One type of column is a *subcolumn*. Suppose you open a Balance Sheet Summary report to view account balances as of the end of the current period. A subcolumn can display, for example, the prior period's dollar amounts, or the current period amounts expressed as a percent of the prior period. There are other subcolumn types available.

Summary reports also enable you to see a different column for each value of a field you select. Suppose you decide to show totals by Vendor. The Profit & Loss Standard report (a summary report, despite its name) shows income and expense accounts in rows, and if you choose to show totals by Vendor it also shows the income or expense amount for each different vendor in columns. Other fields you can use to create columns in a summary report include Class, Item (both detail and type), Job within Customer, Employee, and various date spans such as Two Week and Half Month.

Filtering reports

Summary and detail reports provide a means of limiting the records used. You can always establish a date range for the report in the report itself, by means either of the Date dropdown or the From and To edit boxes. Other selection criteria are available through the Modify Report button.

Clicking Modify Report and then clicking the Filters tab gives you access to a Filter list box. Use the list box to select one or more fields you want to use as a criterion to include or exclude certain records from the report. The criteria tend to apply specifically to transactions (such as invoices, or bills, or sales receipts), and there are about 50 fields you can use as transaction filters in a Balance Sheet Detail or Profit & Loss Detail report. Other reports that focus on lists, such as the Item Listing, have their own filters that pertain directly to the list in question.

More detailed information about using the record filter in reports appears later in this chapter. If you're not interested right now in a tutorial on using the QuickBooks record-filtering mechanism, there's no need to bother with it at present. For the time being it's sufficient to be aware that record filters are available, and that you can filter on more than one field at the same time (for example, you could limit a report to all transactions involving the customer Kristy Abercrombie and the item Wood Door Exterior).

Balance sheets and income statements

The two fundamental financial reports, whether you're using QuickBooks or a paper-and-pencil ledger system, are the income statement (or Profit & Loss) and the balance sheet. The reason they're so important is that, accurately and conscientiously prepared, they can paint an informative picture of the company for a creditor or an investor.

They also form the basis of most business decisions the company makes. For example, there are strict rules you must follow as to structuring an income statement as supporting documentation for a tax return, for a bank loan, or an initial public offering. But you can structure an income statement in a variety of different ways when you use it as an internal decision-making tool, to press a sales team in a more demanding direction or to get a swollen inventory back under control. Used as a management tool, the form of an income statement should follow its function.

Therefore the remainder of this chapter explains how you can control the display of the balance sheet and the income statement using different options in QuickBooks. The concluding section looks at inventory reports as an example of how you can manage the contents of more specialized QuickBooks reports.

Using a report's Display tab

The Display tab appears when you click a report's Modify Report button. It is where you control much of a report's content: that is, what columns you want it to display, what its rows are to represent, and what subcolumns should be included. You can also adjust the date range for the report in the Display tab, without having to go back to the report to use its Dates dropdown or its From and To edit boxes.

Balance sheets

Figure 1.1 shows a Balance Sheet Summary report.

FIGURE 1.1

The balance sheet shows a snapshot of asset and liability accounts as of a particular day.

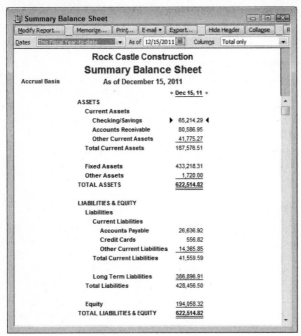

FIGURE 1.2

The appearance of the Display tab varies depending on the type of active report.

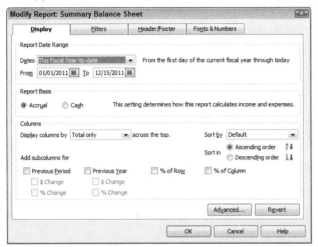

The balance sheet shown in Figure 1.1 uses the framework you'll see if you open the Balance Sheet Summary report using any company file. Only the major divisions within the assets and the liabilities-and-equity sections appear; no accounts or subaccounts and certainly no individual transactions. It's seldom that you can modify the detail level of the information in the rows of a summary report (see the previous section "Collapsing a report"), but you do have some control over what appears in its columns.

> **TIP** Notice in Figure 1.1 that the date and time the report was prepared do not appear, although the default configuration of any QuickBooks report calls for that information. To suppress it in all reports, as is done throughout this book, choose Edit Preferences Reports and Graphs. Click the Company Preferences tab and then click the Format button. Clear the Date Prepared and the Time Prepared checkboxes, and then OK your way out of the Preferences dialog box. Now the date and time prepared is suppressed on all reports you subsequently create.

Figure 1.2 shows the Modify Report dialog box. Its Display tab appears when you click any report's Modify Report button.

Several controls in the Modify Report dialog box interact to determine what you see in a balance sheet report. Of course you decide which control settings you want to use, and this section shows you which choices to make in order to get the display you want.

Using the Dates dropdown

Both the report itself and the Modify Report dialog box have dropdowns that enable you to control the report's Dates. Both dropdowns have the same effect on the report, and the choice of which one to use is purely a matter of which you find more convenient. If the report itself is active and you just want to change the range of dates, use the report's dropdown. If you're using the dialog box to make several changes to the report, it's probably more convenient to use the dialog box's dropdown.

Use the Dates dropdown to establish a range of dates for the report. If you prefer, you can use the From and To edit boxes to establish a range based on particular dates, but if you want to use something such as Last Fiscal Year-to-date, it's probably easier to use the Dates dropdown. The dropdown offers a variety of choices that it would take you a little more time to duplicate using the From and To boxes. The choices available in the Dates dropdown are:

The range of dates you establish does not necessarily have an effect on the appearance of the report, whether it's a balance sheet, a profit-and-loss report, or another type of report. The range of dates determines which transactions QuickBooks will use to populate the report: only those whose transaction date falls within the range of dates you choose.

A balance sheet shows balances as of a specific date. That date always includes the latest in the range of dates you select (and depending on which other options you select, earlier dates might also appear). So changing the range of dates from, say, This Quarter-to-date to This Year-to-date has no effect on which is the latest date in the range of dates.

If you opted to display only one date, therefore, extending the range of dates so that it begins on an earlier date has no effect on the appearance of the balance sheet report.

Using the Columns dropdown

Like the Dates dropdown, the Columns dropdown is found both in the report itself and in the Modify Report dialog box. However, in the dialog box, the dropdown is labeled Display Columns By. Again, which dropdown you use is a matter of your convenience.

In general, the Columns dropdown tells QuickBooks how it should slice up the range of dates. If you've chosen a year for the range of dates and then choose Quarter for the report's columns, you'll get a column for each quarter in the year.

The columns do not venture beyond the limits of the date range. For example, if you choose a date range of one week, say from December 9 through December 15, and then choose to have each column represent a month, you'll get one column only, for December 15. Any earlier quarter is outside the date range you established.

You can select any of the following time slices from the Columns (or the Display Columns By) dropdown:

For example, if you use the default value for Display Columns By, which is Total Only, then the balance sheet report's appearance will not differ when you select different date ranges such as This Quarter-to-date or This Month-to-date. Again, the balance sheet shows account balances as of a particular date. Regardless of the range of dates you select in the Dates dropdown or what you enter in the dialog box's From and To edit boxes, the balance sheet report shows account balances in the report's As Of date.

The Total Only option for columns is special, largely because it's the only option that does not specify a particular time slice. It shows you only one column, which displays the balances for the final day in the date range you selected. For example, if the current date is December 15, 2011, and you choose Next Fiscal Year from the Dates dropdown and Total Only from the Columns dropdown, you will see the balances as of December 15, 2012.

In most cases, though, if you have chosen a sufficiently wide range of dates, your choice in the Columns dropdown provides additional information in the balance sheet. Suppose that you establish 1/1/11 to 12/15/11 as the report's date range. If you now choose Quarter from the

FIGURE 1.3

Notice that the Columns dropdown selects Quarter instead of the default Total Only.

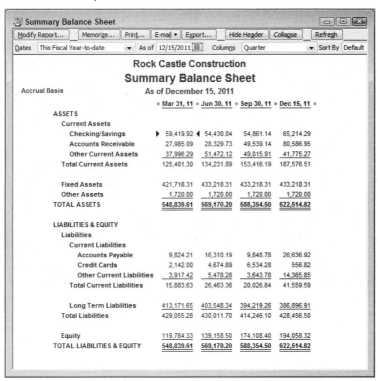

Display Columns By dropdown, and if there is data to display within the date range, you'll see the balance sheet amounts as of the end of each quarter within that range. See Figure 1.3 for an example.

Compare Figure 1.3 with Figure 1.2, and notice that both figures have a Dates dropdown. Both dropdowns have the same choices as shown immediately prior: Total Only, Day, Week, and so on. The report shown in Figure 1.3 has an As Of edit box (as does every balance sheet report), and its function is identical to the To edit box in the Modify Report dialog box shown in Figure 1.2.

> **TIP** Other report types, such as Profit & Loss, have a From and To edit box (instead of As Of) in the report itself. If you use one or both of them to alter the report's date range, be sure to tell QuickBooks to fetch different data by clicking the Refresh button.

FIGURE 1.4

A Previous Period or Previous Year subcolumn might pre-date the Dates range you specified.

Rock Castle Construction
Summary Balance Sheet
As of December 15, 2011

Accrual Basis

	Dec 15, 11	Dec 31, 10	% Change
ASSETS			
Current Assets			
Checking/Savings	65,214.29	53,191.19	22.6%
Accounts Receivable	80,586.95	21,249.39	279.2%
Other Current Assets	41,775.27	38,536.97	8.4%
Total Current Assets	187,576.51	112,977.55	66.0%
Fixed Assets	433,218.31	421,718.31	2.7%
Other Assets	1,720.00	1,720.00	0.0%
TOTAL ASSETS	622,514.82	536,415.86	16.1%
LIABILITIES & EQUITY			
Liabilities			
Current Liabilities			
Accounts Payable	26,636.92	13,100.00	103.3%
Credit Cards	556.82	530.00	5.1%
Other Current Liabilities	14,365.85	72.18	19,802.8%
Total Current Liabilities	41,559.59	13,702.18	203.3%
Long Term Liabilities	386,896.91	421,675.06	-8.3%
Total Liabilities	428,456.50	435,377.24	-1.6%
Equity	194,058.32	101,038.62	92.1%
TOTAL LIABILITIES & EQUITY	622,514.82	536,415.86	16.1%

Showing subcolumns

The term *subcolumn* in QuickBooks is misleading. I say that because there are other structures in QuickBooks that use the *sub* prefix appropriately. Two good examples are subaccounts and subitems. A subaccount is subordinate to, or nested within, a parent account. A subitem is subordinate to a parent item. You don't find a subaccount associated with two different parent accounts, even though subaccounts may have similar, even identical names.

Reports have subcolumns, but they are in no sense subordinate to a parent column. Don't be misled by the terminology into expecting subcolumns to behave the way you see subaccounts behave. A subcolumn in a report is simply a column that helps you put its associated column in context.

There are two types of subcolumn: Previous Period and Previous Year. Each type can appear as either dollars or percent change, or both. Figure 1.4 has one column and two subcolumns.

Compare the information shown in Figure 1.4 with that in Figure 1.1. The only difference is that the user has called for subcolumns in Figure 1.4. Now the report shows:

So in Figure 1.4, the Checking/Savings balance on December 15, 2011, is 22.6% greater than the Checking/Savings balance on December 31, 2010.

The user arranged for the subcolumns by filling, in the Modify Report dialog box, the Previous Period checkbox and its associated % Change checkbox (see Figure 1.2). The Previous Period checkbox calls for the dollar balances headed "Dec 31, 10" in Figure 1.4. The % Change checkbox calls for the percentages subcolumn.

Compare the information shown in Figure 1.4 with that in Figure 1.1. The only difference is in the context of a report, a *period* is whatever you have selected in the Columns dropdown in the report or, equivalently, in the Display Columns By dropdown in the Display tab (refer to Figure 1.2).

Notice that the report shown in Figure 1.4 establishes the date range as This Fiscal Year-to-date. As to *columns*, that means you won't see a column header dated earlier than the start of the current fiscal year. But subcolumns aren't subject to the specified date range. For example, if you choose This Quarter-to-date as your date range, you won't get a column for a date earlier than the start of the current quarter. If you also call for a prior period or prior year subcolumn, it will pre-date the start of the current quarter.

The final date in the date range is special. There will always be a column associated with that date in a balance sheet report. If you call for a previous period subcolumn, the date for that subcolumn is not the final day in the previous period, but instead is exactly one period prior to the final date in the date range.

Suppose the final date in the date range is December 15 and you have chosen to show Quarter in columns. Then the subcolumn associated with December 15 is for September 15, exactly one quarter earlier. By contrast, the same report might also have a column for the quarter ending September 30; that column is associated with a subcolumn for the quarter ending on June 30.

Percent of Row and Percent of Column

Two more checkboxes in the Modify Report dialog box for balance sheets are % of Row and % of Column. The data they display is the basis of what are called comparative balance sheets (or, more generally, comparative financial statements). Each checkbox adds a subcolumn to a report. The % of Row checkbox is most useful when you are comparing one period's results with another's (see Figure 1.5).

The percentages give you a quicker grasp of the company's performance over the three-year time span than do the raw dollar amounts. It's heartening to see that the increase in shareholders' equity outstrips the growth in total liabilities, which is actually negative, declining by 16% from the first though the third year.

FIGURE 1.5

You can see that the company's position is improving year to year by comparing percentages.

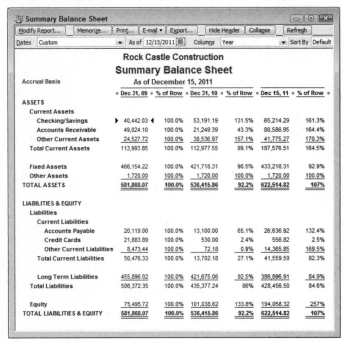

To get this report, take these steps:

1. Open a Balance Sheet Summary report and click the Modify Report button.

2. Click the From button and enter 1/1/2009 to get a three year report ending in December 2011. You can't call for this span of time using the Dates dropdown.

3. Choose Year from the Display Columns By dropdown.

4. Fill the % of Row checkbox and click OK.

The one aspect of this report that departs slightly from traditional practice is its use of the first year for all comparisons. That is, to get a percent change for 2010 over 2009, a 2010 value is divided by its corresponding 2009 value. So far that's standard practice. But for 2011, QuickBooks also divides a 2011 value by its corresponding 2009 value.

There's nothing really wrong with that comparison, but it's somewhat nonstandard (standard practice would be to divide 2011 values by 2010 values) and thus potentially confusing to an audience. Further, it tends to be more immediately informative to see change between consecutive years than nonconsecutive years.

FIGURE 1.6

The divisor for each line is Total Assets (or, equivalently, Total Liabilities & Equity).

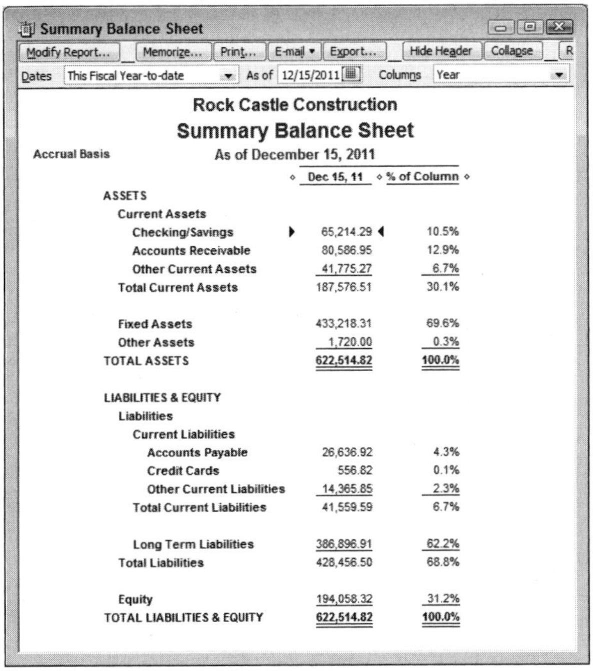

Summary Balance Sheet

Modify Report... | Memorize... | Print... | E-mail ▾ | Export... | Hide Header | Collapse | R

Dates: This Fiscal Year-to-date | As of 12/15/2011 | Columns: Year

Rock Castle Construction

Summary Balance Sheet

Accrual Basis — As of December 15, 2011

	Dec 15, 11	% of Column
ASSETS		
Current Assets		
Checking/Savings	65,214.29	10.5%
Accounts Receivable	80,586.95	12.9%
Other Current Assets	41,775.27	6.7%
Total Current Assets	187,576.51	30.1%
Fixed Assets	433,218.31	69.6%
Other Assets	1,720.00	0.3%
TOTAL ASSETS	622,514.82	100.0%
LIABILITIES & EQUITY		
Liabilities		
Current Liabilities		
Accounts Payable	26,636.92	4.3%
Credit Cards	556.82	0.1%
Other Current Liabilities	14,365.85	2.3%
Total Current Liabilities	41,559.59	6.7%
Long Term Liabilities	386,896.91	62.2%
Total Liabilities	428,456.50	68.8%
Equity	194,058.32	31.2%
TOTAL LIABILITIES & EQUITY	622,514.82	100.0%

Figure 1.6 shows a balance sheet for one year only, with a subcolumn for % of Column.

Even a highly abbreviated summary report such as the balance sheet shown in this chapter can tell you quite a lot about a business's financial status, especially if it includes % of Column data as in Figure 1.6. A quick glance at the percentages for Total Current Assets and Total Current Liabilities tells you that the company's current ratio is over 4.0, its equity ratio is 31.2% (see Chapter 6), and their dollar amounts tell you that the company has about $140,000 in working capital (see Chapter 5).

You might want to enrich the information a bit and have a look at how the percentages differ from one year to the next. To do so, just click the report's Modify Report button and change the From date to a year earlier — in this example, you'd change it from 1/1/2011 to 1/1/2010. With Year selected in the Display Columns By dropdown, Figure 1.7 shows what you'd get.

The news in Figure 1.7 is still good, but it helps you focus on one or two items that you might want to look at more carefully. In particular, the component percentage for current liabilities has increased from 2010 to 2011, from 2.6% to 6.7%. Much of that is due to the increase in accounts payable and that's a normal pattern for a startup. But there's a big jump

FIGURE 1.7

This view of the balance sheet is not as cheery as that in Figure 1.6.

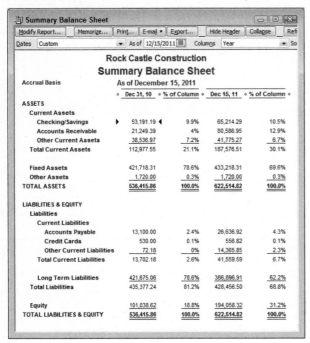

in other current liabilities as well, and you should probably inquire about the reason for that jump.

There's an important conceptual difference between the kind of information presented in Figure 1.5 and that in Figure 1.7. They are both summary balance sheets and both show how component percentages change over time. However:

The % of Row view, in Figure 1.5, shows the rate of growth or decline in a given dollar measure, over time. The % of Column view, in Figure 1.7, shows the rate of growth or decline in a given measurement's *relative importance* over time. They're both important indicators, but they speak to different issues.

Modifying the Balance Sheet Detail report

Detail reports in QuickBooks answer the same kind of questions as the corresponding summary reports, but they present the underlying information in a radically different fashion. Detail reports show each transaction that occurred in an account (or with a customer, or a vendor, or an item, and so on) during a particular time period, whereas summary reports roll up the transactions and the unit of analysis becomes the account (or customer, vendor, or item).

Because the unit of analysis in a detail report is the transaction, there are many fields available for use in a detail report that are not available in a summary report. You can choose to display any of those fields as a report column, and you can use any of them as a data filter.

Just as with the Balance Sheet Summary report, you access the options to modify the display of a detail report by clicking the report's Modify Report button. The Display tab for the Balance Sheet Detail report appears in Figure 1.8.

There are 40 columns available in the Balance Sheet Detail report and you show any of them simply by clicking on it. You cannot get subcolumns such as prior period or prior year in a detail report because the report's unit of analysis is the transaction: it makes no sense to ask what the value of a transaction was in a prior period.

Different detail reports have different columns available (although the Balance Sheet Detail and the Profit & Loss Detail reports offer the same set of 40 columns). Most of the column names are self-explanatory, but two shown in Figure 1.8 deserve mention:

■ The fields you use as columns in detail reports can also be used as filters, and you tell QuickBooks which data to select for the report by means of the Filters tab in the Modify Report dialog box. You can make good use of filters in most detail reports, usually because you want to structure an ad hoc inquiry. For example, if you wanted to view all the inventory transactions that involved an adjustment to an item's quantity on hand, you could open the Inventory Valuation Detail report and use its filters to limit the transaction types to Inventory Adjustments.

There are remarkably few reasons you would want to use a filter in a Balance Sheet Detail report. Again, the purpose of that report is to give you a snapshot of account balances while displaying information about the individual transactions that brought the balances about. Only in an extremely unusual situation would you want to exclude, say, invoices that have been paid from the balance sheet.

FIGURE 1.8

In detail reports, Columns replace subcolumns.

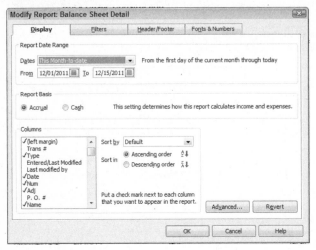

The Profit & Loss report

Figure 1.9 shows a Profit & Loss Standard report.

A balance sheet shows how much money is in a given account at a specific *point* in time. By contrast, a profit and loss statement (often termed an *income statement*) shows how much money has entered a given account over a specific *period* of time.

Subcolumns in the Profit & Loss Standard report

The Display tab of the Modify Report dialog box for the Profit & Loss Standard report is not quite the same as the Display tab for a balance sheet report. Compare the Display tab in Figure 1.10 with that shown in Figure 1.2.

There are additional subcolumns available for the Profit & Loss Standard report that do not appear in a balance sheet report. This report's default date range is This Month to Date. It's convenient, then, that you should be able to fill the Year-To-Date checkbox in the Display tab and obtain a subcolumn that shows the year-to-date figures in dollars, and optionally in percentages. That makes for an easy comparison of your current month's results with your results so far this year.

Of course, you can get the identical report by selecting Profit & Loss YTD Comparison from the Reports menu in the first place.

You'll want to take a little more care in using the other four subcolumns, % of Row, % of Column, % of Income, and % of Expenses. At least understand why you might as well ignore the % of Row and % of Column options.

FIGURE 1.9

The Profit & Loss Standard report is actually a summary report.

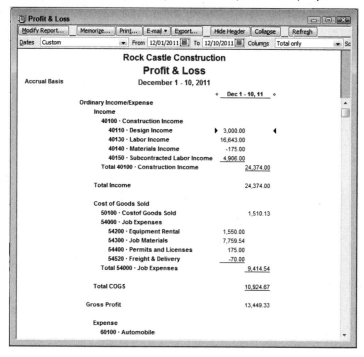

The % of Row option is useful only if you use the Columns dropdown to arrange for more than one range of dates, such as months or quarters within an overall date range of, say, a year. If you do so, the report will show both the dollar amounts for each time period and their percent of the account total. You will not see a percent for a subcolumn, and if you have one column only then all the percentages will be 100%.

The % of Column option is not useful. The basis for the percentages is Net Income: the profit that is left after the cost of goods sold (COGS) and operating expenses have been subtracted from Income (also known as *sales* or *revenue*). With Net Income as the basis, you will see nonsense such as −572.6% in % of Column for Construction Income. (The percentage can be negative if the net income in the report is itself negative.)

Even if the percentage is positive, it's not informative to know that Construction Income is almost six times as great as Net Income. It's much more sensible in a Profit & Loss statement (and it's also traditional) to base column percentages on Income (again, sales or revenue) rather than on Net Income. And that's what the % of Income checkbox gives you (see Figure 1.11).

Many analysts also find it helpful to view expenses as a percentage of total sales, because it shows them how large a claim each expense category makes on the company's revenues. But

FIGURE 1.10

The Profit & Loss Standard report's Display tab adds some options to the Subcolumns area.

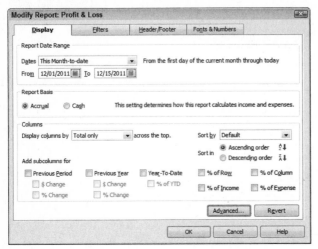

another option in the Display tab, % of Expense, shows more directly each expense category's contribution to total expenses.

It is much less helpful to view income categories as percents of total expenses. Most analysts prefer to view income categories and expense categories as percents of total income, and also to view expense categories as percents of total expenses.

Using the Dates dropdown

Recall that a balance sheet is a snapshot of balances in asset and liability/equity accounts as of a particular date. Even if you arrange to display multiple dates in the report by choosing something such as Month in the Columns dropdown, each column is a snapshot of a particular day.

By contrast, a Profit & Loss report shows income and expense accounts, and it shows cumulative amounts over a period of time. The line for Net Income, for example, shows the dollar amount that entered the Net Income account during the period of time you specify in the Dates dropdown. So when you change the date range from, say, This Fiscal Year-to-date to This Fiscal Quarter-to-date, you are changing the period of time during which amounts can accumulate. The usual result is that the amounts displayed change as the period of time is changed.

Choosing Week from the Columns dropdown results in a report display such as is shown in Figure 1.12.

It's important to be able to display different periods of time in different columns because, when you're analyzing a company's performance with a Profit & Loss report, it's often informative to examine the sources and uses of capital over time. At times you're doing something fairly

FIGURE 1.11

Viewing COGS and sources of income as percents of Total Income helps you gauge how you're creating profits.

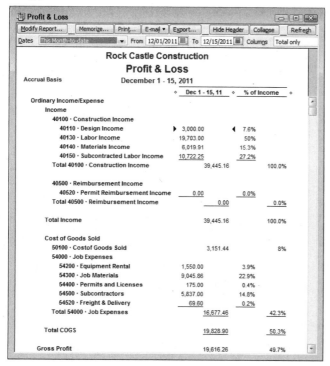

sophisticated with the numbers, such as a quantitative forecast based on weekly results. If not, it usually makes more sense to break the data down by a longer time frame such as month, quarter, or year, and each of those breakpoints are available from the Display Columns drop-down.

Notice in Figure 1.12 that QuickBooks distinguishes a full week from a partial week. The From and To edit boxes together define a time span of 10 days. QuickBooks always begins a week with Sunday in its reports, so the particular 10 days in Figure 1.12 occupy part of one week and all the next. A full week is denoted in the column header by the words *Week of*.

Using report filters

In many software applications, including QuickBooks, the verb *filter* means to exclude some records from a report or other type of analysis. It's an important capability, especially when you want to examine a particular type of report and focus on a specific customer, or item, or transaction type, and so on.

FIGURE 1.12

The date range for a Week column always begins with a Sunday.

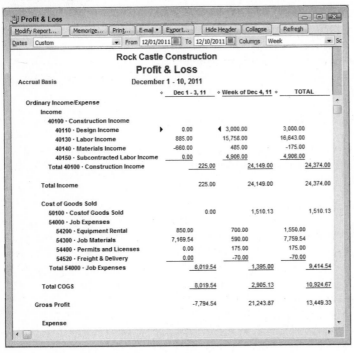

In some ways QuickBooks filters are quite sophisticated and efficient. Still, there are times when they seem to produce more frustration than enlightenment. For example, it's very handy to filter for All Current Assets or All Assembly Items without having to call out each individual current asset account or each assembly item. And by using the Multiple option in a report filter, you can request two or more different instances from the same field simultaneously: for example, Cabinet Pulls and Locking Doorknobs from the Items field, or Accounts Receivable and Undeposited Funds from the Accounts field.

On the other hand, it sometimes seems as though QuickBooks filters have never met the not-equal symbol <>. The analyst cannot filter for all accounts other than current assets, or for all items other than assembly items. Apart from handy groupings such as All Fixed Assets, it can be difficult to create a filter with any real complexity. If you want to apply a filter such as "show all inventory items and all noninventory parts and nothing else," you're better off omitting the filter entirely. You should just report on all records, export the results to another application such as Excel, and use its data filtering capabilities (briefly described at the end of this chapter).

The current section covers report filters and illustrates their use. Because record filters are seldom of real use in a balance sheet or profit-and-loss report, inventory reports are used as a basis for the chapter's examples.

If a company is a manufacturer, wholesaler or retailer, inventory management is crucial to the company's financial status. Inventory often accounts for the majority of current assets, and — as it contributes to COGS — it usually takes the largest bite out of the company's revenues. Therefore, staying informed about the status of inventories is a critical management function. Chapter 7 covers inventory valuation reports in detail.

In QuickBooks, the best way to determine a company's inventory status is by way of the Inventory Valuation Detail and Inventory Valuation Summary reports. In this book, I use them as a basis for describing report filters; because both the detail and the summary report use the same filtering options, the focus is on the Inventory Valuation Detail report. An example of the report itself appears in Figure 1.13.

By default the Inventory Valuation Detail report uses two filters:

The date range is simply a matter of your preference and you can modify it directly in the report as described earlier in this chapter. It is sensible and appropriate to base the report on inventory and assembly items only, because indictors such as quantity on hand and average cost cannot properly be applied to, for example, discounts or fixed assets.

Selecting a single instance from a field

Suppose you wanted to limit the report to one item only, such as Cabinet Pulls. A specific item such as Cabinet Pulls is an instance of the Item field. To select that instance only, take these steps:

1. Open the Inventory Valuation Detail report.
2. Click the Modify Report button and then click the Filters tab.
3. Item is already in use as a filter, so you can click Item either in the Choose Filter list box or in the Current Filter Choices list box.
4. A new dropdown labeled Item appears next to the Choose Filter list box. Use the dropdown to select Cabinet Pulls, as shown in Figure 1.14.
5. Click OK to apply the filter to the report. The result is shown in Figure 1.15.

If you want to add another field from the list of available filters, repeat steps 1 through 5, being sure to select a filter not already listed in the Current Filter Choices list box. If you select a filter that's already selected, you will merely replace one instance of that filter with another — for example, Cabinet Pulls with Locking Doorknobs. Selecting multiple instances of the same field is covered next.

FIGURE 1.13

As usual in detail reports, each record represents a specific transaction. (For space reasons, I have removed some of the columns that appear by default in an Inventory Valuation Detail report.)

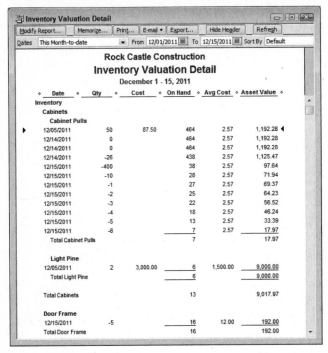

Selecting multiple instances of the same field

Getting a filter to return more than one instance from a field is only a little more complicated than selecting one instance only. Suppose you wanted to examine the inventory valuation for both Cabinet Pulls and Locking Doorknobs. Begin as you would if you wanted to select one instance only, taking steps 1 through 3 earlier. In step 4, select Multiple Items in the Item dropdown.

You generally find Multiple Items as the second instance shown in the dropdown. As soon as you click it, the Select Item dialog box appears as shown in Figure 1.16.

Just click any instances of the field — here, Cabinet Pulls and Locking Doorknobs — from the field — here, Item — that you want to filter on. Then OK your way back to the report, which will now appear as in Figure 1.17.

FIGURE 1.14

Notice the checkmark immediately to the left of a selected item.

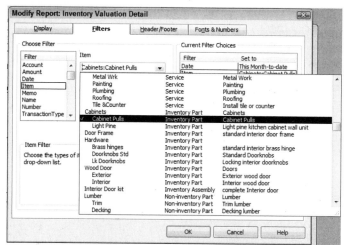

FIGURE 1.15

A positive number in the Qty column normally indicates a purchase to inventory; a negative number normally indicates a sale from inventory.

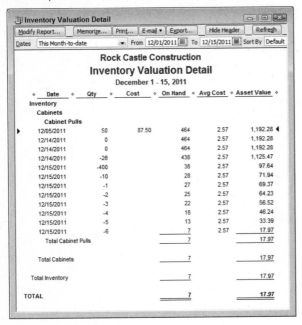

FIGURE 1.16

The name of the dialog box is Select Item, but you can select more than one in its list box.

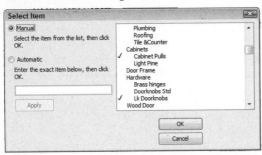

FIGURE 1.17

Only the bottom portion of the report appears here, and only the Cabinet Pulls and Locking Doorknobs items enter the report.

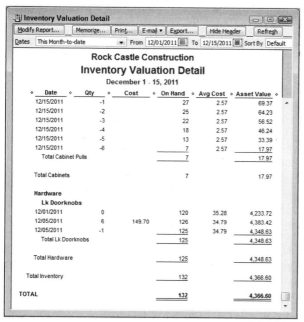

Excel as an Adjunct to Report Analysis

Suppose you've decided, for reasons such as applying more complex filters than are available in QuickBooks, to get the data out of QuickBooks and into another program for analysis. Two excellent choices for that other program are Excel and Access. This book explains how to get the detailed information out of QuickBooks and into other programs in Chapter 2. For now, this chapter outlines some of the reasons you'd want to do so and introduces some of the ways to do it.

Excel started life as a pure spreadsheet application, something Microsoft tossed into the market in an effort to compete with existing applications such as Lotus 1-2-3 and VisiCalc. You can even see Excel's heritage in its eccentricities. For example, one of Excel's depreciation functions uses a constant to calculate depreciation. The constant is rounded to three decimals. It is an artifact of the memory and calculation constraints that applied during the 1980s, and it miscalculates accumulated depreciation by about $2.50 on an asset costing $12,000 over a five-year period.

My point is not that Excel has a quirk. All software has quirks. My point is that Excel has been proving itself in financial and business analysis ever since it was released in 1985. And Excel has a long list of tools you can use on QuickBooks data to get a better handle on what's going on with your business. Before taking a quick look at that toolbox, here's an overview of how you can pipe your report data from QuickBooks to Excel.

Exporting reports

Exporting is probably the quickest way to go from QuickBooks to Excel (or, for that matter, any application that can read files from your working disk). It's also the dirtiest. When you have a QuickBooks report open — a P&L or a Sales by Item Summary — you can move its data to a new text file, to an Excel workbook that you've already saved, or to a new Excel workbook.

As you'll see in the next chapter, there are problems with Excel workbooks that are built from exported QuickBooks reports. Among the problems are cell formats that interfere with calculations, outmoded formulas that calculate subtotals and totals, and cell formulas that turn into error values when you try to copy and paste them.

Still, this approach can be very useful if you want a snapshot of what's going on in a business. For example, one measure of a company's health is the *current ratio*, a measure of a company's ability to pay its debts (see Chapter 6 for an explanation of the current and other ratios). The current ratio is simply the ratio of the company's current assets to its current liabilities. A current ratio that's too low suggests that the company might default on existing liabilities — the company's resources are illiquid — whereas too high a ratio might mean the company's resources aren't invested in ways that contribute effectively to its profitability — the resources are *too* liquid.

FIGURE 1.18

You can save the report to a new CSV file or in an Excel workbook.

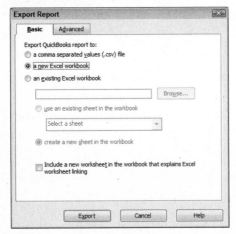

And, because QuickBooks has no built-in report that returns the current ratio, the surest way to get it is to open the Standard Balance Sheet report, export it to Excel, and then put a formula in a worksheet cell that divides the current assets by the current liabilities.

Figure 1.18 shows the QuickBooks dialog box that appears when you click a report's Export button.

Notice that the first option you have is to save the report as a comma-separated values (CSV) file. A CSV file contains nothing but simple text and numbers, and you can open it using Excel, Access, Oracle, Crystal Reports (using the proper connection type), even the lowly Notepad. It's a good way to save a report because it's not cluttered with a lot of formats and formulas you probably don't need. It's a bad way to save a report because you may have a fair amount of work to do after you've opened it.

If you want to save time and effort, and if you're happy to pipe the report data to Excel, just select the A New Excel Workbook option and click OK. Excel will start if it is not already running, and a new workbook will be created that contains your report data in a worksheet. All this is covered in detail in the next chapter.

Manipulating QuickBooks report data in Excel

Once you have the report data exported to Excel, there is a variety of analytic techniques you can apply to the data. For example, if you've exported a Balance Sheet Summary report, you can use Excel to quickly divide current assets by current liabilities and return the current ratio. If you've exported a Profit & Loss Standard report, you can get the operating expense ratio from the total operating expenses and net sales.

FIGURE 1.19

Use the Custom Transaction Detail report to avoid interspersed subtotal lines.

	A	B	C	D	E	F
1	Type	Date	Name	Account	Debit	Credit
2	Check	12/01/2011	Abercrombie, Kristy:Remode	10100 · Checking		711.15
3	Check	12/01/2011	Abercrombie, Kristy:Remode	11000 · Accounts Receivable	711.15	
4	Credit Memo	12/01/2011	Abercrombie, Kristy:Remode	11000 · Accounts Receivable		711.15
5	Credit Memo	12/01/2011	Abercrombie, Kristy:Remode	40140 · Materials Income	660.00	
6	Credit Memo	12/01/2011	State Board of Equalization	25500 · Sales Tax Payable	51.15	
7	Bill	12/01/2011	Fay, Maureen Lynn, CPA	20000 · Accounts Payable		250.00
8	Bill	12/01/2011	Overhead	63610 · Accounting	250.00	
9	Bill Pmt -Check	12/01/2011	Larson Flooring	10100 · Checking		2,700.00
10	Bill Pmt -Check	12/01/2011	Larson Flooring	20000 · Accounts Payable	2,700.00	
11	Check	12/01/2011	Gregg O. Schneider	10100 · Checking		62.00
12	Check	12/01/2011	Gregg O. Schneider	12800 · Employee Advances	62.00	
13	Invoice	12/01/2011	Roche, Diarmuid:Garage rep	11000 · Accounts Receivable	440.00	
14	Invoice	12/01/2011	Roche, Diarmuid:Garage rep	40130 · Labor Income		440.00
15	Invoice	12/01/2011	State Board of Equalization	25500 · Sales Tax Payable	0.00	
16	Bill	12/01/2011	Timberloft Lumber	20000 · Accounts Payable		80.50
17	Bill	12/01/2011	Robson, Darci:Robson Clinic	54300 · Job Materials	45.50	
18	Bill	12/01/2011	Robson, Darci:Robson Clinic	54300 · Job Materials	35.00	
19	Invoice	12/01/2011	Robson, Darci:Robson Clinic	11000 · Accounts Receivable	445.00	
20	Invoice	12/01/2011	Robson, Darci:Robson Clinic	40130 · Labor Income		280.00
21	Invoice	12/01/2011	Robson, Darci:Robson Clinic	40130 · Labor Income		165.00

FIGURE 1.20

Filtering by means of more than one dropdown is equivalent to connecting two conditionals with a logical AND operator.

	A	B	C	D	E	F
1	Type ▼	Date ▼	Name ▼	Account ▼	Deb ▼	Cred ▼
2	(All)	12/01/2011	Abercrombie, Kristy:Remode	10100 · Checking		711.15
3	(Top 10...)	12/01/2011	Abercrombie, Kristy:Remode	11000 · Accounts Receivable	711.15	
4	(Custom...) Bill	12/01/2011	Abercrombie, Kristy:Remode	11000 · Accounts Receivable		711.15
5	Bill Pmt -Check	12/01/2011	Abercrombie, Kristy:Remode	40140 · Materials Income	660.00	
6	Build Assembly Check	12/01/2011	State Board of Equalization	25500 · Sales Tax Payable	51.15	
7	Credit	12/01/2011	Fay, Maureen Lynn, CPA	20000 · Accounts Payable		250.00
8	Credit Card Char	12/01/2011	Overhead	63610 · Accounting	250.00	
9	Credit Memo	12/01/2011	Larson Flooring	10100 · Checking		2,700.00
10	Deposit General Journal	12/01/2011	Larson Flooring	20000 · Accounts Payable	2,700.00	
11	Inventory Adjust	12/01/2011	Gregg O. Schneider	10100 · Checking		62.00
12	Invoice	12/01/2011	Gregg O. Schneider	12800 · Employee Advances	62.00	
13	Item Receipt Liability Check	12/01/2011	Roche, Diarmuid:Garage rep	11000 · Accounts Receivable	440.00	
14	Paycheck	12/01/2011	Roche, Diarmuid:Garage rep	40130 · Labor Income		440.00
15	Payment	12/01/2011	State Board of Equalization	25500 · Sales Tax Payable	0.00	
16	Sales Receipt Sales Tax Paymer	12/01/2011	Timberloft Lumber	20000 · Accounts Payable		80.50
17	Bill	12/01/2011	Robson, Darci:Robson Clinic	54300 · Job Materials	45.50	
18	Bill	12/01/2011	Robson, Darci:Robson Clinic	54300 · Job Materials	35.00	
19	Invoice	12/01/2011	Robson, Darci:Robson Clinic	11000 · Accounts Receivable	445.00	
20	Invoice	12/01/2011	Robson, Darci:Robson Clinic	40130 · Labor Income		280.00
21	Invoice	12/01/2011	Robson, Darci:Robson Clinic	40130 · Labor Income		165.00

If your purpose is to examine individual transactions, or to analyze a subset of transactions, you're well placed if you use a Custom Transaction Detail report and export it to Excel. Figure 1.19 shows that report in an Excel worksheet.

It takes only a couple of commands to get the report data in this layout in Excel — you'll want to delete one nearly blank column and one completely blank row. Now a quick and highly interactive way to manipulate what's displayed is to use Excel's AutoFilter. Select any cell in the populated range and choose Data Filter AutoFilter. Doing so places a dropdown arrow at the top of each column. You can use them singly or in combination to display any subset of records you want. Figure 1.20 shows the data in Figure 1.19 with AutoFilter enabled.

Furthermore, you can select items that do *not* equal one or more values that you specify — just select Custom from the dropdown and choose Does Not Equal as the operator.

AutoFilter is an option that can be enabled from the Advanced tab options of the Export Report dialog box. I recommend that you *not* enable AutoFilter from there; instead, wait until the report is in Excel to enable the AutoFilter.

There are two reasons for my recommendation:

■ The remaining chapters in this book build on this brief introduction to the use of QuickBooks reports for business and financial analysis. Often, you will want to export a report before starting your analysis activities, but this is not always the case — there are times that the QuickBooks report can provide what you're looking for with just a little tweaking of its display.

There is potentially a rich source of information buried in the tables that make up your company file. Reports are often the best way to get at that information, and the next chapter details some powerful and flexible methods for adjusting the reports so that they better meet your needs.

Exporting Data from QuickBooks

To bring a broader array of tools to bear on the data you've entered into QuickBooks, you really need some straightforward ways to make the data available to other applications. Although QuickBooks has various methods you can use to carry out business analysis without leaving its comfortable and familiar user interface, you just can't do it all in QuickBooks. Sometimes you need to send it out.

Exporting Reports to Excel Workbooks

One method you can use to get data from QuickBooks into another application is the export of a report. To export a QuickBooks report is to make its data available to another application such as Excel. As you'll see in this chapter, the information in a report can be placed in an Excel worksheet where you can analyze the data more fully than is possible in QuickBooks.

The very nature of most QuickBooks reports is to summarize data. Even the detail reports have data summaries that provide totals and subtotals for their detail lines.

The summaries can be helpful because they classify values that otherwise you'd have to deal with yourself: COGS (cost of goods sold) versus office supplies, for example. At the same time the summaries can create problems because they often roll up, and therefore repeat, information already in the report in the form of details. Much of the knowledge needed to analyze business data comes from learning what to keep and what to pitch.

IN THIS CHAPTER

Exporting Reports to Excel Workbooks

Formatting and Layout Problems

Exporting to Text Files

Analyzing QuickBooks Data with Pivot Tables

Formatting and Layout Problems

Suppose you want to export an income statement (known to QuickBooks as a Profit & Loss report) from QuickBooks to Excel. There are various reasons you might want to export a report, and perhaps the most typical is so that you can quickly calculate measures such as a Current Ratio or a Times Interest Earned Ratio. Figure 2.1 shows how the QuickBooks report might look.

You start the export process by clicking the Export button at the top of the report. When you do so, the Export Report dialog box shown in Figure 2.2 appears.

The comma-separated values (CSV) option looks like it will take you down a pretty boring road: Saving a report to a simple text file doesn't look nearly as slick as choosing any of the Excel options. But don't ignore the CSV option. Exporting a report in CSV format to a text file can save you plenty of heartburn, especially if you haven't dusted off your Excel skills in a while. See the "Exporting to Text Files" section later in this chapter for more information.

FIGURE 2.1

If you customize the report, your modifications appear in the exported version.

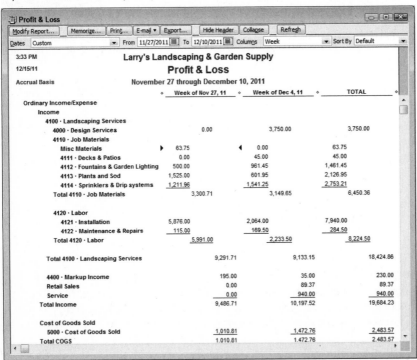

FIGURE 2.2

There are some traps in the Export Report dialog box. Be sure you understand the effects that the options will have on the exported report.

If you want the report to go directly to Excel, you have two principal choices: a new Excel workbook or an existing workbook. If you export to a new workbook, QuickBooks starts Excel if necessary, establishes a new workbook, and places the report data into it.

NOTE The name of the new workbook will be something like Book2, or Book4, or Book6, etc., depending on whether Excel is already open with unsaved workbooks active. New workbooks established by QuickBooks are incremented by 2: Book2, Book4, and so on.

Choosing a new workbook

In the Export Report dialog box shown in Figure 2.2, if you export to a new workbook and click OK, your worksheet will look similar to that shown in Figure 2.3, which is based on the report in Figure 2.1.

There are several ways that you might change the worksheet created by the QuickBooks export:

Naming the worksheet

It would be helpful for QuickBooks to give the worksheet the name of the report it is based on, instead of the nondescript default of Sheet1. I urge you to do that yourself, especially if you intend to store additional reports in the same workbook. To rename the worksheet:

FIGURE 2.3

Report subheadings are indented within their headings by using different columns.

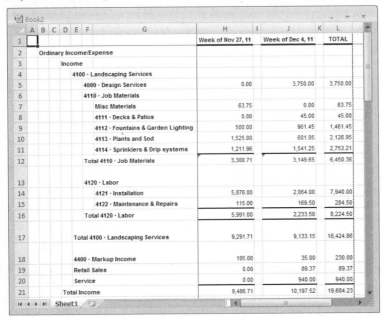

		Week of Nov 27, 11	Week of Dec 4, 11	TOTAL
1				
2	Ordinary Income/Expense			
3	Income			
4	4100 · Landscaping Services			
5	4000 · Design Services	0.00	3,750.00	3,750.00
6	4110 · Job Materials			
7	Misc Materials	63.75	0.00	63.75
8	4111 · Decks & Patios	0.00	45.00	45.00
9	4112 · Fountains & Garden Lighting	500.00	961.45	1,461.45
10	4113 · Plants and Sod	1,525.00	601.95	2,126.95
11	4114 · Sprinklers & Drip systems	1,211.96	1,541.25	2,753.21
12	Total 4110 · Job Materials	3,300.71	3,149.65	6,450.36
13	4120 · Labor			
14	4121 · Installation	5,876.00	2,064.00	7,940.00
15	4122 · Maintenance & Repairs	115.00	169.50	284.50
16	Total 4120 · Labor	5,991.00	2,233.50	8,224.50
17	Total 4100 · Landscaping Services	9,291.71	9,133.15	18,424.86
18	4400 · Markup Income	195.00	35.00	230.00
19	Retail Sales	0.00	89.37	89.37
20	Service	0.00	940.00	940.00
21	Total Income	9,486.71	10,197.52	19,684.23

1. Right-click the tab at the bottom of the worksheet. In Figure 2.3, the tab contains the name Sheet1.

2. Choose Rename from the contextual menu.

3. The worksheet tab is highlighted. Type a new name and press Enter.

TIP You can use up to 31 characters in a worksheet name. If you want to name it *P&L*, you can do so, but you can't use any of these characters: / \ ? * : [ ]

Dealing with error warnings

If you're using Excel 2002 (part of Office XP) or later, you might see a mysterious triangle in the upper-left corner of some cells — for example, cell H12 in Figure 2.3. This triangle is a warning that a cell's contents might not be doing what you intend. The warning usually means that the cell contains a formula that doesn't conform precisely to what Excel expects, and so Microsoft wags its finger at you by way of that mysterious triangle.

If you select the cell, a yellow icon with an exclamation point appears next to it. Clicking that icon reveals a menu, headed by a description of what Excel thinks might be an error.

In the case of an exported QuickBooks report, the potential error (1) isn't an error, and (2) almost always means that a formula omits a value in a neighboring cell. Consider cell H12 in Figure 2.3. That cell contains the formula:

```
=ROUND(SUM(H6:H11),5)
```

This formula tells Excel to take the sum of the values in cells H6 through H11, round the sum to five decimal places, and display the result in the cell that contains the formula. (Not all five decimals appear because the cell's numeric format is Currency. In Excel, a cell's appearance is normally determined more by its format than by its contents.)

QuickBooks is responsible for putting that formula in H12, and it could have done a slightly better job. This formula's purpose is to show you the sum of the dollars associated with Job Materials subaccounts. Those dollar amounts occupy cells H7 through H11, and the formula should really be:

```
=ROUND(SUM(H7:H11),5)
```

As it is, though, Excel notices that cell H5 contains a value, and therefore thinks it is possible that the formula was supposed to include cell H5 in the formula — it's a value in a cell that's adjacent to the cells that the formula sums. So Excel warns you that you might have omitted an important value, and it warns you with that triangle in the upper-left corner of the cell.

You know it's not an error, though, and here are the ways you can deal with the error indicator:

- Ignore it.
- Select the cell with the error indicator. Click the yellow warning icon and choose Ignore Error from the contextual menu. This removes the indicator from the active cell only.
- Select the cell, click the yellow icon, and choose Error Checking Options from the contextual menu. The Excel Options dialog box shown in Figure 2.4 appears. Clear the checkbox labeled Formula Omits Cells in Region and click OK to clear the error indicator, as well as any other instances of the error warning that might be in other cells.

Dealing with the text format

I have been using Excel since the early 1990s, but it still took me around 10 minutes to figure out why a QuickBooks report that I exported to Excel refused to take seriously formulas that I subsequently entered in the worksheet. The following example might save you from wasting the time that I did.

Suppose that you have called for a Profit & Loss Summary report in QuickBooks that has each of two weeks' results in two columns, and their total in a third column. Figure 2.5 shows how the exported report might appear in Excel.

If it's my company, I'd be curious to know how we did in the week leading up to December 4, compared to how we did in the week before November 27. One way to do that is to look at Gross Profit. I'd want to know what percent of the total Gross Profit of $17,200.66 was earned in each of those weeks.

I'd start by entering this formula in cell I25:

```
=H25/L25
```

FIGURE 2.4

To get to the error-checking options in Excel 2007, click the Formulas tab and then click Error Checking in the Formula Auditing group. In earlier versions, choose Tools ▶ Options and click the Error Checking tab.

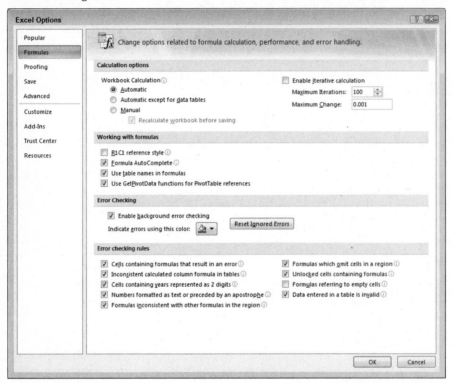

expecting it to return a value of something around 50%. I'd be surprised instead to see this in cell I25:

    =H25/L25

The cell is not evaluating the formula and displaying its result (actually, 49.3%) but merely displaying the formula itself, as though it were a text value such as *Gross Profit*.

This is very unusual behavior for Excel, and at first it took a while to solve. When QuickBooks lays out the new worksheet, it gives a Text format to the cells in the print area that contain neither numeric values nor formulas.

You can do the same thing in Excel by right-clicking a cell, choosing Format Cells from the contextual menu, and choosing Text from the Category list box. If you then enter a formula into the active cell, all you will see is the formula, not its result.

FIGURE 2.5

You can call for or suppress blank intervening columns via the Advanced tab of QuickBooks' Export Report dialog box.

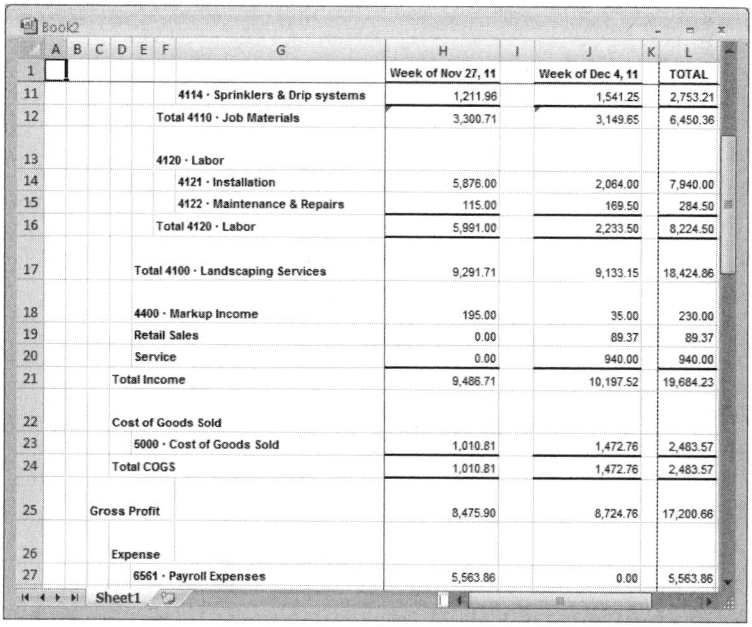

	A B C D E F	G	H	I	J	K	L
1			Week of Nov 27, 11		Week of Dec 4, 11		TOTAL
11		4114 · Sprinklers & Drip systems	1,211.96		1,541.25		2,753.21
12		Total 4110 · Job Materials	3,300.71		3,149.65		6,450.36
13		4120 · Labor					
14		4121 · Installation	5,876.00		2,064.00		7,940.00
15		4122 · Maintenance & Repairs	115.00		169.50		284.50
16		Total 4120 · Labor	5,991.00		2,233.50		8,224.50
17		Total 4100 · Landscaping Services	9,291.71		9,133.15		18,424.86
18		4400 · Markup Income	195.00		35.00		230.00
19		Retail Sales	0.00		89.37		89.37
20		Service	0.00		940.00		940.00
21		Total Income	9,486.71		10,197.52		19,684.23
22		Cost of Goods Sold					
23		5000 · Cost of Goods Sold	1,010.81		1,472.76		2,483.57
24		Total COGS	1,010.81		1,472.76		2,483.57
25		Gross Profit	8,475.90		8,724.76		17,200.66
26		Expense					
27		6561 · Payroll Expenses	5,563.86		0.00		5,563.86

The way to undo this mischief is to select a column whose cells do not now contain numbers or formulas: for example, column I in Figure 2.5. Right-click the column header, choose Format Cells, choose General from the Category list box (you could also choose Percentage or Number if you prefer) and click OK. Now any formula that you enter in the cell will display as its result. If there's already a formula in the cell, click it in the formula box and either press Enter or click the green checkmark icon, to force it to recalculate.

Moving cells with formulas

Skip this section if you consider yourself an experienced Excel user. Otherwise …

From time to time I see a plaintive question in the QuickBooks user forums from someone who tried to copy an exported report into another worksheet. Usually, that other worksheet is intended as a management report of some sort, and someone wants to add information, exported from QuickBooks, to the report. Then, the added information makes no sense.

Notice in Figure 2.6 that the data is captured starting in row 12 of the exported report. The data is intended to appear in row 3 of the target report. Figure 2.7 shows the result of copying cells H12:J12 in the exported report into cells C3:E3 of the management report.

FIGURE 2.6

If you want to copy exported QuickBooks data to another Excel worksheet, convert the formulas to values.

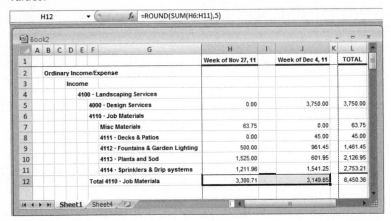

FIGURE 2.7

The formulas are trying to calculate the sums of cells that don't exist.

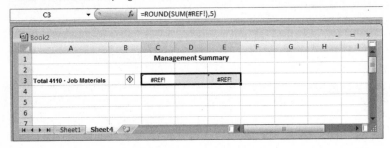

That's an annoying outcome. Here's why it happens, and what you can do about it.

Look at the formula box shown in Figure 2.6 — that's the box located above the workbook, and above specifically columns G and H in the figure. There you'll see that cell H12 contains this formula:

```
=ROUND(SUM(H6:H11),5)
```

You've seen the formula earlier in this chapter, in the section "Dealing with error warnings." The formula's range address includes all the cells from H6 through H11. The formula itself is found in cell H12, so the formula is calling for the sum of the values in the cells that are from one to six rows above H12: H11, H10, H9, H8, H7, and H6.

FIGURE 2.8

The "Formats" in the Values and Number Formats option pertains only to number formats such as currency, not to more broadly defined formats such as boldface and italics.

When you copy cell H12, you are copying its contents, and it contains a formula. When you then paste it into another cell, you are pasting that formula. If you try to paste it into, say, cell C3, you are pasting a formula that calls for the sum of values from one to six rows above the cell that contains the formula. But there aren't six rows above cell C3. Neither are there five rows above it, nor four, nor three.

Pasting a formula that refers to cells that don't exist always results in the #REF! error value, just as shown in Figure 2.7.

Here's the way to manage things, if you want to do something similar to what's shown in Figures 2.6 and 2.7 — assuming additionally that you want it to actually work:

1. In the exported QuickBooks report, select the cells that you want to move. In Figure 2.6, that's H12:J12.

2. You can choose Edit ▶ Copy, or press Ctrl+C, or in Excel 2007 click Copy on the Home tab.

3. Switch to the target worksheet, and select the cell where you want the paste operation to start. (This cell will contain whatever was in cell H12 in the QuickBooks export.)

4. Right-click the selected cell, or choose Edit, and then choose Paste Special. The Paste Special dialog box shown in Figure 2.8 appears.

5. In the Paste section, click the Values and Number Formats option, and then click OK.

Now, when the paste operation is complete, you have not formulas but values (and the number formats in use in the copied cells) in the target worksheet. With values, there are no missing cells for a formula to look for, and therefore no #REF! error values. What you have lost is access to the cells the formula was based on, but since you weren't copying those cells anyway you've lost nothing you need.

TIP   If you want to copy and paste several parts of the QuickBooks report to another worksheet, it can be quicker to begin by converting all the formulas to values in one operation. Click Excel's Select All button, which is the rectangle to the left of the column A header and above the row 1 header, to select all the cells. Next do your copy, and paste-special back to their *original location*. Now all the formulas will have become values in the QuickBooks export, and you can copy and paste them directly to the target sheet.

Exporting to an existing workbook

In Figure 2.2 you'll notice that one of the options in the Export Report dialog box is to export the report to an existing Excel workbook. Using an existing Excel workbook can be an attractive option for several reasons:

■ You can store several different reports in the same Excel workbook.

■ You can store a QuickBooks report that is run after each of several different accounting periods in the same workbook.

■ If you have several different company files, you can store a balance sheet and income statement from each company in one summary Excel workbook.

■ You can run a QuickBooks report on each of several different product lines and have each copy of the report occupy a different worksheet in the same workbook.

And so on. To use an existing workbook, select the option labeled An Existing Excel Workbook (refer to Figure 2.2). When you select this option, the edit box and the Browse button become enabled.

Whatever your reason to store a QuickBooks report in an existing Excel workbook, there are a few minor points that will save you time in the long run. The two main issues to keep in mind are where the workbook is located and which worksheet to use.

Locating the workbook

If you want to use an existing workbook to store the exported report, you have to tell QuickBooks where to find the workbook. If you want, you can type its path and name directly into the edit box. But most of us find that it's a lot easier to click the Browse button and use the familiar Windows navigation windows to locate the file. When you get to the file, click the file's name and then click Open.

A couple of items to take care of before you start the export:

■ The target workbook must be closed.

   You cannot export a QuickBooks report to an open, unsaved Excel workbook. The Export Report dialog box asks you to browse to the saved location of the target workbook, and an unsaved workbook by definition has no saved location.

If you try to export a QuickBooks report to an open, saved Excel workbook, QuickBooks will complain and refuse to comply. This situation comes about when you have saved the Excel workbook but have left the workbook open in the Excel application window.

If you encounter this problem, just switch to Excel and close the workbook, re-saving it if necessary. Then return to QuickBooks and proceed with the export. If a different user has the workbook open, you have two options: You can wait for the other user to finish and close the workbook (Excel has a notification option for this situation). Or you can use Windows to make a copy of the workbook and have QuickBooks export to the copy. Of course you'll first have to specify the name of the copy in the Export Report dialog box.

■ **The workbook must be saved on a disk or network location visible to your logon.**

If an existing file is closed, it must be saved somewhere. If the Excel file is sitting on a server, be sure that you're logged on with a user name that has permission to read and modify the file.

Choosing the worksheet

You have the option of exporting the report to a new or an existing worksheet in an existing workbook. To select a particular worksheet, select the Use an Existing Sheet in the Workbook option. When you do so, the list box becomes enabled so that you can choose among existing sheets.

And here too there are some considerations:

■ **Overwriting existing data.** If you choose to export a QuickBooks report to an existing worksheet, all data, formulas, and formats in that worksheet will be deleted by the export.

Deleting the contents of the existing worksheet might seem okay. All you're doing is replacing an older export with a newer one. And you may well be right to do so. QuickBooks' exporting tips even suggest this method.

As someone who has used Excel on a daily basis for about 20 years, as the author or co-author of more than 15 books on Excel, and as the recipient of several Microsoft Excel MVP awards, I offer you this advice: Don't.

The QuickBooks Export Tips notwithstanding (see the section "Ignoring the QuickBooks Export Tips" for more information), it's likely to get you into difficulties. And even if you have good reason to replace the contents of the existing worksheet, there are better ways to go about it. You're better off exporting to a new worksheet.

■ **Exporting to a new worksheet.** If you export a QuickBooks report to a new worksheet in an existing Excel workbook, you run no risk of overwriting existing data. Once QuickBooks has created the new worksheet, you'll want to find it, and it helps to keep in mind the following:

Every Excel workbook has an *active sheet* that you see when the workbook is open, and whose title bar is *not* dimmed if there is more than one sheet visible in different windows. Even a closed workbook has an active sheet. When you export to a new worksheet, QuickBooks puts that new worksheet immediately to the left of the active worksheet in the tab area. (This is consistent with Excel's behavior when you insert a worksheet via the Excel user interface.)

Ignoring the QuickBook Export Tips worksheet

As Figure 2.2 shows, QuickBooks' Export Report dialog box has an Include a New Worksheet in the Workbook that Explains Excel Worksheet Linking checkbox. If you fill that checkbox and export the report to a new or an existing Excel workbook, QuickBooks adds another worksheet to the workbook named QuickBooks Export Tips. The Export Tips worksheet goes beyond the topic of worksheet linking and mentions some other issues.

The topic "Where did my worksheet go?" tells you where QuickBooks locates the worksheet in the workbook. Another tells you that you can suppress the QuickBooks Export Tips worksheet in the future by clearing the checkbox.

Then the tip sheet gets into cell linkages, and things start to fall apart. The basic idea is that you might want to export a QuickBooks report to an Excel worksheet. Then, you would put formulas into another Excel worksheet, formulas that link to cells in the exported worksheet, in places that make more sense to you — perhaps to structure a report that hits only certain highlights. (See the "Establishing Links" section for an example of how to create this type of link.)

The idea that the tip sheet is trying to get across is that once these links are set up, you can re-export data repeatedly to the source worksheet and see the values update accordingly in the target worksheet.

The Export Tip sheet refers to the worksheet you export to variously as *QuickBooks summary report, your source worksheet, an existing worksheet, a QuickBooks data worksheet, the current report*, and *the exported data sheet which serves as data source*. It may help to standardize the jargon; I refer to the sheet that you export the QuickBooks data to as the *export sheet*, and the sheet that you want to customize either for functional or esthetic purposes as the *custom sheet*.

Establishing links

Figure 2.9 shows an export sheet with a Profit & Loss from QuickBooks.

Figure 2.10 shows the Profit & Loss in a custom sheet, as you want it to appear, for a board meeting perhaps, or just for your files, where you're not interested in maintaining subaccount information.

The way that the data in Figure 2.10 gets there is very different from the method outlined in the section "Moving Cells with Formulas." In the earlier section, you saw how to copy a *formula* and paste it into another cell as a *value*. The numbers in Figure 2.10 are also formulas, but they are formulas created by the user, not by QuickBooks. Figure 2.11 shows the data in Figure 2.9 (top) and Figure 2.10 (bottom), but instead of showing the results in the custom sheet as in Figure 2.10, it shows the formulas.

FIGURE 2.9

The original export from QuickBooks

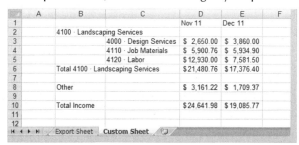

	Nov 11	Dec 11
Ordinary Income/Expense		
Income		
4100 · Landscaping Services		
4000 · Design Services	2,650.00	3,860.00
4110 · Job Materials		
Misc Materials	12.30	129.00
4111 · Decks & Patios	0.00	45.00
4112 · Fountains & Garden Lighting	2,903.50	2,311.95
4113 · Plants and Sod	1,272.00	1,907.70
4114 · Sprinklers & Drip systems	1,712.96	1,541.25
Total 4110 · Job Materials	5,900.76	5,934.90
4120 · Labor		
4121 · Installation	11,440.00	7,296.00
4122 · Maintenance & Repairs	1,490.00	285.50
Total 4120 · Labor	12,930.00	7,581.50
Total 4100 · Landscaping Services	21,480.76	17,376.40
4400 · Markup Income	610.00	120.00
Retail Sales	101.22	89.37
Service	2,450.00	1,500.00
Total Income	24,641.98	19,085.77

Export Sheet / Custom Sheet

FIGURE 2.10

The exported data, laid out according to your preferences in a custom sheet.

	A	B	C	D	E	F
1				Nov 11	Dec 11	
2		4100 · Landscaping Services				
3			4000 · Design Services	$ 2,650.00	$ 3,860.00	
4			4110 · Job Materials	$ 5,900.76	$ 5,934.90	
5			4120 · Labor	$12,930.00	$ 7,581.50	
6		Total 4100 · Landscaping Services		$21,480.76	$17,376.40	
7						
8		Other		$ 3,161.22	$ 1,709.37	
9						
10		Total Income		$24,641.98	$19,085.77	
11						
12						

Export Sheet / **Custom Sheet**

The most convenient, and probably the surest way to get those formulas into the custom sheet is to follow these steps (for just one cell — you'd have to adapt the steps slightly for other cells):

1. Select cell D3 in the custom sheet.

2. Type = (an equal sign).

3. To continue entering the formula, click in cell H5 in the export sheet. The formula should look like this:
   ```
   ='Export Sheet'!H5
   ```

4. Press Enter or click the green checkmark in the Formula Bar to establish the formula.

FIGURE 2.11

Each formula is just a link to a cell in the export sheet.

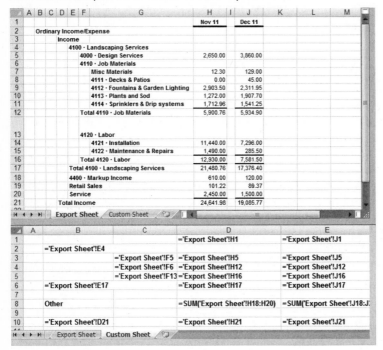

In words, the formula tells Excel to let cell D3 in the custom sheet equal whatever is contained in cell H5 in the export sheet. The Excel Export Tips sheet, as well as Excel itself, terms this formula a *link*.

In theory, this approach can be handy. It's a way to cherry-pick the values you want to see and skip the ones you don't. In this example, I'm cobbling together a report that shows income from parent accounts, and doesn't bother breaking those figures out by sub-subaccounts.

Breaking links

The preceding approach works best when the data source — in this case, the export sheet — does not vary from export to export. For example, suppose you export the income statement on November 11, and you would like the figure for Design Services in cell H5 to also appear in cell H5 when you export the income statement on December 11. The actual numeric figure may well be different a month later, but you would still hope to find it in the same cell as you did a month earlier.

In that case, the cells that the links in your custom sheet point to contain the same sort of information they did when you constructed them one or more months earlier: the values may differ, but if the cell contained a figure for Design Services in November's export, you expect it to contain a figure for Design Services in December's export. If you can depend on H5 in the export sheet to always contain Design Services income, regardless of when you export the report, then you can also depend on cell D3 in the custom sheet to display Design Services income.

But that's not what happens with QuickBooks reports. There are many ways that the P&L (or any QuickBooks report) can vary from month to month, simply as a function of normal financial events. The Export Tips sheet itself warns you of some of them, for example:

- **You have added, deleted, made active or deactivated even one item.** This adds a row that wasn't there before in an item-driven report, or removes a row that was there before. Your formulas point to the same cells they did before, but the information in those cells is different: not just a different value, that's to be expected, but a different source for that value.

- **An account has activity during one period but not during another.** Account-driven reports — reports that show different accounts on different lines — might rearrange themselves without letting you know. During November, for example, the income account named Books About Software might carry a $10 total. During December, when nobody buys books about software, that account might have no activity and disappear from the report. Then every subsequent line would get pulled up by one, but your links would still point at their original sources in the export sheet.

The QuickBooks' Export Tips worksheet recommends that before exporting you modify the report to show all rows. It does not tell you what to do about the fact that this modification snaps back to active rows when you're through. Sure, memorize the report, but are you certain you'll remember to use the memorized version next month? Furthermore, following that recommendation does not protect you against the consequences of adding a new item between exports.

Doing it the expert way

Here's how to build more sophisticated links in Excel: links that will survive even if your report's rows unexpectedly appear or disappear between the dates that you run your report.

This approach is based on the fact that many QuickBooks reports can be depended on to always have certain important labels, and that they are always in the same columns. For example, regardless of the company file or when you create the report, the Balance Sheet Standard report has these labels in an export to an Excel worksheet:

- Total Current Assets in column B
- XXXX Inventory Asset in column D (where XXXX is an account number, if used)
- Total Current Liabilities in column C

Suppose you want to create a custom report that shows your company's Current Ratio and its Quick Ratio. You want to glance at these ratios each month. Your approach is to export a

Balance Sheet Standard report to an existing workbook at the end of each month. The report will always be exported to the same worksheet in that workbook.

Your custom sheet will contain links to the export sheet, and your immediate goal is to structure those links so that they work even if rows in the export sheet come and go from month to month. These links take just a little more time to create than do the simple point-and-shoot links explained in the prior section. But because you will use them over and over again, without having to worry about whether you structured the export report properly, the benefits are well worth the upfront time.

Figure 2.12 shows an example of the export sheet and the custom sheet.

Start by copying the labels of the values you're interested in seeing from the export sheet to the custom sheet. In this case, you want the building blocks of the current ratio and the quick ratio: total current assets, inventory assets, and total current liabilities. Copy these labels from cells B18, D15, and C44, respectively, in the export sheet and paste them into cells A2, A4, and A6 in the custom sheet. (The result is shown in Figure 2.12, column A in the custom sheet.)

Next, you want to build a formula in the custom sheet that finds the Total Current Assets label in the export sheet and displays the dollar figure associated with the label. To do so, start with Excel's MATCH function. In the custom report sheet, you would start by entering this formula, which uses MATCH, in cell B2:

```
=MATCH(A2,Export!B:B,0)
```

The formula returns the value 18, meaning that the value in A2, Total Current Assets, is matched by the value in the 18th row column B in the sheet named Export. The general syntax of the MATCH function is:

```
=MATCH(value to match, search location, match type)
```

where, in this case:

- ■ Total Current Assets is the value to match,
- ■ Column B in the sheet named Export is where to look for a match, and
- ■ 0 is the match type, meaning that values in the search location are not necessarily in ascending numeric or alphabetical order.

The point is to locate the Total Current Assets value in the export sheet, regardless of how many rows precede it, therefore, regardless of which accounts appear in the report. Once you have located that label, it's easy to find the dollar amount associated with it. Meet Excel's OFFSET function:

```
=OFFSET(Export!$A$1,17,6)
```

FIGURE 2.12

If your company has cash, A/R amounts, undeposited funds, or inventory, it has current assets.

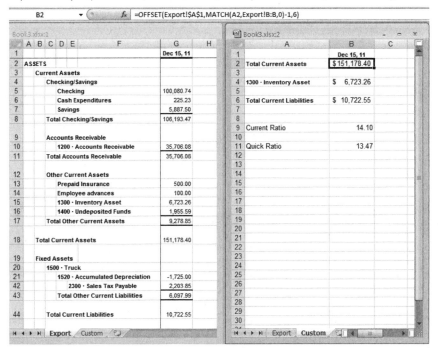

This formula, making use of OFFSET, returns the value 151178.40. That is the value in the cell *offset* by 17 rows and 6 columns from cell A1 in the sheet named Export. Not coincidentally, it's the amount of the total current assets shown in the balance sheet report.

TIP   Notice the dollar signs in the reference to cell A1 in the OFFSET formula. The $'s make it what Excel terms an *absolute* reference. If you copy the formula and paste it to a different cell, it will still refer to cell A1. In contrast, a relative reference to cell A1, without the dollar signs, would change, depending on how many rows down or columns across you pasted it into. By using the absolute reference, you can more easily replicate the formula in other cells, to pick up the inventory asset and the total current liabilities.

How do you know to use 17 rows and 6 columns in the OFFSET function? Well, in the standard balance sheet report, the dollar figures are always found in column G of the exported worksheet. Column G is the seventh column — it is *offset* six columns from cell A1.

The value Total Current Assets is found in the 18th row of column B, located there by the MATCH function described earlier. Therefore, it's *offset* by 17 rows from cell A1.

If you take the six-column offset as a constant, and by using MATCH allow for a variable number of rows to appear before the Total Current Assets value, you can get the associated dollar value directly by nesting MATCH within OFFSET:

```
=OFFSET(Export!$A$1,MATCH(A2,Export!B:B,0)-1,6)
```

to return, using just one formula, the value for the total current assets in the export sheet from QuickBooks.

> **TIP** When you work with more complex formulas like this one, peek inside the formula to see what's going on. One way is to select the cell that contains the formula, click the Formula tab, and click Evaluate Formula in the Formula Auditing group (prior to Excel 2007, choose Tools ▸ Formula Auditing ▸ Evaluate Formula). You will see, step-by-step, how Excel interprets the formula.

Now two more simple steps will give you the value for the inventory asset and the total current liabilities:

1. Copy the formula from its location in cell B2 in the custom sheet (shown in Figure 2.12) and paste it into cells B4 and B6, immediately to the right of the labels in column A that you're looking for in the export sheet.

2. For the inventory value, change B:B in the formula to D:D, so Excel will know which column to look in for the inventory asset label. For the current liabilities, change B:B to C:C, for the same reason.

The reference to cell A2, in the formula that picks up the total current assets, is a relative reference. Therefore, when you copy and paste it into cells B4 and B6, it automatically adjusts to a reference to A4 and A6. You will wind up with these formulas in cells B4 and B6:

```
=OFFSET(Export!$A$1,MATCH(A4,Export!D:D,0)-1,6)
=OFFSET(Export!$A$1,MATCH(A6,Export!C:C,0)-1,6)
```

To get the current ratio, enter this formula in cell B9 (or whatever other cell you prefer):

```
=B2/B6
```

and for the quick ratio (which removes inventory from the current assets to better estimate the assets that are already cash or that can be converted to cash quickly):

```
=(B2-B4)/B6
```

If this is your first time through this sort of formula development, it might seem complicated and unduly exacting. By the time you've done it three or four times it starts to seem old hat. Bear these points in mind:

1. You need do it only once, in your custom sheet.

2. Regardless of what changes push the row containing the current assets (or the inventory asset or the current liabilities) up or down in your export sheet, the MATCH and OFFSET functions cause your formulas to return the correct values for the ratios you want.

And you don't have to worry about all those warnings in the QuickBooks Export Tips worksheet.

Exporting to Text Files

In Figure 2.2 you'll notice that your first available option is to export to a comma-separated values (CSV) file, which has the filename extension `.csv`. A CSV file can be used as a data source for most applications that work with user-supplied data: for example, a spreadsheet program such as Excel, a presentation program such as Adobe Acrobat, a database such as Oracle, or a statistical analysis package such as R. (QuickBooks can read data similar to CSV files too, but imposes extra requirements and refers to them as IIF files.)

Understanding the CSV file structure

A QuickBooks report exported to a CSV file has a particular structure, and it is much like an Excel worksheet list, or a data sheet in a database. Each row contains a different record, and each column contains a different field. If you are exporting a P&L or a balance sheet report, a field on the left corresponds to, say, a parent account, subaccount names appear in the next column, and sub-subaccounts appear in the subsequent columns. The final column or columns is for the numbers that apply to the accounts.

Figure 2.13 shows a CSV file as it appears in a simple application like Notepad:

The ninth row in the file is:

```
,"Invoice","12/12/2011","Stinson, Tracy", "129",-200,"",2670,0.18,480.6
```

There are nine fields in each row of this CSV file. Each pair of adjacent fields is separated by a comma. Text fields, such as customer name, are surrounded by quote marks (and may include a comma that *doesn't* separate two fields). Empty fields, where there is no value given for a particular record, are indicated by consecutive commas (,,) or in text fields by two quotation marks within commas (,"",). The ninth row shown earlier begins with an empty field; there's nothing to the left of the first comma.

Both Microsoft Excel and Microsoft Access recognize these patterns. Figure 2.14 shows how this row appears in an Excel worksheet.

Deciding on a CSV file for a report export

QuickBooks export files that use the CSV structure are not as fancy as their Excel worksheet counterparts. For example:

- **The currency fields have no currency formats.** If you open a CSV file in Excel, you see no dollar signs, thousands separators, or red fonts to indicate negative values.
- **Subtotals and totals are pure numeric values.** In a direct export to an Excel worksheet, subtotals and totals are formulas using (normally) the SUM function. (The absence of formulas is not necessarily a drawback. Even experienced Excel users some-

FIGURE 2.13

Commas separate fields in a comma-separated values file.

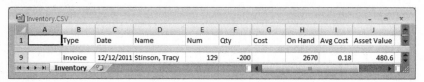

```
Inventory.CSV - Notepad
File   Edit   Format   View   Help
,"Type","Date","Name","Num","Qty","Cost","On Hand","Avg Cost","Asset Value"
"Inventory",,,,,,,"",""
"Irrigation Hose",,,,,,"","",
"1/2"" Line",,,,,,,
,"Invoice","12/1/2011","Theurer-Davis, Vicki:Irrigation & Lawn","119",-425,"",1858,0.12,222.96
,"Invoice","12/12/2011","Rummens, Susie:2877 S Rosebush","128",-75,"",1783,0.12,213.96
"Total 1/2"" Line",,,,,,1783.00,,213.96
"3/4"" Line",,,,,,,
,"Invoice","12/12/2011","Stinson, Tracy","129",-200,"",2670,0.18,480.60
"Total 3/4"" Line",,,,,,2670.00,,480.60
"Total Irrigation Hose",,,,,,4453.00,,694.56
```

FIGURE 2.14

Excel can distinguish numeric values from text, but you have to tell it if a field contains a currency value.

	A	B	C	D	E	F	G	H	I	J
1		Type	Date	Name	Num	Qty	Cost	On Hand	Avg Cost	Asset Value
9		Invoice	12/12/2011	Stinson, Tracy	129	-200		2670	0.18	480.6

Inventory.CSV — Inventory

times insert an extraneous value where it will be used, erroneously, by an existing SUM function.)

- **Particularly in reports that display information for subaccounts, the indenting you normally see might be absent.** Figure 2.15 shows the same balance sheet, once as exported via a CSV file named `Balance Sheet.csv` and opened in Excel, and as exported directly to an Excel worksheet. Note that the report exported directly to Excel uses indentation, and simulates section breaks by varying row heights (for example, rows 9 and 12 in Sheet1 in Figure 2.15).

Generally, it makes more sense to export a report to an Excel worksheet than to a CSV file. If the export is to take advantage of Excel's broad scope of mathematical, financial, and statistical functions, there's usually little reason to take the extra step of exporting to a CSV file and then opening that file using Excel.

But if you want to put a QuickBooks report into an application such as a database, a CSV file makes good sense — and you don't even need a table in the database whose field structure matches the fields that you're going to export.

Why would you bother to import data from QuickBooks into a true database at all? There are several good reasons to import QuickBooks data into Excel. Excel has superior charting capa-

FIGURE 2.15

Notice that the indents indicating parent-subaccount relationships are missing from the CSV file.

	A	B		A B C D E	F	G	H
1		15-Dec-11	1			Dec 15, 11	
2	ASSETS		2	ASSETS			
3	Current Assets		3	Current Assets			
4	Checking/Savings		4	Checking/Savings			
5	Checking	100080.74	5	Checking		100,080.74	
6	Cash Expenditures	225.23	6	Cash Expenditures		225.23	
7	Savings	5887.5	7	Savings		5,887.50	
8	Total Checking/Savings	106193.47	8	Total Checking/Savings		106,193.47	
9	Accounts Receivable						
10	1200 · Accounts Receivable	35706.08	9	Accounts Receivable			
11	Total Accounts Receivable	35706.08	10	1200 · Accounts Receivable		35,706.08	
12	Other Current Assets		11	Total Accounts Receivable		35,706.08	
13	Prepaid Insurance	500					
14	Employee advances	100	12	Other Current Assets			
15	1300 · Inventory Asset	6723.26	13	Prepaid Insurance		500.00	
16	1400 · Undeposited Funds	1955.59	14	Employee advances		100.00	
17	Total Other Current Assets	9278.85	15	1300 · Inventory Asset		6,723.26	
18	Total Current Assets	151178.4	16	1400 · Undeposited Funds		1,955.59	
19	Fixed Assets		17	Total Other Current Assets		9,278.85	
20	1500 · Truck						
21	1520 · Accumulated Depreciation	-1725	18	Total Current Assets		151,178.40	
22	1510 · Original Purchase	13750					
23	Total 1500 · Truck	12025	19	Fixed Assets			
24	Total Fixed Assets	12025	20	1500 · Truck			
25	TOTAL ASSETS	163203.4	21	1520 · Accumulated Depreciation		-1,725.00	

Balance sheet / Sheet1   Balance sheet / **Sheet1**

bilities, analysis tools, and financial functions, and Excel can calculate key financial ratios. But a database, such as Access, SQL Server, or Oracle, has little of this sort of capability.

In fact, you don't get much of a return by moving most QuickBooks reports into a true database. The standard reports are either almost all subtotals and totals (the summary reports) or individual records interspersed with subtotals and totals (the detail reports). Neither of these is much use in a database, which works best when all the records occupy the same level of detail.

One type of report, though, that you can move into a database to good effect is a custom transaction report. This report has great design flexibility. You can have subtotals if you want, using just about any field in your company file: account, item, customer, and so on. Or, if you want to handle data summaries in a different way, you can suppress subtotals, calling for totals only, and export the result to a CSV file for use in a database. Exported in this fashion, the records imported into the database are individual transactions.

Still, what's the point? Well, suppose that you want to analyze your business results by something other than QuickBook's built-in methods: items, or customers, or accounts, or fiscal years, and so on. What if you market to four regions of the country and want to view your revenues by region? Or, what if you have several different kinds of business to transact — say, Design, Landscaping, and Maintenance — and you want to see which business is the most profitable over time?

That's why QuickBooks provides the option of assigning transactions to a *class*. You can enable classes for a company file by choosing Edit ▶ Preferences ▶ Accounting and clicking the Company Preferences tab. Once enabled, you can define classes. You might define a different class for each of four regions: Northwest, Northeast, Southeast, and Southwest, for instance.

The difficulty arises when you want to use the class to represent different ways of slicing up your results. Suppose that in addition to line of business or geographic region, you also want to categorize transactions according to a department, say, Catalog Sales and Direct Sales. You can create these two new classes to represent your departments by choosing Lists ▶ Class List, clicking the Class list box and then clicking New in the list box.

Setting up the two new classes to represent departments isn't the problem. The problem is that you can assign only one class to a given transaction. If you sell 12 argyle sweaters via your catalog to a customer in Idaho, do you assign that transaction to the Catalog class or to the Northwest class? You can't assign it to both since a given transaction can belong to one class only.

The usual advice is to create subclasses. So Catalog and Direct could be subclasses of Northwest, subclasses of Northeast, and so on. The subclass approach can sometimes be a good solution, but not in this case. Beyond the simple esthetics of having to look at something such as Northwest:Catalog Sales, or Design:Direct Sales (you can't suppress a parent class the way you can suppress a parent account) there is the more important issue of properly representing reality. It would make sense if you were to define the sales territories of Washington, Oregon, and Idaho as sub-classes of a Northwest class: states are logically and, usually, structurally subordinate to regions in a company's organization.

But distribution channels, such as catalog sales and direct sales, are not normally subordinate to regions. Channels *cross* regions; they are not nested within them. The same is often true of sales channels and lines of business.

So, to develop a way to classify transactions using more than one type of class, you normally need to go beyond the fields that QuickBooks gives you. Furthermore, true databases are ideally suited to adding new fields to a data set. (Better even than Excel, which offers only rudimentary database management capabilities.)

QuickBooks custom fields don't help here, because they belong to customer records, vendor records, employee records, and item records. They do not belong to transactions, which is what you're looking for. Yes, you could create a sales rep named Catalog, but that doesn't put you in a position to analyze all direct sales versus all catalog sales. QuickBooks reports would contrast each sales rep versus the entire catalog.

Still, you're stuck with how to classify transactions along more than one dimension. One way involves using the reference number field in QuickBooks (titled Num in QuickBooks' reports that show individual transactions). Continuing the example, you might consider entering the letter "C" at the start of each transaction that is a Catalog sale and the letter "D" if it is a Direct sale. After the data has been exported to a CSV file and imported into a database, it's easy to add to the database a field named Sales Channel and populate it by an update query that uses the reference number. You'll see one way in the "Opening the CSV File in Access" section.

Opening the CSV file in Excel

It's easy to open a CSV file in Excel. Suppose that you have exported a report to a CSV file on the Desktop. To open it in Excel, just take these steps:

1. Choose File ◗ Open.
2. Use the Open window to browse to the Desktop.
3. Click the Files of Type list box at the bottom of the Open window and choose Text Files (*.prn, *.txt, *.csv). Only files with one of those three extensions will appear in the Open window.
4. Click the name of your exported CSV file and click Open.

Opening the CSV file in Access

With Access, you can create an entirely new table in a database just by importing the CSV file. Access will use any labels it finds in the file's first row as field names. Importing a CSV file is probably the most straightforward way to get data out of QuickBooks and into a database.

While Excel can open the CSV file directly using File ◗ Open, Access guides you through its options by means of a wizard. Suppose that you have exported the Custom Transaction Detail report from QuickBooks. Open a database in Access 2007 (the steps for Access 2003 and before are similar but not identical) and then take these steps:

1. Click External Data on the Ribbon and click Text File.
2. In the Select the Source and Destination of the Data window, use the Browse button to navigate to the location of the CSV file. When you click Browse, the File Open window appears.
3. Browse to the location where you saved the CSV report export file. Text Files (*.txt; *. csv; *.tab; *.asc) is the default file type, so you'll see any CSV files that you've saved in that location.
4. Select the CSV file and click Open. You are returned to the Source and Destination of the Data window. At this point you choose whether to import the data into the database or link to the data source. This choice is conceptually similar to using values in a report exported to Excel, or using linked formulas (explained earlier in the "Doing it the expert way" section). Your choice has no effect on completing the wizard, so assume you accept the default Import, and click OK.
5. Click the Delimited or Fixed width option (see Figure 2.16). Because the fields in your file are delimited by commas, make sure the Delimited option is selected and click Next. (Files intended for a printer usually have fixed width columns and a .prn file-name extension.)

FIGURE 2.16

Consecutive commas in a CSV file indicate empty fields.

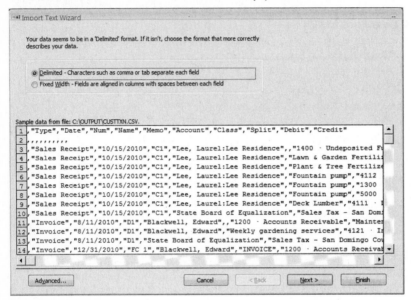

FIGURE 2.17

The structure of the file won't be apparent until you choose a comma as the delimiter and a quote mark as the text qualifier.

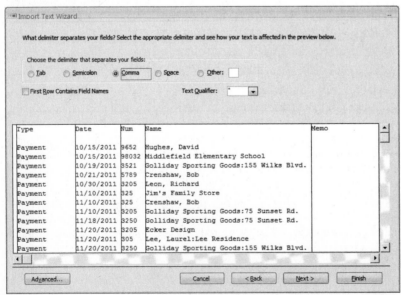

6. Select the Comma delimiter option (see Figure 2.17), choose the quotation mark from the list box as the text qualifier, and fill the First Row Contains Field Names checkbox. Most QuickBooks reports, including the Inventory Valuation reports, have columns with labels in the first row. However, the first column often has nothing in its first row, and the wizard will warn you of that situation. Access will replace a missing or unacceptable field name with something such as Field1. Dismiss the warning and click Next.

7. Next you can specify certain options for each field: the name the field will carry in the database, its numeric format, whether to skip the field, and whether to index it. It's a good idea to specify the Currency format for columns in a QuickBooks report that contains dollar values (see Figure 2.18). Do not index a field unless you're familiar with concepts such as primary keys and foreign keys. When you're finished, click Next.

8. Add a primary key to the table. A primary key is a value that uniquely identifies a record in a table in a database. All QuickBooks transactions and members of lists have primary keys, but you can't get at them through exported reports. The decision to use a primary key is much more complicated than is implied by this step (see Figure 2.19) but it will not slow things down much and could conceivably help. Choose Let Access Add a Primary Key and click Next.

9. In the wizard's final step, give the newly imported table a name and click Finish.

10. There's one more thing: Don't forget that the table is based on a QuickBooks report. That report has a total row, which you don't want in your database table. Scroll down to the bottom of the table to locate the total row, click to select it, and then press Delete to remove the row.

A portion of the imported table appears in Figure 2.20. Notice that the values in the Num field begin with either a C or a D: before the data was exported from QuickBooks, one or the other of those letters was added to indicate a Catalog or a Direct sale. The next task is to add a Sales Channel field to the database, and then classify the sales records according to their channel using the Num field. Here are the specific steps:

1. Click the Home tab on the Ribbon and choose Design View from the View list box. The window shown in Figure 2.21 appears.

2. Click the first empty cell in the Field Name column, and type a name for the new Sales Channel field.

> **TIP** In Access, names without embedded blanks are a little easier to deal with and you might consider a name such as SalesChannel or Sales_Channel.

3. On the same row, click in the cell in the Data Type column and choose Text in the list box.

4. Close the table by clicking the X in its upper-right corner. Respond Yes when Access asks you if you want to save changes to the table.

FIGURE 2.18

Click anywhere in a column to select it and specify its attributes, such as numeric format and whether to skip the field.

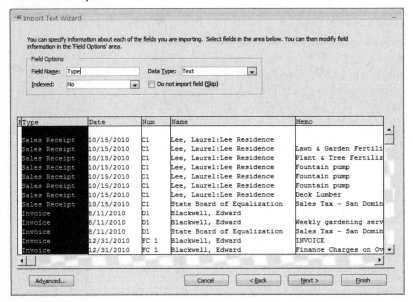

FIGURE 2.19

A primary key must have unique values, and QuickBooks reports provide no field that you can depend on to have a different value on each record.

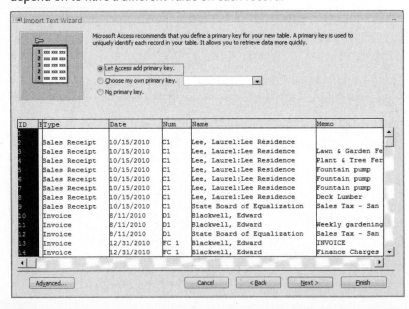

FIGURE 2.20

Access assigned the previously unnamed field the name FIELD1. You can change it later if you want.

ID	Field1	Type	Date	Num	Name	Memo	Account	Class	Debit	Credit
1										
2		Sales Receipt	10/15/2010	C1	Lee, Laurel:Lee Residence		1400 · Undeposited Funds	Maintenance	117.23	
3		Sales Receipt	10/15/2010	C1	Lee, Laurel:Lee Residence	Lawn & Garden	Retail Sales	Maintenance		18.90
4		Sales Receipt	10/15/2010	C1	Lee, Laurel:Lee Residence	Plant & Tree Fe	Retail Sales	Maintenance		14.90
5		Sales Receipt	10/15/2010	C1	Lee, Laurel:Lee Residence	Fountain pump	4112 · Fountains & Garden Lighting	Landscaping		75.00
6		Sales Receipt	10/15/2010	C1	Lee, Laurel:Lee Residence	Fountain pump	1300 · Inventory Asset	Landscaping		56.00
7		Sales Receipt	10/15/2010	C1	Lee, Laurel:Lee Residence	Fountain pump	5000 · Cost of Goods Sold	Landscaping	56.00	
8		Sales Receipt	10/15/2010	C1	Lee, Laurel:Lee Residence	Deck Lumber	4111 · Decks & Patios	Maintenance	0.00	
9		Sales Receipt	10/15/2010	C1	State Board of Equalization	Sales Tax - San	2300 · Sales Tax Payable			8.43
10		Invoice	8/11/2010	D1	Blackwell, Edward		1200 · Accounts Receivable	Maintenance	480.00	
11		Invoice	8/11/2010	D1	Blackwell, Edward	Weekly garden	4121 · Installation	Maintenance		480.00
12		Invoice	8/11/2010	D1	State Board of Equalization	Sales Tax - San	2300 · Sales Tax Payable	Maintenance	0.00	
15		Sales Receipt	12/10/2010	C2	Sonnenschein, Russ		Checking	Maintenance	274.95	
16		Sales Receipt	12/10/2010	C2	Sonnenschein, Russ	Lawn & Garden	Retail Sales	Maintenance		37.80
17		Sales Receipt	12/10/2010	C2	Sonnenschein, Russ	Plant & Tree Fe	Retail Sales	Maintenance		19.37
18		Sales Receipt	12/10/2010	C2	Sonnenschein, Russ	Citrus Tree - 50	4113 · Plants and Sod	Landscaping		198.00
19		Sales Receipt	12/10/2010	C2	State Board of Equalization	Sales Tax - San	2300 · Sales Tax Payable			19.78

FIGURE 2.21

An AutoNumber field provides numeric values that are either incremental or randomly generated. It's a useful way to create a primary key if you don't already have one in the table.

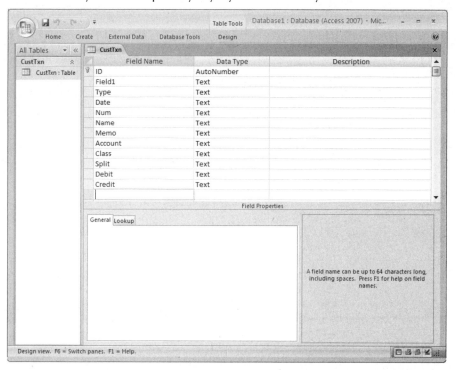

FIGURE 2.22

When a database has more than one table, you often must add two or more tables to the design grid from the Show Table window.

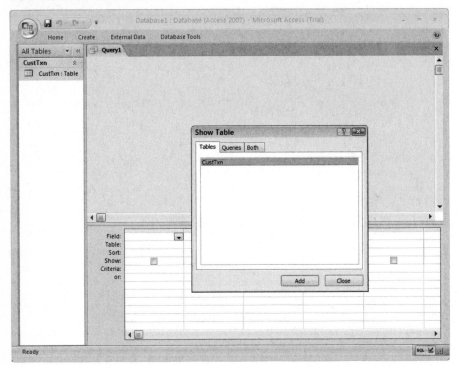

5. With the new field — which will contain the classes QuickBooks could not manage separately from the existing Class — defined, you can create an update query to populate the new field. Click the Create tab and click Query Design on the Ribbon (see Figure 2.22).

6. With just one table, it will be selected in the Show Table window. Click Add and then click Close.

7. Click Update in the Query Type group. The query design grid changes and will appear as shown in Figure 2.23.

8. Click the Num field from the data table and drag it to the cell in the design grid's first column, in its Field row.

9. Click in the first column's Criteria row and type
   Left([Num],1)="C"
   This expression, used as a criterion, tells Access to work only with records that have the letter "C" as their leftmost single character; that is, if the one character at the left end of the Num value is "C," include that record among those to process.

NOTE The brackets surrounding the Num field name are not strictly necessary in Structured Query Language, but they are proper query syntax and help identify the names of fields, queries, tables, and so on. The brackets are needed when you're working with a field name that contains an embedded blank.

10. Click and drag the Sales Channel field name from the data table to the design grid's second column, in its Field row.

11. Click in the second column's Update To row and type this value, including the quote marks: `"Catalog"`. The query window should now appear as shown in Figure 2.23.

12. Click Run in the Results group. The query runs, putting the value `"Catalog"` in the Sales Channel field for all records whose Num field begins with "C."

13. To get the "Direct" values into the Sales Channel field, change "C" to "D" in the design grid's Criteria row, and change `"Catalog"` to `"Direct"` in the Update To row. Then click Run again.

To see the results of your query, double-click the table in the Navigation pane to open it in datasheet view. You will see the values in the Sales Channel field that correspond to the values you used in the update query: in this example, Catalog and Direct. See Figure 2.24 for an example.

But the datasheet view is too detailed to tell you much about how, if at all, Sales Channel and the Class you're using interact to bring about different levels of revenue or profit. The best way is by means of a pivot table.

Microsoft Access does offer pivot tables, but they are not as fully functioned or informative as are pivot tables in Excel. The next section shows you how to build a pivot table in Access, and one way to get the pivot table into Excel.

Analyzing QuickBooks Data with Pivot Tables

Once you have created a table in Access based on a CSV file from QuickBooks, most of the heavy lifting is finished and you're just a few mouse clicks away from a true data analysis. If you've followed the information and instructions in the prior section, you now have a table open in Access. To get a look at that table in a way that gives you some management information, follow these steps:

1. With a table open, click the Home tab if necessary and then choose PivotTable view from the View list box in the Views group. A window that shows the schematic for a pivot table appears as shown in Figure 2.25.

FIGURE 2.23

To see what the query looks like in Structured Query Language, click the View list box in the Results group and click SQL View.

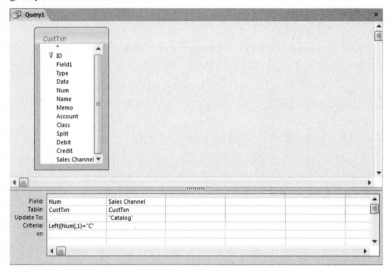

FIGURE 2.24

You should delete the first data row: it's just a blank row in the QuickBooks report that separates the column headers from the data.

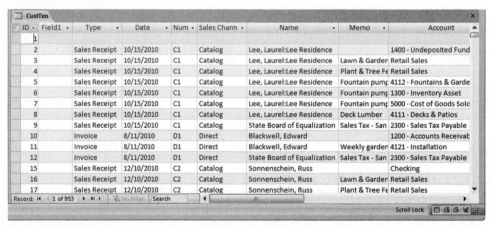

FIGURE 2.25

The Filter Fields area works much as does the Page Fields area in an Excel pivot table.

FIGURE 2.26

With details shown, you get no summary information, but it can sometimes be helpful to see the specific values behind a summary result.

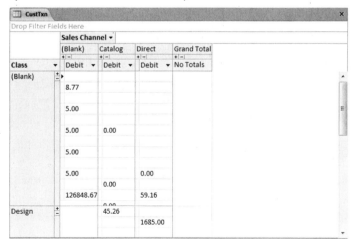

To see the percent of revenue coming from different combinations of Class and Sales Channel, click the Show As button and choose Percent of Grand Total.

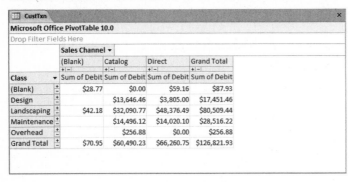

2. If you don't see the PivotTable Field List box shown in Figure 2.25, click the Field List button in the Show/Hide group on the Design tab. Drag the Class icon into the rectangle in the table schematic labeled Drop Row Fields Here.

3. Drag the Sales Channel icon into the rectangle labeled Drop Column Fields Here.

4. Drag the Debit icon into the main body of the schematic, labeled Drop Totals or Detail Fields Here.

5. At first you might see individual Debit values in the pivot table's data area, as shown in Figure 2.26. You can get sums of dollar values for each combination of Class and Sales Channel by clicking the Hide Details (the – [minus sign] icon) next to each value of either the Class field or the Sales Channel Field. When you do so, the pivot table appears as shown in Figure 2.27.

TIP If your pivot table appears like the one in Figure 2.27 but no sums appear, make sure that you have defined the Debit field as Currency (begin by clicking View ▸ Design View). The default summary for a Text field is Count, not Sum.

This type of analysis is not feasible in QuickBooks. You sometimes need to export transaction data (or even list data) out of QuickBooks and into an application that might not be intended for bookkeeping, but that performs powerful numeric analysis.

Pivot tables in Access are useful, but they're even more useful in Excel. You can export the pivot table you created In Access to an Excel workbook; it will retain all the functionality it has in Access. Just click the Ribbon's Design tab, and then click Export to Excel in the Data group.

Digging Deeper with Pivot Tables

C hapter 2 ended with a brief description of building a pivot table from QuickBooks data. Because of the great flexibility of analysis that pivot tables offer you, and because it is so easy to port data from QuickBooks into Excel, this chapter describes the pivot tables features in much greater depth. You will see how to bring pivot tables to bear on QuickBooks data and explore patterns in your data that you simply can't uncover in the QuickBooks user interface.

Pivot tables do take some getting used to. Before you can begin to feel comfortable with them you have to learn a few special terms. And pivot tables are so powerful and flexible that you need some experience before new ways to use them become clear. The next section gets some of that housekeeping out of the way with an overview of pivot table fields.

A Sample Pivot Table

Figure 3.1 shows a mildly complicated pivot table based on QuickBooks' Rock Castle Construction sample file.

Notice in Figure 3.1 that you can see the joint effect of City and Class on the company's revenues. It's important to know whether there is a difference in how your products do according to your customers' locations. One reason is that knowing where different products perform best enables you to focus your marketing efforts.

In QuickBooks, you can view a report of sales by item. You can customize a transaction report that shows sales by, say, customer city.

FIGURE 3.1

Pivot tables can show you breakdowns that just aren't available in QuickBooks reports.

Sum of Amount	Class			
Name City	New Construction	Remodel	(blank)	Grand Total
Bayshore	$154,540	$117,465		$272,005
East Bayshore	$40,710	$45,772		$86,481
Middlefield	$76,722	$15,906		$92,629
Millbrae	$13,900	$167,755		$181,655
San Mateo		$24,005		$24,005
West Bear		$700		$700
(blank)			$15	$15
Grand Total	$285,872	$371,604	$15	$657,490

But you can't see whether pine cabinets sell better in Millbrae or in Bayshore. A pivot table makes that kind of information both straightforward and easy to get.

It will help you to understand pivot tables if you begin by understanding some of their terminology.

Pivot table terminology

The explanation of terms might as well start with the term pivot table itself. When Microsoft first introduced pivot tables in the mid-1990s, it chose to call them "pivottables," which it continues to do so today. So, if you want to look up information about pivot tables in Microsoft Help documents or online, you might get more information if you spell it as one word, without a space. This book uses the less gimmicky term "pivot table."

A table pivots on a worksheet in the sense that the user can change the orientation of a field in the table by dragging it from a row orientation to a column orientation, or vice versa. So doing is called p*ivoting the table*. It's fun to watch once or twice, and it leads to an initially intriguing term, but even if you (like me) find that you have created thousands of pivot tables over the years, you'll be hard-pressed to think of a time that you pivoted a table for a reason more important than just watching the wheels go around.

Pivot tables have four kinds of fields: row, column, data, and page.

Row fields

A row field is one that occupies rows in a pivot table. In Figure 3.2, the field called Name City is the row field. The designation Name City is due to QuickBooks. Several address fields are qualified by the word Name, to indicate that they are associated with the Customer Name: Name Street1, Name State, Name Zip, and so on.

The individual rows associated with the row field are each occupied by a row item. The row items in Figure 3.2 are Bayshore, East Bayshore, Middlefield, and so on. Notice that there is one row item labeled (blank). This is to account for items that have no value in Name City. You can use the dropdown labeled Name City to suppress the (blank) item by clearing its checkbox. See Figure 3.3.

FIGURE 3.2

This is the same pivot table as in Figure 3.1, but the column field has been removed.

Sum of Amount	
Name City ▾	Total
Bayshore	$272,005
East Bayshore	$86,481
Middlefield	$92,629
Millbrae	$181,655
San Mateo	$24,005
West Bear	$700
(blank)	$15
Grand Total	$657,490

FIGURE 3.3

There is a similar dropdown for column fields. The dropdown always contains the items that make up the field.

FIGURE 3.4

Individual items in row and column fields usually represent categories.

Sum of Amount	Name City ▾							
	Bayshore	East Bayshore	Middlefield	Millbrae	San Mateo	West Bear	(blank)	Grand Total
Total	$272,005	$86,481	$92,629	$181,655	$24,005	$700	$15	$657,490

Column fields

Figure 3.4 shows the pivot table from Figure 3.2 with Name City moved (or pivoted) to act as a column field. Its different items now occupy separate columns, whereas in Figure 3.2, as a row field, its items occupied separate rows.

Compare Figures 3.1, 3.2, and 3.4. Figure 3.1 is the usual way of displaying a table that has two fields: One is used as a row and the other as a column. Figures 3.2 and 3.4 show that you can use other considerations, such as a report layout, to decide whether to treat a pivot table's single field as a row or as a column field. This is strictly a look-and-feel decision and has nothing at all to do with the results of the analysis.

Data fields

In pivot table parlance, Figures 3.2 and 3.4 actually have two fields each (and Figure 3.1 has three fields). The reason is that pivot tables consider the data that's totaled to be a field. This is consistent with how QuickBooks regards the data. In Figures 3.1, 3.2, and 3.4, the data that's totaled and shown as currency is QuickBooks' Amount field: You can tell because there's a cell labeled Sum of Amount. This label tells you that the Amount field has been summed, and the sums appear in the cells occupied by the table's data field.

> **NOTE** There are several functions that you can use to summarize the data field. So far this chapter has shown only the SUM function. For example, Figure 3.1 shows you the sum of the Amount field for Remodel class sales that took place in Bayshore summed to $117,465. Other functions available are the COUNT function (such as the number of sales of the Remodel class in Bayshore), AVERAGE, MAX, MIN, STANDARD DEVIATION, and VARIANCE. (The most useful of these for business analysis are SUM, COUNT, and AVERAGE.) Excel refers to all these functions as *totals*, even though only one, SUM, has anything to do with getting a total.

Page fields

A fourth type of field in a pivot table is the Page field. It hasn't yet appeared in this chapter's figures, but you'll see one in Figure 3.5.

QuickBooks has a field named Type (some reports in QuickBooks refer to it as Transaction Type). Its possible values include Invoice, Sales Receipt, Payment, Deposit, and so on. Used as a Page field in Figure 3.5, you can call for specific transactions: those that are invoices. You could use its dropdown to select any other type of transaction that appears in the report exported from QuickBooks. In Figure 3.5, only those transactions that are invoices contribute their data to the pivot table. For example, invoices for the Remodel class in Middlefield sum to $15,906.

If, instead, you wanted to see the sum of Sales Receipt transactions by class and city, you would choose Sales Receipt from the Type dropdown. (It is labeled Type because that's the name the QuickBooks report gives the field. If a QuickBooks report calls it Transaction Type, that's the label you'd see on the dropdown.)

Multiple fields, one orientation

There can be more than one row, column, data, or page field in a pivot table. The considerations are different for row and column fields than they are for page fields, or for the data field.

Here, Type is used as the Page Field, and Invoice is the selected Type.

Type	Invoice					
Sum of Amount	Class					
Name City	New Construction	Remodel	(blank)		Grand Total
Bayshore	$154,540	$117,465			$272,005
East Bayshore	$40,710	$45,772			$86,481
Middlefield	$76,722	$15,906			$92,629
Millbrae	$13,900	$167,755			$181,655
San Mateo		$24,005			$24,005
West Bear		$700			$700
(blank)			$15		$15
Grand Total	$285,872	$371,604	$15		$657,490

Multiple row or column fields

Suppose that you wanted the breakdown shown in Figure 3.1 but instead of Class in columns and City in rows, you wanted both Class and City in rows. That's entirely feasible and it might look like the table shown in Figure 3.6.

Figure 3.6 shows what happens when you treat, in this case, the Class field as a secondary or inner row field instead of as a column field. Compare Figure 3.6 to Figure 3.1. The total amounts for each combination of Class and City are the same in both figures. All that differs is the layout.

The pivot table has two row fields, termed an *inner* field and an *outer* field.

Type	Invoice		
Sum of Amount			
Name City	Class		Total
Bayshore	New Construction		$154,540
	Remodel		$117,465
Bayshore Total			$272,005
East Bayshore	New Construction		$40,710
	Remodel		$45,772
East Bayshore Total			$86,481
Middlefield	New Construction		$76,722
	Remodel		$15,906
Middlefield Total			$92,629
Millbrae	New Construction		$13,900
	Remodel		$167,755
Millbrae Total			$181,655
San Mateo	Remodel		$24,005
San Mateo Total			$24,005
West Bear	Remodel		$700
West Bear Total			$700
(blank)	(blank)		$15
(blank) Total			$15
Grand Total			$657,490

FIGURE 3.7

The Layout & Print tab gives you control over the placement of item labels.

But some people find it easier to locate a particular combination of Class and City when the fields are laid out as an inner and an outer row field. And if a field has more than three or four items, it can stretch too far, left to right, if it's treated as a column field. You get a taller, skinnier table if you use two row fields.

You also get a denser table structure. The totals for a particular City or Class are no longer found by looking to the end of a row or the bottom of a column. Instead, to find the subtotal for, say, East Bayshore, you have to look below the rows for East Bayshore New Construction and for East Bayshore Remodel; then you get to the subtotal for East Bayshore.

There's also the issue of subtotals for the inner row field. Notice in Figure 3.1 that the total across all cities for the Remodel class is $371,604. You don't find that total anywhere in Figure 3.6 because as the table is structured there is no place for the Remodel total.

In this situation, where you want an inner and an outer field, take these steps to get subtotals for the inner field:

1. Right-click any cell that contains a value for the inner field, such as New Construction in Figure 3.6.

2. Choose Field Settings from the contextual menu.

3. The Field Settings dialog box appears (see Figure 3.7). Choose Custom under Subtotals, and click Sum in the list box. Then click OK to close the dialog box.

The result of taking Steps 1 through 3 earlier appears in Figure 3.8.

FIGURE 3.8

The inner field's subtotals are called *block totals*.

Type	Invoice	

Sum of Amount		
Name City ▼	**Class** ▼	**Total**
⊟Bayshore	New Construction	$154,540
	Remodel	$117,465
Bayshore Total		$272,005
⊟East Bayshore	New Construction	$40,710
	Remodel	$45,772
East Bayshore Total		$86,481
⊟Middlefield	New Construction	$76,722
	Remodel	$15,906
Middlefield Total		$92,629
⊟Millbrae	New Construction	$13,900
	Remodel	$167,755
Millbrae Total		$181,655
⊟San Mateo	Remodel	$24,005
San Mateo Total		$24,005
⊟West Bear	Remodel	$700
West Bear Total		$700
⊟(blank)	(blank)	$15
(blank) Total		$15
	New Construction Sum	$285,872
	Remodel Sum	$371,604
	(blank) Sum	$15
Grand Total		$657,490

Notice near the bottom of the pivot table, just before the Grand Total row, you find three subtotals, sometimes called block totals, one for each Class (including the records with blank values on Class). The values are the same as the column totals shown in Figure 3.1.

Multiple data fields

You can display more than just one data field in a pivot table. The data fields might represent different underlying fields, such as Amount and Open Balance. Or they might show two ways of viewing the same field, such as Sum of Amount and Count of Amount. Figure 3.9 shows an example.

To keep the pivot table from becoming too complex, only one row field and one page field appear in Figure 3.9; there is no column field. As in prior figures, the transactions summarized by the pivot table are limited to Invoices by means of the page field.

By arranging to show both the count and the sum of the transactions' amounts, you can tell how important a particular city is to the business, in terms both of dollars billed and in terms of frequency of transactions.

Notice in Figure 3.9 that the two data fields, Count and Sum of Amount, are stacked vertically within each City item. In Excel 2003 and earlier, this is the default arrangement when you call for two or more data fields. But particularly when you have no column field, you might want to arrange the data fields side by side. Compare Figure 3.10 to Figure 3.9.

FIGURE 3.9

It's often useful to know how many transactions form the basis of a sum.

Type	Invoice	
Name City ▾	Data	Total
Bayshore	Count of Amount	526
	Sum of Amount	$272,004.85
East Bayshore	Count of Amount	198
	Sum of Amount	$86,481.21
Middlefield	Count of Amount	126
	Sum of Amount	$92,628.93
Millbrae	Count of Amount	54
	Sum of Amount	$181,655.00
San Mateo	Count of Amount	49
	Sum of Amount	$24,005.24
West Bear	Count of Amount	1
	Sum of Amount	$700.00
(blank)	Count of Amount	9
	Sum of Amount	$15.00
Total Count of Amount		963
Total Sum of Amount		$657,490.23

FIGURE 3.10

Showing data fields side by side can result in a more compact pivot table.

Type	Invoice	
	Data	
Name City ▾	Sum of Amount	Count of Amount
Bayshore	$272,004.85	526
East Bayshore	$86,481.21	198
Middlefield	$92,628.93	126
Millbrae	$181,655.00	54
San Mateo	$24,005.24	49
West Bear	$700.00	1
(blank)	$15.00	9
Grand Total	$657,490.23	963

To arrange the layout shown in Figure 3.10, start with the arrangement shown in Figure 3.9. Then take these steps:

1. Move the mouse pointer over the button labeled Data.

2. When the mouse pointer turns into a crosshairs, press the mouse button and hold it down.

3. Drag the Data button one column to the right and release the mouse button.

If you want to stack the data fields vertically, take Steps 1 and 2 earlier, but drag the Data button one row down and one column to the left before releasing it.

The default arrangement of multiple data fields in Excel 2007 is side by side, and the button is labeled Values instead of Data. Otherwise the procedures are as given immediately prior.

FIGURE 3.11

Selecting for Invoice transactions keeps Sales Receipts out of the analysis and focuses on credit sales.

| Account | 40130 · Labor Income | ▾ |
| Type | Invoice | ▾ |

Sum of Amount	
Name City ▾	Total
Bayshore	$59,829.50
East Bayshore	$18,208.25
Middlefield	$19,276.50
Millbrae	$129,090.00
San Mateo	$1,175.00
West Bear	$700.00
Grand Total	$228,279.25

Multiple page fields

The section "Page fields" earlier in this chapter noted that you use a pivot table's page field as a record-selection device. For example, if the underlying data set includes various transaction types, you can set the Page field to Invoice to limit the records summarized by the pivot table to only Invoice transactions.

You could limit the records even further by including another page field in the pivot table. If the additional page field represented Account, you could select the Labor Income item. Then the pivot table summaries would be based on invoice transactions that are posted to the Labor Income account. Figure 3.11 shows how this arrangement might look.

The important issue here is that adding a second page field to a pivot table connects the two page field items by a logical AND. That is, in Figure 3.11, the records that are summarized by the sum and count functions are those that are Invoice transactions and that post to Labor Income.

TIP To arrange page fields side by side, right-click a cell in the pivot table and choose PivotTable Options from the contextual menu. Change the Display Fields in Report Filter Area from Down, Then Over to Over, Then Down.

Data summaries

The previous section explained how to manage the use of multiple fields as row fields, page fields, and data fields. When you have more than one data field it's often because you want to display the field using different kinds of totals: as a sum, as a count, as an average, and so on. Here's how to change a data field's summary function:

Suppose you have already established Amount as a data field in a pivot table, and that the data field appears as the Sum of Amount. If you want to change that to Count instead, take these steps:

1. Right click any cell in the pivot table's Data area — in this example, that means any cell that contains a sum for the Amount field.

2. Choose Value Field Settings from the contextual menu.

3. The Value Field Settings dialog box appears as shown in Figure 3.12. (When you're working with a Data field, the dialog box's appearance differs from that shown in Figure 3.7.)

4. Choose Count in the Summarize Value Field By list box.

NOTE If a field has even one missing value — a blank cell — or text value in the pivot table's data source, then Excel uses COUNT as the default totaling method. If all the field's values are numeric, then the default totaling method is SUM.

Number formats in Data fields

Pivot tables offer a special method of formatting Data fields. Suppose that you just now finished creating the pivot table shown in Figure 3.11. The number format of the Data field is by default General, so you would see no dollar signs or commas in the data field totals. You would prefer that the format be Currency.

The normal way to format cells is to select them and then use Format Cells, either from the Formatting toolbar, or from the Excel 2007 Ribbon, or by right-clicking the cells and using the contextual menu.

These methods all associate the selected format with the cells that the Data field occupies, not necessarily with the Data field itself. Under some circumstances, when you modify the pivot table structure, you can lose that cell formatting. Furthermore, if you change a SUM field to a COUNT field, the cell formatting can make it look like East Bayshore has $198.00 transactions instead of 198 transactions.

FIGURE 3.12

You can edit the field's name in the Custom Name edit box, but it's best to include the totaling method as part of the name.

So the best way to set a number format for a Data field is to use its field settings. Right-click in a Data field cell and choose Value Field Settings from the contextual menu. Click the Number Format button in the Value Field Settings dialog box and select the number format you want for the field.

If you subsequently change the totaling method for the Data field from, for example, SUM to COUNT, Excel acts as though you have changed the Data field itself, not just its totaling method. Therefore Excel does not apply the currency format you established for the SUM to the field when it shows COUNT instead. It applies the General number format, or some other number format that you have specified for the data field when it shows counts.

And if you change the structure of the table, you can be confident that the Data field will retain the number format you assigned to it, whether you change a row field to a column orientation or vice versa.

Using other totals

At times you will want to view your QuickBooks data using a totaling method other than Sum and Count. As the earlier section "Data fields" mentioned, there are several other totals that you might find useful. These include AVERAGE, MIN, and MAX.

If you have read Chapter 10, you know that some sales are more efficient than others. The sale of a product with a higher contribution margin is generally more profitable than the sale of a product with a lower contribution margin.

A similar line of thought, applied to total sales revenue and number of sales, shows that the notion of average sales revenue can be important. If it takes 200 sales to reach $20,000 in revenue, then there's something about those sales that makes them less efficient than 100 different sales that get you to the same revenue figure. A more rigorous analysis would look at both revenue and variable costs, along with a breakdown by item sold, sales territory, and sales rep. But you can get a quick idea by comparing a total revenue analysis with an average revenue analysis — perhaps something such as in Figure 3.13.

FIGURE 3.13

These three pivot tables sort the cities by descending total revenue, by descending transaction counts, and by descending average revenue.

Sum of Amount			Count of Amount			Average of Amount	
Name City	Total		Name City	Total		Name City	Total
Bayshore	$272,004.85		Bayshore	526		Millbrae	$3,363.98
Millbrae	$181,655.00		East Bayshore	198		Middlefield	$735.15
Middlefield	$92,628.93		Middlefield	126		West Bear	$700.00
East Bayshore	$86,481.21		Millbrae	54		Bayshore	$517.12
San Mateo	$24,005.24		San Mateo	49		San Mateo	$489.90
West Bear	$700.00		West Bear	1		East Bayshore	$436.77
(blank)	$15.00		(blank)	9		(blank)	$1.67
Grand Total	$657,490.23		Grand Total	963		Grand Total	$682.75

FIGURE 3.14

If you choose Name City instead of Sum of Amount, you can get an alphabetic sort of the row field by the name of the city.

Figure 3.13 shows that the company realizes the greatest portion of its revenue from sales in Bayshore, and the second largest portion from Millbrae — the difference between the two is over $90,000. Bayshore looks like a good sales patch.

But if you look at the average sales, you see that Bayshore falls from first place in total revenue to fourth place in average revenue. The culprit is the number of sales in Bayshore: 526 versus 198 in East Bayshore. Much depends on how the company makes its sales: Online, for example, entails a lot less overhead than cold calls. Still, those Bayshore sales have to be eating up a lot of G&A dollars, and a manager at Rock Castle Construction should probably be looking hard at how the company's sales force is deployed.

You can't make that kind of inference from just looking at total revenue. You have to look at averages and perhaps counts as well.

It's important to recognize that there's no QuickBooks report that will give you this sort of analysis. But if you don't have it, you have no quantitative basis to manage your company's sales. You need something that looks at total and average revenue by fields such as territory, sales rep, or item sold.

Sorting row fields

Figure 3.13 shows the same data set sorted three ways: by Sum of Amount, by Count of Amount, and by Average of Amount. You could arrange these data sorts by the usual Excel method of selecting the range and then choosing Sort from the Data menu (in Excel 2007, you choose Sort & Filter from either the Home or the Data tab).

But if you do that, you might have to do it again if you restructure the pivot table in some way. If you know that you'll always want to sort a pivot table in a particular way, take these steps in Excel 2007:

FIGURE 3.15

Both the actual counts and the resulting percentages are shown for comparison.

Type	Invoice ▾		Type	Invoice ▾
Count of Amount			Count of Amount	
Class ▾	Total		Class ▾	Total
New Construction	46.52%		New Construction	448
Remodel	52.54%		Remodel	506
(blank)	0.93%		(blank)	9
Grand Total	100.00%		Grand Total	963

1. Right-click a row field item. In Figure 3.13 you might choose Bayshore under Name City.

2. Choose Sort from the contextual menu.

3. Click More Options. The Sort (Name City) dialog box shown in Figure 3.14 appears.

4. To replicate the setup in Figure 3.13, click the Descending (Z to A) dropdown in the Sort Options dialog box.

5. Choose Sum of Amount from the Descending (Z to A) dropdown.

6. Click OK.

In versions earlier than Excel 2007, choose Field Settings in Step 2 and click the Advanced button in Step 3.

Displaying data as percents

Thus far, this chapter has focused on showing actual dollar amounts, or counts of transactions, in pivot table data fields. You can also view them as percents. For example, you might wonder what percent of a company's revenue comes from different classes of sales. The Rock Castle Construction Company uses New Construction, Remodel, and Overhead as its three classes. Figure 3.15 shows how invoiced sales amounts are distributed across the company's classes.

To get an analysis such as the one shown in Figure 3.15, take these steps:

1. Build or redesign the pivot table so that it has the Row field and the Data field you want. Use the Data field's settings to choose the totaling method you want — most likely, SUM, COUNT, or AVERAGE.

2. Right-click a Data field cell and choose Value Field Settings from the contextual menu.

3. Click the Show Values As tab, and choose % of Column from the Show Values As dropdown.

4. Click OK.

Note that the sequence is functionally the same in Excel 2003 and earlier.

Most of the choices you have in the Show Data As dropdown are different sorts of percents: percent of row, percent of or percent difference from some other item, and so on. You are unlikely to need or want to use any of these options, but you might want to keep in mind that they're there.

> **NOTE** One useful option in the Show Data As dropdown is the Running Total In option. This option can be useful when you need to re-create balance sheet accounts for consecutive accounting periods. You would set the base field to Date.

Moving Data into a Pivot Table

So far, I have focused on how you can use pivot tables, configured in different ways, to answer questions about a business's operations that can't be addressed directly in the QuickBooks user interface. There are more such examples in the remainder of the chapter, but it's time to see how to build a pivot table from data that you have exported from QuickBooks via reports. (Chapters 1 and 2 cover in detail the considerations involved in exporting reports to Excel.)

Bear in mind as you glance through the following material that you do not need to complete the processes for every pivot table you build. It's quite enough to export a new report when your company data has changed significantly — depending on how active your company file is, you might want to re-export data weekly, monthly, or even quarterly.

This chapter also shows you a little-known way to update all your pivot tables with fresh data from QuickBooks without doing anything more than exporting a new report. Implementing that technique can save you large amounts of time, even in the short run.

Sources of data for pivot tables

Depending on the version, Excel supports three or four sources of data for a pivot table. At least one must be in place before you can build a pivot table. This book concentrates on just one data source: the list. The next section explores the relationship between Excel lists and QuickBooks reports.

An Excel pivot table can also be built using data in another application such as an Oracle, SQL Server, or Access database. The database must support open database connectivity (ODBC), a standard software interface that enables the exchange of data between applications. QuickBooks' support for ODBC is very limited, though, and you can't depend on its availability from version to version, or even for all datasets within a specific version. (Some ODBC drivers are available from third-party vendors.)

Two other data sources have very limited applicability. Multiple Consolidation Ranges, which is no longer available in Excel 2007, was never a truly feasible source. Another Pivot Table as a data source had significant drawbacks and has also been dropped as an option from Excel 2007.

NOTE   **The drawbacks have to do with the shared cache. For example, if two pivot tables share the same data cache and a field is grouped in a particular way in one pivot table, it is automatically grouped the same way in the other pivot table. This was generally regarded as an annoying situation.**

That leaves Excel lists. An Excel list is an informal structure and in fact is little more than a set of guidelines for laying out data. In Excel 2007, lists have become formal structures, but are known as tables.

If you want to apply Excel's powerful analytic technology to QuickBooks data, it's essential that you understand the basics of Excel lists and tables. Fortunately, QuickBooks' transaction reports work beautifully with Excel list and table structures.

In Excel 2007, a table is not the same as a pivot table. An Excel 2007 table is a list with a few bells and whistles added into the mix. If you identify a list as a table by clicking the Ribbon's Insert tab and then clicking Table in the Tables group, Excel does the following:

- Adds AutoFilter dropdowns in the table's first row.
- Enables the addition of a totals row to the end of the table.
- Adds shading to the rows and columns.
- Creates a named range that identifies the table.

Of these actions, the fourth is useful. Later sections of this chapter explain named ranges in more detail; for now, simply know that you can tell Excel to use a named range as a pivot table's data source.

Excel lists

Figure 3.16 shows an example of a QuickBooks report after it's been exported to Excel.

You can create this list of QuickBooks data in Excel by following the steps described in Chapter 2. Once you're used to exporting a report, it's almost second nature and you can get the data out of QuickBooks and into Excel in three steps: Open the report, modify it as needed, and export it to Excel.

Once the report is there, you still have a couple of quick steps to conform to Excel's list structure:

- Delete mostly blank rows starting at row 2. Notice row 2 in Figure 13.16. QuickBooks puts it there to show the date label in the Custom Transaction Detail report if the user has specified a date range other than All. An Excel list should not have a row of blank cells immediately following the field names in the first row, so in this case you would delete row 2. QuickBooks often puts more blank rows at the top of other detail reports (for example, the Profit & Loss Detail report), and then you would delete each blank row to draw the start of the actual data up to just below the field names.

FIGURE 3.16

Notice that the list structure largely conforms to the QuickBooks detail report format.

	Type	Date	Name	Name City	Account	Class	Amount
1	Type	Date	Name	Name City	Account	Class	Amount
2							
3	Bill	09/30/2011	Sloan Roofing	Bayshore	20000 · Accounts Payable		-500.00
4	Bill	09/30/2011	Abercrombie, Kristy:Remodel Bathro	Bayshore	54300 · Job Materials	Remodel	500.00
5	Bill	10/01/2011	McClain Appliances	Middlefield	20000 · Accounts Payable		-1,780.00
6	Bill	10/01/2011	Cook, Brian:Kitchen	Middlefield	54300 · Job Materials	Remodel	475.00
7	Bill	10/01/2011	Cook, Brian:Kitchen	Middlefield	54300 · Job Materials	Remodel	385.00
8	Bill	10/01/2011	Cook, Brian:Kitchen	Middlefield	54300 · Job Materials	Remodel	255.00
9	Bill	10/01/2011	Cook, Brian:Kitchen	Middlefield	54300 · Job Materials	Remodel	375.00
10	Bill	10/01/2011	Cook, Brian:Kitchen	Middlefield	54300 · Job Materials	Remodel	195.00
11	Bill	10/01/2011	Cook, Brian:Kitchen	Middlefield	54300 · Job Materials	Remodel	95.00
12	Bill	10/03/2011	Hamlin Metal	Bayshore	20000 · Accounts Payable		-239.00
13	Bill	10/03/2011	Pretell Real Estate:155 Wilks Blvd.	Middlefield	54500 · Subcontractors	New Construction	239.00
14	Invoice	10/05/2011	Teschner, Anton:Sun Room	Bayshore	11000 · Accounts Receiva	New Construction	1,960.00
15	Invoice	10/05/2011	Teschner, Anton:Sun Room	Bayshore	40130 · Labor Income	New Construction	-1,960.00
16	Invoice	10/05/2011	State Board of Equalization	Sacramento	25500 · Sales Tax Payable	New Construction	0.00

■ Delete any rows that contain subtotals. QuickBooks knows that those rows are sub-totals, but Excel doesn't, so Excel interprets a subtotal row as a separate record. The effect is to falsely inflate the dollar totals in the resulting pivot table.

After you have deleted blank rows beginning with row 2, and subtotal rows, you are left with a range of data in the worksheet that conforms to what Excel calls a list. A list has column labels and different records in different rows; it should not have blank columns interspersed as separators.

Column labels

An Excel list has the names of the fields in its first row; they are often termed *column labels*. This characteristic of lists is useful for analysis techniques other than pivot tables. Excel can use column labels in chart legends, to make it easier to sort data and filter it, and for use with other utilities such as the analysis toolpack.

While you can get away with omitting column labels with data that you'll chart, sort, or filter, these labels are required in a pivot table's data source. If you omit the column headers, Excel will think your first row of data represents the column headers.

Records in rows

Each row in a list constitutes a different record. The records need not be sorted, although of course they can be. It is technically permissible but inconvenient for there to be blank rows in the list, so you should delete any that exist. As noted earlier, you should also delete any subtotal and total rows from the exported report.

Custom Transaction Detail report

QuickBooks' Custom Transaction Detail report is nearly ideal as a data source for an Excel pivot table. That is so for several reasons, as follows.

All transactions included

Most QuickBooks detail reports include at least one filter. The Profit & Loss Detail report filters for all income and expense accounts. The Sales by Customer Detail report filters for all sales items and all customers/jobs. The Inventory Valuation Detail report filters for all inventory and assembly items.

By contrast, the only filter that the Custom Transaction Detail report includes is Dates, which defaults to This Month-to-date. If you set that filter to All before exporting, you'll get all transactions, regardless of date, transaction type, account, or any other criterion.

This is helpful because you can use Excel's pivot table page fields to limit the records you analyze to a particular period, or class, account, and so on. To get a different view, you just choose a different item in the page field — you don't need to re-run the report with a different filter.

> **NOTE** There are times when it is useful to use a filter to the Custom Transaction Detail report before you export it. For example, without a good bit of spadework it is difficult to show all income accounts, and only income accounts, using a pivot table's page field. In a case like that, it's usually better to include the field as a row field and use the field's dropdown to select individual items. Even this approach can be onerous, but if you use the QuickBooks Account filter before exporting the report it's very easy to limit the analysis to the accounts you're interested in.

Most fields included

The Custom Transaction Detail Transaction report can display 71 fields. This does not include all the fields available in QuickBooks but it does account for most of the fields that you're likely to want to analyze. Calculated fields such as the current average cost of an inventory item and some specialized fields such as Vehicle Mileage Rate are not included. Figure 3.17 shows the fields available in the Custom Transaction Detail report.

Memorize the report

I recommend that you make two changes to the Custom Transaction Detail report and then have QuickBooks memorize the report with your changes. The changes are as follows:

- Change the report's dates to All.
- Include all the fields in the report. Click the report's Modify Report tab and use the Columns list box to select all fields. If you don't want to include all fields, at least include all the fields that you might ever want to access. Omit the *(left margin)* column, which isn't a field at all but is just some padding on the left edge of the report.

After you have made those changes, click the report's Memorize button, give it a meaningful name such as Custom Transaction Detail for Pivot Tables, and click OK.

The reason to make these changes, and to memorize them, is that there are likely to be several pivot tables that you will want to examine on a periodic basis — monthly, quarterly, weekly, whatever. If you set things up correctly, you won't have to re-create those pivot tables every time another period has elapsed. You just run the report again and export it to the existing

FIGURE 3.17

The field categories are arbitrary.

Customer/ Vendor/ Employee	Financial information	Transaction Identification	Payroll and taxes
Name	Terms	Entered/Last Modified	SSN/Tax ID
Source Name	Due Date	Last modified by	Payroll Item
Name Address	Billed Date	Date	Tax Table Version
Name Street1	Paid Through	State	Income Subject To Tax
Name Street2	Discount Available	Action	Wage Base
Name City	Sales Tax Code	Adj	Wage Base (Tips)
Name State	Clr	User Edit?	Tax Line
Name Zip	Pay Meth	Trans #	WC Rate
Name Contact	Aging		Exp. Mod.
Name Phone #	Open Balance	**Item information**	WC Code
Name Fax #	Billing Status	Item	
Name E-Mail	Split	Item Description	**Miscellaneous**
Name Account #	Debit	Qty	Type
Rep	Credit	U/M	Num
Contract #	Amount	Sales Price	P. O. #
	Paid		S. O. #
Shipping information	Balance		Memo
Ship Date	Account		Class
Deliv Date	Account Type		Print
FOB	Calculated Amount		Estimate Active
Via	Amount Difference		

Excel workbook. When you have that workbook set up as described in the next section, your pivot tables will automatically refresh themselves with the new set of exported data.

If you know that you're always getting all transactions from your company file, regardless of their date, you can be confident that your periodic exports update the workbook accurately. (You can always filter for particular dates in the pivot table itself.)

The reason to include all the available fields in the report is partly practical and partly technical. As a practical matter, by exporting all the fields in the same report, you can base several pivot tables on the same set of source data. And if something in an analysis piques your interest, it might be that you already have some other field available that will help you explore further.

As a technical matter, exporting all the fields the first time means that you won't have to add a field later on. If you have to add one later, you might have to rebuild your pivot tables. If a pivot table sees a field name that wasn't there when it was built, difficulties can arise when the table updates itself based on the new set of data.

Use a named range

Excel has a feature called *range names*. If you give a name, such as Data_For_Pivot_Tables, to a range of contiguous cells in a worksheet, you can use that name when you're asked to identify the location of a pivot table's source data.

NOTE Named ranges have many other uses in Excel. As just one example, you can use them in formulas as data sources for charts. But the other uses go beyond the scope of this book, and well beyond the scope of this chapter.

Quick and easy dynamic range names

If you're not interested (or not interested just now) in the technical underpinnings of dynamic range names, skip the next section, "Creating dynamic range names." You can use the information in this section when you're ready to build the pivot table. Later, if you get curious, you might want to come back to the next section.

After you have exported the Custom Transaction Detail report from QuickBooks, you'll want to delete its second, blank row and any subtotal or total rows it contains. These deletions were explained in the earlier section "Excel lists."

NOTE You should leave column A alone, even though it's mostly blank and often completely so. If you delete a blank column A so that the main data range starts there, you'll have to delete column A again the next time you export to this sheet. If you do that, you'll induce a #REF! error in the definition of the dynamic range name.

Now name the range by taking the following steps. (You need take them once only.)

1. Select the cell in the uppermost row and the leftmost column in the exported report. In the course of events as described here, that's cell B1. (Although you'll see any applicable dates in column A, the actual report data starts in column B.)

2. If you're using Excel 2007, click the Formulas tab on the Ribbon and then click Define Name in the Defined Names group. If you're using an earlier version of Excel, choose Insert ▶ Name ▶ Define. The New Name dialog box for Excel 2007 appears in Figure 3.18; the Define Name dialog box in prior versions differs only slightly.

3. Type the name Data_For_Pivot_Tables into the Name edit box. Of course, you can use just about any name you want, as long as it doesn't contain spaces and doesn't resemble a cell reference like D15. (There are other rules but it's hard to break them unless you're really working at it.)

4. Assuming that you began in Step 1 by selecting cell B1, enter the following in the Refers To edit box:
   ```
   =OFFSET(Sheet1!$B$1,0,0,COUNTA(Sheet1!$B:$B),
   COUNTA(Sheet1!$1:$1)).
   ```

5. Click OK.

Creating dynamic range names

Here's the background, technical information on the formula at the end of the previous section. Again, you can skip this if you want.

What you're aiming for is a way to update several — perhaps many — pivot tables in an Excel workbook when you export new data to the workbook from a QuickBooks report. When you first create the pivot tables, you tell Excel to look for the source data in a range named — well, whatever name you want. This chapter is using, as its example of a range name, Data_For_Pivot_Tables.

FIGURE 3.18

Excel names can refer to ranges, constants, and even formulas.

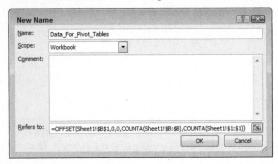

 **The technique described here works equally well for automatically updating Excel charts with new data.**

When you define a range name, you include a reference to worksheet cells. For example, in the Refers To edit box, you could enter this:

```
=Sheet1!$A$1:$E$5
```

Then the name would refer to that worksheet range in the worksheet named Sheet1. (By convention, Excel uses an exclamation point to separate the name of a worksheet from a cell or range address.) The dollar signs in $A$1 and $E$5 anchor the reference to the range A1:E5.

The problem is that a range defined by a reference to fixed column letters and row numbers is static. No matter whether the data you export from QuickBooks occupies five rows or 500, five columns or 50, the name you defined as referring to Sheet1!$A$1:$E$5 stubbornly continues to refer to those specific 25 cells.

But if you create a *dynamic* range name, you can replace the old data with new, a smaller range with a larger one, and the name will *redefine itself* to capture all the new data. If you set up the pivot tables so that they look to a named range for their source data rather than to a specific address, the pivot tables will also capture the new data.

The way to do that is to use something similar to this formula in the New Name dialog box:

```
=OFFSET(Sheet1!$B$1,0,0,COUNTA(Sheet1!$B:$B),COUNTA(Sheet1!$1:$1))
```

The formula uses Excel's OFFSET function, which defines the location, and number of rows and columns, of a worksheet range. Its syntax is:

```
=OFFSET(Reference,Rows,Columns,Height,Width)
```

The address that OFFSET assembles is based on its *reference* argument. Suppose the reference is cell $B$1, as in the prior example. Then the remaining arguments to the function have these effects:

- The Rows argument defines how far away from B1, in rows, that the new range starts.
- The Columns argument defines how far away from B1, in columns, that the new range starts.
- Height is the number of rows occupied by the new range.
- Width is the number of columns occupied by the new range.

So, the formula

```
=OFFSET($B$1,1,1,3,4)
```

returns an address that is one row down and one column right of B1. It is three rows high and four columns wide. So the OFFSET function with those arguments returns the range C2:F4.

In the example, this section is using the following for the pivot table's source data:

```
=OFFSET(Sheet1!$B$1,0,0,COUNTA(Sheet1!$B:$B),COUNTA(Sheet1!$1:$1))
```

The reference cell is Sheet1!$B$1, and the new range starts zero rows down and zero columns over from $B$1 — that is, the new range's upper-left corner is cell $B$1.

The entire point of defining a range name in this way is to make the reference sensitive to the number of rows and columns it occupies. Therefore, the number of rows and columns that contain data must be counted. The results of those counts determine the number of rows and columns in the named range.

The COUNTA function is used to count the number of values, whether numeric or not, in a range of cells. For example, in

```
=COUNTA(Sheet1!$1:$1)
```

the COUNTA function returns the number of values in row 1 of Sheet1.

And in

```
=COUNTA(Sheet1!$B:$B
```

the COUNTA function returns the number of values in column B of Sheet1. This is why I prefer to suppress (left margin) in the report's display, and to be certain that the report's first column contains a field such as Trans # or Type that is sure to have a value in every transaction. That way, I'll get an accurate count of the number of transactions that the exported QuickBooks report contains. I don't want the first data column to contain a field such as Debit, which is overwhelmingly likely to contain fewer values than there are exported records.

So, if the exported report contains 70 columns and 1,500 rows, then the range definition

```
=OFFSET(Sheet1!$B$1,0,0,COUNTA(Sheet1!$B:$B),COUNTA(Sheet1!$1:$1))
```

resolves to this:

```
=OFFSET(Sheet1!$B$1,0,0,1500,70)
```

or, more simply, Sheet1!B1:BS1500. That's the address of the range occupied by a report exported to Sheet1 when the report has 1,500 rows and 70 columns. If the range is named Data_For_Pivot_Tables, any and all pivot tables in the workbook that base their source data on the range Data_For_Pivot_Tables will get their data from Sheet1!B1:BS1500.

Back to the entire point of doing all this. (Doing it just once, remember.) The *next* time that you export the report to Sheet1 in this workbook, it's liable to have more rows: More time will have elapsed and more transactions will have been recorded, therefore the Custom Transaction Detail report will have more rows (unless, of course, you add a filter to it; the technique described here handles that situation, too).

Because you created a *dynamic* range name, the range redefines itself when the new data arrives. The OFFSET formula re-counts the number of values in the first column and extends the range reference to encompass all the new rows. The pivot tables that use the range for their source data now refer to the newly extended range.

The same is true of the number of columns in the range. I advised you earlier, in the section "Memorize the report," to use the same number of fields — all of them — when you export the report. In case you decide not to follow that advice, the OFFSET formula counts not only the rows but the columns in the exported report.

> **NOTE** Suppose you decide to establish a shorter range of dates for the report prior to re-exporting it. Won't that result in a smaller range? If so, what happens to the data in the earlier, larger range? QuickBooks warns you, when you're exporting to an existing worksheet, that it will overwrite existing data. It doesn't tell you that it first deletes all the data in the worksheet. Therefore, you don't need to worry about earlier data remaining. (You *do* need to worry about data that you don't want to lose, even if it's outside the range occupied by the exported QuickBooks report.)

> **CAUTION** Be sure that you don't put any extraneous data in column B or row 1, outside the range occupied by the exported report. If you do, the COUNTA functions in the range definition will count those values and will give the range too many rows or too many columns, or both.

Building the pivot table

Once you have exported the report to Excel into a dynamic named range, as described in the previous section, you're ready to build a pivot table.

> **NOTE** If you have already built one or more pivot table reports based on exported QuickBooks reports, as described in the earlier section "Use a named range," you do not need to rebuild the pivot tables. The instructions in the previous section are designed to provide a basis that responds accurately to new data in an exported QuickBooks report. The existing pivot tables do need to cite the range's name, such as Data_For_Pivot_Tables, as their data source.

To build a new pivot table, take these steps:

FIGURE 3.19

The External Data Source option is not generally useful with QuickBooks data sources.

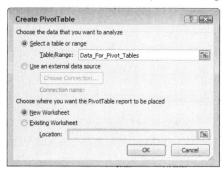

1. In Excel 2007, click the Ribbon's Insert tab and then click PivotTable in the Tables group. In earlier versions of Excel, choose Data ▶ PivotTable and PivotChart Report.

2. Excel 2007 displays the Create PivotTable dialog box shown in Figure 3.19. In the Table/Range edit box, enter the name of the dynamic range you established for the exported QuickBooks report. This example uses Data_For_Pivot_Tables.

3. Leave the New Worksheet option selected and click OK.

Versions of Excel earlier than Excel 2007 use a three-step wizard. Use its first step to indicate that the data source is an Excel list. Supply the name of the dynamic range in the second step, and specify a new worksheet in the third step.

Excel 2007 displays the worksheet and the PivotTable Field List dialog box shown in Figure 3.20 when you leave the Create PivotTable dialog box.

Versions earlier than Excel 2007 present a somewhat different interface. The functionality is identical but you can drag fields from the Field List directly into their areas in the worksheet (for example, Drop Page Fields Here and Drop Data Items Here).

Using the field list

Using the PivotTable Field List dialog box shown in Figure 3.20, drag the fields from the list box labeled Choose Fields to Add to Report into the boxes where you want them:

- The Report Filter box represents a pivot table's page fields.
- The Column Labels and Row Labels boxes represent a pivot table's Column and Row fields, respectively.
- The Values box represents a pivot table's Data fields.

If you filled the Defer Layout Update checkbox, you can click the Update button at any time to view the pivot table's current structure. When you have finished the initial design, close the dialog box. Figure 3.21 shows one possible result.

FIGURE 3.20

Fill the Defer Layout Update checkbox to keep the pivot table placeholder in the worksheet as you add more fields.

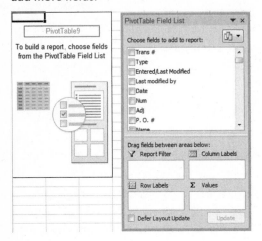

FIGURE 3.21

Use the Terms dropdown to display or suppress individual items.

Count of Debit Terms	Total
1% 10 Net 30	2
Due on receipt	22
Net 15	64
Net 30	208
Net 60	20
(blank)	60
Grand Total	376

You can, of course, create other pivot tables to cut the data in different ways. Let each pivot table get its data from the same named range — again, this example has used the range name Data_For_Pivot_Tables. When each pivot table is based on the same data range, you can be more confident that you're not comparing apples and bowling balls. When you're through designing the pivot tables, be sure to save the workbook.

Refreshing pivot tables

A pivot table doesn't automatically respond to a change in its source data the way a worksheet formula does. Suppose you use the SUM function in a formula to get the total of the values in A1:A5. Then you change the value in, say, A3. Unless you've gone to the trouble of turning off automatic recalculation, the formula with the SUM function immediately recalculates and takes account of the changed value.

Pivot tables don't work like that. When their data source changes, they don't automatically recalculate themselves. You have to arrange for that to happen. There are three basic methods:

Manual refreshes

Updating a pivot table to reflect new data is called *refreshing the pivot table*. To do this manually, right-click any cell in the pivot table and choose Refresh from the contextual menu (in versions earlier than Excel 2007, the menu item is Refresh Data).

Semi-automatic refreshes

You can, if you want, use the pivot table's options to call for the pivot table to refresh itself when the workbook is opened. This approach has value when the pivot table's data source is not a range in a worksheet, as explained in this chapter, but a connection to an external database. In that case, whenever you open the workbook, the pivot table refreshes itself from the latest information in the database.

QuickBooks does not generally support that sort of live connection. So, if you want to take this approach, you would have to update the workbook with new data from a QuickBooks report as described earlier in this chapter, then save and close the workbook, and then cause the pivot table or tables to refresh themselves by reopening the workbook.

Automatic refreshes

This is probably the most convenient method in the long run, but it requires some up-front work. The idea is to cause VBA code to run automatically whenever you activate a worksheet that contains one or more pivot tables. (VBA is Microsoft's Visual Basic for Applications scripting language, which Excel uses.) In turn, the VBA code causes the pivot tables to refresh. This approach is superior to manual or semi-automatic refreshes because you don't have to remember to do it every time you export a QuickBooks report.

Here are the steps to arrange automatic refreshes:

1. Right-click the worksheet tab of a worksheet that contains one or more pivot tables.

2. Choose View Code from the contextual menu.

3. The Visual Basic Editor window opens, as shown in Figure 3.22.

4. There are two dropdowns at the top of the Code window. The one on the left, by default, displays General. Choose Worksheet from that dropdown.

5. The dropdown on the right changes to display *SelectionChange* and two VBA statements appear in the Code window. You can select and delete them if you want. They do no harm if you decide to keep them.

6. Choose Activate from the dropdown on the right. The following statements appear in the code window, with a blank row between them:

   ```
   Private Sub Worksheet_Activate()
   End Sub
   ```

FIGURE 3.22

You can switch back to the worksheet view by clicking the Excel icon at the left of the upper toolbar.

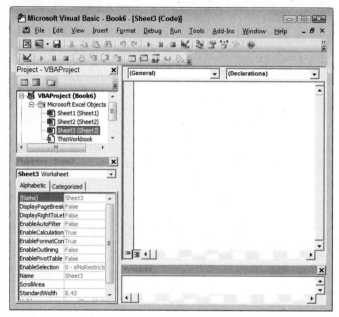

7. Enter the following code between the Private Sub and the End Sub statements:

```
Dim pt As PivotTable
For Each pt In ActiveSheet.PivotTables
    pt.RefreshTable
Next pt
```

8. Switch back to the Excel workbook window and save the workbook.

Now whenever you activate the worksheet, any pivot table in that worksheet will be refreshed with the most current data in its data source.

Updating the saved workbook

With all the spadework done, it's easy to update the pivot tables later, perhaps at the beginning of the next accounting period. Just export the version of the Custom Transaction Detail report you had QuickBooks memorize. If any transactions occurred in the meantime, they will be included in the new export.

The steps to perform an initial export have been described in detail in Chapter 2. Follow those steps to export the report to a new Excel workbook. Then follow the steps described earlier in this chapter, in the section "Excel lists." Create the dynamic named range, design the pivot tables, and save the workbook.

Now you're ready to update the workbook — and thus the dynamic named range and the associated pivot tables — with new data:

1. Make sure that the Excel workbook you want to update is closed. Excel itself can be open. (If the workbook is open, QuickBooks will wait until you're ready to export; then QuickBooks will tell you that you need to close the workbook first.)

2. Open the memorized report in QuickBooks and click the Export button.

3. Choose An Existing Excel Workbook.

4. Click Browse, and navigate to the location where the pivot table workbook is stored, and click Open.

5. Choose Use an Existing Sheet in the Workbook. Choose the name of the worksheet that contains the exported data from the Select a Sheet dropdown.

6. Be sure the Include a New Worksheet checkbox is cleared.

7. Click Export.

When the export is complete, proceed as described earlier in the section "Excel lists." You just have to delete the second, blank row and any subtotal rows. The dynamic range name now takes over and recalculates its rows and columns so that all the pertinent data is captured. Your pivot tables will update according to your choice of manual, semi-automatic, or automatic refreshes, described earlier in this section.

Special Features of Pivot Tables

Since Microsoft introduced Excel pivot tables in the mid-1990s, they have become more and more integrated into the full workbook interface. Related features, such as pivot charts, have been implemented. (This section is not intended as a treatise on Excel or its pivot tables. But it often helps to know that a particular feature exists. That way, if you decide at some point that you might want to use it, you'll know it's there and you'll know what terms to look up for further information.)

Handling pivot table fields

Even though you have set up the pivot tables to do the analyses that you're interested in, from time to time you'll want to fine-tune them, or make them do something special so that you can peer into the data summary more closely. Some of the associated techniques are explained here.

Managing subtotals

Figure 3.6 shows an example of a pivot table with two row fields: an outer row field (Name City) and an inner row field (Class). A subtotal for each Name City item appears after the final Class item for that city. Usually you'll want to see those subtotals, but you can suppress them if you don't:

1. Right-click any cell in the column that shows the names of the outer row field's items.

2. Choose Field Settings from the contextual menu. The Field Settings dialog box appears.

3. Click None in the Subtotals area, and then click OK.

You can also use the Field Settings dialog box to change the name of the field as it's displayed in the pivot table. The field will still point to its original column in the pivot table's data source.

Other settings in the Field Settings dialog box are more idiosyncratic. You can, for example, call for a subtotal that uses a different type of summary than is shown for the individual row items. For example, each value for Name City could show the Sum of Amount. But then the subtotal for Class could show the Average of Amount. (It would take an unusual analysis requirement to get you to make that sort of arrangement.) There are some other layout options on the Layout & Print tab, such as including a page break at each change in a field's item.

Grouping numeric fields

Row and column fields in a pivot table are usually best reserved for fields that identify categories, such as individual cities and states, or inventory items, or sales reps. A row field isn't often used to display each individual value found in a numeric field such as Amount.

At times, though, you would like to group numeric values into categories such as Low, Medium, and High. Suppose that you're thinking of altering your company's sales commission plan to include bonuses for sales that fall within certain revenue categories. Before you implement the plan, it would be wise to determine the number of past sales in each category.

The way to do that is to group the Amount field in categories. Here are the steps:

1. Establish a pivot table with Amount as both the row field and the data field.

2. With Amount in the data field, its total will usually default to Count, but if it doesn't then use the Field Settings dialog box to set the total method to Count.

3. Right-click in one of the row field cells and choose Group from the contextual menu.

4. The Grouping dialog box appears as shown in Figure 3.23. Set its Starting At edit box to zero.

5. You should normally leave the Ending At edit box alone, but you can modify it if desired.

6. Set the By value to the group size you're after. For example, if you want group boundaries to go up in $10,000 increments, enter **10000** in the By edit box.

7. Click OK.

The result will look something like the pivot table in Figure 3.24.

The process of grouping a continuous variable is the same in Excel versions earlier than Excel 2007. However, Excel 2007 has fixed an annoying problem that existed in earlier versions: If the field that you wanted to group contained a blank value somewhere in the underlying data set, you could not group on that field. It did not help to suppress blanks. You had to go to

FIGURE 3.23

By default, the smallest and largest values in the data source are placed in the Start At and the End At edit boxes.

FIGURE 3.24

All group boundaries are equidistant.

Row Labels	Count of Amount
0-10000	2659
10000-20000	65
20000-30000	14
30000-40000	4
40000-50000	2
>50000	5
Grand Total	2749

the data source and either eliminate the record, or provide it with a nonblank value, and then rebuild the pivot table. Fortunately this has been fixed in Excel 2007.

The labels of a grouped numeric field do not use any special formatting that you might have applied to the numeric field itself. For example, if Amount has been formatted in the pivot table as Currency, the dollar signs, commas, and decimal points are not preserved in the group labels.

If the field that you're grouping is a date field, the grouping options recognize the field's characteristics and present you with a different set of choices. (See Figure 3.25.)

If, as you normally will, you want to show months in one year separate from months in a different year, you should click both Years and Months in the By list box. If you click Months only, then (for example) February 2010 and February 2011 will be combined in the same pivot table row. The same is true for Quarters.

Integrating pivot tables with worksheets

At times, you want to use pivot table information directly in worksheet cells. There are two pivot table features that you'll find useful for getting data out of a pivot table.

FIGURE 3.25

To group by week, choose Days and set the number of days to 7.

The GETPIVOTDATA function

GETPIVOTDATA is a worksheet function that you can enter in a cell, just like SUM or IF. Its syntax is complicated, though, and if you enter it yourself with the keyboard you're liable to make mistakes. Fortunately, there's an easier way.

Suppose you wanted to show a value in a pivot table in some other worksheet cell or even in a different worksheet. Type = in that cell, perhaps cell J15, just as you would to initiate any worksheet formula. Then click in the pivot table, in the cell whose value you want to show in J15. The GETPIVOTDATA function is automatically completed on your behalf. It might look something like this:

```
=GETPIVOTDATA("Amount",$A$3,"Name City","Millbrae","Class","Remodel")
```

(You can see why you might want it generated automatically.) Now you can restructure the pivot table, within limits, and the GETPIVOTDATA function will continue to return the Amount value for the Millbrae item of Name City when the Class is Remodel.

The ability to generate the GETPIVOTDATA function is a toggle. In Excel 2007, select a pivot table cell and then click the Options tab on the Ribbon. Click Options in the PivotTable group and then click Generate GetPivotData. It's more complicated in earlier versions; see the documentation for the version you're using.

Double-click to drill down

From time to time I see a value in a pivot table that doesn't make much sense to me. Long experience has taught me that it's not the pivot table going wrong. Either I did something I shouldn't have when I designed the table, or there's something strange in the pivot table's data source.

It should be faster to find something strange in the data than to figure out what I did wrong designing the table. But QuickBooks reports can send thousands and thousands of records to

Excel, and it could take a while to find the records in question. That's when a drill-down can be helpful.

I just double-click the cell in the pivot table's data field that looks odd, and Excel responds by inserting a new worksheet that contains all the fields in the underlying data source and all the individual records that are summarized in that data cell. Sometimes the problem is nothing more than a typographical error I made while entering the data in QuickBooks.

That makes it much easier to find the problem, if the problem is in the data. If it's not, then I know to look to my pivot table design. When I'm through examining the individual records I just delete the worksheet that Excel added.

For this technique to work, you need to have the proper option set. To see if it's set, right-click a cell in a pivot table and choose PivotTable Options from the contextual menu. In the PivotTable Options dialog box, on the Data tab, make sure Enable Show Details is checked.

Pivot table formulas

Pivot tables enable you to create new fields and items within fields, right in the pivot table. This feature is both limited and useful:

- It's limited because you can create a *calculated field* for use only as a data field — you can't use a calculated field as a row or column field. You can create a calculated *item* only for use in a row or column field.
- It's useful because you might want to analyze a QuickBooks field that is not easily exported — assuming you can export it at all.

There are good reasons to create a calculated data field in a pivot table that uses QuickBooks data; some are described in the remainder of this section. But the analysis of the sort of data you can obtain from QuickBooks is not normally enhanced by the addition of calculated items in row or column fields. (This book does not explain calculated items further.)

Calculated fields

Suppose you're interested in assessing your company's monthly gross profit over time. QuickBooks offers a chart (by choosing Reports ▶ Company & Financial ▶ Income & Expense Graph), but it shows income and expense separately, and does not focus on gross profit as the difference between total sales and cost of goods sold.

On the other hand, QuickBooks detail reports do not show a calculated field such as Gross Profit. So if your exported report is a detail report, you'll have to create a calculated field in the pivot table named Gross Profit. (You could calculate the field in a worksheet and incorporate the results into the pivot table's data source. But that approach creates complications when you next export from QuickBooks.)

FIGURE 3.26

Use the Name dropdown to view any existing calculated fields, along with their formulas.

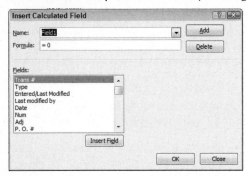

> **NOTE** You could export the Profit & Loss Standard report, with months in columns. Once the report has been exported to Excel, select the range of monthly dates (they are used as the column headers) and the corresponding range of Gross Margin values. With that multiple selection, create a standard line chart. However, if you export the standard report, you lose the ability to examine underlying detail records. Furthermore, you might be running an ad hoc analysis and prefer not to create and export a report simply to satisfy a momentary curiosity. In this sort of very common situation, a calculated field is a good alternative.

To create the calculated Gross Profit field in the pivot table, take these steps in Excel 2007:

1. Select any cell in the pivot table to activate the Options tab for PivotTable Tools.

2. Click Formulas in the Tools group and then choose Calculated Field in the dropdown list.

3. The Insert Calculated Field dialog box appears as shown in Figure 3.26. Type the name **Gross Profit** in the Name edit box.

4. In the Formula edit box, enter this formula:
   ```
   =Credit-Debit
   ```

5. Click OK.

In earlier versions of Excel, right-click a cell in the pivot table and choose Show PivotTable Toolbar in the contextual menu. On the toolbar, choose Formulas from the PivotTable dropdown and proceed with Step 2.

Now you have established the calculated field in the pivot table, but you can't yet see it. Here's one way to display it, which assumes that you have exported the Custom Transaction Detail report and that you have included at least these fields: Date, Debit, Credit, and Account Type.

1. If you can't see the PivotTable Field List dialog box, right-click a cell in the pivot table and choose Field List from the contextual menu.

2. Drag Date from the Choose Fields list box into the Row Labels box.

3. If you have filled the Defer Update checkbox, click the Update button.

4. Right-click one of the dates in the pivot table's row area. Choose Group from the contextual menu.

5. In the Grouping dialog box, make sure that both Years and Months are selected in the By list box. Click OK. The pivot table updates to show months within years instead of individual dates

6. In the PivotTable Field List dialog box, drag Account Type from the Choose Fields list box into the Report Filter box, and drag Gross Profit (your newly calculated field) into the Values box.

7. If the Gross Profit field is not using SUM as its totaling method, click its dropdown arrow in the Values box, choose Value Field Settings from the menu, and select Sum from the Summarize list box. While you're there, you might as well click the Number Format button to choose Currency as the number format. Click OK twice to close the Value Field Settings dialog box.

8. Click the dropdown on the right of Account Type in the pivot table's page field. If necessary, select the Multiple Items checkbox. Clear the All checkbox to clear all account type checkboxes, and then select the Cost of Goods Sold checkbox and the Income checkbox.

9. Click OK. The result appears in Figure 3.27.

FIGURE 3.27

Compare the Sum of Gross Profit values with the Gross Profit line in the Profit & Loss Standard report.

Account Type	(Multiple Items)	

Row Labels	Sum of Gross Profit
⊟2009	
Nov	$15,299.50
Dec	$30,716.85
⊟2010	
Jan	$12,865.42
Feb	$4,803.40
Mar	$9,000.00
Apr	$5,943.65
May	$9,000.00
Jun	$6,330.00
Jul	$2,670.81
Aug	$17,680.13
Sep	$8,790.00
Oct	$12,508.58
Nov	$4,892.83
Dec	$3,408.00
⊟2011	
Jan	$16,377.70
Feb	$19,566.75
Mar	$19,385.11
Apr	$17,483.71

FIGURE 3.28

It makes sense to remove the legend in a one-series chart. Click it and press Delete.

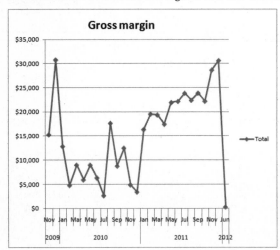

As shown in Figure 3.27, you now have a pivot table that displays the gross profit — income less cost of goods sold — for each month within the data range you selected when you exported your report from QuickBooks. The next section shows you how to chart your results.

Pivot charts

Pivot charts came along several years after pivot tables first arrived in Excel, and it shows: They are not as mature a feature as pivot tables, but they continue to improve. There are some things that you can do with standard Excel reports that you cannot do with pivot charts, but because the reverse is also true it's helpful to know about both.

If you worked your way through the previous section on creating a calculated field in a pivot table, you're ready to show the results in a pivot chart. It's a quick process:

1. Select any cell in the pivot table.

2. Click the Ribbon's Options tab, under PivotTable Tools.

3. Click the PivotChart button in the Tools group.

4. Select one of the Line chart types in the Insert PivotChart dialog box, and click OK. A new pivot chart appears, embedded in the active worksheet. (You can relocate it to its own chart sheet if you prefer.)

5. To change the default chart title of Total, click the title to select it, drag across the characters to select them, and type what you want to use as the title. Click anything else to deselect the title.

FIGURE 3.29

A report to show when outstanding balances are due, and how much payment can be expected, by customer.

Account Type	Accounts Receivable ✓					
Sum of Open Balance	**Column Labels** ✓					
Row Labels ✓	**Qtr1**		Qtr2	Qtr3	Qtr4	**Grand Total**
Allard, Robert:Remodel	$0		$0	$14,510	$0	$14,510
Mackey's Nursery and Garden Supply	$0		$0		$13,900	$13,900
Campbell, Heather:Remodel	$0		$0		$13,900	$13,900
Robson, Darci:Robson Clinic	$12,421		$0		$0	$12,421
Melton, Johnny:Dental office	$0		$0		$8,619	$8,619
Cook, Brian:2nd story addition	$0		$0		$5,418	$5,418
Pretell Real Estate:155 Wilks Blvd.	$1,715		$0		$3,312	$5,027
Violette, Mike:Workshop	$4,732		$0		$0	$4,732
Hendro Riyadi:Remodel Kitchen	$0		$0		$4,223	$4,223
Cook, Brian:Kitchen	$1,643		$0		$2,337	$3,979
Jacobsen, Doug:Kitchen	$0		$0		$2,320	$2,320
Ecker Designs:Office Repairs	$0		$0		$1,468	$1,468
Burch, Jason:Room Addition	$0		$0		$1,005	$1,005
Vitton, David:Remodel Kitchen	$0		$0		$700	$700
Teschner, Anton:Sun Room	$0		$0		$566	$566
Lew Plumbing - C:Storage Expansion	$220		$0		$0	$220
Abercrombie, Kristy	$16		$0		$0	$16
Grand Total	**$20,747**		**$0**	**$14,510**	**$57,767**	**$93,024**

I sometimes find that the final month in the pivot table — and therefore in the pivot chart — really represents only partial results. Therefore I suppress it by clicking the Row Labels drop-down at the top of the pivot table and clearing the checkbox for the period that I want to omit from the table. When the complete results are in for the month, I can re-export the report, refresh the pivot table, and select that month's checkbox.

The pivot chart based on the pivot table in Figure 3.27 appears in Figure 3.28.

Sample Pivot Tables from QuickBooks Data

This chapter concludes with two pivot table reports based on QuickBooks sample file data, exported through the Custom Transaction Detail report. They show types of analysis that I have found helpful in my own business, but that QuickBooks does not do a good job of supplying.

Figure 3.29 shows a pivot table of customer by quarter during which payment comes due. More formally:

■ It uses the QuickBooks Contact field rather than the Name field. In this way the table avoids a different row for each combination of customer and job, which would make for a much more complicated table.

■ It groups on the Due Date field, showing it by quarter rather than by individual date due.

■ It shows invoices only, and of the invoices it shows only those that are still in Accounts Receivable.

FIGURE 3.30

Without an item type field it's not possible to group items as QuickBooks does.

Type	(Multiple Items)		
Account	(Multiple Items)		
Name City	(All)		
Sum of Revenue	**Column Labels**		
Row Labels	**New Construction**	**Remodel**	**Grand Total**
Appliance	$1,200	$16,743	$17,943
Blueprints	$2,400	$1,000	$3,400
Cabinets - Custom	$2,843	$9,621	$12,464
Cabinets:Cabinet Pulls	$425	-$4	$422
Cabinets:Light Pine	$2,598	-$1,900	$698
Concrete Slab	$8,377	$450	$8,827
Counter	$0	$3,070	$3,070
Deposit	$0	$0	$0
Door Frame	$0	$10	$10
East Bayshore	$28	$51	$79
Electrical Materials	$0	$2,400	$2,400
Equip Rental	$1,350	$2,000	$3,350
Fin Chg	$141	$6	$147
Floor Plans	$3,153	$33,577	$36,729

QuickBooks does a good job of displaying aging data, but that applies only to overdue payments. Another useful report is Open Invoices, which shows open balances, but although it shows due dates it doesn't classify by them. It's good to know who's late and by how much, but it's also good to know how much to expect in the future.

Figure 3.30 contains a report of total revenue associated with each item sold, by class (remodel vs. new construction). To get the correct figures, these special steps were needed:

- Define a calculated field, Revenue, as Credit minus Debit.
- In the Transaction Type filter, select Sales Receipts and Invoices.
- In the Account filter, select all accounts except Inventory Asset.

A filter for Name City is also used, so that the user can easily switch between job locales.

You can create the report in Figure 3.30 in QuickBooks by using the Custom Transaction Summary Report. But there's a problem: If you want to include a text field such as Name City as a filter, you might find that it's too inclusive. The QuickBooks description on the Filters tab of the Modify Report dialog box says, "Enter the words (or characters) that must be in the Name City field."

Of course, the name of the field varies when you change the field you want to filter on. The point is that whatever you enter in the edit box as a filter criterion must be *in* the field for a record to be selected — not be *equal to*, but be *in*. That means if you enter **Bayshore** in the edit box, the filter returns records for Bayshore, for East Bayshore, and for E. Bayshore.

This probably isn't what you want. This sort of fuzzy search absolutely has a place in filtering, but this isn't it. The filter used in the pivot table report returns what you ask for, and nothing else.

Figure 3.31 shows the QuickBooks version of the report so that you can compare it to the pivot table.

FIGURE 3.31

The report returns more categories but is more difficult to interpret.

	New Construction	Remodel	TOTAL
Inventory			
Cabinets			
Cabinet Pulls	425.43	-3.59	421.84
Light Pine	2,598.00	-1,900.00	698.00
Total Cabinets	3,023.43	-1,903.59	1,119.84
Door Frame	0.00	9.60	9.60
Hardware			
Brass hinges	0.00	2.40	2.40
Doorknobs Std	33.99	30.77	64.76
Lk Doorknobs	39.81	19.19	59.00
Total Hardware	73.80	52.36	126.16
Wood Door			
Exterior	22.81	41.53	64.34
Interior	86.96	197.21	284.17
Total Wood Door	109.77	238.74	348.51
Total Inventory	3,207.00	-1,602.89	1,604.11

Part II
Analyzing Financial Statements

Comparative Balance Sheets and Profit & Loss Statements

Chapter 1 touches briefly on the reasons you might want to use QuickBooks to prepare financial statements such as comparative balance sheets and comparative income statements. That chapter also goes into detail on the mechanics of structuring that kind of statement in QuickBooks. This chapter goes into the rationale for comparative statements in more depth, and explains how that rationale helps you decide how to structure those statements.

Reasons for Comparative Analysis

In its simplest form, a comparative financial statement merely shows you two, or occasionally three, periods of financial data so you can compare across time periods the results of doing business. In theory, the periods could represent anything from days to decades, but in practice people usually look at years or quarters. Of course, both periods should be of the same duration, so you would compare Year 3 with Year 4, or Quarter 1 with Quarter 2.

If it's year-end and you want to compare last year's income statement with this year's, it seems that the thing to do is to use QuickBooks reports to print a couple of income statements. The dates would be January 1 through December 31 for each year. Then just look at them and see what's changed.

Suppose you do just that with a merchandising company, and find that the company's COGS (cost of goods sold) increased by $230 from one year to the next. That doesn't seem like much. It's so small, in fact, that it could even be the result of cumulative rounding errors in QuickBooks' average cost algorithm.

But what if you also noticed that the company's revenues increased by $60,000 from Year 1 to Year 2? Does that put an almost-constant COGS value in a different light? How can revenue increase by $60,000 while COGS increases by $230? If you're genuinely interested in what's going on with this company, you have some spadework to do.

It's for that sort of reason that comparative financial statements often express raw dollar amounts both in dollars and in percentages. When you express several dollar amounts — one amount for each account, usually — as percentages, all the percentages must use the same basis; else, you find yourself trying to compare 25% of one thing with 15% of another.

To say that the percentages must have the same basis doesn't mean that the basis must be the same number, but it must be the same kind of measure. You would divide the income account amounts for Year 1 by total income in Year 1, and those for Year 2 by total income in Year 2.

This approach, which casts the dollar amounts in the common metric of percentages, is called *common sizing*. Its use makes comparative statements more informative. Furthermore, it makes it possible to compare one company's financials with the published financials of another company, or even group of companies, usually from the same industrial grouping or Standard Industrial Classification (SIC).

Now, if you find that COGS is 47% of sales in Year 1 and 38% of sales in Year 2, it doesn't much matter what the actual dollar amounts are. As a percentage of sales dollars, there's a large year-over-year dropoff in COGS. Did the company emulate Southwest Airlines and use hedging strategies to lock in low costs before increasing its sales prices in Year 2? Did the company make a major purchase, enough to fulfill sales for two or more years, early in Year 1?

To find the reason for the apparent disconnect between COGS and revenue, you'd have to take a look at the balance sheet in addition to the income statement. Of course, you should use a comparative balance sheet and it should also be common-sized. It's typical, and most useful, to common-size an income statement by total income, and to common-size a balance sheet by total assets.

Using QuickBooks to Create Comparative Financial Statements

Suppose you want to examine Rock Castle Construction's income statement (also known as its Profit & Loss report) for two consecutive years to compare its performance year-to-year. One way is to call for a Profit & Loss Prev Year Comparison report. An excerpt from the report appears in Figure 4.1.

Notice the dates that head the two columns of actuals. The report was run December 15, 2011, and the current fiscal year is not quite over. QuickBooks calls the column that contains the previous year's data a *subcolumn*. A subcolumn uses the same date range as the main column. Therefore, in Figure 4.1 the main column (January 1 through December 15, 2011) and the sub

FIGURE 4.1

The change columns are both year-to-year; note that the more recent year's actuals are on the left.

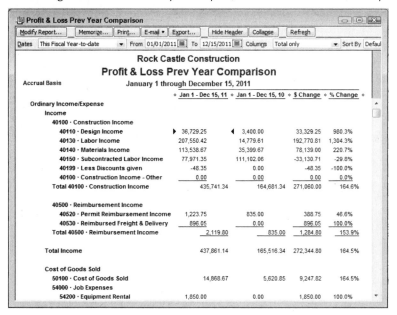

column (January 1 through December 15, 2010) are based on the same 349-day range within consecutive years.

NOTE **You can verify that the prior year's data is shown as a subcolumn, not a column, by clicking the report's Modify Report button. In the Modify Report dialog box, notice that in the Subcolumns area, the Previous Year checkbox has been selected. This is the default setting for both the Profit & Loss and the Balance Sheet Prev Year Comparison reports (see Figure 4.2 for an example).**

The report in Figure 4.1 shows the actual dollar values in each income and expense account during each year, and it also shows the dollar and percent changes, account by account, from year to year. The report supplies good information but it's not all you want. The percentages, for example, are strictly year-over-year changes, following this pattern:

```
($ Year 2 - $ Year 1) / ($ Year 1)
```

That is, for each account, subtract the value for Year 1 from the value for Year 2, and divide the difference by the value for Year 1. It's helpful to know that, and you'll want it for a full analysis, but it's horizontal only, a measure of year-to-year change. For a fuller picture you need a vertical analysis, which shows you how each account contributed to total income (or to total expenses) during each year.

FIGURE 4.2

The Modify Report dialog box for the Profit & Loss Prev Year Comparison report

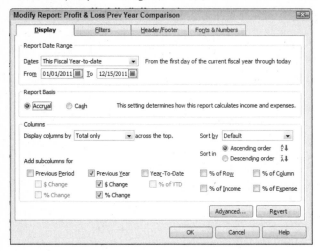

The vertical analysis is necessary because it gives you a context for interpreting a year-to-year change. An account that shows a 300% growth rate year-to-year is exciting at first glance, but when you find that the same account is responsible for 0.5% of total income, you're less excited about its growth rate.

The Profit & Loss Prev Year Comparison report shown in Figure 4.1 does not provide information about percentage of total income. For that information you might resort to the Profit & Loss Standard report (see Figure 4.3).

The report in Figure 4.3 is abbreviated, to fit in this book's page size. It omits two columns at the right, which on screen would show each account's total dollars for two years and its percent of the two-year income.

The four visible numeric columns show, for both 2010 and 2011, the actual dollars and the percent of income in each account. (The income referred to in the % of Income column headers is Total Income, sometimes labeled *Revenue* or *Total Sales*. Whatever term used, it is the proper basis for component percentages in a comparative Profit & Loss report.)

Those percentages represent the data missing from the Profit & Loss Prev Year Comparison report shown in Figure 4.1. The columns that show the percent of income accounts give you the component percentage of each source of income during each year. For the expense accounts, they show what percentage of total income is used to pay for the various expense categories that help produce revenue.

The Profit & Loss Standard report is not a complete comparative report because it's missing the year-to-year change data shown in the Profit & Loss Prev Year Comparison report. And there

FIGURE 4.3

The Profit & Loss Standard report, with the default options modified

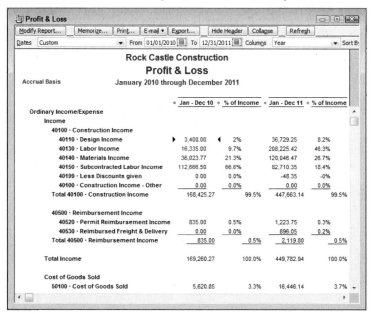

are problems with its legibility. It's slightly more difficult to compare the percentages for Year 2010 with those for Year 2011 because they are separated by the dollar amounts for Year 2011.

No single report

You cannot get the vertical (account by total income) and the horizontal (year-to-year change) analyses in one QuickBooks report. The reason is that QuickBooks shows year-to-year change as a percentage only for the combination of a column with a subcolumn: for example, in the Profit & Loss Prev Year Comparison report. But QuickBooks does not analyze percent of income for a subcolumn. And the % of Row option (see Figure 4.2) is not helpful because it is not a rate of change but a component rate: For example, the % of Row option might tell you that 25% of the total two-year COGS was spent in Year 1 and 75% in Year 2.

Nor is the Custom Transaction Summary report an answer. It is possible to structure that report with rows that show Income Statement accounts and columns that show annualized results. But it does not provide a percent of total income analysis — only a percent of column analysis, and those two are very different things. With income and expense accounts as the report's rows, the % of Column option shows each row's dollar amount as a percent of net income, not total income.

Still, you have one report that shows the year-to-year changes and another that shows the figures for percent of total income. Why not run both reports and combine them somehow, perhaps by exporting them to Excel? There are at least two good reasons *not* to do that, explained next.

Watching reports' date ranges

If you intend to combine or compare two or more different QuickBooks reports, you must take care that they use the same date ranges. For example, suppose you open a Profit & Loss Prev Year Comparison report, when today's date is December 15, 2011 and you're not quite to the end of the fiscal year. Both the main column (for the current year) and the subcolumn (for the previous year, 2010) capture data for the first 349 days of the year, January 1 through December 15.

Then, you want to compare that report with a Profit & Loss Standard report, for the same two years. You use a different report (Standard instead of Prev Year Comparison) because you want the % of Income column. The % of Income information is available only for columns, not subcolumns (various aspects of this distinction are explained later), and the Prev Year Comparison report shows the prior year as a subcolumn. Therefore you cannot get % of Income for both years in a Prev Year Comparison report.

So you open the Profit & Loss Standard report, set the date range to start at January 1, 2010, and set the columns to display by Year. You click Modify Report and in the Display tab, call for % of Income, and click OK.

Now you're ready to compare the Profit & Loss Standard report with the Profit & Loss Prev Year Comparison report, but there are two problems that make a comparison tricky: the order in which the report displays the dates, and ensuring that all the pertinent accounts appear.

Reversed dates

The Profit & Loss Prev Year Comparison report shows 2011 figures to the left of 2010 figures. This is because the report shows 2010 as a subcolumn, and a subcolumn appears to the right of a main column. In contrast, the Profit & Loss Standard report, structured as just described, shows two main columns, one for 2010 and one for 2011. When both years are shown as main columns, QuickBooks puts them in chronological order, left to right.

So when you compare the two reports you'll need to keep in mind that their column order is not the same.

Missing accounts

The second difficulty in comparing the two reports arises in a Profit & Loss report, which displays cumulative data, but not in a Balance Sheet report, which displays balances as of a particular date. The Profit & Loss Prev Year Comparison report provides a subcolumn based on the same dates, one year earlier, as are used for the main column. So if the main column's end date is 12/15/2011, the subcolumn's end date is 12/15/2010.

The same is not true of a Profit & Loss Standard report, where you set the date range to capture everything from 1/1/2010 through 12/15/2011, and you display columns by Year. In this case the column for 2010 captures activity for the full 365-day year, but the Prev Year Comparison report shows only the first 349 days of 2010.

There are various ways that the difference in date ranges for the two Profit & Loss reports, Standard and Prev Year Comparison, can throw you off. One way is that the only activity in an account for 2010 might occur after December 15. The default option for displaying rows in a report is to show active rows only. Therefore, you might wind up with account activity in the Profit & Loss Standard report (which shows data through 12/31/2010) but not in the apparently complementary Profit & Loss Prev Year Comparison report, where the 2010 subcolumn stops at the same date as the main column, December 15.

The way to manage the problems concerning date ranges, and at the same time create a more readable report, is to stick with one report. You export its data to Excel to complete the analysis. That way you don't have to worry about inconsistencies in the two reports that are due solely to the way that reports are structured. The process of exporting one report and completing the analysis in Excel is detailed in the next section.

You'll still need two reports, a Profit & Loss and a Balance Sheet, but you'll find that you need to export only one of each.

Combining Vertical and Horizontal Analyses

The most straightforward way to get the data out of QuickBooks and into Excel is to export two reports. One is a Profit & Loss Prev Year Comparison report that has a main column for Year 2 and a subcolumn for Year 1. This enables you to call for the previous year comparison, both in dollars and in percentages. You also want a similarly structured Balance Sheet report. You could get Excel to make those prior-year comparisons for you, but there's little reason not to leave the comparisons to QuickBooks. (There is one potential problem though; see the section "The trouble with the SIGN function.")

You'll also want each account as a percentage of income, for the Profit & Loss report, and as a percentage of total assets, for the Balance Sheet report. It's those comparisons that you'll get Excel to make for you.

Here are the steps to get the data out of QuickBooks and into Excel. The process is broken into two main tasks: exporting the Profit & Loss and exporting the Balance Sheet. Within each task you'll find steps first for exporting the report and then for completing the calculations.

Exporting the Profit & Loss report

This example continues to use the Rock Castle Construction file, a QuickBooks sample file. When you open a sample file, QuickBooks sets the effective date to a particular date, and this example uses December 15, 2011 as the effective date. The following steps allow for that setting.

To export the Profit & Loss, follow these steps:

1. Choose Reports ▶ Company & Financial ▶ Profit & Loss Prev Year Comparison.

2. The report opens. Change the date in the To edit box to December 31, 2011. (More generally, change the To date to the end of the current fiscal year.)

3. Click the Refresh button to force QuickBooks to update the report to capture the full year for both 2011 and the previous year, 2010.

4. Verify that the report shows raw dollar amounts for 2011 and 2010, the year-to-year dollar change and percent change.

5. Click the Export button.

6. In the Export Report dialog box, choose A New Excel Workbook. Clear the Include a New Worksheet checkbox.

7. Click the Advanced tab in the Export Report dialog box.

8. In the Advanced tab, select the Send Header to Screen in Excel. If necessary, clear the Space Between Columns checkbox.

9. Click OK to complete the export.

If Excel is not already running, the application starts. A new workbook is added to any open workbooks and the data from the QuickBooks Profit & Loss Prev Year Comparison report is written to a worksheet in that workbook. Switch to Excel and verify that the exported report resembles the one shown in Figure 4.4.

Step 8 advises you to use the Advanced tab option labeled Send Header to Screen in Excel. That's a mildly misleading label. QuickBooks *always* sends report headers to Excel, including the report title (such as Profit & Loss Standard), the pertinent From and To dates and the basis for the figures (accrual versus cash). QuickBooks sends that information either to the worksheet that contains the report data, or to Page Setup.

When QuickBooks sends the header to the Screen, the header actually goes to the worksheet. In that case the header information occupies the worksheet's first few rows. When QuickBooks sends the header to Page Setup, it is stored not in the worksheet itself but as data that's shown only when you print, or print-preview, the worksheet. Stored as page setup information, it's available to you but out of your way when you're editing the worksheet.

Step 8 suggests that you put the header information in the worksheet, just to keep it straight which report you're looking at.

If you find the information is in your way in the worksheet, just delete the rows it occupies. Page Setup is the default destination, so simply skip setting the header option in the future.

> **TIP** To edit a header that's already been sent to Excel's Page Setup, choose File ▶ Page Setup (in Excel 2007, click the Page Layout tab and then click Print Titles in the Page Setup group). Click the Header/Footer tab in the Page Setup dialog box and then click the Custom Header button. You'll find the header supplied by QuickBooks in the Center Header edit box, where you can modify it as you see fit, including formatting elements.

FIGURE 4.4

Exporting the report title is a good way to keep track of which QuickBooks report you're looking at.

					F	G	H	I	J
1	Rock Castle Construction								
2	Profit & Loss Prev Year Comparison								
3	January through December 2011								Accrual Basis
4									
5						Jan - Dec 11	Jan - Dec 10	$ Change	% Change
6		Ordinary Income/Expense							
7			Income						
8				40100 · Construction Income					
9					40110 · Design Income	36,729.25	3,400.00	33,329.25	980.27%
10					40130 · Labor Income	208,225.42	16,335.00	191,890.42	1,174.72%
11					40140 · Materials Income	120,046.47	36,023.77	84,022.70	233.24%
12					40150 · Subcontracted Labor Income	82,710.35	112,666.50	-29,956.15	-26.59%
13					40199 · Less Discounts given	-48.35	0.00	-48.35	-100.0%
14					40100 · Construction Income - Other	0.00	0.00	0.00	0.0%
15				Total 40100 · Construction Income		447,663.14	168,425.27	279,237.87	165.79%
16									
17				40500 · Reimbursement Income					
17					40520 · Permit Reimbursement Income	1,223.75	835.00	388.75	46.56%
18					40530 · Reimbursed Freight & Delivery	896.05	0.00	896.05	100.0%
19				Total 40500 · Reimbursement Income		2,119.80	835.00	1,284.80	153.87%
20			Total Income			449,782.94	169,260.27	280,522.67	165.74%
21		Cost of Goods Sold							
22				50100 · Cost of Goods Sold		16,446.14	5,620.85	10,825.29	192.59%

Step 8 in the prior list also advises you to clear the Space Between Columns checkbox. If the checkbox is selected, QuickBooks places an empty column between columns that contain data; some people prefer this arrangement as visually clearer. However, it can complicate matters if you intend to add formulas to the worksheet and the formulas rely on data found in different columns. That's the case here, and you'll find it easier to create, and duplicate, the formulas if you have omitted intervening, blank columns.

Preparing the analysis

So far, you have exported the account names, dollar amounts for each of two years, and the dollar and percent changes year-to-year. It remains to get the percent of total income represented by each account. To do so, take these steps:

1. Using a worksheet layout such as that shown in Figure 4.4, enter this formula in cell K9:

   `=IF(G9<>"",G9/G$20,"")`

2. If necessary, re-select cell K9. Click the Percent Style button in Excel's Formatting toolbar; if you're using Excel 2007, click the Home tab, then click the Percent Style button in the Number group.

3. Position your cursor over the small black box in the cell's lower-right corner (the box is called the *fill handle*). Your cursor turns into a crosshairs.

4. Drag one column to the right, and release the mouse button. You should now have two percent values appearing in cells K9:L9, the result of dividing Design Income by Total Income, for 2011 in column K and for 2010 in column L. The process described in this step is called *autofill*.

FIGURE 4.5

If you structure the formula in K9 correctly, you need to enter it once only.

/ECCE	F	G	H	I	J	K	L
1	Rock Castle Construction						
2	Profit & Loss Prev Year Comparison						
3	January through December 2011				Accrual Basis		
4							
5		Jan - Dec 11	Jan - Dec 10	$ Change	% Change	Component	Component
6	Ordinary Income/Expense					%, 2011	%, 2010
7	Income						
8	40100 · Construction Income						
9	40110 · Design Income	36,729.25	3,400.00	33,329.25	980.27%	8.17%	2.01%
10	40130 · Labor Income	208,225.42	16,335.00	191,890.42	1,174.72%	46.29%	9.65%
11	40140 · Materials Income	120,046.47	36,023.77	84,022.70	233.24%	26.69%	21.28%
12	40150 · Subcontracted Labor Income	82,710.35	112,666.50	-29,956.15	-26.59%	18.39%	66.56%
13	40199 · Less Discounts given	-48.35	0.00	-48.35	-100.0%	-0.01%	0.0%
14	40100 · Construction Income - Other	0.00	0.00	0.00	0.0%	0.0%	0.0%
15	Total 40100 · Construction Income	447,663.14	168,425.27	279,237.87	165.79%	99.53%	99.51%
16	40500 · Reimbursement Income						
17	40520 · Permit Reimbursement Income	1,223.75	835.00	388.75	46.56%	0.27%	0.49%
18	40530 · Reimbursed Freight & Delivery	896.05	0.00	896.05	100.0%	0.2%	0.0%
19	Total 40500 · Reimbursement Income	2,119.80	835.00	1,284.80	153.87%	0.47%	0.49%
20	Total Income	449,782.94	169,260.27	280,522.87	165.74%	100.0%	100.0%
21	Cost of Goods Sold						
22	50100 · Cost of Goods Sold	16,446.14	5,620.85	10,825.29	192.59%	3.66%	3.32%
23	54000 · Job Expenses						

5. Make the multiple selection of cells K9:L9. (To make a multiple selection of these two adjacent cells, select K9, continue to hold down the mouse button, drag into L9, and release the mouse button.)

6. The fill handle will now appear in the lower-right corner of cell L9. Click it and, while holding down the mouse button, drag down to the end of the report. Release the mouse button.

7. In row 5 (and row 6 if necessary) add descriptive labels for the component percentages in columns K and L.

Your worksheet should now resemble the one shown in Figure 4.5.

Understanding the formula

It will help to examine the formula in Step 1 more closely. It's usually best to examine a formula from the inside out, so start with this fragment of the formula as it's first entered into cell K9 in Figure 4.5:

```
G9/G$20
```

This fragment returns the result of dividing the value in cell G9 by the value in cell G20. In this case, the expression divides the total Design Income during 2011 by the Total Income for 2011, or 8.17%.

The dollar sign between the G and the 20 in G20 anchors the formula to row 20. No matter where you copy and paste this formula, the divisor is found somewhere in row 20.

For example, if you look at the formula as it's autofilled into cell K10 (one row down from K9), you'll find this:

```
=IF(G10<>"",G10/G$20,"")
```

The numerator in the division expression now refers to G10, one row down from where you originally entered it. But the denominator is still a cell in row 20, and that's because of the dollar sign. It anchors the row reference.

> **NOTE** This type of Excel cell reference is called a *mixed reference*. If there were no dollar sign at all, it would be a *relative reference*. If both the column letter and the row number were preceded by a dollar sign, it would be an *absolute reference*. The F4 key makes it easy to cycle through a sequence of reference types: Select the reference you want to change and press F4 repeatedly. So doing cycles the reference through the styles A1, $A$1, A$1, $A1, and back to A1.

Now enclose the division expression in an IF structure. The IF function has this syntax in Excel worksheets:

```
=IF(Condition, Result if Condition is TRUE, Result if Condition is
    FALSE)
```

In cell K9, the condition is:

```
G9<>""
```

This expression is TRUE if cell G9 contains any value or formula, and FALSE otherwise.

If the condition is TRUE, the result is the division expression:

```
G9/G$20
```

If the condition is FALSE, the result is the empty quotation marks:

```
""
```

Suppose first that G9 contains a numeric value, as it will when row 9 represents a particular account such as Design Income and not a category of accounts such as Construction Income. In this case you want to calculate a percentage based on the value in G9. (Because QuickBooks faithfully keeps dollar amounts in different columns than labels such as account names, you can be confident that you won't find a dollar amount in G9 and a label in G10.)

So, when the condition is TRUE, because G9 contains a value, show the result of the division expression in K9, because that is the result when the condition is TRUE.

On the other hand, suppose there's nothing in cell G9. It's empty, as indicated by the empty quotation marks in the condition. Then the condition is FALSE, and Excel shows the result for a FALSE condition. As the formula is written, it's a blank — again, the empty quotation marks.

When there's nothing in cell G9, putting the division expression in cell K9 results in the value 0: If you divide a blank cell by a numeric value, the result is 0. If you do not test for blank cells in the numerator, you get a 0 in every cell, such as K16, where the corresponding cell in column G is empty — that's an undesirable outcome. It's uninformative and it clutters up the analysis.

Therefore, the formula tests for a value in column G of the current row. If the formula finds a value there, the division is performed and the result displayed. If the formula finds no value in the current row of column G, the IF test returns, and displays, a blank. You could characterize all this as cosmetic. You could also characterize it as an effort to make the analysis legible.

Report legibility

Notice in the worksheet in Figure 4.5 that columns J, K, and L contain the relevant percentages: percent change, percent of total income for 2011, and percent of total income for 2010. Because they are adjacent, it is much easier to compare them than in the original QuickBooks reports. Furthermore, the gridlines help you read across from a percentage that gets your attention to the actual dollar amounts that underlie the percentages.

And the columns are in the same year order: Columns G and H show 2011 and 2010, respectively, as do columns K and L. That's not the case with the Profit & Loss Standard report, which is how you get component percentages in QuickBooks by calling for a % of Income subcolumn. There, the years are in chronological order, reading left to right — the reverse of what you get with the Profit & Loss Prev Year Comparison.

These may seem like small things — whether columns of interest are adjacent, whether columns are in the same order, whether there are gridlines separating columns and rows, and so on. But they have a cumulative effect, and the way you handle these matters results in reports that are either easy to misread or easy to interpret correctly. By exporting the basic framework of the Profit & Loss Prev Year Comparison report to Excel, and then using its data to derive component percentages by way of formulas, you wind up with a report layout that is much easier to interpret correctly.

Figure 4.6 shows another benefit of putting a QuickBooks report in an Excel worksheet: You can hide uninteresting, uninformative rows in a long report, making it easy to see the rows and the numbers you want to compare. Notice in Figure 4.6, for example, that rows 16 through 19 are hidden.

To hide a row, right-click on the row number and choose Hide from the contextual menu. To show a hidden row, make a multiple selection of the visible row above the hidden row and the row below it. Right-click either row number and choose Unhide from the contextual menu.

> **TIP** To make a multiple selection of two or more rows, click the row number you want to select. Then Shift+click the row number of the other row. The two rows you clicked, and any intervening rows, are now selected.

You'll see an example of how useful this technique can be in the section "Interpreting the Profit & Loss report."

FIGURE 4.6

Rows with minuscule year-to-year changes are hidden.

	F	G	H	I	J
1	Rock Castle Construction				
2	Profit & Loss Prev Year Comparison				
3	January through December 2011				Accrual Basis
4					
5		Jan - Dec 11	Jan - Dec 10	$ Change	% Change
6	Ordinary Income/Expense				
7	Income				
8	40100 · Construction Income				
9	40110 · Design Incor	36,729.25	3,400.00	33,329.25	980.27%
10	40130 · Labor Incom	208,225.42	16,335.00	191,890.42	1,174.72%
11	40140 · Materials Inc	120,046.47	36,023.77	84,022.70	233.24%
12	40150 · Subcontract	82,710.35	112,666.50	-29,956.15	-26.59%
15	Total 40100 · Constructi	447,663.14	168,425.27	279,237.87	165.79%
20	Total Income	449,782.94	169,260.27	280,522.67	165.74%
21	Cost of Goods Sold				
22	50100 · Cost of Goods S	16,446.14	5,620.85	10,825.29	192.59%
23	54000 · Job Expenses				
24	54200 · Equipment R	1,850.00	0.00	1,850.00	100.0%
25	54300 · Job Material:	98,935.90	12,171.60	86,764.30	712.84%
26	54400 · Permits and	700.00	225.00	475.00	211.11%
27	54500 · Subcontract	63,217.95	53,350.00	9,867.95	18.5%
30	Total 54000 · Job Expens	165,299.14	65,746.60	99,552.54	151.42%
31	Total COGS	181,745.28	71,367.45	110,377.83	154.66%
32	Gross Profit	268,037.66	97,892.82	170,144.84	173.81%

Understanding the QuickBooks formulas

When QuickBooks exports a report to Excel, some of the resulting cells may contain formulas rather than values. For example, cell G9 in Figure 4.6 contains the value 36729.25. But cell G15, which contains the sum of all the Construction Income accounts, contains the formula:

```
=ROUND(SUM(G8:G14),5)
```

This formula takes the sum of the values in cells G8:G14 and rounds the sum to 5 decimal places. That's pretty straightforward, but consider this formula in cell J9:

```
=ROUND(IF(G9=0, IF(H9=0, 0, SIGN(-H9)), IF(H9=0, SIGN(G9),
    (G9-H9)/H9)),5)
```

Strip it down a bit by getting rid of the portion of the formula that does nothing but round its result to five decimals:

```
=IF(G9=0, IF(H9=0, 0, SIGN(-H9)), IF(H9=0, SIGN(G9), (G9-H9)/H9))
```

Notice there are three IF functions in the formula, the second and the third nested inside the first. It's still complicated enough that I don't intend to disentangle it here. If you're not interested in how it works, explaining it will just make your eyes glaze over. If you are interested, you'll learn more prying it apart yourself than reading about it.

> **TIP** Excel 2002 and later versions have a way to help you peer inside a complex formula. Start by selecting the cell containing the formula. Then, in Excel 2002 and 2003, choose Tools ▶ Formula Auditing ▶ Evaluate Formula. In Excel 2007, click the Formulas tab and then choose Evaluate Formula in the Formula Auditing group. You'll get a dialog box that you can step through, where each step shows you which part of the formula is being evaluated and the current result.

I will explain, though, that the SIGN function used in the formula merely returns one of three values, 1, 0, or –1, depending on whether the value presented to the function is positive, zero, or negative. So:

```
SIGN(8) = 1
SIGN(0) = 0
SIGN(-15) = -1
```

The magnitude of the number presented to SIGN is irrelevant.

In the great majority of cases, both the values the formula tests are positive numbers, and so there is no problem with the result. With two positive numbers, the formula returns the result of this expression (in row 9; in other rows, the only changes are to the row references):

```
(G9-H9)/H9
```

But the formula presents problems when cell G19 is positive and cell H9, the cell in the divisor, has a value of zero. In this case, the formula in cell J9 evaluates to return SIGN(G9). When G9 is positive, the result of SIGN(G9) is 1.0, and formatted as a percent 1.0 is 100%. That means that if the annual cumulative value for an account is zero for the first year, and is a positive number for the second year, the year-to-year growth percentage is taken to be 100%.

This is a simple decision rule, but it's terribly misleading. For example, a cumulative value of $1 in year 1 and of $10 in year 2 represents a growth rate of 900%. It is therefore senseless to say that growing from $0 to $10 represents a 100% growth rate. It would be much better to simply divide by zero and allow Excel to assign the error value of #DIV/0! to the result. But doing so would mean that the native QuickBooks report and the report as exported to Excel would not be identical.

The next section highlights this problem and how it can throw you off when you're interpreting a Profit & Loss report.

Interpreting the Profit & Loss report

Figure 4.7 shows the Profit & Loss report from top to bottom, with most of the rows hidden and only the rows of greatest interest remaining visible. See the earlier section "Report legibility" for information about how to hide rows, and to subsequently show them.

Rock Castle Construction had a good year in 2011, at least as compared to 2010. Total income was up by nearly 166% (cell J20). Total COGS went up too, but not by quite so great a degree as income. Net income as a percent of total income is healthy in both years (cells K82 and L82). Even Procter & Gamble managed only about 14% in 2007 and 2008. (See this chapter's "Making comparisons to other companies" section.)

But some figures don't seem quite right. In particular, the net income is growing by more than 300% year-to-year. At first glance that figure doesn't fit with a growth in total income of 166%. To determine the reason for the apparent discrepancy you need to look both at how the expenses have behaved during that period, and also the relative importance (as gauged by percent of total income) of different accounts.

Total COGS, for example, grows at about 155% (cell J31), a figure that's just a bit lower than the growth in total income. When your revenues grow faster than your costs, your profitability inevitably rises, whether it's measured in dollars or in percentages. The cost of the goods themselves rises faster than total income (193 versus 166%, in cells J22 and J20, respectively). Note, though, that the cost of goods is only about 4% of total income and therefore is not a major cost driver.

But at the same time you have another COGS component, Job Materials, increasing at almost 713% per year (cell J25), a huge rate. Looking a little further, you see that the cost of Subcontractors has increased only about 18% (cell J27).

Now you check the component percentages for Job Materials and Subcontractors, and find that they account for nearly all the COGS. Take just 2010, for example. Total COGS is 42% of total income (cell L31). Job Materials is 7% (cell L25) and Subcontractors is 31% (cell L27) of total income, so together they account for nearly all of Total COGS. Job Materials may have increased year-to-year by 713%, but in 2010 it was only 7% of total income. All that growth in Job Materials is mitigated by the far more moderate 18% increase in Subcontractors, which started at 31% of total income and finished at 14%, still an appreciable component percentage.

An increase in the cost of subcontractors is probably inevitable when total income increase 166%. But 713% for Job Materials is not sustainable, especially when its component percentage rises to 22% of total income in 2011 (cell K25). A manager at Rock Castle Construction should be watching the company's use of subcontractors during 2012.

Continuing down the report into the Expense section, you see that Total Expenses grew by 127% (cell J74). That's a significantly lower rate of growth than occurred in total income, 166%. And from 2010 to 2011, Total Expenses as a percent of total income dropped from 43% to 37% (cells L74 and K74, respectively).

Quantifying the combined effects of costs and expenses

There are two effects at work in this Profit & Loss analysis: total income growing faster than COGS, and total income growing much faster than expenses. The combination of those effects results in the dramatic increase of over 300% in net income. How those effects combine can be seen more easily by working directly with percentages, as shown in Figure 4.8.

FIGURE 4.7

The combination of percent change in column J with the percent of total income in columns K and L points you to the interesting drivers.

	F	G	H	I	J	K	L
1	Rock Castle Construction						
2	Profit & Loss Prev Year Comparison						
3	January through December 2011				Accrual Basis		
4							
5		Jan - Dec 11	Jan - Dec 10	$ Change	% Change	Component	Component
6	Ordinary Income/Expense					%, 2011	%, 2010
7	Income						
8	40100 · Construction Income						
9	40110 · Design Income	36,729.25	3,400.00	33,329.25	980.27%	8.17%	2.01%
10	40130 · Labor Income	208,225.42	16,335.00	191,890.42	1,174.72%	46.29%	9.65%
11	40140 · Materials Income	120,046.47	36,023.77	84,022.70	233.24%	26.69%	21.28%
12	40150 · Subcontracted Labor Income	82,710.35	112,666.50	-29,956.15	-26.59%	18.39%	66.56%
15	Total 40100 · Construction Income	447,663.14	168,425.27	279,237.87	165.79%	99.53%	99.51%
20	Total Income	449,782.94	169,260.27	280,522.67	165.74%	100.00%	100.00%
21	Cost of Goods Sold						
22	50100 · Cost of Goods Sold	16,446.14	5,620.85	10,825.29	192.59%	3.66%	3.32%
23	54000 · Job Expenses						
24	54200 · Equipment Rental	1,850.00	0.00	1,850.00	100.0%	0.41%	0.00%
25	54300 · Job Materials	98,935.90	12,171.60	86,764.30	712.84%	22.00%	7.19%
26	54400 · Permits and Licenses	700.00	225.00	475.00	211.11%	0.16%	0.13%
27	54500 · Subcontractors	63,217.95	53,350.00	9,867.95	18.5%	14.06%	31.52%
30	Total 54000 · Job Expenses	165,299.14	65,746.60	99,552.54	151.42%	36.75%	38.84%
31	Total COGS	181,745.28	71,367.45	110,377.83	154.66%	40.41%	42.16%
32	Gross Profit	268,037.66	97,892.82	170,144.84	173.81%	59.59%	57.84%
33	Expense						
47	62710 · Gross Wages	110,400.10	0.00	110,400.10	100.0%	24.55%	0.00%
51	Total 62700 · Payroll Expenses	120,347.21	0.00	120,347.21	100.0%	26.76%	0.00%
74	Total Expense	165,082.08	72,630.95	92,451.13	127.29%	36.7%	42.91%
75	Net Ordinary Income	102,955.58	25,261.87	77,693.71	307.55%	22.89%	14.92%
82	Net Income	103,331.54	25,542.90	77,788.64	304.54%	22.97%	15.09%

Figure 4.8 summarizes the principal effects that bring about a 307% growth in Net Income from 2010 to 2011. Columns B and D show the actual component percentages for Total Income, Total COGS and Total Expense during 2011 and 2010; although the Gross Profit and Net Income percentages are derived by subtraction, they match the figures in the original report.

Column C takes into account the percentage increase in Total Income, 2010 to 2011. The *growth* reported in the Profit & Loss is 166%, but the *ratio* of 2011 Total Income to 2010 Total Income is 266%, or 2.66. The original component percentages for 2011 were based on 2011

Total Income. Multiplying the 2011 percentages by 2.66 makes the percentages commensurate with the 2010 percentages.

Subtracting Total COGS and Total Expenses from Total Income results in a Net Income of 15% for 2010 and 61% for 2011, where both percentages are relative to 2010 Total Income. Their growth rate of 307% agrees with the 307% shown in the Profit & Loss report.

This analysis is meant to emphasize how combining a strong increase in sales with increases in costs and expenses that are not so strong can result in a truly dramatic increase in net income. And you can perform similar analysis with comparative, common-sized reports on other companies and other years. Notice that while it's necessary to interpret the growth rates over time, those rates are not informative if you don't know what component percentages they represent.

FIGURE 4.8

Applying the math to the percentages makes it clear how smaller differences combine to create very large differences.

	A	B	C	D
1	(2011 Total Sales) / (2010 Total Sales): 2.66			
2				
3		2011		2010
4		Percentage	Percentage times multiplier	Percentage
5	Total sales	100%	266%	100%
6				
7	Total COGS	40%	107%	42%
8				
9	Gross profit	60%	158%	58%
10				
11	Total expense	37%	98%	43%
12				
13	Net income	23%	61%	15%
14				
15	Net Income growth	307%		

The trouble with the SIGN function

Refer to Figure 4.7 and notice the percent year-to-year change in payroll expenses (cell J51). It is shown as 100%. As you analyze this Profit & Loss report, you're looking for percentage changes that are on roughly the same order of magnitude as the change in total income, 166%, or larger, and a change of "only" 100% does not really jump out at you.

Have another look at the formula that calculates the year-to-year percentage change rate, shorn of its irrelevant ROUND function:

```
=IF(G51=0, IF(H51=0, 0, SIGN(-H51)), IF(H51=0, SIGN(G51), (G51-H51)/H51))
```

In this case, G51 is greater than 0 and H51 is exactly 0: no wages or other payroll expenses were reported for 2010. Evaluating the formula shows that under those conditions, the formula returns the result of SIGN(G51). The figure in G51 is positive, so SIGN(G51) returns 1.0, and formatted as a percent, the result is shows as 100%.

In effect, for QuickBooks to use this formulation is to redefine mathematics. To derive a growth rate when both G51 and H51 are positive numbers, the growth rate is calculated as the difference between the payrolls for 2010 and 2011, divided by the payroll for 2010. But when the payroll for 2010 (the denominator) is 0, the result of the division is undefined in a mathematical sense. To avoid showing an error value, QuickBooks defines the result of division by 0 as 100%.

There's nothing terribly wrong about that. Certainly it's not as goofy as the Indiana Pi Bill of 1897. But the result makes a potential problem easy to miss. *Notice that if the company had paid $1 in wages and payroll expenses during 2010, the calculated growth rate would have been over 12 million percent, and that really would have stood out.*

FIGURE 4.9

When you interpret the balance sheet, bear in mind that the dollar figures are snapshots, not cumulative amounts as on a P&L.

	A	B	C	D
1	(2011 Total Income) / (2010 Total Income):	2.66		
2				
3		2011		2010
4		Percentage	Percentage times multiplier	Percentage
5	Total Income	100%	266%	100%
6				
7	Total COGS	40%	107%	42%
8				
9	Gross profit	60%	158%	58%
10				
11	Total expense	37%	98%	43%
12				
13	Net income	23%	61%	15%
14				
15	Net Income growth	307%		

NOTE The problem just described is not merely an artifact of exporting a report from QuickBooks to Excel. It is native to QuickBooks. To prove it to yourself, open the Rock Castle Construction sample file and pay a $1 bonus to an employee for a previous year in which there is at present no payroll expense. Then open a P&L Prev Year Comparison report and check the % Change column.

A manager at Rock Castle needs to watch the increase in payroll expenses. Although QuickBooks says that the year-over-year increase was 100%, the dollar increase is over

$120,000 and its component percentage goes from 0% to over 26%. That sort of payroll growth is just not sustainable any more than a 713% increase in Job Materials, even when subcontractor costs are falling. But the payroll expense growth is hidden by the use of 100% to represent the percent change. Remember that this occurs in a Profit & Loss report at a period in the company's history when three-digit growth rates are the norm.

The lesson once again is that you can't look just at growth rates. You need to look at dollar changes and component percentages for context. But you also need to bear in mind that QuickBooks' formulas can sometimes paint a misleading picture.

Exporting and interpreting the Balance Sheet report

The considerations involved in selecting and exporting a balance sheet from QuickBooks are largely the same as those involved in exporting a Profit & Loss report. You want to see the actual dollars and rates of change year-to-year for each asset and liability/equity account, so you need a previous year comparison report.

The Balance Sheet Standard report offers a % of Column option, which is based on Total Assets and therefore is better behaved than the % of Column option in the Profit & Loss Standard report. Still, the % of Column subcolumns in the Balance Sheet Standard report are neither

FIGURE 4.10

Total Assets should always equal Total Liabilities & Equity, so you can use either as the denominator for the component percentages.

	F	G	H	I	J	K	L
1	**Rock Castle Construction**						
2	**Balance Sheet Prev Year Comparison**						
3	As of December 31, 2011				Accrual Basis		
4							
5		Dec 31, 11	Dec 31, 10	$ Change	% Change	Component	Component
6	ASSETS					%, 2011	%, 2010
7	Current Assets						
8	Checking/Savings						
9	10100 · Checking	63,604.10	36,810.16	26,793.94	72.79%	10.04%	6.86%
10	10300 · Savings	1,110.19	15,881.03	-14,770.84	-93.01%	0.18%	2.96%
11	10400 · Petty Cash	500.00	500.00	0.00	0.0%	0.08%	0.09%
12	Total Checking/Savings	65,214.29	53,191.19	12,023.10	22.6%	10.30%	9.92%
13	Accounts Receivable						
14	11000 · Accounts Receivable	93,024.10	21,249.39	71,774.71	337.77%	14.69%	3.96%
15	Total Accounts Receivable	93,024.10	21,249.39	71,774.71	337.77%	14.69%	3.96%
16	Other Current Assets						
17	12000 · Undeposited Funds	2,559.39	18,252.08	-15,692.69	-85.98%	0.40%	3.40%
18	12100 · Inventory Asset	28,952.59	12,775.15	16,177.44	126.63%	4.57%	2.38%
19	12800 · Employee Advances	832.00	770.00	62.00	8.05%	0.13%	0.14%
20	13100 · Pre-paid Insurance	4,050.00	4,943.02	-893.02	-18.07%	0.64%	0.92%
21	13400 · Retainage Receivable	3,703.02	1,796.72	1,906.30	106.1%	0.58%	0.33%
22	Total Other Current Assets	40,097.00	38,536.97	1,560.03	4.05%	6.33%	7.18%
23	Total Current Assets	198,335.39	112,977.55	85,357.84	75.55%	31.32%	21.06%
24	Fixed Assets						
25	15000 · Furniture and Equipment	34,326.00	22,826.00	11,500.00	50.38%	5.42%	4.26%

adjacent nor in the same order as in the Balance Sheet Prev Year Comparison report. So again you're better off using just the comparative balance sheet report and entering the component percentage formulas yourself.

The process of opening and modifying the Balance Sheet Prev Year Comparison report is identical to the process used for the Profit & Loss Prev Year Comparison, described earlier in this chapter in the section "Exporting the Profit & Loss report." The exported balance sheet should resemble the one excerpted in Figure 4.9.

Once the comparative report is exported, you can calculate the component percentages just as you did for the Profit & Loss Prev Year Comparison report. The one difference is that you use Total Assets (or, equivalently, Total Liabilities & Equity) as the denominator for component percentages instead of total income.

Using the layout as shown in Figure 4.9, you would begin by entering this formula in cell K9:

```
=IF(G9<>"",G9/G$35,"")
```

where cell G35 contains Total Assets for 2011. Don't forget the dollar sign in the denominator's cell address, to make the reference a mixed reference and anchor the denominator to a value in row 35. Then autofill the formula into column H, and down through the remaining rows in the report as described earlier, again in the "Exporting the Profit & Loss report" section.

Part II: Analyzing Financial Statements

FIGURE 4.11

The zeroes in the dollar and percent change columns for Long Term Liabilities are unexpected.

	F	G	H	I	J	K	L
1	**Rock Castle Construction**						
2	**Balance Sheet Prev Year Comparison**						
3	As of December 31, 2011				Accrual Basis		
4							
5		Dec 31, 11	Dec 31, 10	$ Change	% Change	Component	Component
6						%, 2011	%, 2010
60	Total Current Liabilities	42,006.63	13,702.18	28,304.45	206.57%	6.63%	2.55%
61	Long Term Liabilities						
62	23000 · Loan - Vehicles (Van)	10,501.47	16,290.52	-5,789.05	-35.54%	1.66%	3.04%
63	23100 · Loan - Vehicles (Utility Truck)	19,936.91	19,936.91	0.00	0.0%	3.15%	3.72%
64	23200 · Loan - Vehicles (Pickup Truck)	22,641.00	22,641.00	0.00	0.0%	3.58%	4.22%
65	28100 · Loan - Construction Equipment	13,911.32	14,343.11	-431.79	-3.01%	2.20%	2.67%
66	28200 · Loan - Furniture/Office Equip	21,000.00	21,000.00	0.00	0.0%	3.32%	3.91%
67	28700 · Note Payable - Bank of Anycity	2,623.21	31,180.52	-28,557.31	-91.59%	0.41%	5.81%
68	28900 · Mortgage - Office Building	296,283.00	296,283.00	0.00	0.0%	46.79%	55.23%
69	Total Long Term Liabilities	386,896.91	421,675.06	-34,778.15	-8.25%	61.09%	78.61%
70	Total Liabilities	428,903.54	435,377.24	-6,473.70	-1.49%	67.73%	81.16%
71	Equity						
72	30000 · Opening Bal Equity	38,773.75	38,773.75	0.00	0.0%	6.12%	7.23%
73	30100 · Capital Stock	500.00	500.00	0.00	0.0%	0.08%	0.09%
74	32000 · Retained Earnings	61,764.87	36,221.97	25,542.90	70.52%	9.75%	6.75%
75	Net Income	103,331.54	25,542.90	77,788.64	304.54%	16.32%	4.76%
76	Total Equity	204,370.16	101,038.62	103,331.54	102.27%	32.27%	18.84%
77	**TOTAL LIABILITIES & EQUITY**	633,273.70	536,415.86	96,857.84	18.06%	100.0%	100.0%

When you have finished adding the formulas, the Excel worksheet should look something like Figure 4.10.

It's clear, looking at the increases in accounts receivable and inventory, that the company is going through the early growing process typical of successful startups. The company develops a larger customer base over time and therefore sends out more invoices — and accounts receivable grows. Similarly, the company requires more in the way of physical resources to complete its work, and the inventory asset grows.

As it happens, this balance sheet suggests there is some sound financial management to accompany the entrepreneurial activity that's taking place during 2010 and 2011. For example, see Figure 4.11, which displays the Balance Sheet report's sections for Long Term Liabilities and for Equity accounts.

Overall, you can tell from the decrease in Total Liabilities and the increase in Equity that the company is shifting its sources of capital from debt to equity. This would be regarded as a good move by those who prefer a conservative approach to financial management. Equally, it might be regarded as unduly conservative if the company's return on assets is higher than the interest rates it is paying for its loans.

There's something strange about the figures in the balance sheet, however: No payments have been made on four of the long-term loans during 2011; have a look at cells I63, I64, I66, and I68. Perhaps this accounts for the increase of almost $27,000 in the company's checking accounts, shown in Figure 4.10. More likely, it's simply an oversight in a sample QuickBooks company file. Again, you need to look at both the Profit & Loss and the Balance Sheet. Unless you were quite familiar with this company's finances anyway, you would not be able to spot these odd loan balances from a Profit & Loss alone.

Another useful aspect of a common-sized balance sheet is that some standard ratios are derived automatically. You can read more about these ratios in Chapter 6, and two of them are the debt ratio and its complement, the equity ratio. The former is the result of dividing Total Liabilities by Total Liabilities & Equity, and the latter is the result of dividing Total Equity by Total Liabilities & Equity.

Either one tells you the degree to which the company relies on borrowing, or on investment, for its funds. Using the comparative, common-sized balance sheet, you can find the debt ratio for this company during 2011 and during 2010 in cells K69:L69 of Figure 4.11. The equity ratio values are found in cells K76:L76.

Making Comparisons to Other Companies

Many companies, particularly very large and publicly traded corporations, make their financial statements available on the Web. Even if you can't find the statements on a company's Web site, you can often find them on the sites maintained by brokerages or by content providers like Yahoo. Sometimes it can be illuminating to compare your company's finances with a Fortune 500 company, although the differences in scale can make such comparisons suspect — if not entirely bogus.

Suppose yours is a small company that manufactures a household product, perhaps a specialty wood polish. You manufacture it and even assist with local marketing but you do not act as a retailer. Instead, you sell it on a wholesale basis to the few small hardware and home goods stores that have not yet been driven out of business by Home Depot and Wal-Mart.

As a percent of total income, how does your gross profit compare to a firm that's in a similar line of business, albeit much, much larger? You could find, for example, Procter & Gamble's income statements for 2007 and 2008, and copy them into an Excel worksheet. Then, by doing the same kinds of calculations described in this chapter for exported QuickBooks reports, you could compare your company's Gross Profit (or any other component) to P&G's on the common metric, percent of sales.

To do so, browse to a Web page with an income statement (or balance sheet, and some sites also publish cash flow statements). Select the statement's numbers by dragging through the statement on the Web page. Use any of a variety of methods (your Web browser's menu, or right-clicking, or a button on the Web page) to copy the matrix of selected numbers to the Windows Clipboard.

Then switch to Excel and, with a blank worksheet active, right-click in, say, cell A1. Choose Paste Special from the contextual menu. Figure 4.12 shows the Paste Special dialog box.

FIGURE 4.12

This version of the Paste Special dialog box appears when you are pasting HTML data.

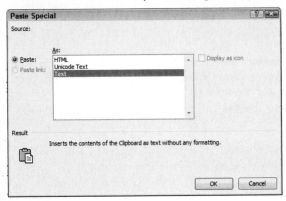

FIGURE 4.13

The income statement, copied and pasted from the Web page.

	A	B	C	D	E
1	PERIOD ENDING			30-Jun-08	30-Jun-07
2	Total Revenue			83,503,000	76,476,000
3	Cost of Revenue			40,695,000	36,686,000
4	Gross Profit			42,808,000	39,790,000
5			Operating Expenses		
6			Selling General and Administrative	25,725,000	24,340,000
7			Total Operating Expenses	-	-
8	Operating Income or Loss			17,083,000	15,450,000
9			Income from Continuing Operations		
10			Total Other Income/Expenses Net	462,000	564,000
11			Earnings Before Interest And Taxes	17,545,000	16,014,000
12			Interest Expense	1,467,000	1,304,000
13			Income Before Tax	16,078,000	14,710,000
14			Income Tax Expense	4,003,000	4,370,000
15			Minority Interest	-	-
16			Net Income From Continuing Ops	12,075,000	10,340,000
17	Net Income			12,075,000	10,340,000

Click the Text option in the As list box and click OK. You'll get a result that looks much like the worksheet in Figure 4.13. It may be necessary to adjust column widths, to get very large numbers to appear correctly in the cells.

Don't choose the HTML option in the Paste Special dialog box. If you do, you're likely to get graphics and controls such as buttons that you copied, usually unintentionally, from the Web page. These objects just get in the way of your analysis.

And don't choose the Unicode option. Unicode is a sort of extended ASCII (the encoding standard for text and symbols on computers), and it includes some nonprinting characters that

FIGURE 4.14

Component percentages in consecutive years for Procter & Gamble's published income statements appear in columns F and G.

	A B	C	D	E	F	G
1	PERIOD ENDING		30-Jun-08	30-Jun-07	30-Jun-08	30-Jun-07
2	Total Revenue		83,503,000	76,476,000	100%	100%
3	Cost of Revenue		40,695,000	36,686,000	49%	48%
4	Gross Profit		42,808,000	39,790,000	51%	52%
5	Operating Expenses					
6	Selling General and Administrative		25,725,000	24,340,000	31%	32%
7	Operating Income or Loss		17,083,000	15,450,000	20%	20%
8	Income from Continuing Operations					
9	Total Other Income/Expenses Net		462,000	564,000	1%	1%
10	Earnings Before Interest And Taxes		17,545,000	16,014,000	21%	21%
11	Interest Expense		1,467,000	1,304,000	2%	2%
12	Income Before Tax		16,078,000	14,710,000	19%	19%
13	Income Tax Expense		4,003,000	4,370,000	5%	6%
14	Minority Interest					
15	Net Income From Continuing Ops		12,075,000	10,340,000	14%	14%
16	Net Income		12,075,000	10,340,000	14%	14%

Excel has trouble dealing with (particularly HTML's ` `, which is a nonbreaking space character and can't be removed by Excel's `TRIM` function).

Your best bet is to paste the copied data into the worksheet as Text. Despite the name Text, Excel will normally paste pure ASCII and Excel will interpret a number as a numeric value.

Now just enter the formulas presented in this chapter to obtain the component percentages. (These formulas were described earlier in this chapter in the sections "Exporting the Profit &

Loss report" and "Exporting and interpreting the Balance Sheet report.") Figure 4.14 shows an example of what the formulas will return to the worksheet.

You're now in a position to compare the component percentages for your company with those reported by a member of the Dow Jones 30 Industrials.

Notice in Figure 4.14 how stable the component percentages are year-to-year, even though there's considerable growth in all components over time. The dollar values are reported in $1000s, so you're looking at revenues and costs that are measured in tens of billions of dollars. With such large amounts of money, it takes a huge shift of $360 million in COGS to get it to budge from 48% to 49%. In my own business, I can move my COGS from 40% to 50% just by spilling a glass of water on a laptop's keyboard.

With that degree of inertia in the component percentages, it doesn't make much sense to compare year-to-year percentage changes with annual changes that QuickBooks reports in your company file. But it makes good sense to aim to get your COGS (or any given expense category) to a level similar to that reported by a large and mature company, one that shares your company's SIC code. Presumably, one of the ways they got to be large and mature is by managing their costs sensibly.

Working Capital and Cash Flow Analysis

W̲e all like cash. Cash is liquid — you can spend it. As distinct
from, say, a barrel of oil or a bushel of wheat, you know pretty
closely how much it will be worth next week or next month.
Stashed into the right money market instrument, it can even earn some
interest, enough to slow, even if just slightly, the erosion of inflation.

But cash isn't really working for you. It just sits there, ready to meet
upcoming obligations, perhaps newly converted from accounts receivable
or deposited from an investor's capital infusion or a creditor's loan. Cash
isn't really pulling its weight.

But it is a current asset and obviously it has value. Other current assets
have value, and they are invested in creating income. Inventory, if you're
regularly turning it over, contributes to your profits. Accounts receivable,
if you're collecting them regularly, turn your older investments into cash
you can use to make new investments. Prepaid expenses are viewed as
unexpired assets: that is, assets that have not yet been used, such as the
remaining coverage on a 12-month fire insurance policy.

Of course, you normally have liabilities that make claims on those assets.
Accounts payable, salaries payable, and so on are typical current liabilities,
those that are coming due within the next year. Because these liabilities
already exist as claims on your assets, any accurate assessment of the
company's resources has to take account of those obligations. A $500,000
balance in a bank account means less when you consider that you have
$490,000 in accounts payable.

This sort of consideration leads to the notion of *working capital*, a concept
that's much broader than just cash on hand. It encompasses all the assets

that the company could, in the normal course of business, convert to cash in the near future, and takes account of the liabilities that must be met in the same time frame.

Working capital is a realistic view of the extent of the resources you have available. Examining how and why its value changes over time can give you a good sense of how a company has been managing its assets.

Determining Working Capital

Working capital has a deceptively simple definition: current assets minus current liabilities. That is, working capital is the amount of a company's assets that can be converted to cash in the near future, taking into account the payments that have to be made. The result is the amount of funds available for investment to generate new business.

QuickBooks makes it easy to calculate a company's current assets and current liabilities, and therefore its working capital, as of any date that the company has been in business.

FIGURE 5.1

The Balance Sheet Summary is a handy way to get balances for the major account categories.

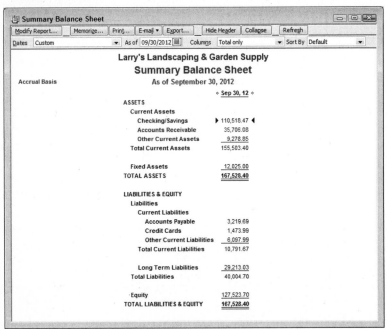

Current assets and liabilities

Figure 5.1 shows a summary balance sheet as of the end of the company's fiscal year for Larry's Landscaping, a sample company included with the QuickBooks software. It will be necessary to use a more complex version of the balance sheet later in this chapter, but the information in Figure 5.1 is all that's needed to calculate the company's amount of working capital.

With the definition of working capital in mind, it's easy to see that the company has $155,503.40 in current assets, $10,791.67 in current liabilities, and therefore $155,503.40 – $10,791.67 = $144,711.73 in working capital.

Changes to current accounts

It's helpful to get a sense of what does and doesn't have an effect on the amount of working capital available, because that can clarify the concept.

The first aspect to notice is that any change involving only current accounts has no net effect on working capital (Figure 5.2 shows an example).

Paying a $100 bill on October 4 reduces a bank account — and therefore current assets — by $100. That also reduces accounts payable by $100, so there is no net effect on working capital. But, obviously, the *components* of working capital are changing constantly.

FIGURE 5.2

Satisfying an account payable involves only current accounts, and there is no effect on working capital.

				D	E	F	G
1					Oct 4, 12		Sep 30, 12
2	ASSETS						
3		Current Assets					
4			Checking/Savings		110,418.47		110,518.47
5			Accounts Receivable		35,706.08		35,706.08
6			Other Current Assets		9,278.85		9,278.85
7		Total Current Assets			155,403.40		155,503.40
8		Fixed Assets			12,025.00		12,025.00
9	TOTAL ASSETS				167,428.40		167,528.40
10	LIABILITIES & EQUITY						
11		Liabilities					
12			Current Liabilities				
13				Accounts Payable	3,119.69		3,219.69
14				Credit Cards	1,473.99		1,473.99
15				Other Current Liabilities	6,097.99		6,097.99
16			Total Current Liabilities		10,691.67		10,791.67
17			Long Term Liabilities		29,213.03		29,213.03
18		Total Liabilities			39,904.70		40,004.70
19		Equity			127,523.70		127,523.70
20	TOTAL LIABILITIES & EQUITY				167,428.40		167,528.40
21							
22				Working capital	144,711.73		144,711.73

Similarly, when a customer sends a check for $200 to pay an invoice, you reduce accounts receivable by $200 and increase a bank account (even if only eventually via undeposited funds, another current asset) by $200. No change to total current assets, so no change to working capital.

Changes to noncurrent accounts

If you have an algebraic turn of mind, you might consider the following sequence, beginning with the fundamental accounting equation Assets = Liabilities + Equity.

Now, using these abbreviations,

- CA = Current Assets
- NCA = Noncurrent Assets, including both fixed and other assets
- CL = Current Liabilities
- NCL = Noncurrent Liabilities, including long-term and other liabilities

we can get to an algebraic definition of working capital:

```
CA + NCA = CL + NCL + Equity
CA - CL + NCA = NCL + Equity
Working Capital + NCA = NCL + Equity
Working Capital = NCL + Equity - NCA
```

FIGURE 5.3

A change in the balance of a noncurrent account often, but not always, changes the amount of working capital.

				D	E	F	G
1					Oct 4, 12		Sep 30, 12
2	ASSETS						
3		Current Assets					
4				Checking/Savings	125,518.47		110,518.47
5				Accounts Receivable	35,706.08		35,706.08
6				Other Current Assets	9,278.85		9,278.85
7			Total Current Assets		170,503.40		155,503.40
8			Fixed Assets		12,025.00		12,025.00
9	TOTAL ASSETS				182,528.40		167,528.40
10	LIABILITIES & EQUITY						
11		Liabilities					
12			Current Liabilities				
13				Accounts Payable	3,219.69		3,219.69
14				Credit Cards	1,473.99		1,473.99
15				Other Current Liabilities	6,097.99		6,097.99
16			Total Current Liabilities		10,791.67		10,791.67
17			Long Term Liabilities		44,213.03		29,213.03
18		Total Liabilities			55,004.70		40,004.70
19		Equity			127,523.70		127,523.70
20	TOTAL LIABILITIES & EQUITY				182,528.40		167,528.40
21							
22				Working capital	159,711.73		144,711.73

So, as distinct from changes involving only current accounts, a change to a noncurrent account (a noncurrent asset, a noncurrent liability, or an equity account) can change the amount of working capital. If Rock Castle Construction takes out a three-year loan for $15,000 and deposits the funds in a bank account, working capital increases by $15,000. The liability account that records the loan is a long-term liability, not a current liability. So current liabilities remain unchanged and both current assets and working capital increase by $15,000 (see Figure 5.3).

Of course, a company's primary source of working capital in the long run is net income, the excess of revenues over expenses, and that's the principal financial reason for being in business at all. From an accounting perspective, how do current assets such as inventory and accounts receivable get to be noncurrent, so that they affect working capital?

Don Lenney starts a new company called Goleta Floors, a sole proprietorship, at the end of April and provides it with startup funds by depositing $25,000 in its bank account. At this point, the company has no liabilities, current or otherwise, and a current asset (and owner's equity) of $25,000. The company's working capital is therefore $25,000 at the outset. Lenney then records the following transactions:

- A deposit of another $15,000 from his personal funds into the company's checking account, and also recorded as paid-in equity.
- The purchase of $28,000 in inventory for resale.
- The sale of $21,000 worth of inventory for $33,000.
- The receipt of $15,000 in payments from customers for their $33,000 worth of purchases. Those payments post first into Undeposited Funds, and then post into the company's checking account. The total of the customers' outstanding balances, $18,000, remains in accounts payable.
- The receipt of bills for the $28,000 worth of inventory from his vendors, and the payment of $18,000, leaving $10,000 in accounts payable.
- Lenney pays $8,500 in various operating expenses such as travel and communications.
- Lenney also purchases a small, two-room office in a shopette for $22,000, paying for it with $15,000 in cash and $7,000 from a six-month bank loan.
- The withdrawal of $1,000 for his personal use, as an owner's draw.

Figure 5.4 shows a P&L report for Goleta Floors as of the end of May.

The net income of $3,500 during May acts as a source of working capital. To see how it gets there, first see Figure 5.5. There, the assets portion of the balance sheet shows that the current assets, including cash, accounts receivable, and inventory, total $37,500.

Figure 5.6 shows the Liabilities and Equity section of the balance sheet. The current liabilities entry provides the other number you need to find the working capital.

FIGURE 5.4

On the balance sheet, the net income appears in Equity, a noncurrent account.

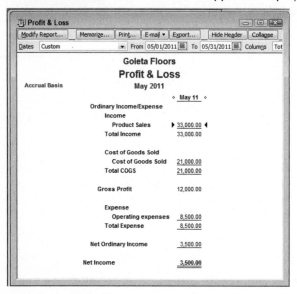

FIGURE 5.5

$22,000 of current assets have been converted to fixed assets by the purchase of the office space.

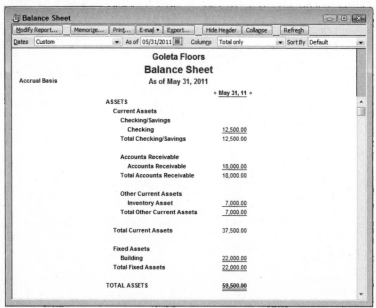

FIGURE 5.6

Notice that the net income shown on the P&L in Figure 5.4 flows to the Balance Sheet Equity section.

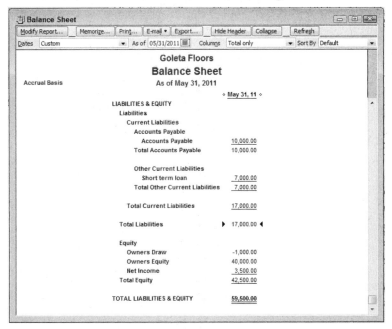

Current assets of $37,500 less current liabilities of $17,000 result in working capital of $20,500. Goleta Floors started out with $25,000 in working capital. It has earned $3,500 in net income. But its cash account has fallen to $12,500 and its working capital is down from $25,000 to $20,500.

How does this come about? Looking into the matter helps you get a clearer understanding of how the company does business. Each transaction listed later has an effect on the amount of working capital available, subsequent to Lenney's initial $25,000 investment. Be sure you see that none of the transactions involves solely current accounts. Other activities the company undertakes, such as purchasing inventory, are not listed because they involve only current accounts and therefore have no net effect on working capital.

1. Lenney's second investment increases working capital by $15,000 to $40,000.

2. Product sales bring in $12,000 in gross profit, increasing working capital to $52,000.

3. The company pays $8,500 in operating expenses, decreasing working capital to $43,500.

4. A check for $15,000 is written as a partial payment for the office space. Working capital is now $28,500.

5. Accounts payable is increased by $7,000 as a result of the short-term loan to pay the remaining balance owed on the office space. Working capital is $21,500.

6. Lenney withdraws $1,000 for his personal use, decreasing both his equity and working capital by $1,000, leaving working capital at $20,500.

So, after the initial investment of $25,000, various purchases, sales, and other transactions reduce the company's working capital to $20,500. This amount agrees with the result of subtracting, on May 31, current liabilities from current assets. It's obviously a lot quicker to do one simple subtraction than it is to trace every transaction during the period, particularly when a company typically has many more transactions than the six listed earlier.

This simple subtraction is informative, certainly — it's the quickest way to determine working capital and therefore how it varies over time. But it doesn't give you any real insight into how the company is carrying out the process of investing and disinvesting that creates profit (or loses it).

Analyzing components of working capital

The first step in that direction is to put together a statement of changes in financial position. This is usually done by categorizing the components, not according to when they occurred — as in the preceding list — but according to whether transactions constitute sources of working capital, or uses of working capital. In the current example, you can categorize the transactions as shown in Figure 5.7.

Any transaction that involves changes to both a current and a noncurrent account is either a source or use of working capital: It causes funds to flow into or from the company. These transactions either increase or reduce working capital. The transactions shown in Figure 5.7 conform to that condition. Lenney's second investment of $15,000 increases Owner's Equity (noncurrent) as well as the Cash account (current) and is therefore a source of working capital.

Similarly, the net income of $3,500 for the month is the excess of sales (current account) over costs and expenses (current accounts). At the close of an accounting period, these funds are transferred as net income to the retained earnings account (a noncurrent, equity account). At that point, the net income becomes a source of working capital, involving the transfer from current accounts to the noncurrent account.

Figure 5.7 also shows the usage of working capital. The office, a fixed asset, was acquired with the use of cash (a current account) and a short-term note (another current account). The funds left the company, so this transaction was a use of working capital. Last, when Lenney withdrew $1,000 for his personal use, both the current account Cash and the noncurrent Owner's Equity were decreased, establishing the transaction as a use of working capital.

Notice the agreement between the two approaches to calculating the change in working capital shown in Figure 5.7. You can subtract the uses of working capital (cell E5) from the sources (cell E2) and find that the change in the company's working capital is negative, a decrease of

FIGURE 5.7

A review of noncurrent accounts explains the reasons behind changes in working capital, not the amount of working capital itself.

	A	B	C	D	E
1	Sources	Net income	$ 3,500		
2		New capital investment	$ 15,000	Total sources	$ 18,500
3					
4	Uses	Purchase of office space	$ 22,000		
5		Owner's draw	$ 1,000	Total uses	$ 23,000
6					
7				Decrease	$ 4,500
8					
9		Working capital, 4/30	$ 25,000		
10		Working capital, 5/31	$ 20,500		
11		Decrease in working capital	$ 4,500		
12					

$4,500. You can also subtract the working capital at the end of April from that at the end of May, and get the same decrease of $4,500.

Looking at changes in financial condition from the point of view of sources and uses is more informative than merely calculating the overall change, and these sources and uses appear perfectly reasonable for a newly established company. Working capital did drop during the first month, and that situation cannot continue — if it does, the company will run out of resources and be forced to suspend operations or close entirely. But the principal use of working capital, the purchase of office space, is very likely a nonrecurring cost. And the secondary investment by the owner is probably also a nonrecurring event. If you take those two transactions out of the mix, the company's working capital would have increased by $2,500 instead of falling by $4,500.

The notion of working capital focuses on assets that are available for use in the near term as well as liabilities that must be satisfied in the near term. It is the difference between the two amounts, so the amount of working capital is the company's accessible assets less the near-term liabilities that it has already incurred. It is the amount of resources available to invest in new business, by converting cash to equipment, hiring additional staff, purchasing additional inventory, and so on.

What doesn't affect working capital

Earlier in this chapter, I noted that transactions involving only current accounts have no net effect on the amount of working capital. That sort of transaction affects the *components* of working capital, of course, but not the result of subtracting current liabilities from current assets.

The same is true of noncurrent accounts. A transaction that does not involve a current account does not change the amount of working capital. An example is depreciation.

Suppose your business owns a truck that it bought for $20,000. You keep it on your books as a fixed asset worth $20,000. But the truck loses value over time — that is, it depreciates — and you record that amount of loss periodically. The amount of loss you record is determined by which one of several methods for determining depreciation you and your accountant decide on.

That method might tell you to record $300 in depreciation for the first month your company owned the truck. You record $300 as a debit to an expense account, perhaps named Depreciation, and also as a credit to a fixed asset account, perhaps named Truck:Accumulated Depreciation. Neither account is a current asset account, therefore the transaction has no effect on working capital.

NOTE Although depreciation is recorded in expense and in fixed asset accounts, and thus does not affect working capital, it still needs to be accounted for when you're *calculating* working capital. This issue is explained in the "Tracking changes in working capital" section of this chapter.

What does affect working capital

There are some transactions that are typical in the increase and decrease of working capital. Among them are the following:

- **Net income.** The sale of product for more than it cost to acquire the product is a typical source of working capital. But net income often must be adjusted before adding it in with other sources. The reason is that some expenses that are subtracted from gross profit to arrive at net income do not involve current accounts. In fact, one of the purposes of analyzing the sources and uses of working capital is to clarify the reasons for a difference between net income and working capital provided by a company's operations.

- **Acquisition of fixed assets.** Buying equipment with cash, including cash obtained via borrowing, is a typical use of working capital. Acquiring the asset in exchange for stock involves no current account and has no effect on working capital.

- **Paying off long-term debt.** Assuming, as is usually the case, that a company uses current assets to retire a long-term debt, paying off the debt is a use of working capital. A long-term debt is not carried in the current accounts payable liability account.

- **Acquiring long-term debt.** When a company takes out a long-term loan, the money borrowed goes into a current asset, usually a cash account. The company also acquires a noncurrent liability, the debt itself. This transaction involves a current asset and a noncurrent liability, and is therefore a source of working capital.

- **Selling a fixed asset.** A company might occasionally sell equipment, a building, or even land in return for cash, because the company no longer has use for the asset or is in desperate need of funds. This involves a current and a noncurrent account and is therefore a source of working capital. Suppose the asset is sold at a loss: A building purchased for $200,000 in 2005 is sold for $150,000 in 2009. Even though the sale represents a loss, it nevertheless increases working capital by $150,000.

Tracking Changes in Working Capital

It's helpful to know that a company has increased — or decreased — its working capital from one period to the next. Knowing that is often more helpful than knowing the change in cash assets, or net sales, or even net income. But merely knowing that a company's working capital increased by $103,355.59 during 2011 doesn't help you to understand how it's being managed. It's good to know that the company has over a hundred thousand dollars more to work with, but whether you're a potential employee, a manager, a stockholder, or creditor, you should want to know more.

What's the main source of the increase in working capital?

- Long-term debt? Then maybe you should be extra careful about loaning the company more money.

- A recent stock issue? If newly floated shares were snapped up, maybe you should seriously consider the job offer they gave you.

- Net income? The only people who are unhappy when net income builds a company's working capital are the short-sellers.

Using the Balance Sheet Standard report

The route to learning how and why a company has experienced an increase or a decrease in working capital begins with the balance sheet, as shown in Figures 5.8 through 5.11.

FIGURE 5.8

In most cases, you want access to both Current Assets and Fixed Assets.

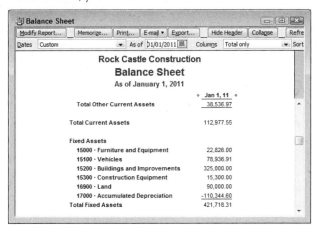

FIGURE 5.9

Compare to Figure 5.8: There is a change to only one Fixed Asset account.

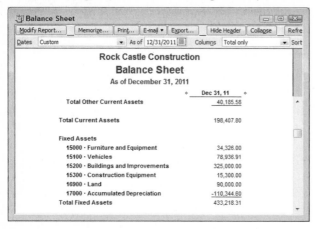

FIGURE 5.10

Notice that there is no Net Income account listed; it was restated in Retained Earnings at the start of the fiscal year.

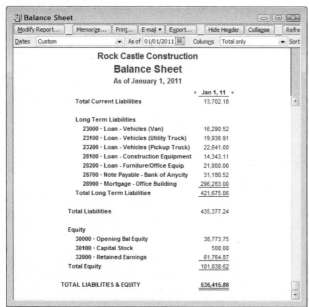

FIGURE 5.11

Net Income is ready to be transferred to Retained Earnings.

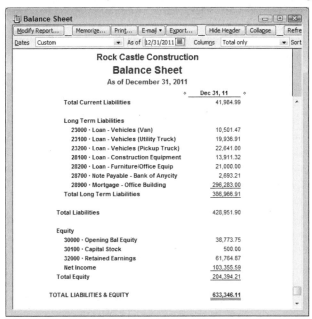

It will help to bear in mind a few aspects of the balance sheet excerpts shown in Figures 5.8 through 5.11.

Using selected accounts

Figures 5.8 through 5.11 display selected accounts: in particular, total current assets and liabilities, and the long-term liability and equity accounts. Because of the way working capital is tracked, only the totals of the current accounts, and the specific noncurrent accounts, are needed.

Beginning and ending dates

To track increases and decreases in working capital during an accounting period, and to determine why those changes occurred, you need to know several account balances at the beginning and at the end of the period.

QuickBooks automatically sweeps the net income from one fiscal year into a Retained Earnings account on the first day of the next fiscal year. This gives you zero dollars in net income at the start of the year, which is convenient for a variety of reasons. One reason is that your net income figure at the end of the fiscal year represents the amount of net income for the full year, unmixed with amounts from prior periods.

To keep everything as neat and tidy as possible, it's a good idea to compare balance sheet accounts on the first day of the fiscal year with the final day of the year. You might think that the Balance Sheet Prev Year Comparison report would do that, but it reports the final day of both the current and the previous year. You cannot tweak that report to show the first day of the year and the last day of the year. Therefore, use the Balance Sheet Standard report for the working capital analysis. Run it twice: once as of the first day of the period, and once as of the final day.

> **NOTE** **If you use the Premier Accountant or Enterprise edition of QuickBooks, you have access to a tool that enables you to build a single balance sheet that shows the first and last days of a given year. Depending on the year of release of your software, this tool might be called the Financial Statement Designer or the Intuit Statement Writer.**

Getting enough detail

The Balance Sheet Summary report can be a handy one, because it does not drill down through as many levels of subaccounts as does the standard balance sheet. Using it, you can often get a useful account summary report on one sheet of paper. Still, it gives you enough detail that you can compare total current assets with total current liabilities and come up with a current amount of working capital.

However, it's not usually enough simply to know the amount of working capital. You want to know how and why it varies over time, and for that you need access to balances in specific non-current accounts.

Preparing the analysis

QuickBooks does not supply a built-in analysis of working capital and its report options are not flexible enough to enable you to cobble one together. The best way is to export the balance sheets to an Excel workbook and use its linking capabilities to put the analysis together.

There are several ways to get the data from a report such as the Balance Sheet Standard into an Excel worksheet. Chapter 2 goes into more detail on this topic. Probably the worst way is to try to type the values you see in a report directly into a worksheet's cells. One handy (if not bullet-proof) method is to export the report to an Excel workbook and insert a new worksheet in that workbook. Then, enter formulas in the new worksheet that simply point to values you want to pick up from the exported sheet. For example, in a new worksheet named Sheet4, the cell that shows net income might contain the formula

```
=Sheet1!J20
```

You'll see the process illustrated in the remainder of this section.

Exporting the balance sheets to Excel

If this is your first time through the exporting process it's going to seem painstaking and unwieldy. Once you work your way through it a couple of times you'll find that it quickly becomes second-nature.

Suppose you want to analyze the change in working capital for the Rock Castle Construction sample file that accompanies QuickBooks, for fiscal year 2011. Take these steps:

1. With the company file open, choose Reports ▶ Company & Financial ▶ Balance Sheet Standard.

2. In the As Of edit box, enter the first date of the fiscal year (or, more generally, the accounting period) you want to analyze. In this example, that's 1/1/2011.

3. Click the Refresh button at the top of the report to update the balances per the date you entered in Step 2.

4. Click the Export button. In the Export Report dialog box, make sure that you select the option labeled A New Excel Workbook and then click Export. If Excel was not already running, QuickBooks opens it for you.

5. When the export is complete, switch to Excel. The exported report will be visible in a new, unsaved workbook. Double-click the active worksheet's tab (the tab at the bottom of the worksheet that says Sheet1). When you do so, it will become highlighted and you can type **First Day**. Press Enter to finish renaming the worksheet.

6. Select an empty cell in the worksheet; to make it easy to find later, I suggest a cell near the bottom of the balance sheet.

7. Type = (an equal sign), then click in the cell that contains the value for Total Current Assets. Type − (a minus sign) and click in the cell that contains the value for Total Current Liabilities. Press Enter. You have now calculated the working capital available on the first day of the fiscal year.

8. Switch back to QuickBooks. With the standard balance sheet report active, change the As Of date to the last day of the period. In this example, that's 12/31/2011. Repeat Steps 3 and 4 to export the report with the new date.

9. Switch back to Excel and if necessary activate the workbook with the closing date for the accounting period. Double-click its sheet tab to rename it Last Day.

10. With the Last Day worksheet still active, right-click its sheet tab and choose Move or Copy from the contextual menu to open the dialog box shown in Figure 5.12.

11. From the To Book dropdown, choose the workbook that contains the worksheet named First Day. Click the (Move to End) item in the Before Sheet list. Select the Create a Copy checkbox and click OK.

12. The workbook with both worksheets, First Day and Last Day, is now active. Switch to the workbook that contains only the Last Day worksheet and close it without bothering to save. You have already copied its important information into the other workbook.

13. Activate the Last Day worksheet and repeat Steps 6 and 7 to get the working capital on the final day of the fiscal year.

FIGURE 5.12

If you did not tell QuickBooks to include a tips worksheet, you'll be forced to create a copy: a workbook cannot have fewer than one visible worksheet.

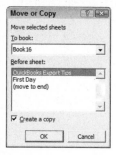

Deriving the working capital analysis from the account balances

You now have an Excel workbook with these worksheets:

- A worksheet named First Day that contains a balance sheet as of the first day of the fiscal year.

- A worksheet named Last Day that contains a balance sheet as of the final day of the fiscal year.

- (Possibly) a worksheet named QuickBooks Export Tips. You can delete this worksheet if you'd like. Right-click its sheet tab and choose Delete from the contextual menu.

To make sure you don't lose your work, you might as well save the workbook now, giving it a file name such as Working Capital Analysis. The next sequence of steps completes the numeric portion of the analysis. When that's finished, it remains for you to examine the sources and uses of working capital, as well as their dollar amounts, and to decide whether you regard them as reasonable and prudent.

In Figures 5.8 and 5.9, notice that the fixed asset Furniture and Equipment increases during the fiscal year. You will account for this increase when you build the analysis in the next sequence of steps.

Now compare Figures 5.10 and 5.11, and notice that there are three loans whose balances changed between the start and the end of the year: the loan for the van, for the construction equipment, and the note payable to the bank. Payments that reduce the principal of each loan are made during the year, constituting uses of working capital, and you're about to account for them as well.

The worksheet shown in Figure 5.13 contains the structure for the working capital analysis. The following steps make reference to its cell addresses.

To create the analysis, take these steps:

FIGURE 5.13

In practice you'll defer entering the labels in cells B5:B8 until you have finished linking to the balance sheets.

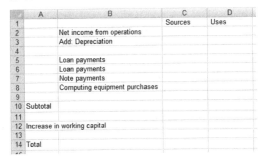

1. Insert a new worksheet into the workbook. Right-click any worksheet tab and choose Insert. In the Insert dialog box, select the worksheet icon and click OK.

2. Rename the new worksheet something such as Analysis Sheet.

3. Enter the labels shown in Figure 5.13.

4. Select cell C2 and type =. Do not press Enter.

5. Select the Last Day worksheet by clicking its worksheet tab. Select the cell in the balance sheet that has the total income for the fiscal year and now press Enter. That cell will be near the bottom of the balance sheet and will have the label Net Income to its left, in column A.

6. Select cell D5. Type =, activate the First Day worksheet, and click in the cell with the amount for the loan on the van and then type –. The partial formula in cell D5 should now look like this:
   ```
   ='First Day'!F46-
   ```

7. Activate the Last Day worksheet, click the cell with the ending balance for the loan on the van and press Enter. The formula in cell D5 in the analysis worksheet should now appear something like this (depending on the actual locations in the two balance sheets):
   ```
   ='First Day'!F46-'Last Day'!G58
   ```

8. Repeat Steps 6 and 7 for the construction equipment loan and for the bank note. Put the linking formulas in cells D6 and D7.

   Repeat Steps 6 and 7 for the fixed asset Furniture and Equipment, putting the linking formula in cell D8. However, begin by selecting the Last Day worksheet instead of the First Day worksheet. The formula in cell D8 should look something like
   ```
   ='Last Day'!G21-'First Day'!F21
   ```
   The idea is to get the differences in the account balances into the analysis sheet as positive numbers in the Uses column. Whereas the long-term liabilities tend to decrease over time, the fixed assets tend to increase over time. That is why the formulas for the

liabilities subtract the last day from the first, and why the formula for the fixed assets subtracts the first day from the last.

9. Now get the change in working capital during the year. In the analysis sheet, select cell D12. Type =, activate the Last Day worksheet, and click in the cell where you entered the formula for the working capital at the end of the year. Type −.

10. Activate the First Day worksheet and select the cell that contains the working capital at the start of the year. Press Enter. Cell D12 now contains a formula that looks something like this:

    ```
    ='Last Day'!I73-'First Day'!H60
    ```

11. Select cell C10 in the analysis worksheet and enter this formula:

    ```
    =SUM(C2:C8)
    ```

    If necessary, reselect cell C10. Move your mouse pointer over the small black square on the cell's lower-right corner (its fill handle). Pressing the left mouse button, drag one column to the right. This autofills the formula into cell D10. You now have subtotals of the Sources and Uses of working capital during the fiscal year.

12. Select cell C14 and enter this formula:

    ```
    =SUM(C10:C12)
    ```

    As in Step 11, autofill the formula into cell D14.

No depreciation is recorded for the fiscal year ending in 2011, so don't worry about putting an entry in cell C3. (You can check the depreciation status by comparing the Accumulated Depreciation amount on the First Day worksheet with that on the Last Day worksheet.)

The report's appearance now resembles that shown in Figure 5.14.

> **TIP**
>
> To get the single and double underlines shown in rows 10 and 14 in Figure 5.14, right-click in a cell and choose Format Cells. Click the Font tab and choose Single Accounting or Double Accounting in the Underline dropdown.

> **NOTE**
>
> Even if you use the Rock Castle Construction sample file when you take these steps, you might not get precisely the same results. The sample files differ as to transaction amounts in different releases of QuickBooks, and what QuickBooks considers to be the current date also varies.

Interpreting the analysis

In Figure 5.14, the subtotal of the Sources and Uses of working capital that took place during the year is shown in row 10. Row 12 shows, as the Increase in Working Capital, the difference in the amount of working capital between the beginning and the end of the fiscal year. Notice that this figure brings into balance the totals of the Sources and Uses of working capital during the fiscal year, shown in row 14.

There is another, conceptually richer way of looking at this information. The company created $103,355.59 in working capital during the fiscal year (cell C2). It used $46,208.15 of that working capital (cell D10). The difference between the two amounts, 57,147.44, represents the change in working capital during the year — the amount of new working capital created but not used.

FIGURE 5.14

The totals balance and you can now apply your judgment regarding the company's use of working funds during the fiscal year.

	A	B	C	D
			Sources	Uses
1				
2		Net income from operations	$ 103,355.59	
3		Add: Depreciation		
4				
5		Loan payments		$ 5,789.05
6		Loan payments		$ 431.79
7		Note payments		$ 28,487.31
8		Furniture and Equipment		$ 11,500.00
9				
10	Subtotal		$ 103,355.59	$ 46,208.15
11				
12	Increase in working capital			$ 57,147.44
13				
14	Total		$ 103,355.59	$ 103,355.59

Be sure you understand that the change in working capital shown in cell D12 comes from the comparison of current assets and current liabilities, *not* from subtracting the total Uses in D10 from the total Sources in C10. This issue is explored in the next section.

Arranging for greater detail

This analysis, as far as it goes, illustrates that the two ways used to calculate the change in working capital agree: the difference between working capital amounts at the beginning and the end of the fiscal year, and the difference between the total sources and uses of working capital during that year.

If the totals had not balanced, you would know there was an error somewhere and would have to start tracking it down. That they are in balance is not a guarantee that the analysis is error-free, but because they do balance it's now reasonable to look further into the nature of the Sources and Uses of the working capital.

For example, Figure 5.14 shows that the company used $11,500 in the Furniture and Equipment fixed asset account, but from the balance sheet alone you have no way of knowing whether the $11,500 went for workstations and servers or for a couple of gold-and-burgundy floral-pattern shower curtains.

Perhaps the quickest way to find out is, with QuickBooks active, to choose Lists ▶ Chart of Accounts and double-click Furniture and Equipment in the list of accounts. A window containing the register for this account opens with information about transactions in the account. (To see even more detail, click the transaction you're interested in and choose Edit Transaction.) In this example, you would learn that the $11,500 went for two PCs and a server. At least, the company's records say that is where the money went (see Figure 5.15).

In this example, you don't have to go quite so far to learn about the way working capital was used to reduce long-term liabilities. The numbers are in the balance sheets (see Figures 5.10 and 5.11) to tell you that the balances on two loans and one note were reduced by $5,789.05, $431.79, and $28,487.31, as shown in Figure 5.14, for a total of $34,708.15.

Working capital in another company

Another sample company file included with your QuickBooks software is Larry's Landscaping. Larry doesn't appear to be managing his company's resources quite as skillfully as the people running Rock Castle Construction. A working capital analysis is probably in order, and once again the Balance Sheet Standard report is a good place to start. Figures 5.16 through 5.19 show the assets and the liabilities portions of the company's balance sheet at the start and at the end of the fiscal year.

The procedures to move the balance sheets into Excel and to create the analysis worksheet are identical to the steps described in this chapter's previous two sections. There is one additional task: moving depreciation onto the analysis worksheet, which now appears as shown in Figure 5.20. As with other entries such as the partial retirement of loans, the entry for depreciation in Figure 5.20 is the difference between accumulated depreciation account balance at the beginning of the period and at the end of the period.

In the process of building an income statement, depreciation is subtracted from gross profit (among other expenses) to arrive at a figure for net income. The net income is then transferred to the balance sheets, as shown in Figures 5.18 and 5.19. Depreciation does reduce net income (and therefore plays a role in reducing corporate income taxes), but it does not reduce working capital: Recording depreciation is not a transaction that involves both a current account and a noncurrent account. Depreciation must be added back to net income to calculate the total of sources of working capital.

Don't let this step confuse you. Some people look at an analysis such as the one in Figure 5.20, see depreciation added to net income, and conclude that depreciation somehow increases a company's funds. It does not: The addition of depreciation to net income is simply the recognition that depreciation does not decrease working capital. Having been subtracted from gross profit to arrive at net income, depreciation must be added back in so as to accurately calculate working capital.

Note the entry of $23,645.97 as a change in equity accounts. If you examine the individual transactions in the company's Opening Balance Equity account, you see that over $40,000 was transferred between Opening Balance Equity and Retained Earnings. This transaction involves two noncurrent equity accounts, and therefore has no effect on working capital.

The remaining transactions in the Opening Balance Equity account involve current accounts (Payroll Liabilities, Inventory, and Checking/Savings) and result in a net use of working capital. Figure 5.21 details these transactions.

In all, the working capital analysis does not suggest that Larry's Landscaping is in great shape at the end of the 2010-11 fiscal year. It helps to highlight the existence of two loans taken out just prior to the fiscal year's end, and in the absence of further information, one would have to wonder if those loans were properly collateralized. A potential creditor or potential employee of this business would surely have plenty of questions to ask after seeing these figures.

Of course, it's a sample file, and so will probably remain solvent for several more editions of QuickBooks.

FIGURE 5.15

Greater detail in the working capital analysis gives you a better picture of how the company is using its assets.

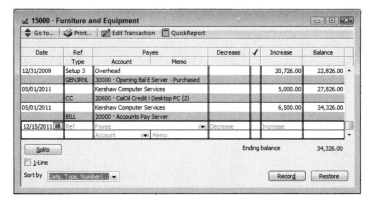

FIGURE 5.16

Larry's Landscaping uses October 1 as the start of its fiscal year.

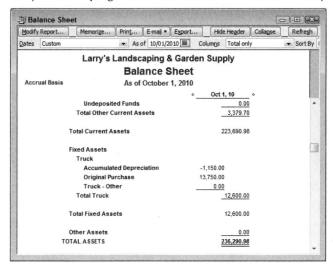

FIGURE 5.17

Compare to Figure 5.16. This company records $575 in depreciation during the year shown.

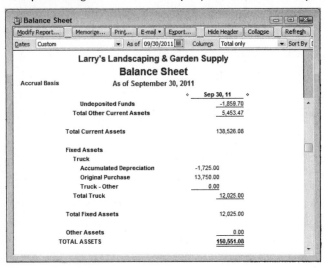

FIGURE 5.18

Net Income is zero as of the first day of the fiscal year.

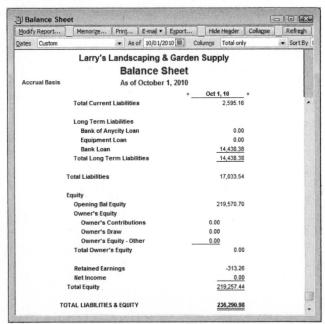

FIGURE 5.19

The business lost money over the course of the year.

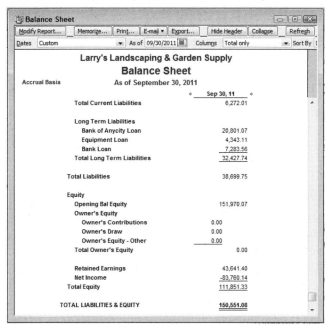

FIGURE 5.20

Depreciation must be returned to Net Income.

	A	B	C	D
1			Sources	Uses
2		Net income from operations	$(83,760.14)	
3		Add: Depreciation	$ 575.00	
4				
5		New loan	$ 20,801.07	
6		New loan	$ 4,343.11	
7		Loan payments		$ 7,154.82
8		Changes to equity accounts		$ 23,645.97
9				
10	Subtotal		$ (58,040.96)	$ 30,800.79
11				
12	Increase in working capital			$(88,841.75)
13				
14	Total		$ (58,040.96)	$ (58,040.96)

FIGURE 5.21

The inventory adjustments, possibly due to a corrected physical inventory, result in a higher asset valuation.

	A	B	C
1	Transactions involving current and equity accounts	Debit	Credit
2	New loan		$ 20,801.07
3	New loan		$ 4,343.11
4	Inventory adjustment	$ 885.00	
5	Inventory adjustment	$ 1,575.00	
6	Payroll liabilities		$ 961.79
7			
8	Totals	$ 2,460.00	$ 26,105.97
9			
10	Net use		$ 23,645.97

Getting all the accounts

The previous two sections have arranged the export of balance sheets to Excel in a layout that requires the use of links to calculate the differences between account balances. For example, the working capital analysis sheet includes a formula for the change in a loan amount that points both at a worksheet for the starting date and at a worksheet for the closing date.

There are two reasons for this approach. One is that this book is principally about QuickBooks, and only secondarily about using Excel to augment analysis that can be done in QuickBooks. The second reason is that keeping the balance sheets separate emphasizes the notion of changes in account balances to explain changes in working capital.

But there is an option in QuickBooks that you should be aware of if you want to carry out working capital analysis on a routine basis — or any other analysis that requires the use of one or more QuickBooks reports as of different dates.

One default option for QuickBooks' reports is to show only nonzero accounts. With a report active, if you click Modify Report and then click the Advanced button in the Modify Report dialog box, you see the window shown in Figure 5.22.

With the default, nonzero option in effect, you can easily find an account in an end-of-year balance sheet that does not appear in the balance sheet as of the start of the year. In turn, this means that you cannot easily line up the rows to create your own comparative balance sheet.

However, if you select the All option, in the Display Rows area, for both balance sheets, you get the same accounts in both sheets regardless of their current balances, and they appear in the same rows on both sheets. The reason this is useful is that it makes it easier to get changes in account balances in Excel. Figure 5.23 has an example.

To get the differences in account balances between the start and end date, begin as described in the "Exporting the balance sheets to Excel" section. Once you have the Last Day sheet in Excel, select its contents — both the account labels and the dollar values — and copy and paste them in the First Day worksheet as shown in Figure 5.23.

FIGURE 5.22

The Active option displays only rows with accounts (or other elements) that have any activity during the period covered by the report.

FIGURE 5.23

With the accounts lined up, it's easy to calculate all the balance differences.

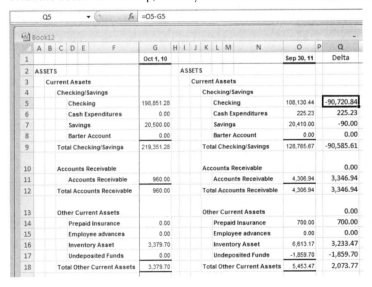

Then select the cell in the first row that contains dollar amounts, and in the first column to the right of the Last Day balances. In Figure 5.23, that's cell Q5. Enter a formula, as shown in the formula bar, that subtracts the value for the first day's balance from the last day's balance. Then, with that cell selected, copy it, and paste it down through the remaining rows in the report.

You now have the differences in the account balances. As you're assembling the working capital analysis (explained in the section "Deriving the working capital analysis from the account balances"), just link to the cells containing the differences.

Tracking Cash Flow

The Statement of Cash Flows report is sometimes helpful in understanding changes in a company's financial position. An example, using the Rock Castle Construction sample file and based on the same date range as the earlier examples in this chapter, is shown in Figures 5.24 and 5.25. This report is available by choosing Reports ❯ Company & Financial ❯ Statement of Cash Flows.

Some companies are small enough, and their financial activities sufficiently uncomplicated, that a cash basis for accounting makes sense: The additional and more accurate information provided by the accrual basis does not justify the added time and effort needed. Thus, if a company uses accrual as the basis for its accounting, income statements that allow for the accrual of income and expense are the best guide to the company's financial position. Furthermore, in an accrual situation, a working capital analysis is a better guide than a cash flow statement.

But cash is the most liquid of liquid assets, and the ways a company uses cash show how it goes about managing its investments and expenditures, as well as its disinvestments and receipts. A cash flow statement can also provide information in support of a working capital analysis.

The data in Figure 5.24, for instance, shows that the company had $103,355.59 in net income during the 2011 fiscal year. Figure 5.14 shows that the company had an increase in working capital of $57,147.44. How is it, then, that Figure 5.25 shows a net cash loss for the period?

FIGURE 5.24

Negative amounts in this report reduce the amount of cash available.

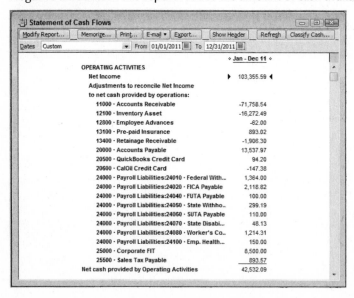

FIGURE 5.25

The cash flow report can help reconcile a positive net income with a reduction in cash position.

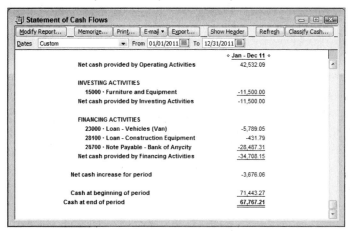

The answer is found partly in the adjustments shown in Figure 5.24. There remains over $71,000 in accounts receivable — as-yet-uncollected receipts — and a relatively small amount in accounts payable, indicating that the company may have stayed more current in its payments than in its receipts. Furthermore, Figure 5.25 shows $34,708.15 in the reduction of principal on three loans and the expenditure of $11,500 on new equipment (which I established earlier was for PCs and a server).

All in all, the cash statement echoes the message of the working capital analysis: This is a healthy firm, with all its working capital during 2011 coming from operations. However, both the absolute amount of funds in Accounts Receivable, as well as the fact that it is more than five times greater than Accounts Payable, suggests that the company might want to revisit its collections procedures.

Ratio Analysis

There are certain numbers that appear in your company's income statement and balance sheet that, combined properly, can give you much more insight into how the company is performing than just the raw dollars. The combinations usually take the form of ratios, such as the ratio of current assets to current liabilities.

Some ratios are of greater interest depending on your role. As a potential creditor, for example, you would probably be more interested in a company's debt ratio than in its inventory turns ratio. A manager will likely attend more closely to the operating expense ratio than to the times interest earned ratio. But anyone with a financial interest in a company should want to know how the company is performing as measured by its return on assets.

Some ratios need extra context. For example, it's nice to know the current ratio is 3, but it doesn't mean as much unless you know the amount of working capital that ratio represents.

The ratios group themselves naturally into several categories, such as liquidity ratios and activity ratios. You'll find them covered in sections that comprise related ratios.

In this chapter I explain some of the most useful financial ratios and describe how you can obtain them either directly from QuickBooks' financial reports or with assistance from exports to Microsoft Excel.

IN THIS CHAPTER

Liquidity Ratios

Profitability Ratios

Leverage Ratios

Activity Ratios

Liquidity Ratios

Liquidity ratios give the business analyst a sense of how well the company is positioned to convert its assets to cash, should it need to do so in a hurry, in order to meet its liabilities — liabilities that might be either expected or unanticipated.

Current ratio

The current ratio (and its close cousin, the quick ratio) is one measure of a company's ability to meet its short term obligations. Creditors and potential creditors typically pay attention to the current ratio because it tells them if the company is in a position to pay off its liabilities with assets that it can quickly access.

The definition of the current ratio is:

```
(Current Assets) / (Current Liabilities)
```

Current assets are usually defined as those that can be converted to cash within a year, and current liabilities are obligations that come due within a year. So, if a company has a current ratio of 3, it can pay its known liabilities three times over from existing, relatively liquid resources. A current ratio of 3 would tend to be regarded as fairly high — a current ratio of 2 or more is usually considered satisfactory by creditors.

But a company's current ratio can be *too* high, even though the higher the current ratio, the better creditors like it. When too much of a company's resources are in current assets (cash, accounts receivable, inventory, and prepaid expenses usually account for most of a company's current assets), it may be that the resources are not being invested to the company's best advantage. Having $30,000 in a cash account does not tend to support the creation of new revenue; having $30,000 invested in a new delivery van does.

It's usually a good idea to look at a company's current ratio along with a closely related measure, *working capital*. The current ratio is the ratio of current assets to current liabilities, whereas working capital is the result of subtracting current liabilities from current assets. Chapter 5 has much more to say about working capital. For the moment, consider two companies, one with current assets of $30,000 and current liabilities of $10,000, and one with current assets of $300,000 and current liabilities of $100,000. Both have current ratios of 3. But the first company's working capital is $10,000 while the second company has $200,000 in working capital. Clearly, the second company will have a much easier time qualifying for a loan than the first company.

QuickBooks' Summary Balance Sheet report is the easiest way to get the current ratio (as well as the quick ratio, explained in the next section). To get the report, choose Reports ▶ Company & Financial ▶ Balance Sheet Summary (see Figure 6.1).

FIGURE 6.1

The current ratio based on these figures is probably much too high for management's comfort.

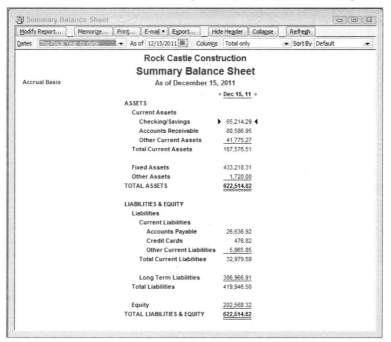

Once you've pulled up this report, you can tell the company's current ratio, at least roughly, with just a glance at the total current assets and the total current liabilities. In the figure it's between 5 and 6, which is unusually high, and a large fraction of the current assets is in accounts receivable. If you were a creditor, you'd take comfort in these figures, but if you were a stockholder you might want less liquidity and more investment in the company's future — something should be done with that $155,000 in working capital. And if you were a manager in the company, you'd probably want to look at the company's average collection period (see the final section in this chapter).

Quick ratio

The quick ratio, sometimes called the *acid test*, takes an even more conservative look at a company's liquidity than does the current ratio. The idea is that some current assets are more current than others. In particular, it takes longer to convert inventory to cash than to convert receivables; the same is true of prepaid expenses, some of which may not be convertible to cash at all. Cash is cash, of course, and the company can press for payment of receivables if necessary.

Some analysts therefore want to look at the quick ratio as well as the current ratio. The quick ratio subtracts inventory from current assets in the ratio's numerator. Formally:

```
Quick ratio = (Current Assets - Inventory) / (Current liabilities)
```

In Figure 6.1 you can see that the company's quick ratio is between 4 and 5: about $146,000 in cash and receivables, and about $33,000 in current liabilities.

As with the current ratio and working capital, it can help to evaluate the quick ratio in the context of another figure, the average collection period (again, see the final section in this chapter). If the length of time that the company has to pay its vendors is roughly the same as its average collection period, then payment and receipt schedules are in line with one another and a quick ratio of 1 is acceptable.

But if it takes a company 60 days or longer, on average, to collect its receivables and its vendors are pressing for net 30, there might be much less liquidity than a quick ratio of 1 would normally suggest.

If you don't feel like glancing at the balance sheet and doing the addition and division mentally, just click the report's Export button and move the data to an Excel workbook. There you can compute both the current ratio and the quick ratio directly, as shown in Figure 6.2.

FIGURE 6.2

You can calculate a variety of financial ratios directly from the Balance Sheet Summary report.

	A B C	D	E	F	G	H
	H7		f_x	=(E4+E5)/E17		
1			Dec 15, 11			
2	ASSETS					
3		Current Assets				
4		Checking/Savings	65,214.29			
5		Accounts Receivable	80,586.95			
6		Other Current Assets	41,775.27			
7		Total Current Assets	187,576.51	Quick ratio:		4.420954
8		Fixed Assets	433,218.31	Current ratio:		5.687654
9		Other Assets	1,720.00			
10	TOTAL ASSETS		622,514.82			
11	LIABILITIES & EQUITY					
12		Liabilities				
13		Current Liabilities				
14		Accounts Payable	26,636.92			
15		Credit Cards	476.82			
16		Other Current Liabilities	5,865.85			
17		Total Current Liabilities	32,979.59			
18		Long Term Liabilities	386,966.91			
19		Total Liabilities	419,946.50			
20		Equity	202,568.32			
21	TOTAL LIABILITIES & EQUITY		622,514.82			

Profitability Ratios

It's one thing to note in your P&L that your company made net income of $100,000 during the last fiscal year. It's quite another to find that it would have been $200,000 if you'd had a better handle on cost of sales, or that the company had $3 million in assets available and used it to generate a 3% return. Numbers such as net sales and total assets give you a context with which to evaluate the raw dollar figures.

Operating expense ratio

As a manager, and possibly the owner, of a company that seeks to conduct its operations without actually losing money, you know that you have more control over how the company spends its money than you do over how your customers spend their money. Much of your time goes to making sure that expenses are under control and, where possible, staying focused on creating more revenue.

One indicator that's useful in the control of expenses is the operating expense ratio, particularly when you view it across more than one accounting period using a comparative P&L. Figure 6.3 shows a comparative P&L summary. To obtain it, choose Reports ▶ Company & Financial ▶ Profit & Loss Prev Year Comparison. Because we're looking primarily at percent changes, the default dollar change column is suppressed: click the Modify Report button and clear the $ Change checkbox under Previous Year.

At first glance, this report looks like good news: Sales are up over 27% year to year. But the bad news immediately sets in when you look at the cost and expense categories. The COGS is up over 33%, and gross profit must fall when COGS rises more than sales. This can happen when a company reduces its sales price, usually in an effort to increase volume, but its vendors hold the line or even increase their pricing.

Then the General and Administrative (G&A) expenses have increased, also more than sales, so they are eating up more of the gross profit during the second year than they did during the first. It is particularly troubling when G&A rises faster than sales. Although some G&A costs rise and fall in line with sales (bonuses, for example), many administrative costs such as office space leases are fixed or, perhaps, semi-variable. So you generally expect to see G&A costs rising *slower* than sales, not faster.

You would have to look further than a P&L allows to determine the reasons that sales expenses rose nearly two-thirds when sales rose less than one-third. It's possible that in trying to increase sales, commissions were boosted, or there was more travel. Whatever the reason, it did not pay off, at least not so far, with a commensurate increase in revenues.

As an owner or manager, it's not sufficient that you pursue increased revenue. You want to pursue *profitable* revenue. And when operating expenses are rising faster than sales, as is the case in this example with G&A and sales expenses, you need to investigate the reasons. It could easily be due to something reasonable and one-time, such as additional office space to accommo

FIGURE 6.3

The Percent Change in QuickBooks' comparative reports use the earlier period's value as the denominator.

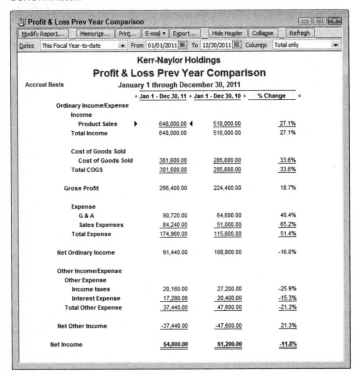

date new staff. But if it's due to things such as a $1,400 wastebasket for the CEO, then there are problems looming that had better be corrected before the costs outstrip the sales.

It does help to focus on the expenses where you have more, or more immediate, control, and the operating expense ratio can tell you if you need to delve further. The ratio is defined simply as follows:

```
(Operating Expenses) / (Net Sales)
```

In this example, for the year 2010, the ratio is 115,600 to 510,000, or 22.7%. For the year 2011, it's 174, 960 to 648,000, or 27.0%. That may not seem like too much, a difference of 4.3%, but if operating expenses just kept pace with sales in 2011, then net income would have grown 15.6% instead of falling by 11.8%. Figure 6.4 shows that analysis. The reports are exported to Excel for more effective comparison.

FIGURE 6.4

Comparative income statements with rising, and with constant, operating expense ratios

	A	B	C	D	E	F	G	H	I	J
1		2011	2010		Pct Change		2011	2010		Pct Change
2	Net sales	$648,000	$510,000		27.1%		$ 648,000	$510,000		27.1%
3	COGS	$381,600	$285,600		33.6%		$ 381,600	$285,600		33.6%
4	Gross profit	$266,400	$224,400		18.7%		$ 266,400	$224,400		18.7%
5										
6	Operating Expenses									
7	Selling expenses	$ 84,240	$ 51,000		65.2%		$ 64,821	$ 51,000		27.1%
8	Administrative expenses	$ 90,720	$ 64,600		40.4%		$ 82,107	$ 64,600		27.1%
9	Total Operating Expenses	$174,960	$115,600		51.3%		$ 146,928	$115,600		27.1%
10										
11	Operating Income	$ 91,440	$108,800		-16.0%		$ 119,472	$108,800		9.8%
12										
13	Interest expense	$ 17,280	$ 20,400		-15.3%		$ 17,280	$ 20,400		-15.3%
14	Income before Taxes	$ 74,160	$ 88,400		-16.1%		$ 102,192	$ 88,400		15.6%
15										
16	Income Taxes	$ 20,160	$ 27,200		-25.9%		$ 31,444	$ 27,200		15.6%
17	Net Income	$ 54,000	$ 61,200		-11.8%		$ 70,749	$ 61,200		15.6%
18										
19										
20	Operating expense ratio:	27.0%	22.7%				22.7%	22.7%		

In Figure 6.4, columns B, C, and E show the comparative P&L data from the QuickBooks report in Figure 6.3. The total operating expenses increase by 51.3% from 2010 to 2011 (cell E9) as net sales are rising 27.1% (cell E2). The result is that net income falls by 11.8% (cell E17).

Now look at columns G, H, and J. The only differences are in operating expenses in rows 7 through 9, which have been constrained in 2011 to the same rate of change (27.1%) as net sales in row 2. Because the expenses are lower, the income tax for 2011 is higher than it was when the operating expenses were greater (compare cells B16 and G16). And yet, even with an additional $11,284 in income taxes, the company's percent change in net income rose from –11.8% to 15.6%.

Notice also that the operating expense ratios in cells G20 and H20 are identical, whereas the ratio increases by 4.3%, as noted in the figure, in cells B20 and C20.

Return on assets

The concept of the return on assets (ROA) is fundamental to an assessment of how well a company's management is handling its resources. Conceptually, ROA is a measure of the income earned, adjusted for the amount of assets available to support the earnings process. More objectively, it is defined as follows:

```
(Net Income) / (Total Assets)
```

If you have $1,000 available in the form of assets — cash, equipment, supplies — and you create $100 by using those assets, your ROA is 10%. If you manage the $1,000 in assets a little more effectively and create $140 in net income, your ROA is a slightly more robust 14%.

Calculating ROA

More specifically yet, the "net income" that's the numerator in the ROA ratio usually has interest payments added back in. The reason is that the net income calculation subtracts COGS, salaries, supplies, and other costs from gross profit. Among those other costs are interest payments on loans taken out to increase the company's total assets. The cost of acquiring the assets that are to be managed should not count against the manager's effectiveness in generating income with those assets. Therefore interest payments are added back in to net income before calculating the ROA.

Bear in mind that the P&L shows the accumulation of income and expenses over time: for example, the current year to date, or current quarter, or some other time span that's important to you. The balance sheet, in contrast, represents a snapshot, the amount of money that the company has invested in different accounts and that it owes in the form of various liabilities, as of the report date. It's a good idea, therefore, to get a measure of the company's total assets over the full period of time covered by the P&L. One way to do that is to take the average of the total assets at the beginning of the period and at the end of the period.

Figure 6.5 shows a variation of the balance sheet in Figure 6.1. Figure 6.5 shows a *comparative* balance sheet, one that makes it easy to compare account balances on December 15, 2011, with those from exactly one year earlier. With the total assets at the beginning and at the end of the period in view, it's easy to average them for a slightly more accurate ROA estimate.

To get the sort of comparative statement shown in Figure 6.5, take these steps:

1. Open a Balance Sheet Summary report by choosing Reports ▶ Company & Financial ▶ Balance Sheet Summary.

2. Click Modify Report. The Display tab appears as shown in Figure 6.6.

3. Fill the Previous Year checkbox and click OK.

Using the average of the start and end of the period as an estimate of total assets is better than a single-date snapshot, but it's still a relatively crude estimate and it's a relic of times when a balance sheet as of any given date could not be quickly and easily obtained. If you're concerned about getting a more accurate estimate of the typical level of total assets during, say, a year of the company's operations, you can get it for each month and then take the average across 12 evenly-spaced dates, not just two.

To do so, first refer back to Figure 6.6. Instead of filling the Previous Year checkbox in the Modify Report dialog box, use the Display Columns By dropdown at the top of the report itself and choose Month. Then, after you click OK, the report will appear as shown in Figure 6.7.

FIGURE 6.5

By tradition, comparative statements show the more recent accounting periods on the left.

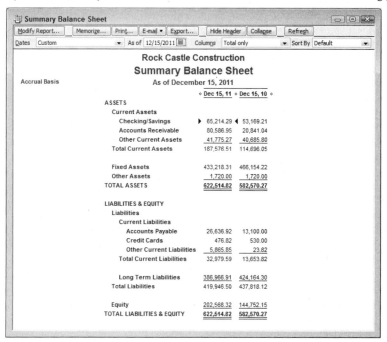

FIGURE 6.6

You can choose a range of dates, but the results are shown for only the ending date.

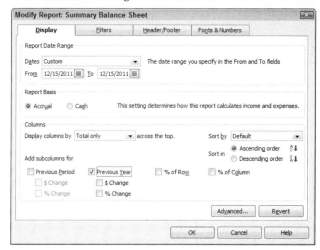

FIGURE 6.7

You can't see it here, but the columns extend through December 15, 2011.

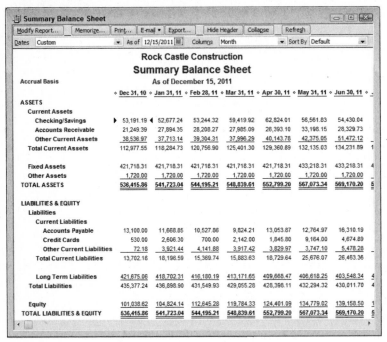

Of course it's a lot more difficult to take the average of 12 asset values in your head than just two, so it's a good idea to export this report to an Excel workbook and then compute the average.

The corresponding P&L appears in Figure 6.8. Notice that it covers the period from December 15, 2010, through December 15, 2011.

Only a portion of the P&L is shown in Figure 6.8. Notice that an Expand button appears at the top of the report. This button is a toggle. If it were clicked, subaccounts would appear in the report and the button's caption would change from Expand to Collapse. With the report collapsed, the user can see that interest expense for the period shown is $2,217.31. Adding interest back in to net income results in $57,816.17 + $2,217.31, or $60,033.48.

Using the data from Figure 6.5, the average total assets at the beginning and end of the 12-month period is $602,542.55. The ROA is therefore $60,033.48 ÷ $602,542.55, or almost exactly 10%. Is that good, bad, or indifferent? The ROA from other, similar companies — a type of *vertical* analysis — can help determine whether the company is operating more or less efficiently than its competitors. It can also be useful to compute the ROA on the same company but from other years — a *horizontal* analysis that can help determine whether a company is operating more or less efficiently over time.

FIGURE 6.8

The custom report dates are chosen to align the data more closely with the report in Figure 6.7.

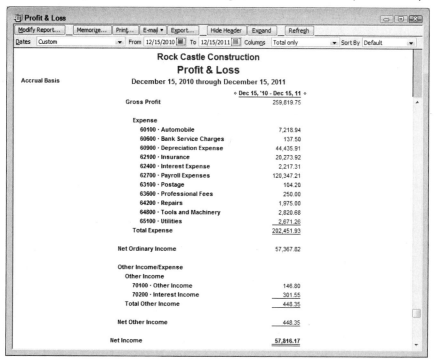

ROA and leverage

But perhaps the best context to use in assessing a company's ROA is its cost of borrowing capital: the interest rate it is paying on loans. Consider this situation, which is oversimplified to make the point:

You take out a $50,000 loan to purchase new equipment, at an annual 9.5% interest rate. Even at simple interest, that loan will cost you $4,750 in interest payments alone. Suppose now that the company's overall ROA of 10% applies to the equipment asset you acquired with the loan. In that case, you make net income (before interest, because of the way ROA is defined) of $5,000. You are *leveraging*, to your advantage, the loan and the equipment you bought with it. Even if you charge the $4,750 in interest against the incremental income produced by the new equipment, you are ahead by $250. And if you can manage to squeeze out a 15% ROA on that equipment, you'll be increasing net income by $7,500, while the interest payments hold steady at 9.5%.

NOTE The formal definition of *leverage* is the purchase of assets with money that's either loaned to the company or through issuing preferred stock. (Holders of preferred stock have an earlier claim on the company's assets if it is liquidated; on the other hand, preferred stock usually carries no voting rights.)

Suppose you don't do quite so well with the equipment you bought, and it returns only 5% in net income before interest payments. In that case, you make $2,500 from the equipment, but you're still paying $4,750 for the privilege. You're losing $2,250 per year on the deal. The creditor doesn't mind: As long as you stay in business and don't retire the loan, he'll make 9.5% per year on his money. But the business owner and/or its stockholders will get hurt.

That's leverage. When the investment you make with borrowed funds does well, the leverage magnifies your returns. When it doesn't turn out well enough, the leverage magnifies your losses.

Calculating a loan's interest rate

If you don't know what interest rate you're paying on a loan you can calculate it quickly in Excel. You need to know the loan's original principal amount, the number of payments to be made, and the amount of each payment.

Suppose that the loan is for $60,000, it is to be repaid in 24 equal payments, and the monthly payment is $2,710.90. In an Excel worksheet cell, enter the formula

```
=(1+RATE(24,-2710.90,60000))^12-1
```

This formula returns the annualized interest rate for the loan. Notice that the monthly payment is entered as a negative number. Because of the way Excel's algorithm for the family of payment functions is written, at least one argument must be negative; else the function returns an error value.

If you're not sure of the principal, number of payments, and size of each payment, take these steps:

1. Open the company's Balance Sheet Standard report and locate the loan's balance line, probably in the Long Term Liabilities section but possibly among the Current Liabilities.

2. Double-click the amount shown for the loan to open the Transactions by Account report.

3. You should be able to pick up the principal — the opening balance — at the top of the report.

4. You can enter the actual number of payments or estimate the number of payments by counting the number of payments made already; then estimate the number of payments remaining by comparing the unpaid balance with the size of the recent payment amounts.

5. Double-click in any payment's row to open the window (typically the Write Checks window), which will show you the total payment, summing together the principal and interest for the payment.

With that information on principal amount, number of periods, and amount of each payment, you can use the formula given earlier to obtain the loan's interest rate. Compare it to the estimated ROA for whatever you used the loan to acquire, to determine whether the leverage is working on your behalf or against you.

If the interest rate you're paying on loans to purchase assets exceeds your ROA, your best move is to get more out of those assets. If that's not feasible, look into retiring the loans early.

Leverage Ratios

Two complementary ratios that help you assess how a company finances its assets are the equity ratio and the debt ratio. It's usually true that a company finances the acquisition of its assets through borrowing or by using its equity (capital investments plus retained earnings).

The fundamental equation in accounting is that a company's total assets equal its total liabilities. The liabilities comprise its debt and its equity. Therefore, the company's debt and its equity total to its liabilities, and therefore to its assets.

The equity ratio is equity divided by total assets. The debt ratio is debt divided by total assets. (You could of course divide debt by total liabilities instead of by total assets, but it's conventional to define these two ratios in this fashion.) The two ratios therefore sum to 1.0, and if you know one you know the other.

Equity ratio

The Balance Sheet Summary, shown in Figure 6.1, and in worksheet format in Figure 6.2, make it very easy to determine the company's equity ratio:

```
(Total Equity) / (Total Assets)
```

Just divide the value in cell E20 of Figure 6.2 (the company's total equity) by the value in cell E10 (the company's total assets). In this case that's $202,568.32 divided by $622,514.82, or 33%.

If you hold stock in this company, you should watch its ROA carefully. A low equity ratio (and 33% is rather low) shows that the company has acquired most of its assets through borrowing rather than by using its equity. As described in the earlier section on ROA, leverage magnifies the effect of borrowing, whether that's good or bad. If the ROA is less than the rate paid to service the debt, the degree of leverage accelerates the loss. And the equity ratio is one measure of the amount of leverage the company is using.

The danger to the company becomes more apparent when you put yourself in the position of a stockholder. The company has in this example financed two-thirds of its assets through borrowing. If the return on those assets is less than the company is paying to finance the debt, then your return in the form of dividends or stock price also suffers. You could do better by lending the company money than you can by investing your funds in it.

The combination of a low equity ratio (therefore, high leverage) and a relatively poor ROA would pressure you, as a stockholder, to sell your stock if feasible. So will other stockholders. And that makes it very difficult for the company to raise money in the capital markets.

On the other hand, if the ROA is greater than the debt service, you can do better as an investor than you can as a creditor. The lesson is that if the company has a relatively low equity ratio, an investor needs to watch its ROA and its debt service.

Debt ratio

As mentioned in the prior section, the debt ratio is the complement of the equity ratio. You can find it either by subtracting the equity ratio, calculated earlier, from 1.0, or directly by the formula

```
(Total Liabilities) / (Total Assets)
```

In Figure 6.2, that's cell E19 divided by cell E10, or 67%.

If you were a creditor you'd prefer to see a debt ratio that's a lot closer to 33% than 67%. Suppose that the company loses value precipitously and must liquidate its assets. The assets themselves then lose value, and a high debt ratio suggests there might not be enough in the way of devalued assets to pay off all the creditors. A low debt ratio, and a correspondingly high equity ratio, provides more protection to creditors against a reduction in the company's asset value.

Times interest earned ratio

The ratio called "times interest earned" can be considered a leverage ratio because it depends in part on the amount of debt service a company must pay during an accounting period, typically a year. But while the debt ratio looks at total liabilities as a fraction of total assets, the times interest earned ratio looks at the cost of the debt as a fraction of income.

Creditors are of course vitally interested in a company's ability to repay the principal of a loan, but they also want to know to what degree the company is positioned to make its periodic interest payments. That ability is measured by the ratio of income to interest payments, or the multiple of the interest that is represented by income: the number of times that the interest is earned.

The divisor in the ratio is simply the dollars in interest payable during the year. The numerator is the company's operating income, with a couple of adjustments. The income should be *before*

FIGURE 6.9

In a closer case, you should probably export the data to Excel for the calculations.

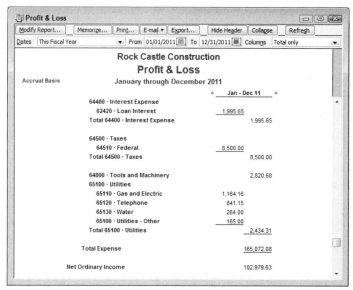

interest and income taxes are deducted to arrive at net income — that is, EBIT, or earnings before interest and taxes. The rationale is that the analyst wants to know how much money is available for interest payments, and therefore those payments should not be subtracted in arriving at the income estimate. Furthermore, because the income tax amounts depend on the deductible interest amounts, they should not be subtracted from the income.

Each value, the interest payments and the pre-interest, pre-tax income can be found on, or easily derived from, the P&L Standard report (see Figure 6.9).

The example in Figure 6.9 clearly returns a very large times interest earned ratio — large enough that you can quickly see that there's no problem lending this company some money. In a closer case, such as a company with a much smaller ratio of EBIT to interest payments, let Excel do the calculations for you. The times interest earned ratio often ranges from 2 to 6, and a ratio between 3 and 4 is typical. Ratios in the 3 and 4 range are strong enough to encourage lending.

Activity Ratios

Turning inventory into income depends heavily on two activities: getting the inventory off the shelves and into the customer's hands, and getting the customer's payments out of accounts receivable and into the bank. The longer goods stay in inventory, the longer their value is static, unavailable for other, more lucrative purposes. And every day your revenues are in accounts receivable is a day you can't reinvest that money. Activity ratios that measure the frequency of the inventory turnover, and how long invoices remain unpaid, are the ways to watch how efficiently a company navigates its business cycle.

Inventory turns ratio

The inventory turns ratio, sometimes called the *inventory turnover ratio*, is an indictor of how well a company manages its investment in merchandise, whether at the wholesale or the retail level.

You may have come across the term *just-in-time inventory*. It refers both to a goal and to procedures that are meant to help meet the goal: to bring goods into inventory no sooner than needed for manufacture, or onto a reseller's shelves no sooner than needed to support revenues. The idea is that the longer a company owns goods, the longer its financial resources are tied up in a static investment and are unavailable to create more profit.

The sales/week ratio

In QuickBooks, when you set up a new inventory item — or when you edit an existing item — you might supply a reorder point on the item record. (Choose Lists ▶ Item List and double-click an item in the list box.) If you do so, it's possible that the reorder point you choose is the result of exhaustive, empirical research into how fast that item sells. It's also possible that you specify a reorder point solely on the basis of your own experience, how pricey it is, and how painful it would be to run out.

Regardless of how you come up with a reorder point, it represents one way to express the idea of a turns ratio. A rational reorder point takes into account how soon you need more of an item and how long it will take your supplier to fulfill your order. If you sell 20 units a week, and if your supplier needs two weeks' lead time, then you should probably reorder when you're down to 40 units in stock.

The phrase "20 units a week" in the preceding sentence is a measure of inventory turns: an inventory level of 20 turns over once a week. But that's too specific a usage. Instead, it's usual to talk in terms of an annual turnover rate, and to generalize the ratio to a dollar value: cost of goods sold, or COGS.

The turns ratio

Before cheap computing power became broadly available, the turns ratio was often calculated in this way:

```
(Annual COGS) / (Average Inventory Asset Value)
```

where the average inventory level was just the inventory value at the start of the year plus the inventory level at the end of the year, divided by 2.

FIGURE 6.10

The sales/week ratio in the final column is a measure of units sold, not dollars reinvested.

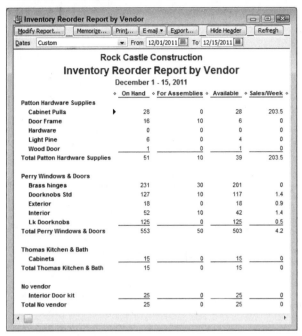

There are problems with that approach. For one thing, companies often arrange their inventory levels to be lowest on the date their fiscal year's start (and end). This is to dress up their financial statements, so it will not appear as though their resources are tied up in stock sitting on shelves, but hard at work generating new profits. Therefore, the average inventory level is often an underestimation of the actual level throughout the year, and the turns ratio was therefore not representative of the actual inventory activity.

Notice that this ratio is calculated in terms of dollars: the cost of goods sold, divided by a measure of typical inventory value. This is handy, because by using a ratio of dollars to dollars it's possible to compare turns ratios across items, or product lines, or even companies. To see the advantage of working with ratios based on currency units, consider the QuickBooks Inventory Reorder Report by Vendor (see Figure 6.10). This report is found in the Premier Manufacturing and Wholesale edition of QuickBooks, but don't worry if you don't use it — my mentioning it is meant only to illustrate why your management decisions should look beyond simple unit counts.

The sales/week ratio shown in Figure 6.10 is a helpful number from the perspective of ordering new inventory from the supplier. You can see, among other fields, how many units you have on hand, how many are committed, how many are available, and how many you have sold per

FIGURE 6.11

The Inventory Valuation Summary report helps you build up a rough estimate of average inventory levels.

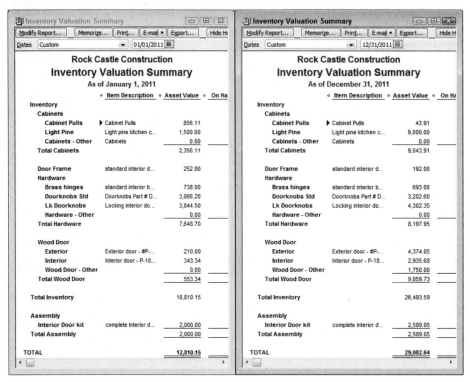

week during the report's time frame. Operationally, the sales/week ratio can be a very useful number because it tells you if you're likely to run out of product in the near future.

But from a business analysis or a management perspective, it's not so useful. Suppose your purpose in looking at inventory status is not to decide when and if to buy more goods, but whether or not a product line moves well enough to justify retaining it in your business mix. Selling cabinet pulls at a 250 per week clip is all well and good, but that number by itself does not address an important issue: How long does it take to deplete your existing stock at that run rate?

That's what the turns ratio is intended to examine. Figure 6.11 shows two Inventory Valuation Summary reports for Rock Castle Construction, for the first and last days of 2011. No customization is needed to produce this report, other than specifying the date for the summary.

It helps to start with the full inventory analysis as a context. Figure 6.11 shows the overall inventory level on 1/1/2011 was $12,810.15. On 12/31/2011, the inventory level was $28,807.29. The average of the two inventory valuation figures is ($12,810.15 + $28,807.29)

FIGURE 6.12

Be careful to pick up the total cost for inventory, not the grand total cost which might include non-inventory parts.

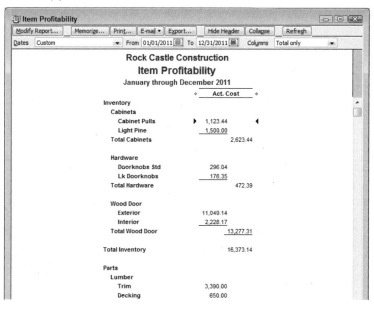

÷ 2 = $20,808.72, a fairly crude but not irrational estimate of how much the company has invested in its inventory on any given day.

Figure 6.12 uses the Item Profitability report to get a COGS figure for the overall inventory during the same period of 12/1/2011 through 12/15/2011. This report has been modified, using the Modify Report button, to show only the Actual Cost column, and to use 1/1/2011 and 12/31/2011 as its starting and ending dates. To display the Item Profitability Summary, choose Reports ▶ Jobs, Time & Mileage ▶ Item Profitability.

The company used $16,373.14 — the COGS — in inventory during the time period in question. So, an estimate of the turns ratio for the company's overall inventory is $16,373.14 ÷ $20,808.72, or almost exactly 0.8. Overall, during the 12 months of 2011, this company runs through 0.8, or 80%, of its inventory. The stock turns over 0.8 times per year.

With that figure as context, here's a look at a particular inventory item. In addition to the overall inventory, Figures 6.11 and 6.12 show the required data for Rock Castle's supply of exterior wooden doors. With a starting inventory of $210.00 and an ending inventory of $4,374.05, the average is $2,292.03. Combined with COGS of $11,049.14, the resulting turns ratio is 4.8. That is, the company's average supply of exterior wood doors turns over not quite five times in 2011. Clearly, some other inventory item or set of items is selling so slowly that it's dragging down the company's overall turns ratio. Only a similar examination of the other inventory items will identify the source of the problem.

And it *is* a problem. Inventory is traditionally and conventionally regarded as a current asset, and the usual definition of a current asset is one that can be converted into cash within a year. This company's inventory is turning over — being converted to cash — less than once a year. Once every 15 months, to be precise. That's not good enough, and if you were the company's owner you would demand to know why you're carrying so much stock, or selling it so slowly, that your overall inventory turns ratio is only 0.8.

There are some other issues to keep in mind with the turns ratio, as the following subsections explain.

Average inventory

Two factors can cause a low turns ratio: a low COGS and a high inventory level. If your company has done its account setup and data entry properly, it's hard to argue with the figure that QuickBooks gives you for COGS. But the average inventory level is another matter.

Earlier in this section, I mentioned that the average of the inventory at the start and the end of the fiscal year might be misleading, because companies sometimes manage to time their fiscal years with periods of low inventory. If you're going to go to the trouble of getting a starting and an ending inventory, you might as well do a little bit of additional work and get the starting inventory for each quarter as well as the end of year level. Add them up and divide by 5 to give you a better estimate of the actual average inventory level. You can go further and get monthly figures to average, as explained later in the "Average collection period" section.

Best would be to determine the asset value in stock for each day during the fiscal year. That's feasible, but it requires exporting the inventory valuation detail report to Excel and then doing some hand-waving to get a value for every calendar day, not just those days on which a transaction occurs. If you do this, bear in mind that any day that has no activity for a given item carries the same total asset value as the most recent day on which a transaction involving that item occurred.

High turns

A high turns ratio is usually regarded as a positive sign, but if it's high compared to similar companies there *may* be a problem. Because part of the ratio is some measure of average stock level, a high ratio can be due more to low stock levels than to high sales. Low stock levels can mean that some customers are turned away or otherwise underserved because the company maintains insufficient stock levels. I mention this only because this point is frequently cited. It actually occurs less frequently than the number of citations suggests.

Relationship to gross profit rate

It often happens that high inventory turns rates are found in companies with low gross profit margins. It's not necessarily cause-and-effect. Instead, it is often due to the fact that companies with low gross profit margins, companies that deal in commodities, for example, must turn their inventories over rapidly in order to make up for the low profit margins. Otherwise, they will not be able to produce an acceptable return on assets.

Measuring turns in days

Some analysts find it easier to think of stock turnover in terms of number of days worth of stock. If you divide 365 by an annual turns ratio, you have the number of days worth of stock on the shelf. In the example given earlier in this section, a turns ratio of 0.8 divided into 365 results in 456 days: a year and three months. This figure is useful in combination with the average collection period, explained next, to determine the length of a company's operating cycle.

Average collection period

The average collection period is analogous to inventory turnover. Inventory turnover analysis tells you how long it takes to deplete your stock of goods, while the average collection period gives you a rough idea of how long it takes to collect money for sales made on credit. Together, the two figures make up the company's operating cycle: the initial investment in goods, holding the goods in stock until they are sold, collecting from the purchaser, and then reinvesting that money in more goods.

The average collection rate tells you how long proceeds from credit sales sit in accounts receivable. Formally, it is defined by the formula

```
(Total Sales - Returns - Cash Sales - Credit Card Purchases) /
   (Average Accounts Receivable)
```

the ratio of net credit sales to an average accounts receivable balance. (In QuickBooks, *net credit sales* means total invoiced amounts, less returns.) If you have made $500,000 in net credit sales for a year and your average monthly A/R balance was $50,000 during that year, you are turning over — that is, depleting accounts receivable by means of collections — at the rate of 10 times per year. Your average collection period is therefore 36.5 days. It's important to note that the net sales in this context are limited to those made on credit; sales for cash or via credit card result in immediate collection, or at worst the two or three days it takes a credit card processing bureau to credit the company's bank account.

Obviously, the calculation as described is a rough estimate. It depends on the comparison of the sales made during one period with the collection of funds for sales made at other times. There are many ways to calculate an average accounts receivable balance — daily average, weekly average, average of starting and ending balances, and so on — and each returns a different result if your receivables bounce around much. Which they do.

Ideally, the analysis of QuickBooks data would begin with a list of all credit transactions (in effect, transaction types would include invoices and payments only) that associate an invoice date, amount, terms, due date, payment date, and payment amount. Only then would it be possible to create a more sensitive analysis. Greater precision would enable, for example, the analysis of collection periods across different payment terms, such as net 15 versus net 30. But

QuickBooks reports do not tie payment transactions to their associated invoices, so a rough estimate is the best that can be done by means of the user interface.

The QuickBooks software development kit enables you to write code that can access an internal table which pairs invoices' unique ID numbers with the associated payments' unique ID numbers. With access to this relationship, one can create the more sensitive analysis just sketched.

Here's how to get the average collection period using QuickBooks reports. So that you can see everything in Figures 6.13 through 6.15, the following instructions pick up data by quarter. Remember that when you run your own analysis, you might want more frequent time slices, and pick up the data by month instead of by quarter.

1. Choose Reports ▶ Custom Summary Report. The Modify Report dialog box automatically appears, along with an empty Custom Summary report.

2. On the Display tab, choose the time span of interest in the Dates dropdown. This example uses Last Fiscal Year.

3. From the Display Columns By dropdown, choose Quarter.

4. Choose Balance Sheet from the Display Rows By dropdown.

5. Click the Filters tab, and choose All Accounts Receivable from the Account dropdown.

6. Click OK. The report appears as shown in Figure 6.13. You might see more or fewer columns, depending on the size of your QuickBooks window, how long the company has been in business, and the time span you selected in Step 3.

7. Click the Export button to export the report to a new Excel workbook.

You now have the basis for getting average accounts receivable. It would be useful if you could get net sales on the same report, but from the balance sheet perspective you'll get a cumulative, not a quarterly, figure. To make the analysis easier in Excel it will be best to get the quarterly actuals instead of a running total. So take the earlier seven steps again, with these modifications:

1. In Step 4, choose Income Statement from the Display Rows By dropdown.

2. In Step 5, choose whatever income account or accounts you post credit sales to. (Using the Rock Castle sample file, as this example does, you would choose the Construction Income account.)

3. While you're still on the Filters tab, choose TransactionType from the Filter list box, and choose Invoice from the TransactionType dropdown. Then click OK and export the report.

You now have two Excel worksheets in two different workbooks. Suppose that the accounts receivable information is in Excel Book3 and the sales income data is in Book5. They appear in Figure 6.14.

FIGURE 6.13

Modify the report dates to match your company's particular history.

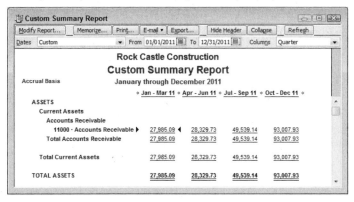

FIGURE 6.14

It's a good idea at this point to check that the dates in the two reports correspond.

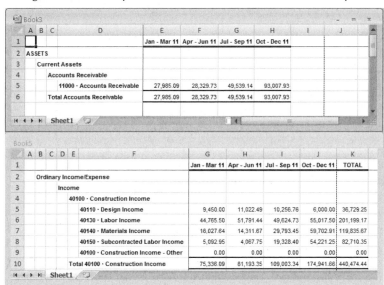

FIGURE 6.15

It takes this company an average of 41.2 days to collect on its credit sales.

	A	B	C	D	E	F	G	H
				E13	▾	*fx*	=SUM(E11:H11)	
					Jan - Mar 11	Apr - Jun 11	Jul - Sep 11	Oct - Dec 11
1								
3			Current Assets					
4				Accounts Receivable				
5				11000 · Accounts Receivable	27,985.09	28,329.73	49,539.14	93,007.93
6				Total Accounts Receivable	27,985.09	28,329.73	49,539.14	93,007.93
7				Total Current Assets	27,985.09	28,329.73	49,539.14	93,007.93
8		TOTAL ASSETS			27,985.09	28,329.73	49,539.14	93,007.93
9		LIABILITIES & EQUITY			0.00	0.00	0.00	0.00
10								
11					75,336.09	81,193.35	109,003.34	174,941.66
12								
13					440,474.44			
14					49,715.47			
15					8.9			
16					41.2			

To complete the analysis, take these steps:

1. Switch to Microsoft Excel and activate the workbook named Book5 (the workbook that contains the sales income data.

2. Select the cell that contains the income from credit sales for the earliest quarter. In Figure 6.14, that's cell G10 in Book5.

3. Hold down the Shift key and click in the final quarterly cell in the Total Income row: in Figure 6.14, that's cell J10 in Book5. Steps 2 and 3 select the first quarter, the final quarter, and all the intervening cells.

4. Right-click any cell in the selected range and choose Copy from the contextual menu.

5. Switch to Book3, the workbook with the accounts receivable data. Locate the cell in the column that contains the first quarter's data, and in the first empty row below the report data. In Figure 6.15, that's cell E11.

6. Right-click the cell you located in Step 5 and choose Paste Special from the contextual menu. In the Paste Special dialog box, choose the Values and Number Formats option button, and click OK.

7. Now calculate the summary data. Begin in cell E13 with the formula
   =SUM(E11:H11)
   (See Figure 6.15.) This formula returns the total of the four quarters' net credit sales.

8. In cell E14 enter the formula
   =AVERAGE(E6:H6)
   to obtain the average quarterly accounts receivable.

9. Now enter in cell E15 the ratio of total credit sales to average accounts receivable:
   =E13/E14
   This ratio gives you the collection rate.

10. To get the average collection period on an annualized basis, divide 365 by the collection rate. Enter this formula in cell E16:
    =365/E15

If you have another year's, or more, worth of data, you can repeat Steps 7 through 10 another four columns to the right. Comparison of the annualized data for the two years will tell you whether your average collection period is increasing or decreasing. In turn, that will tell you whether you should take steps to reduce the length of time needed to collect on credit sales, perhaps by adjusting the terms you offer your credit customers.

By adding the average collection period to the inventory turnover period, you can get a measure of how long it takes to turn an investment in goods back into cash. If that length of time is increasing by what is, to you or in your industry, a meaningful amount, that means you are experiencing lower sales and higher investment in inventory. That combination, if left uncorrected, is sure to hurt your profit.

Part III

Controlling Costs and Planning Profits

Inventory Valuation and Gross Margins

I f your company is a consultancy, or if you provide professional services, or if your use of tangible materials in the production of a product can be sensibly viewed as an expense, then you probably have little use for inventory analysis.

But if you're a retailer, wholesaler, or other type of merchandiser, or if you manufacture products, it's likely that most of your operating profit comes from selling goods for more than your acquisition costs. And in that case, the management and valuation of inventory is critically important to the health of your business.

On the balance sheet, it's likely that inventory represents the majority of a merchandiser's current assets. It can be tricky to weigh the need for inventory availability against the costs of acquiring and keeping it in stock.

On the income statement, the gross profit that a merchandising firm realizes during an accounting period is directly attributable to the difference between sales price and the cost of the goods sold (COGS). If you have a mistaken idea of how much the wireless printer you just sold cost you, you also have a mistaken idea of how much money the sale made you.

QuickBooks has tools that help you keep track of how much money you have invested in inventory, how many units you own, and how fast you turn them over. The tools that help you find out how profitable your company is, in conducting its merchandising or manufacturing business, are also available — they just take a little study to find out how they can inform or mislead you.

The key, in QuickBooks anyway, is the idea that every item in your inventory has an average cost.

Average Cost

The fundamental aspect about the value of your company's inventory assets is that you value a unit according to what you paid for it. There are additional considerations that sometimes apply, such as revaluing your inventory according to lower of cost or market rules, or inventory profits, but even these use your cost of acquisition as a basis.

> **NOTE** The *lower of cost or market* principle is a conservative approach to valuation that states that inventory (or other investments, for that matter) should appear on the balance sheet as worth either the lower of what the company paid for them, or their current replacement cost. *Inventory profits* come about when inventory is held in stock for a period of time during which the replacement cost rises, and the inventory assets are more valuable than they were when acquired. Inventory profits present accountants with headaches.

Taking acquisition cost as the building block of an inventory analysis, the next issue that arises is the assignment of unit costs. Suppose that you purchased 100 widgets in June for $5 each. You sell one today for $7. Your revenue on that sale is $7, your COGS is $5, and your gross profit is therefore $2. You still have 99 widgets in stock that you paid $5 apiece for, so your total widget asset is worth $495.

Then in July you buy another 100 widgets for $6 each and put them in a store bin along with the 99 widgets remaining from your original acquisition. That bin now contains $1,095 worth of widgets. A customer grabs one and buys it. You charge him $7, as before, but what is your COGS? Your gross profit? And what are your widgets worth now?

If the customer bought a widget that cost you $5, your COGS was $5 and your gross profit was $2. You have $1,090 worth of widgets.

If he bought a widget that cost you $6, your COGS was $6 and your gross profit was $1. Your widgets are worth $1,089.

Obviously this isn't a tenable situation, and the reason is that you have so many widgets in stock, and that they are relatively inexpensive. It's just not worth your while to keep track of the actual acquisition cost of every single unit that you sell, not when the gross profit is in the one- to two-dollar range.

If you sold custom made surfboards instead of widgets, if you had twenty in stock at any given time and they cost anywhere from $500 to $600 to build, then it might make sense to keep track of the cost of acquiring each one. And this inventory valuation method is used by merchandisers such as jewelers, fine art studios, and classic car dealers — virtually any merchandiser who deals in relatively small numbers of relatively expensive goods. It even has a name: *specific identification*. QuickBooks does not do a good job of supporting the specific identification method of valuing inventory. It can be done, but you have to jump through hoops.

NOTE   Specific identification in large-volume, low-cost situations has become more feasible as point-of-sale scanners that can identify unique units have become more common. But that doesn't help in situations where you cannot point to a unique unit with a unique acquisition cost. A gallon of gasoline, for example.

Another approach that many companies use is FIFO, which stands for *first in, first out.* (There is also the reverse approach, LIFO, or *last in, first out,* that is much more controversial than FIFO.) Under FIFO, you assume that, in the prior example, your customer bought a widget that cost you $5, even though the bin is stocked with both $5 and $6 widgets.

You will continue to assume that your customers are buying $5 widgets until you have sold 100 widgets, the size of your initial buy. At that point you will assume that the next widget sold cost you $6. First in, first out: You assume that you sell nothing but the first batch until you have sold all of them. Only then does the opposite side of the assumption kick in: Until you sell as many units as were in the second batch, that's all you're selling. Under FIFO, you act as though your customers have entered into an agreement with you to pull the oldest widgets out of the bin first.

Even jumping through hoops won't help you here: QuickBooks has no feasible way to track inventory value using FIFO. What about a custom field? At the time of this writing, custom fields in QuickBooks are text-only, and will do you no good in tracking inventory with FIFO methods.

The third broadly defined approach to inventory valuation is *average cost.* You bought 100 widgets for $5 and 100 for $6. Setting aside for a moment the issue of how many you have sold, one way of looking at it is that you bought 200 widgets for a total of $1,100, so the unit cost of any one of those widgets is the average cost, $1,100 ÷ 200, or $5.50.

That average cost is used as the basis for the COGS. If you sell one widget for $7, your COGS is $5.50 and your gross profit is $1.50. Those figures hold true until you buy more widgets at a cost that's something more or less than $5.50 each, whether or not you have run out of widgets.

It's at this point that the basic concept of average cost becomes more complicated. There are two schools of thought about whether or not sales should influence average cost, and each is associated with a different calculation method. Both pass muster with GAAP (Generally Accepted Accounting Practices) but they can yield very different results. I describe them both, starting with the method that QuickBooks does *not* use, but that I'll refer to as the "mainstream" approach to average costing.

The mainstream approach

Using the mainstream approach to average costing, all you do is add up the cost of the units of a given product you have purchased to inventory. Then you count the number of units you bought. You divide the first number by the second, and that's your average cost. Figure 7.1 shows how this approach would calculate the average cost of your widgets.

FIGURE 7.1

Excel's formula box shows the formula in the active cell. It divides total purchases by units purchased.

	J4			f_x	=H4/E4					
	A	B	C	D	E	F	G	H	I	J
1	Date	Number Bought	Unit Cost	Extended Cost	Cumulative Number Bought	Number Sold	Quantity on Hand	Total Cost of Purchases	Total Asset Value	Average Cost
2										
3	06/26/2011	100	$ 5.00	$ 500.00	100		100	$ 500.00	$ 500.00	$ 5.00
4	07/03/2011	100	$ 6.00	$ 600.00	200		200	$ 1,100.00	$ 1,100.00	$ 5.50

FIGURE 7.2

The "extended cost" is just the unit cost multiplied by the number of units purchased.

	J6			f_x	=H6/E6					
	A	B	C	D	E	F	G	H	I	J
1	Date	Number Bought	Unit Cost	Extended Cost	Cumulative Number Bought	Number Sold	Quantity on Hand	Total Cost of Purchases	Total Asset Value	Average Cost
2										
3	06/26/2011	100	$ 5.00	$ 500.00	100		100	$ 500.00	$ 500.00	$ 5.00
4	07/03/2011	100	$ 6.00	$ 600.00	200		200	$ 1,100.00	$ 1,100.00	$ 5.50
5	09/05/2011	50	$ 4.00	$ 200.00	250		250	$ 1,300.00	$ 1,300.00	$ 5.20
6	10/02/2011	50	$ 5.20	$ 260.00	300		300	$ 1,560.00	$ 1,560.00	$ 5.20

Figure 7.1 shows a situation that's about as simple as it gets. On any given date, you add up the dollars you spent and divide by the number you bought.

At any rate, that's the theory. It does get a little more complicated in practice, but only a little. Figure 7.2 complicates matters by adding more purchases at different unit costs.

In Figure 7.2, you see average cost change each time another purchase is made *at a cost per unit that differs from the current average cost*. It doesn't matter how many units are purchased. It doesn't matter whether any units have been sold. Under this approach, if you buy more stock at a unit cost that's different from the current average cost, the average cost changes, and not otherwise.

Figure 7.2 shows the average cost changing in response to the purchase in July and the purchase in September, each of which is made at a unit cost that differs from the average cost immediately prior to the date of the purchase. The fourth purchase is made at a unit cost of $5.20, that equals the average cost immediately prior to the purchase — and therefore the average cost does not change.

Figure 7.3 shows what happens — or, rather, what doesn't happen — when you sell some units.

You see in Figure 7.3 that 100 widgets have been sold in August. That sale has no effect on the average cost — notice that the average cost on the date of the sale is unchanged, and that the average costs following the sale are the same as they would be had the sale not occurred — compare to the average cost figures in Figure 7.2.

FIGURE 7.3

Under the mainstream approach, average cost does not respond to sales of the item.

	J7		f_x	=H7/E7						
	A	B	C	D	E	F	G	H	I	J
1	Date	Number Bought	Unit Cost	Extended Cost	Cumulative Number Bought	Number Sold	Quantity on Hand	Total Cost of Purchases	Total Asset Value	Average Cost
2										
3	06/26/2011	100	$ 5.00	$ 500.00	100		100	$ 500.00	$ 500.00	$ 5.00
4	07/03/2011	100	$ 6.00	$ 600.00	200		200	$ 1,100.00	$ 1,100.00	$ 5.50
5	08/03/2011				200	100	100	$ 1,100.00	$ 550.00	$ 5.50
6	09/05/2011	50	$ 4.00	$ 200.00	250		150	$ 1,300.00	$ 780.00	$ 5.20
7	10/02/2011	50	$ 5.20	$ 260.00	300		200	$ 1,560.00	$ 1,040.00	$ 5.20

Notice, by the way, the COGS associated with the sale made in August shown in Figure 7.3. You can get COGS quickly by comparing the Total Asset Value prior to the sale, in cell I4, with the Total Asset Value as of the sale, in cell I5. The difference is $1,100 – $550, or $550. The COGS for the sale is $550. It is also the result of multiplying the number of units sold, 100, by the average cost just prior to the sale, $5.50.

And that is how QuickBooks arrives at a COGS figure (even though it uses a different method of calculating average cost). QuickBooks multiplies the number of units sold by their average cost to get the COGS. That value is subtracted from the prior Total Asset Value to get a new Total Asset Value. The COGS is also subtracted from the sales price to arrive at a gross profit for the sale.

The average cost formula explained in this section is acceptable under GAAP as a measure of average cost. There are several reasons that many users find it preferable to the approach that QuickBooks uses. Here are three:

1. It is the true average cost of all the items you brought into inventory, not just the items you currently have in stock.

2. It is easier to verify because it is not affected by sales of the item.

3. It is not subject to fluctuations that are as extreme as can occur using the QuickBooks formula, because it uses information about all the purchases of the item that you have made.

The QuickBooks approach

QuickBooks adopts a different approach to calculating the average cost of an item. It too is approved by GAAP, but it would be more accurate to call it "average cost of items on hand." The difference between the QuickBooks method and the mainstream method is that QuickBooks adjusts the number purchased and the total acquisition cost according to any sales that have taken place. Figure 7.4 shows how the QuickBooks approach to average cost changes the outcomes of the transactions shown in Figure 7.3.

FIGURE 7.4

Compare with Figure 7.3. The difference so far is only in average cost after the first sale, in August.

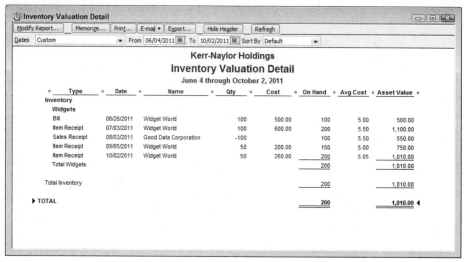

The calculation of average cost by the mainstream approach uses the formula:

```
Average Cost = (Total Purchase Cost) / (Total Quantity Purchased)
```

In contrast, QuickBooks calculates the current average cost of an inventory item as:

```
Average Cost = (Total Asset Value) / (Quantity on Hand)
```

An item's asset value is the total acquisition cost of that item less the total COGS, taking into account such transactions as Inventory Adjustments that can change the dollar value of an item's stock. The item's quantity on hand works the same way, but it is a count of the number of units rather than a total of the dollars currently invested in the units.

One consequence of using this formula is that it makes average cost sensitive to the sales of an item — the formula uses on-hand values, which are the result of combining purchases with sales. This fact is often hidden in the numbers, because you don't usually see a change in an item's average cost until you buy more of it at a different unit cost. A sale affects both the quantity on hand and the total asset value, and therefore it will eventually have an effect on average cost, but not before another purchase is made at a unit cost that differs from the current average cost.

When you sell an item, both its asset value and the quantity on hand change — but its average cost doesn't, because the ratio of value to quantity remains the same. If you start with 100 units at $5 each, and sell 90, the average cost remains unchanged: ($500 ÷ 100 units) gives the same average cost as does the ratio of the resulting total asset value and quantity on hand ($50 ÷ 10

FIGURE 7.5

Average cost helps determine COGS, and therefore your gross profit.

J8			fx	=H8/E8					
	A	B	C	D	E	F	G	H	I	J

	Date	Number Bought	Unit Cost	Extended Cost	Cumulative Number Bought	Number Sold	Quantity on Hand	Total Cost of Purchases	Total Asset Value	Average Cost
1										
2										
3	06/26/2011	100	$ 5.00	$ 500.00	100		100	$ 500.00	$ 500.00	$ 5.00
4	07/03/2011	100	$ 6.00	$ 600.00	200		200	$1,100.00	$1,100.00	$ 5.50
5	08/03/2011		$	$ -	200	100	100	$1,100.00	$ 550.00	$ 5.50
6	09/05/2011	50	$ 4.00	$ 200.00	250		150	$1,300.00	$ 780.00	$ 5.20
7	10/02/2011	50	$ 5.20	$ 260.00	300		200	$1,560.00	$1,040.00	$ 5.20
8	11/02/2011		$	$ -	300	100	100	$1,560.00	$ 520.00	$ 5.20

units). Even though there's no apparent change at this point, the sale has an effect on the average cost later on, when you buy more units at a different price.

In Figure 7.4, the sale of 100 units in August had no immediate effect on the average cost of $5.50, because it did not change the ratio of asset value to quantity on hand. But when the next purchase was made in September, the average cost changed to $5.00 (because September's unit cost of $4.00 is lower than the existing average cost of $5.50) and it is different from the average cost of $5.20 shown in Figure 7.3 because of the differences in the formulas used.

Figure 7.5 returns to the mainstream approach to average costing. Notice that 100 widgets were sold in November. The average cost did not change, because under the mainstream approach sales have no effect on average cost. The asset value changes though, from $1,040 to $520, a drop of $520. That $520 is the COGS for the sale. QuickBooks arrives at the COGS by multiplying the units sold, 100, by the current average cost, $5.20.

Now compare Figure 7.5 with Figure 7.6, which shows how QuickBooks handles the November sale of 100 widgets.

In Figure 7.6, the COGS for the November sale is ($1,010 – $505), or $505. In Figure 7.5, that sale's COGS is $520. The method of calculating COGS, and for calculating gross profit, is the same regardless of which method you use to calculate average cost. But because the two methods calculate average cost differently, the results of the COGS and gross profit calculations differ. Figure 7.7 shows the journal entry for the sale, including QuickBooks' calculation of the COGS.

Using the QuickBooks approach, it's not always easy to figure out why a current average cost has the value it does. You have to track all the increases and the decreases to your holding in a given item — all the purchases, sales, adjustments to quantity, adjustments to valuation, and so on — or you won't arrive at the same figure as QuickBooks.

FIGURE 7.6

The average cost calculated by QuickBooks differs from the calculation shown in Figure 7.5, and therefore the COGS and gross profit are different.

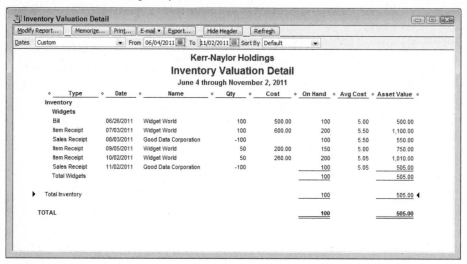

FIGURE 7.7

The profitability of any sale involving inventory depends directly on the COGS and, therefore, on the item's average cost.

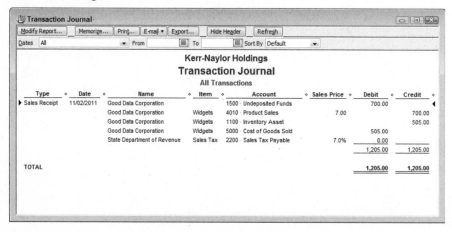

COGS and Gross Margin

There is no danger posed to your company's bottom line by the choice of method to calculate average cost. The method employed by QuickBooks tends to result in a more volatile measure of average cost, and people who have not encountered the QuickBooks method before sometimes have difficulty determining what's going on with their inventory valuation.

But in the long run, neither method is superior to the other as a means of determining COGS for the income statement or the asset value for the balance sheet. Particularly from the standpoint of the taxing authorities, what really matters is to be consistent across product lines and over time.

With all that said, QuickBooks introduces a problem that, if you don't understand its consequences, can immediately create huge headaches for you. Those headaches do nothing but get worse if you don't fix the problem right away. The problem concerns selling more of an item than QuickBooks thinks you have in stock: that is, selling negative. If you sell more of an item than is currently available, that error interacts with the method of calculating average cost. It does so in a way that makes it impossible for you to trust any financial results for that item that come about following the date of the error.

Selling negative

Merely selling out of an item is hardly a catastrophe — not, at least, to your financial statements. It can make you scratch your head when you look at an item's average cost, but if you acquire more of the item, or deactivate or otherwise discontinue it, no harm is done. Still, it will help to understand what's going on with the relatively benign act of selling to exactly zero units on hand.

Selling to zero

When you sell an item down to a zero quantity and then replenish your supply at a different cost, the inventory valuation can appear to be out of whack. If you look again at the formula that QuickBooks uses:

```
Average Cost = (Total Asset Value) / (Quantity on Hand)
```

You see that when an item goes to zero units on hand its average cost is undefined — because you'd be dividing by zero — and that's why QuickBooks temporarily uses the existing average cost. See Figure 7.8 where a sale made in December takes the company's quantity on hand to zero.

Then, when you replenish your supply, the new average cost is based entirely on the cost of that new purchase. The history of prior purchases disappears from the average cost estimate, which is based solely on the units you currently own. Figure 7.9 shows what happens to the average cost when, in January, the company buys 100 widgets at $3 each.

FIGURE 7.8

You may wonder how an item can have any average cost at all when the average's numerator and denominator are both zero.

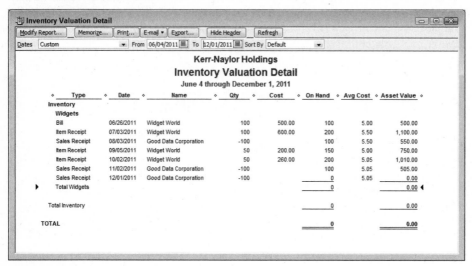

FIGURE 7.9

The new average cost, after an item has been taken to zero and then replenished, is that purchase's unit cost.

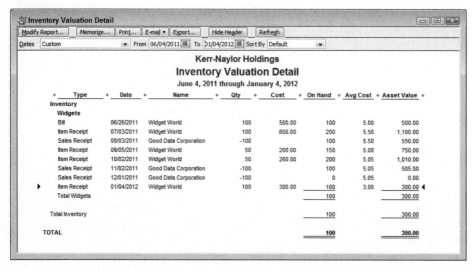

FIGURE 7.10

The new average cost retains the effect of the purchases made before taking the item to a zero quantity.

	J10		f_x	=H10/E10						
	A	B	C	D	E	F	G	H	I	J
1	Date	Number Bought	Unit Cost	Extended Cost	Cumulative Number Bought	Number Sold	Quantity on Hand	Total Cost of Purchases	Total Asset Value	Average Cost
2										
3	06/26/2011	100	$ 5.00	$ 500.00	100		100	$ 500.00	$ 500.00	$ 5.00
4	07/03/2011	100	$ 6.00	$ 600.00	200		200	$1,100.00	$1,100.00	$ 5.50
5	08/03/2011		$ -		200	100	100	$1,100.00	$ 550.00	$ 5.50
6	09/05/2011	50	$ 4.00	$ 200.00	250		150	$1,300.00	$ 780.00	$ 5.20
7	10/02/2011	50	$ 5.20	$ 260.00	300		200	$1,560.00	$1,040.00	$ 5.20
8	11/02/2011		$ -		300	100	100	$1,560.00	$ 520.00	$ 5.20
9	12/01/2011		$ -		300	100	0	$1,560.00	$ -	$ 5.20
10	Jan 4 2012	100	3	$ 300.00	400		100	$1,860.00	$ 465.00	$ 4.65

The current average cost of $3.00, as shown in Figure 7.9, no longer comprises any of the item's prior history. You may or may not regard that effect as desirable. Many users and accountants do not, primarily because this version of average cost is much more volatile when your suppliers are changing the prices they charge you. (GAAP takes no position on the issue of which version is preferable.)

Figure 7.10 is provided so that you can contrast the effects of the two formulas.

So far, what you've seen concerning inventory valuation is entirely due to the two different methods of calculating the average cost of an inventory item:

(Total Purchase Cost) / (Total Units Purchased)

and

(Total Asset Value) / (Quantity on Hand)

The differences in asset valuation are entirely due to different concepts of what should constitute the average cost of an item (the method used by QuickBooks actually has a lot of FIFO in it). But QuickBooks has a quirk that magnifies the effect of the differences you've seen so far. That quirk is the fact that QuickBooks allows the user to sell negative, by selling more of an item than is on hand — and this is nowhere near as benign as just depleting your stock.

Selling below zero

Suppose you have 10 widgets on hand and a customer wants to buy 20. Maybe the customer doesn't need them all right away, or maybe you can borrow ten more from another order that isn't scheduled to ship for a couple of days, or maybe you've just completed a physical inventory and you know that QuickBooks has a short count. Whatever your rationale, you use QuickBooks to establish a sales receipt or invoice transaction that calls for the sale of 10 more widgets than QuickBooks shows you presently have on hand.

FIGURE 7.11

The negative quantity on hand in February will freeze the average cost, but not the asset value.

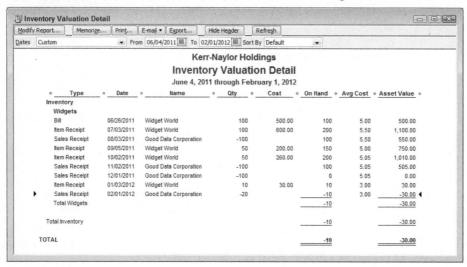

If you've done that before, whether deliberately or by accident, you know that QuickBooks Pro displays the message "You don't have sufficient quantity available to sell 20 of the item: Widgets," where the quantity and the name of the item depends on how much you tried to sell of which item. (The message may be different if you're using QuickBooks Premier, but its substance is the same.) There's an OK button, and after you click it you're back at the Sales Receipt window. Click the Save and Close button and you have succeeded in selling more widgets than QuickBooks thinks you have in stock. QuickBooks now declines, and continues to decline, to recalculate the current average cost for widgets until the quantity on hand turns positive again. Figure 7.11 shows your current inventory situation, with a negative quantity on hand.

Now, suppose you buy five more widgets, at a cost that's different from the current average cost. According to the QuickBooks formula for average cost, this should result in a change in the average cost. Figure 7.12 shows that it actually doesn't.

You've bought five units at $100 each — roughly 20 times what you had been paying. But the average cost doesn't budge. Remember: Average cost won't change until the quantity on hand is once again greater than zero. One consequence of the unchanging average cost appears in the total asset value. You spent $500, but the asset value has increased by only $15.00. That increase of $15.00 occurs because QuickBooks uses the *old* average cost of $3.00 to calculate the effect of your $500 purchase on the asset value: the acquisition of five units at an out-of-date average cost of $3.00 results in an increase in asset value of $15.00, rather than the actual increase of $500 due to purchasing five units for $100 each.

FIGURE 7.12

The unit cost of $100 in March has no effect on the average cost.

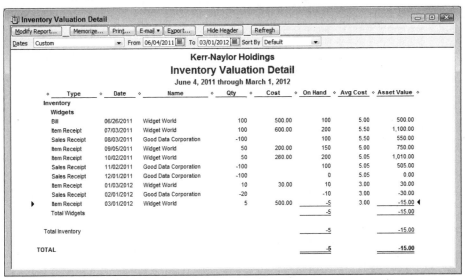

The effect is not limited to asset valuation, but, as you might expect, there's a consequence for COGS and gross profit as well. Figures 7.13 and 7.14 show that when you make another sale and the current quantity on hand is already below zero, the COGS can be based on an erroneous average cost. Figure 7.13 shows the inventory report, and Figure 7.14 shows the journal entry associated with the sale.

Here's what happened. First, using the QuickBooks version of average cost:

Starting in November 2011, the first two sales transactions are entirely normal: You sell 100 units, dropping the quantity on hand to 100, and then sell another 100, completely selling out of the item. As explained earlier, the result of selling to exactly zero is to set the average cost to the same value it had prior to that transaction. In this case, that's $5.05. The purchase of another 10 widgets on 1/3/2012 takes you back into positive territory and resets the average cost based exclusively on that purchase, that is $3.00.

But then, on 2/1/2012, you sell another 20 units. That's 10 more than you had on hand, and you are now in negative territory. Notice that the Total Asset Value is correct. (But that's an accident: Even a broken clock is right twice a day.) You have –10 units, and at an Average Cost of $3, the Asset Value is –$30.00. Nothing has happened so far to change the Average Cost. Remember, sales have no immediate effect on Average Cost.

Now, on 3/1/2012, you buy five units for $500.00. That's $100 apiece, and two errors jump out at you:

FIGURE 7.13

The inventory report has the wrong average cost.

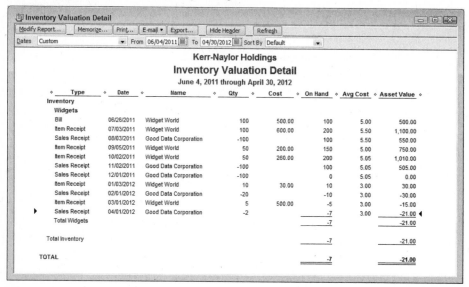

FIGURE 7.14

The journal entry for the sale also uses the wrong COGS.

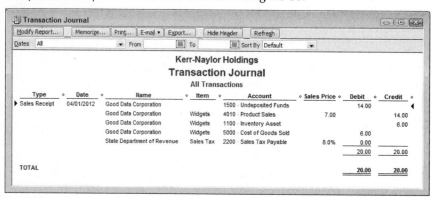

FIGURE 7.15

The misstatement of COGS is the kind of damage that can be caused by selling into a negative quantity on hand.

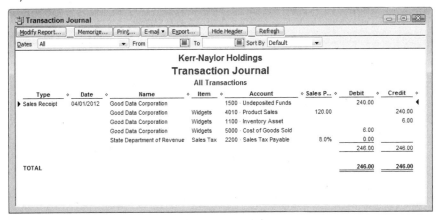

- The Average Value should change from $3, but it does not: You still see an Average Value of $3 as of the purchase.

- The Total Asset Value is now also wrong: The numeric accident that caused an erroneous calculation to return a correct result can't recur when the *true* average cost has changed.

The quantity on hand is correct, but both the Average Cost and the Total Asset Value are wrong. Again: QuickBooks does not recalculate Average Cost when the quantity on hand is zero or below.

You haven't suffered financial damage yet, but you're about to. On 4/1/2012, you sell two units, taking you from −5 on hand to −7 on hand. Because you still have a negative quantity on hand, QuickBooks doesn't yet recalculate the Average Cost. And because you sold two units on 4/1/2012, QuickBooks assigns a COGS of $6 to that sale. Figure 7.15 shows the relevant journal entry.

The journal's COGS entry says that you sold, for $240, inventory items that cost you $6 to acquire. But which physical units did you sell? You had −10 units on 2/1/2012, and although you can sell imaginary units, you can't sell physical units you don't have, so the sale can't have been from the −10 units. So, on 4/1/2012 you must have sold two of the five units you bought on 3/1/2012. You bought them for $100 apiece — but QuickBooks thinks the sale's COGS was $6.

Your apparent gross margin on that sale was therefore $240 revenue less $6 COGS, or $234. You'll be obligated to pay corporate income tax on that profit, after it has been reduced to taxable income by legitimate deductions. But those two widgets actually cost you $200, so in fact your gross margin was $40. From just about every standpoint that you can name — taxes, cash flow, product line analysis — you have problems that are directly traceable to the combination

FIGURE 7.16

You wouldn't know until your accountant told you that something was wrong, unless you make a habit of looking at more than just the current month.

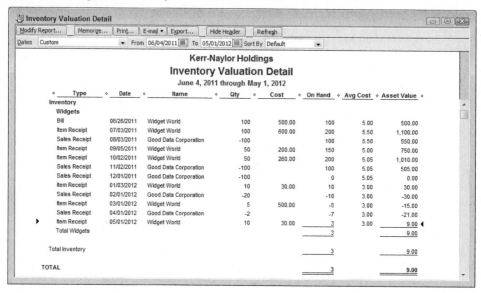

of QuickBooks' method of average costing combined with its feckless response to the act of selling more than you appear to have.

Finally, on 5/1/2012, your quantity on hand turns positive again as you buy 10 more units. And QuickBooks responds by recalculating the Average Cost, although you can't tell that it did, because that purchase is for $3 per unit — the same as the Average Cost that was current before all the quantity on hand went negative and you transacted business with some very different cost structures (see Figure 7.16).

> **NOTE** I could have demonstrated that the Average Cost calculation kicks back in on 5/1/2012 by arranging a purchase at a different unit cost, such as $9, instead of $3. I did it this way to demonstrate how what's really happening with QuickBooks' Average Costs can be masked by the numbers.

Going positive

The best way to avoid these problems is to avoid letting an inventory item go negative at all. There are two general ways to do that: before and after. If you can arrange things so that your apparent quantity on hand doesn't dip below zero, you're managing your inventory before anything bad happens. If for some reason you can't avoid a negative quantity on hand, you can still recover after the fact, but it may take some extra work.

Pending sales

One of the differences between the QuickBooks Pro and Premier editions is support for sales orders — which can be much like backorders, if you're more comfortable with that term. Using QuickBooks Pro, you can emulate Sales Orders as they're handled in a QuickBooks Premier edition — it's just not quite as convenient and you can't duplicate all the functionality.

There are several steps you can take, including establishing a custom field, that make it easier to work with backorders in QuickBooks Pro. Because this book is not intended as a users' guide, I'll skip the details, and just mention the irreducible minimums for dealing with insufficient inventory in Pro and Premier.

Pending sales in QuickBooks Pro

When you create a Sales Receipt or an Invoice in QuickBooks Pro that involves the sale of inventory items, you must enter the number of units of each item you're selling. If you try to sell more units than you have recorded in QuickBooks as on hand, you see the message shown in Figure 7.17.

When you click OK, the warning disappears and you can continue editing the transaction. Before you save it, though, you should right-click the form's header or footer, or click the Edit menu, and select Mark Invoice as Pending. (If you're creating a Sales Receipt, the menu item is Mark Sales Receipt as Pending.)

When you do so, a Pending stamp appears on the form (see Figure 7.18). A pending invoice or sales receipt is known as a "nonposting" transaction. No journal entries occur when you establish a nonposting transaction, and the inventory unit counts are unaffected. This means that you do not create a negative quantity on hand situation, and all the troubles explained earlier in this chapter are prevented, at least for that transaction.

When you know you once again have sufficient inventory, open the order, right-click the header or footer (or use the Edit menu) and choose Mark Order as Final. Now, when you close the order, the numbers post to the proper accounts, and the COGS and average costs will reflect the reality of your inventory status.

> **TIP** A quick way to access pending sales is to choose Reports ▶ Sales ▶ Pending Sales. When you find, on the report, the order you're interested in, double-click it to open the Invoice or the Sales Receipt window.

Sales orders in QuickBooks Premier

QuickBooks Premier Edition includes a nonposting transaction called a Sales Order. You can think of a sales order as a way to collect information about a sale without actually committing it to your company's financial records. Only when the sales order is finalized by turning it into an invoice is the revenue recognized and the posting to various accounts performed.

FIGURE 7.17

This warning is identical for Sales Receipts and Invoices.

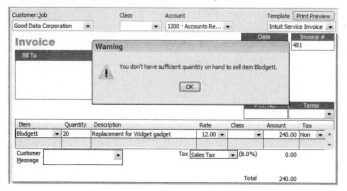

FIGURE 7.18

The Pending stamp disappears when you finalize the order.

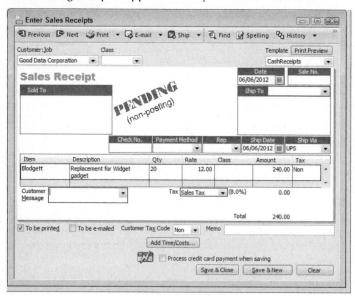

There are various reasons that a company might want to delay recognizing revenue temporarily. The customer might have a large balance due, or a sales manager might want to watch a new sales rep more closely than usual. Or, insufficient inventory might come into play.

If a possible shortage of inventory is the reason for creating a sales order instead of a sales receipt or an invoice, there are additional benefits to Premier's sales orders that are not available in Pro. For example, you can arrange to distinguish between quantity available and quantity on hand. Quantity on hand, in this context, is the number of units on the shelf, ready to ship. Quantity available, by contrast, is the number of units ready to ship that have not already been spoken for by other sales, sales orders, or assembly builds.

In any case, if you enter into a sales order more units of an inventory item than can be shipped, you'll be warned as you are using QuickBooks Pro. It's necessary to have enabled the warning (choose Edit ▶ Preferences ▶ Items and Inventory ▶ Company). Options are available that help you manage orders: for example, whether you want to ship a partial fulfillment or hold the shipment until the entire order can be sent at once.

As with Sales Receipts and Invoices in QuickBooks Pro, you can put a Pending stamp on a sales order from a contextual menu by right-clicking the order's header or footer. In the case of sales orders, though, it's less critical because a sales order is by definition a nonposting transaction.

The main point to keep in mind is that QuickBooks offers you tools that help you record information about a sale without actually committing you to fulfilling it. At the very least, a pending sale or a sales order is an important buffer that can prevent the inventory count on an item from going negative.

Recovering after the fact

A customer has called to tell you he wants to buy all your remaining stock of Princess phones. QuickBooks has warned you that you don't have a sufficient quantity to sell even one, but you know perfectly well that you have had 10 of them gathering dust in dead storage since Ford pardoned Nixon. You'd love to unload them (the phones) and you do so, ignoring the QuickBooks warning that you don't have enough on hand.

Now comes the hangover. QuickBooks thinks you're even farther into negative territory on that item than you were before. The phones' average cost showed up as $75 — a legitimate figure as of your most recent acquisition but not since. You got rid of the phones for a token $100 but the COGS appear in the Journal as $750. And there's no longer a reference market if you wanted to mark them down via a lower-of-cost-or-market adjustment.

Nevertheless, you should do something about it. There are three approaches that QuickBooks would let you take:

Correct your quantity on hand using an Adjustment

Choose Lists ▶ Item List. Click the item in question, and then click the Activities button at the bottom of the window. Choose Adjust Quantity/Value on Hand to display the dialog box shown

FIGURE 7.19

Filling the Value Adjustment checkbox displays a Current Value and a New Value column.

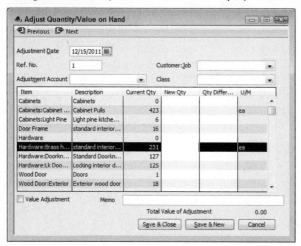

in Figure 7.19. In the row for the item you want to adjust, click in the New Quantity column and enter the quantity really on hand as of the Adjustment Date (see Figure 7.19).

If your quantity adjustment brings the quantity on hand back into positive territory before the date of the sale, the average cost calculation will reflect any subsequent item purchases and the COGS for the sale will be recalculated accordingly. The basic mechanism is the one already mentioned several times: QuickBooks does not recalculate average cost (and therefore does not recalculate COGS) until the quantity on hand is greater than zero.

Using an Inventory Adjustment could be the best approach if the reason that QuickBooks thinks you have fewer than zero units is an erroneous physical inventory.

Correct your quantity on hand by editing an item receipt

Another reason you might show a negative quantity on hand is that you bought more units than you told QuickBooks about. There's nothing unusual about a typographical error and if all you did was type 50 instead of 150, there's nothing wrong with correcting it directly in the Item Receipt. You might want to note in the Memo field that it's a corrected record. If this typo caused a negative quantity on hand, it's very likely that correcting it will turn that quantity positive so that QuickBooks can recalculate subsequent average costs and COGS.

Revise an existing sales record

It's entirely possible that a prior sales record that took you into negative territory is itself wrong. If it states that you sold 100 blodgetts when in fact you sold 10, it could be that correcting the sales receipt or invoice is all that's needed to correct your quantity on hand to a positive value and cause QuickBooks to recalculate subsequent average costs and COGS figures.

Forecasting and Projections in QuickBooks

T he flow of cash in and out of your business is an important gauge of how well you manage your resources. In an established business, it's not as crucial as net income and working capital, but it's still an important way to judge how well you're managing the process of turning products into cash and reinvesting in the business.

Cash management is even more important in the early days of a business, because the cushion is usually fairly thin. And if there's some way to forecast how much money is going to hit the Undeposited Funds account during the next month or two, well, that could be comforting information. Is there a good way to find out? Yes and no — read on.

Using the Cash Flow Projector and the Cash Flow Forecast Report

If you explore the QuickBooks menu structure, you'll find several menu items that refer to forecasting: Set Up Forecast, Cash Flow Projector, Cash Flow Forecast, and so on. It's not necessary to explore all the fine distinctions between these procedures and these reports, but these two are useful when you need to watch your cash position: the Cash Flow Projector and the Cash Flow Forecast report.

Each tool brings something different to the job of forecasting your company's cash position. The Cash Flow Forecast report is more rigid than the Cash Flow Projector, but it does a better job of informing you about your Accounts Receivable. The Cash Flow Projector is an interactive tool, not a static report, but it has some traps that you need to know about before you trust what it tells you. This chapter explores both tools and shows you how to use them as complementary sources of information rather than competing alternatives.

A quick overview of the Cash Flow Projector

Lots of QuickBooks users get confused about the Cash Flow Projector, and it's really no wonder. What is in fact a simple exercise in arithmetic, in adding receivables and subtracting payables, turns into mystic calculus. The whole point of using the Cash Flow Projector is to answer this question: Over the next six weeks, are my current cash assets, plus whatever additional revenue I expect to take in, enough to pay the bills coming due?

That's simple enough. We've all done that kind of analysis on a spare yellow sticky note during a moment of anxiety, at least when we were first building our businesses. Later on, we used a spreadsheet instead of a yellow sticky, but we're trying to answer the same question: Will I be able to pay my bills?

Before you begin using the projector, it helps to have made a few decisions:

■ What bank accounts would you tap for cash if you need to?

■ Do you want to manually enter the cash receipts you expect during the next six weeks, or do you want to use a forecasting equation?

■ Do you want to enter any upcoming expenses apart from the bills you've already recorded in QuickBooks as Accounts Payable?

■ Do you want to use bills that you've entered in Accounts Payable to estimate your near-term costs?

Completing the Cash Flow Projector takes several steps. You're expected to do the following, in line with those decisions:

1. Identify the cash accounts you're interested in.

2. Select a method to project cash inflows, and optionally adjust the projections as you see fit, for the next six weeks.

3. Select expenses that you expect to pay off during the next six weeks.

4. Review and adjust amounts and dates from upcoming Accounts Payable.

5. Review the resulting cash balances.

After reviewing the projected balances, you might want to transfer cash, step up sales efforts, do some belt-tightening, or merely stand pat.

The Cash Flow Projector puts these questions to you in a wizard. You'll see each step in the wizard later in this chapter.

Thinking back over those decisions and actions, you can infer that the Cash Flow Projector takes four basic steps:

1. It finds your current cash balance.

2. It asks you how much money you expect to spend during the next six weeks.

3. It asks you how much money you expect to take in during the next six weeks.

4. It takes your current balance, subtracts your costs, adds your revenues, and tells you the result.

It ain't multivariate calculus, folks.

Working your way through the Cash Flow Projector

A little reflection shows that there are three capabilities in the Cash Flow Projector that might convince you to use it in preference to other tools such as a spreadsheet or that yellow sticky note:

- It identifies the cash accounts that will be of interest, and shows the current balance for each cash account.

- It offers several ways to project six weeks of cash inflows. It creates these forecasts automatically or lets you specify them manually.

- It identifies Accounts Payable dates and amounts that will come due during the six-week window.

Only the projection of cash inflows offers you something that's not entirely under your control. Although you decide when to meet business expenses and pay bills, you do not generally exert control over when customers will buy from you or how much cash you'll take in over the next few weeks. Therefore, it's useful to have a credible and rational way of projecting what those receipts will be, based on history.

NOTE   It's an overstatement to claim that you don't exert control over when or how much your customers are going to pay you. It's true that if you retail consumer goods, the state of the economy and consumer confidence drive your revenues more than any short-term action you can take. But if you manufacture critical parts for hybrid car engines, you're in the happy position of knowing that when you send an invoice it's going to get paid — probably net 15.

Verifying the Cash Flow Projector

One reason the Cash Flow Projector mystifies many users is that it can be difficult to verify the cash receipts that form the basis for the forecasts. It helps a lot to know where those numbers come from.

The next section, "Running the Cash Flow Projector," gets into these issues in more depth, but for now it's useful to know that the projector can forecast your receipts for each of the next six weeks. (You can override this behavior and manually enter estimates of the receipts yourself, but manual entry is just one of the six forecasting methods that the projector offers.)

To create forecasts, the projector uses one of these periods:

FIGURE 8.1

Because this is a custom report, the Modify Report dialog box appears automatically.

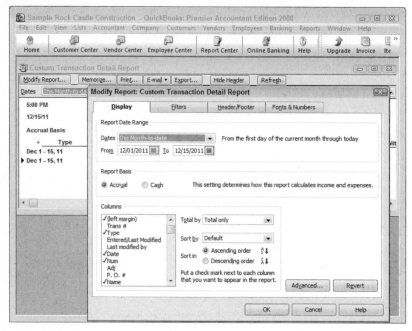

- The last six weeks. If today is 12/11/2011, the last six weeks would extend from 10/30/11 through 12/10/2011.

- The last six weeks from one year ago (so, if today is 12/11/2011, the six-week period would extend from 10/31/2010 to 12/11/2010).

Whether you choose the most recent six-week period or the six-week period that began 58 weeks ago, you can choose to use each week's total receipts or an average of the six weeks' total receipts. (The default option is a weighted average of the most recent six weeks.)

The projector shows you the weekly values (or their average), but it's helpful to compare that to a report. Here's how to create the report:

1. Choose Reports ▶ Custom Transaction Detail Report. An empty report appears, along with the Modify Report dialog box (see Figure 8.1).

2. In the From and To boxes, enter the beginning and ending dates that define the six-week period you want.

3. In the Columns list, clear each checked field name by clicking it. Click the following field names to give them checkmarks: Type, Date, Account and Debit (you'll have to scroll through the list to find all four).

4. In the Total By dropdown, choose Week.

FIGURE 8.2

The region immediately to the right of the Filter list box changes, depending on the field you selected as a filter.

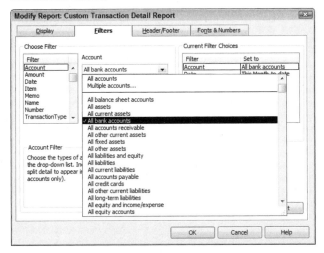

5. Still in the Modify Report dialog box, click the Filters tab. Click on Account in the Filter list box. The Account dropdown appears. In the Account dropdown, click All Bank Accounts (see Figure 8.2).

6. Back in the Filter list box, choose Transaction Type. The Transaction Type dropdown appears. Click Multiple Transaction Types. A new window, Select Transaction Types, appears. Click Deposit, Sales Receipt, Payment and Transfer. Then click OK to close the Select box. (If you are creating this report for real, omit Transfer as a transaction type.)

7. Click OK to close the Modify Report dialog box.

The resulting report appears in Figure 8.7, so that you can compare it with the projector's preliminary results.

You might wonder why Step 6 advises you to include Transfer as a transaction type, along with Deposit, Sales Receipt, and Payment, and then warns you instead to omit it. You shouldn't include transfers as part of the normal procedure. But for the purpose here, you must include transfer transactions, to understand why the projector's results can be confusing.

Running the Cash Flow Projector

You start the Cash Flow Projector by choosing Company ◗ Planning and Budgeting ◗ Cash Flow Projector from the QuickBooks menu. After you click Next to go past an introductory splash screen, you see the window shown in Figure 8.3. Of course, the balances will differ according to the company file you have open. This example uses the sample file supplied by QuickBooks called Sample Product-Based Business, also known as Rock Castle Construction.

FIGURE 8.3

The Cash Flow Projector lets you base the projections on any accounts that might contain cash.

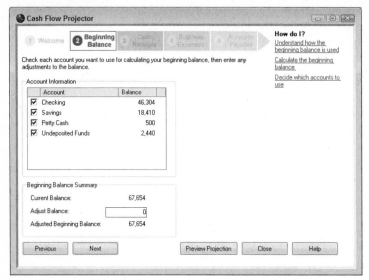

You can choose any or all of the available accounts in the Beginning Balance step — generally Bank accounts and Undeposited Funds (but subaccounts are not shown).

NOTE   **The Undeposited Funds account is an extremely helpful but underused shoebox. You put checks in it to keep them together until you're ready to deposit them all at once. Using Undeposited Funds makes it possible for you to record the deposit of, say, 20 checks without winding up with 20 deposit receipts.**

The Cash Flow Projector needs to know which accounts should be used because it will look back six weeks (or 58 weeks) from the current date to see how much cash has entered each account during each of those weeks. The projector then uses that recent history to project, or forecast, how much cash will come in during the subsequent six weeks.

For this example, I'll specify Checking to keep things simple, but there's another reason: The projector does not manage transfers between accounts properly. Suppose that four weeks ago, you deposited $5,000 into your checking account, and the next day transferred $5,000 from your checking account into your savings account.

If you now choose to project cash flows using both the checking and the savings accounts, the Cash Flow Projector thinks you took in not $5,000 but $10,000; that is, the $5,000 you deposited into checking, plus the $5,000 you transferred out of checking and into savings. The projector's erroneous treatment of the transfer will have a disastrous effect on the accuracy of your projected cash position, as well as any receipts that you forecast using one of the automatic methods. Therefore, if you decide to use this tool, heed this:

FIGURE 8.4

Recent deposits might not appear until you force a recalculation by choosing a different projection method, and then return to Use a Weighted Average of Last 6 Weeks.

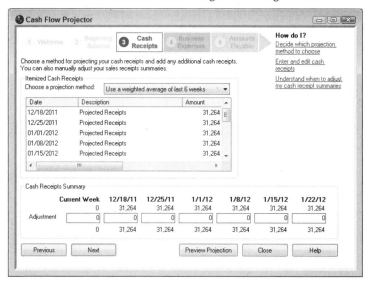

 **Do not select more than one bank account in the Cash Flow Projector's second step.**

Once you've selected an account (or, if you must, accounts) by filling its checkbox, click Next to go to the Cash Receipts window, shown in Figure 8.4.

The projected cash receipts appear in the list box (labeled Itemized Cash Receipts), and also above the edit boxes (labeled Adjustment) where you can enter adjustments to the projections. Where do these projections, each of them 31,264 in this example, come from?

Notice the Choose a Projection Method dropdown. The currently selected item is Use a Weighted Average of Last 6 Weeks. It is the default selection when you first run the Cash Flow Projector, and it specifies the method that results in the projections of 31,264 in Figure 8.4. I have more to say about this method, not all of it good, later. First, here's a description of the other options in the Choose a Projection Method dropdown.

I Want to Project Cash Receipts Manually option

If you choose this option, the projected cash receipts shown in the Figure 8.4 disappear, and you can enter any numbers you want.

In this case, you presumably have some particular knowledge regarding the timing and amount of cash receipts that you can expect during the next six weeks. You might, for example, have

FIGURE 8.5

This warning just means that you're about to replace the projections due to one method with projections calculated by a different method.

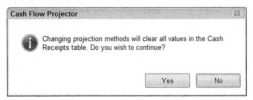

access to a forecast of cash receipts from another source (see the "Going Outside QuickBooks to Project Receipts" section later in this chapter).

Use Last 6 Weeks option

If you select this item, you are telling the projector to assume that your cash receipts for each of the previous six weeks will be repeated for the next six weeks. When you first choose a different projection method from the dropdown, you receive the warning shown in Figure 8.5.

There's no need for concern because you can always get the existing values back by returning to the current method, unless you've been entering cash receipts manually.

> **TIP** The Cash Flow Projector has a disconcerting habit of changing which accounts are selected in Step 2 (refer to Figure 8.3) when you change projection methods. It's a good idea to use the Previous button to check what's selected in Step 2 after you change the projection method in Step 3.

When you click Yes in response to QuickBooks' warning, the projector's Cash Receipts window looks like the one shown in Figure 8.6.

In Figure 8.6, the projector has replaced the projected receipts shown in Figure 8.4 with new amounts, in both the Itemized Cash Receipts box and the Cash Receipts Summary box. Because I started by selecting all accounts (see Figure 8.3), the projector looks back at dollar amounts entered in each account for the past six weeks, and assumes the cash receipts will be the same for the next six weeks.

You can verify the amounts by looking at a report with bank account debits on a weekly basis. One way is by means of the custom detail report, as shown in Figure 8.7.

You can see in Figure 8.7 that the cash receipts in Checking correspond exactly to those in the projector, shown in Figure 8.6.

Figure 8.8 charts the effect of taking the results of the prior six weeks and using them as a forecast of the next six weeks. This charting is easy to do in Excel, using an export from the QuickBooks report into an Excel workbook (see Chapter 2 for information on how to manage the export).

FIGURE 8.6

You can enter numbers in the Adjustment row to show any special revenue amounts that you expect during an upcoming week, but that are not anticipated by QuickBooks.

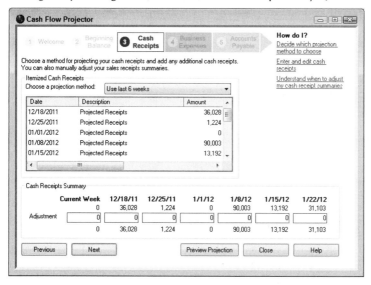

In Figure 8.8, look at what's been going on from January 2011 (shown in the chart as 1/11) through early October (shown as 10/11). It appears that for three weeks of any given month the cash receipts are relatively low, under $10,000, and during one week of the month the receipts spike to between $15,000 and $20,000.

More important, the cash receipts vary between $0 and $20,000 per week from January to October. Then the swings become much larger — look at the spikes of $30,000 and over $90,000 from October on.

The trend is clearly up during the fourth quarter, and to use the prior six weeks as the projection of the next six weeks is to ignore that trend. If this were a real company instead of a sample, I wouldn't be a bit surprised to see the actuals from the end of December and into January that were $10,000 higher than the projections (which are shown in the chart in Figure 8.8 as squares instead of diamonds).

The point to bear in mind is that there's no special reason to use the last six weeks as a stand-in for the next six weeks. It's better than nothing, though, and it could even be the best forecast you can make.

Furthermore, it's about a year better than the next option — unless you know that your business is highly seasonal.

FIGURE 8.7

A report such as this one is essential if you want to validate the figures in the Cash Flow Projector.

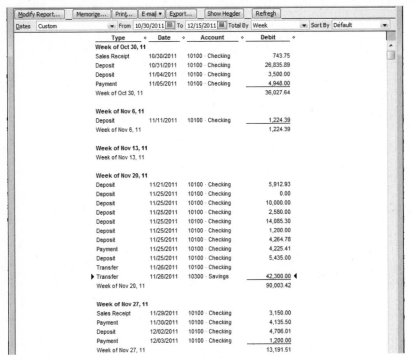

Same 6 Week Period Last Year option

This option from the Choose a Projection Method dropdown means that the forecast values are the same as the values one year earlier. Suppose that today is Thursday, December 15, 2011. The first week that will be forecast starts on Sunday, December 18, 2011. This projection method uses the actual value for a year earlier, the week of Sunday, December 19, 2010.

You can tell from Figure 8.9 and Figure 8.10 why these dates would be a bad choice for this company. Figure 8.9 shows the values from the projector.

Now look at Figure 8.10 which charts the forecast based on receipts from a year earlier in the context of the full year (again, the forecast receipts are shown as squares rather than diamonds).

If your business is highly seasonal, and if you can expect your sales during any given period to be much like they were 52 weeks earlier, you might want to use the Same 6 Week Period Last Year option. But I'd want three or four years worth of data, at the very least, to convince me. Maybe with more data I'd accept a projection like the one in Figure 8.10, where the bottom drops out of the cash receipts at the end of the year.

The six recent weeks are a lot better bet as forecasts than the six weeks from a year ago.

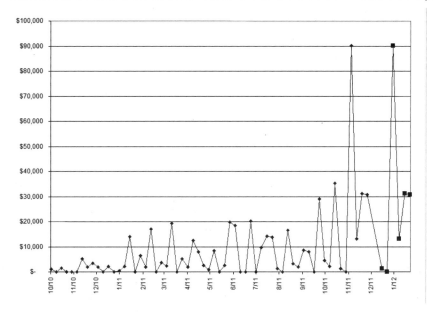

Note that the chosen projection method forecasts using the prior year's receipts.

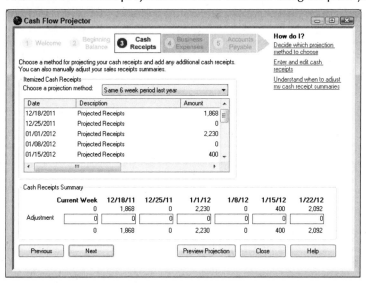

FIGURE 8.10

The receipts from one year earlier were very low compared to recent receipts.

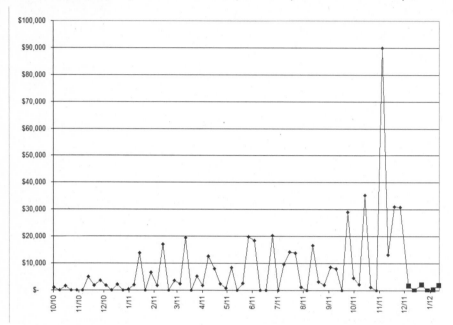

NOTE When you're working with the mists and smokes of forecasts, it's easy to get lost in the numbers and forget where the data is coming from and how you want to use it. Figure 8.10 is a good example of this effect. If the business's revenues are highly seasonal, it's not at all implausible that the upcoming receipts could be as low as projected. On the other hand, if the business was just getting started one year earlier, the relatively low receipts could very well be due to its startup status, not to any seasonality that's inherent in its cash flows. There's no special reason to expect the company to act like a startup at the beginning of every fiscal year.

The preceding two methods, Use Last 6 Weeks and Same 6 Week Period Last Year, provide forecasts that vary from week to week in the same way that the actuals vary from week to week. If the six weeks prior to the current week had cash inflows of $100, $500, $200, $0, $800, and $300 then Use Last 6 Weeks forecasts $100, $500, $200, $0, $800, and $300 for the subsequent six weeks.

The same is true of the Same 6 Week Period Last Year option. The averaging methods explained next use the same periods as the preceding two methods, but they treat the data differently.

FIGURE 8.11

A constant forecast is seldom correct, but sometimes it's less wrong than the alternatives.

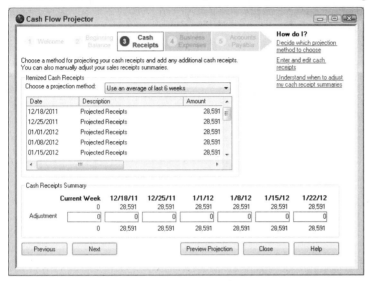

Use an Average of Last Six Weeks option

Another option in the Choose a Projection Method dropdown is Use an Average of Last Six Weeks. If you run the Cash Flow Projector every week, by using Average of Last Six Weeks you wind up forecasting next week's cash receipts by means of a moving average. That is, next week's forecast is always the average of the last six weeks; as time moves forward, so does the basis for the average — thus the term *moving average*.

In Figure 8.6, the projections, which are the actuals for the prior six weeks, are $36,028, $1,224, $0, $90,003, $13,192, and $31,103 (not visible in the projector's window). The average of those six values is $28,591. Figure 8.11 shows the result of choosing Use an Average of Last Six Weeks.

Used in this way — to provide a constant forecast value through several future time periods — the approach is called a *random no-trend* model. That is, applied to cash inflows, it assumes that the receipts are not trending up or down, and that any differences from week to week are due to random errors around the true long-term average.

(The errors would have to do with random events such as rainstorms that keep people at home, or overdrawn checking accounts, or a burglar breaking into your store and stealing all your stock, or a sudden, temporary, and one-time-only surge of customer interest in your product.)

Although this sort of single-forecast model has been popular in the past, it has become much less so as computing power has become generally accessible and applications such as QuickBooks and Excel have made it easy to create even slightly more sophisticated forecasts. A few people would argue that it's okay to use the same single forecast for a subsequent six-week period: Even a broken clock is right twice a day. But they'd be in the minority.

In summary, you might consider using the Cash Flow Projector's Average of Last 6 Weeks method to forecast if you repeat it every week, turning a single-forecast model into a moving average model.

Average of Same 6 week Period Last Year option

The same arguments apply in even greater measure to another option in the Choose a Projection Method dropdown: Average of Same 6 week Period Last Year. Again, the assumption of this model is that the cash inflows from last year are a good predictor of the upcoming cash inflows — only this time, the average of the year-old data is used for each of the next six weeks. In a highly seasonal business, it can make good sense to look back a year, but almost no sense to push an average out six weeks when there are subsequent historical values available.

My advice is to avoid using the six-week average forecasts for more than one period beyond the current week. If you want to use the six-week average, repeat the analysis weekly to turn it into a moving average.

Use a Weighted Average of Last 6 Weeks option

There's one more option in the Choose a Projection Method dropdown: Use a Weighted Average of Last 6 Weeks. It's the default option, the one that's chosen when you first run the Cash Flow Projector. Here's what it does:

In the Average of Last 6 Weeks method, each week's cash receipts carries an equal weight in the average. You just take the sum of the weekly cash receipts and divide by 6. This is an unweighted average.

By contrast, the weighted average multiplies each week's cash receipts by a different factor, or weight, before totaling them; then divides by 6 the number of values being averaged. Figure 8.12 shows what it looks like in an Excel worksheet.

Notice first that the cash receipts in the first column agree with those shown for the most recent six weeks, shown in Figure 8.6. Also notice that the weighted average of $31,264 agrees with the weighted average calculated by the Cash Flow Projector as shown in Figure 8.4.

You can demonstrate the same outcome for yourself by entering the six weights, ranging from 0.1875 to 3, into a worksheet along with your own set of cash receipts for the past six weeks.

Multiply the receipts by the weights and take the average of the results. It should agree with the weighted average as given by the Cash Flow Projector when you run it on your company file.

This projection method, the Weighted Average of the Last Six Weeks, is stronger than the unweighted average shown in Figure 8.11 because, using the unweighted average, each week's cash receipts have equal weight in the average. The weighted average method gives greater weight to more recent receipts. The assumption is that the more recent the observation, the

The weekly weights are the same regardless of the actual receipts in use.

	A	B	C
			Receipts
1	Cash receipts	Weight	times Weight
2	$ 36,028	0.1875	$ 6,755
3	$ 1,224	0.1875	$ 230
4	$ -	0.375	$ -
5	$ 90,003	0.75	$ 67,502
6	$ 13,192	1.5	$ 19,788
7	$ 31,103	3	$ 93,309
8			
9		Weighted Average:	$ 31,264

Half the value of the forecast is due to the prior week's value.

	A	B	C
			Percent of
1	Weeks back	Weight	effect
2	6	0.1875	3.13%
3	5	0.1875	3.13%
4	4	0.375	6.25%
5	3	0.75	12.50%
6	2	1.5	25.00%
7	1	3	50.00%

more likely it is to resemble the next occurrence. If your weekly cash receipts have been trending up from, say, $5,000 six months ago to $8,000 last week, it is rational to project that next week's receipts will be closer to $8,000 than to $5,000.

It's easy to express the relative effect of the weights in percentage terms (see Figure 8.13).

Of course, this assumes that you have no special knowledge about next week. If you know that your business will be closed next week, and that you will make no sales, that's special knowledge, which is difficult to build into a weighted average without seeing your calendar.

If this weighted average approach is better than the unweighted average approach shown in Figure 8.11, it's not all that much better. Three issues are pretty clear:

■ It's still a single-forecast. The Cash Flow Projector is asking you to let it apply weights that get smaller the further back you go. Then it wants to apply the same result in each of the subsequent six weeks (again, see Figure 8.4). That's self-contradictory.

■ The only thing that's special about looking exactly six weeks back is that the projector gives you an analysis of your cash position for the next six weeks. But there's no requirement that the baseline should be the same length as the forecast. In fact, in genuine forecasting applications, the baseline is almost always much longer than the forecast horizon. Why not look back 14 weeks, or 26?

■ Those specific weights are arbitrary. Bear in mind that the same weights, ranging from 0.1875 to 3, are used regardless of the company file that's open. It's just a sequence of numbers, each of which happens to be twice as big as the prior number after the second in the sequence, that add to 6. They're better than nothing, but there's nothing magic about them.

Fortunately, there are much stronger ways to forecast cash (and net income as well) than the methods offered in the QuickBooks Cash Flow Projector. Some are based on least-squares regression, some on what's called *exponential smoothing* — a hifalutin name for a straightforward technique that has lots of intuitive appeal and strong practical applications. The section "Going Outside QuickBooks to Project Receipts," later in this chapter, takes a look at smoothing and regression methods.

The trouble with transfers

Earlier, at the end of the "Verifying the Cash Flow Projector" section, I advised you to include Transfer as Transaction type when you are building a custom report to check the projector's numbers. I also implied that it's wrong to do so in the normal course of events. Here's why:

If the projector has a six-week baseline of transactions that includes even one transfer from one bank account to another, you have to include transfers in the custom report too or, the report's figures won't agree with that of the projector. I didn't want to confuse what the projector does with the fact that it does it wrong, so I postponed explaining transfers until now.

First, why is it wrong to include transfers? Because you want to project cash inflows: *new* funds that you can use to help meet upcoming obligations. That's the whole point of using the Cash Flow Projector, after all — to warn you if your near-term costs exceed your near-term cash assets.

If you transferred $5,000 from Savings to Checking last month, that's not new money. You already had that $5,000. And if the projector looks at that increase in the balance of Checking and decides it's new money, it will overestimate your cash receipts for last month by $5,000.

And in turn, if you ask the projector to forecast cash receipts for the next six weeks, based on the last six weeks, its forecast is guaranteed to be an overestimate. Forecasts are always wrong, and you get used to that, but there's no reason to build a *structural* source of error into a process that has enough *random* error in it already.

I have no idea why the developers of the Cash Flow Projector allowed transfers to sneak into the list of permissible transactions for the forecast of cash inflows. But they did, and there are just three fixes:

■ Don't transfer funds among cash accounts.

■ Void any transfers between cash accounts during the six-week period that you tell the projector to use.

■ Forecast your cash receipts outside of QuickBooks and enter them manually into the Cash Flow Projector.

FIGURE 8.14

The transfers in the fourth and sixth weeks have been voided.

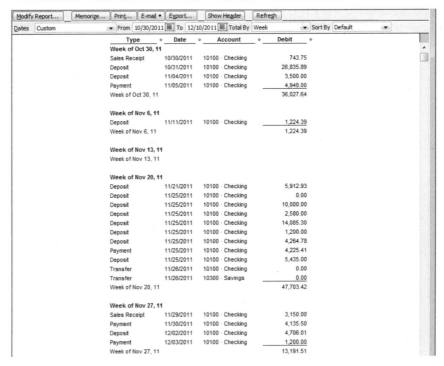

Of these three fixes, the first is impractical, the second requires you to remember to re-establish the transfer after running the projector, and the third requires that you obtain or write a utility to do the work. None of these is a great option. Unfortunately, doing this kind of analysis is too important for your business to skip, so it's best to bite the bullet and choose one.

Figures 8.14 and 8.15 show the custom cash receipts report, and the forecast results in a chart, with the transfer transactions removed. Compare these two figures with Figures 8.7 and 8.8 to see what a dramatic difference the transfers make.

Getting inflow estimates yourself

As explained earlier, there are real problems associated with estimating your cash receipts over the six-week projection period. If you opt for one of the automatic forecasting methods supplied by the projector, you risk running afoul of its disadvantage. If you decide to enter estimated receipts manually, you face the problem of quantifying them — that is, where will the numbers come from?

FIGURE 8.15

FIGURE 8.15

The projected receipts are much lower than in Figure 8.8 because the baseline values are much lower without the transfers

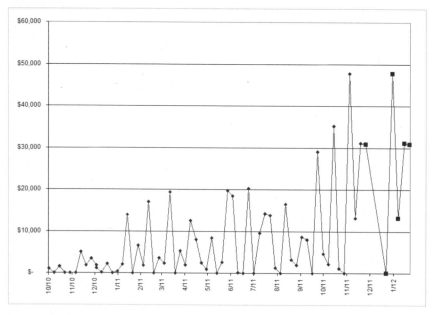

FIGURE 8.16

You'll need to do a little tinkering to get the right figures for the projector.

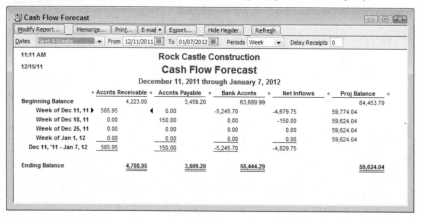

You may have noticed that the projector has a built-in inconsistency: It picks up upcoming costs that you have recorded in QuickBooks automatically, by looking to Accounts Payable. You might expect that it would also pick up upcoming receipts automatically, by looking to Accounts Receivable. But it does not. Perhaps the projector is merely taking the conservative approach of assuming that you will pay your bills on time, but getting paid is a matter for your customer and your customer's conscience. And after all, you can enter Accounts Receivable yourself, if you want. (I'm being as kind as I can manage here.)

So, what's the best way for you to estimate cash receipts during the upcoming six weeks? That depends on how your customers buy from you:

- If your revenue stream relies on invoices and Accounts Receivable, you should use a QuickBooks report to summarize AR on a weekly basis, and then enter the results manually into the projector.

- If your business is the retailing of consumer goods, you have few if any Accounts Receivable to use as the basis for an estimate. You should adopt one of the forecasting methods offered by the projector, or go outside QuickBooks for a forecast that you can then enter — again, manually.

Using the Cash Flow Forecast's Accounts Receivable

The best way to get a forecast of Accounts Receivable is to use the Cash Flow Forecast report. Choose Reports ▶ Company & Financial ▶ Cash Flow Forecast. A sample appears in Figure 8.16.

The figures that you need to move into the projector are your Accounts Receivable, found in the first numeric column in the Cash Flow Forecast report. Notice these two aspects of the report:

- QuickBooks places the date you run the report in its upper-left corner.

- The first column identifies the start of the week for you. When QuickBooks shows "Week of December 11," for example, the data on that row are for December 11 through December 17.

You want to return to the Cash Flow Projector the Accounts Receivable total for the current week and for each of six subsequent weeks. Therefore, make sure that the date you run the report is captured by the first week shown. If it is not, adjust the start date for the report either by overtyping in the From date edit box or by clicking the calendar icon to the right of the box.

You should also adjust the report's To date. By default it shows the current week and three subsequent weeks, followed by the totals for those four weeks and finally by the balance. Either correct the To date in its edit box or click the calendar icon. Set it to a date seven weeks following the To date.

 **Don't forget to click the Refresh button after you've adjusted a report's date range.**

The Cash Flow Forecast report is so useful in this analysis because it assigns Accounts Receivable totals to the correct week by using the due date. Other preset reports in QuickBooks

FIGURE 8.17

For each category, weekly transaction totals are left-aligned and the beginning and ending balances are right-aligned.

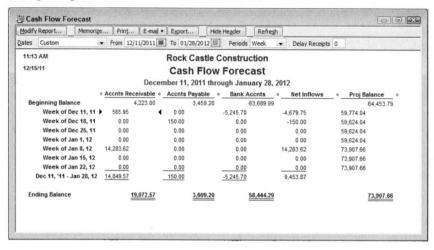

analyze transactions according to the transaction's date. Suppose that you open a Balance Sheet Detail report and set its To and From dates to capture 12/14/11 through 12/27/11. An invoice created on 12/12/11 with a due date of 12/21/11 would not appear in the report. But an invoice created on 12/15/11 with a due date of 12/29/11 would appear. In the case of the Balance Sheet, it's the creation date that governs, because that's when it enters your Accounts Receivable.

But when you're looking at cash flow, it's the due date that matters: the date that you expect to have the cash in hand. So you want a report that attends to the due date instead of the creation date, and that's what the Cash Flow Forecast report provides. To make sure, it's not a bad idea to double-click an entry in the Accounts Receivable column to get a Quick Zoom. There you can verify that the due date for the Accounts Receivable transaction lies within the week where it appears on the Cash Flow Forecast report.

Figure 8.17 shows the Cash Flow Forecast report after adjusting it to capture not just four but seven weeks.

With these figures in hand, you can transcribe them to the Cash Flow Projector's Cash Receipts step. Choose I Want to Project Cash Receipts Manually from the Choose a Projection Method dropdown. Now you can enter the total amount of Accounts Receivable for each week, using either the Itemized Cash Receipts box or the Adjustments boxes.

TIP It's quicker to use the Adjustments boxes. But if you have adjustments that you want to keep separate from Accounts Receivable, use both. QuickBooks combines them in the final projection.

Using the Cash Flow Forecast's Accounts Payable

Another reason to run the Cash Flow Forecaster report with the Cash Flow Projector is that sometimes the projector gets your Accounts Payable wrong.

The reason is unclear. But it is documented that occasionally the projector fails to remove bills that have already been paid from its accounting of Accounts Payable. If this happens, one solution is to restart the projector, running it to completion several times. During this sequence, the projector gradually omits more and more bills that have been paid. Depending on the number of such bills at the outset, the projector might converge on an accurate cash estimate anywhere from the third to the seventh repetition.

Or it might not happen at all. You can see the potential for annoyance.

The Cash Flow Forecast report, by contrast, returns an accurate listing of Accounts Payable (and Accounts Receivable). So while it's not as flexible a tool as the Cash Flow Projector, it's ideal as a check on the results you get from the projector.

It's best to use both methods:

■ Use the Cash Flow Forecast report to get weekly Accounts Receivable and Accounts Payable figures. If you have Accounts Receivable, enter their weekly totals in the projector's Cash Receipts step. Use the Forecast report's Accounts Payable figures as a check against those returned by the projector.

■ Use the Cash Flow Projector, with an assist from the Cash Flow Forecast report, to make adjustments to both upcoming receipts and accounts payable, and to enter expenses that you have not entered into Accounts Payable. Also use the projector if instead of Accounts Receivable you want to use an automatic forecasting method for cash receipts.

Going Outside QuickBooks to Project Receipts

Suppose your business is not the sort that enables you to estimate your upcoming cash receipts by way of a pipeline full of receivables coming due. You're a startup, perhaps, or you sell in small dollar amounts to a large customer base.

If so, the amount of revenue you bring in during the next few weeks is much more a function of your customers' behavior than anything you do as a business owner. In that case, the best guide to the size of your revenue stream in the future is the past. The QuickBooks Cash Flow Projector offers revenue forecasts based on the revenues that came in during the last six weeks, or during the same six-week period one year back.

For the purpose of budgeting your cash position during the next month and a half, those forecasts might be good enough, even with the defects described earlier in "Running the Cash Flow

Projector" section. But if you've used the projector before and haven't been satisfied with the results, or if you think you might like to try forecasting something other than dollar revenues (foot traffic, for example, or units sold for inventory planning), you should think about forecasting with a different software package.

There are many applications that offer good quantitative forecasting functions: R and SAS are two of the more familiar applications. But the application that you're likely to already own, and that's capable of the numeric analysis required, is Microsoft Excel. The remainder of this chapter shows how to export data from QuickBooks so it can be used to forecast in Excel, and then how to move the forecast back into QuickBooks (for use with the Cash Flow Projector, perhaps, or with setting up an operating budget for the next fiscal year).

Forecasting with smoothing

The idea of smoothing is a simple and attractive one. Suppose you have on hand a history of the amount of revenue your company has taken in each week for, say, the past year. At the end of each week, you can forecast the amount of revenue you think you'll bring in next week. After the next week is over, you make another forecast.

When you smooth a series of numbers, weekly revenues in this example, you let each new forecast consist of two parts:

- A part that depends on the amount of revenue taken in during the week just ended
- A part that depends on how much the prior forecast turned out to be wrong

Creating a smoothed forecast

Suppose that it's Friday, January 15, the end of your business week. Your business took in $5,000 from January 9 through January 15. But at close of business on Friday, January 8, one week ago, you forecast that you would take in $4,000 from January 9 through January 15. So your forecast of $4,000 turned out to be too low by $1,000.

You have already decided that for the time being you'll base each forecast on the prior forecast amount (here, $4,000) plus 30% of the amount of error in the last forecast ($5,000 − $4,000) = $1,000. Your forecast for next week is therefore:

```
Next forecast = $4,000 + 30% * $1,000
```

Or $4,300. Just looking at the numbers, that's not very intuitive. But consider the effects of the formula:

- Each new forecast moves the old forecast by an amount, and in a direction, that would have improved the old forecast. The old forecast was too low by $1,000. So in the new forecast, you correct the old one: You increase it by 30% of the amount of the underestimate.
- This value, 30%, is called a *smoothing constant*. (See the next section for more information on this value.)

FIGURE 8.18

The custom summary report is the most convenient way to get receipts by week.

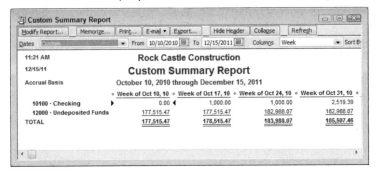

- The result is that the forecasts are self-correcting — they adapt to changes in whatever it is you're forecasting.

Here's an example, starting with a QuickBooks custom summary report. Figure 8.18 shows a portion of that report.

You can structure the report using the following setting in the Modify Report dialog box's Display tab:

- Date range: Custom (for this example, 10/10/2010 to 12/15/2011)
- Display columns by Week
- Display rows by Account list
- No subcolumns

In the Filters tab:

- Accounts: Multiple accounts (Checking, Savings, Petty Cash, and Undeposited Funds
- Transaction Type: Multiple accounts (Sales Receipt, Payment)

To get the report into Excel for analysis:

1. Click the Export button, and choose to export to a new Excel workbook.

2. When you click OK, Excel opens a new workbook with an active worksheet whose final two columns look similar to columns BK and BL in Figure 8.19.

3. Select rows 4 through 6 by dragging through their row headers with your mouse. Choose Format ▶ Cells and set the Number Format to Currency. In Excel 2007, click the Home tab, click Format in the Cells group, and choose Format Cells from the drop-down.

FIGURE 8.19

The cash balances and their dates, exported to an Excel worksheet with smoothing forecasts included.

	BR6 ▼	f_x =0.3*BQ5+0.7*BQ6								
	A	B	BK	BL	BM	BN	BO	BP	BQ	BR
1			Week of Dec 4, 11	Dec 11 - 15, 11						
2	10100 · Checking		34,066.26	55,259.93						
3	12000 · Undeposited Funds		509,616.78	521,692.90						
4	TOTAL		543,683.04	576,952.83	589,881.40	608,912.34	626,112.57	643,862.01	661,446.69	679,080.79
5			6,102.65	33,269.79	12,928.57	19,030.94	17,200.23	17,749.44	17,584.68	17,634.11
6			15,853.97	12,928.57	19,030.94	17,200.23	17,749.44	17,584.68	17,634.11	17,619.28

4. Locate the final Total value in row 4 (this will be a different row if QuickBooks provided weekly data for accounts in addition to Checking and Undeposited Funds). In Figure 8.19 the final Total value is in cell BL4. In the next column, in cell BM4, enter

=BL4+BL6

5. Copy and paste that formula into the next six columns — in effect, extending the range of cash receipts into the future by six weeks, as required by the Cash Flow Projector. For the moment it will appear as though this step does nothing more than extend a constant value into the next six columns.

6. In cell D5, enter

=D4-C4

This formula returns the increase in the balance of the accounts during the second week.

7. Copy and paste the formula in row 5 across as many columns as the QuickBooks report provided data, plus the six you added in Step 4 (in Figure 8.19, the paste goes through cell BR5). You now have the total cash inflows per week from the From date through the To date you selected for the report, plus an additional six weeks to forecast into.

8. In cell E6 enter the formula

=D5

This is your first forecast value. It's called a forecast even though it applies to a date in the past, because it's based on earlier data.

9. In cell F6 enter the formula

=0.3*E5+0.7*E6

10. Copy and paste the formula into cell G6, and on through the column you extended into in Step 4.

The values you arrive at in the final step are your forecasts. You can now enter the final seven values in row 5 into the Cash Flow Projector's Cash Receipts step, using the Adjustment boxes.

It's often helpful to view both the historical cash receipts that you have exported from QuickBooks and the forecasts that result from smoothing. Figure 8.20 displays a chart of actuals and smoothed forecasts over time.

FIGURE 8.20

Notice how the forecasts respond to, or *track*, the actual cash receipts.

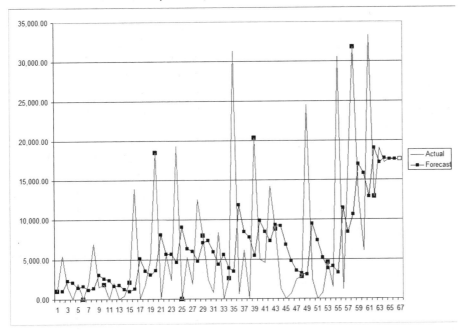

Considerations in smoothed forecasting

The process just described is called *exponential smoothing*. There are a few things to keep in mind:

- **Exponential smoothing is a one-step-ahead method.** Without using a seasonal component, and without using a more complicated method such as double smoothing, it's not typical to use smoothing to forecast more than one step ahead of the current observation. This section uses it anyway, pushing the forecast six weeks into the future, because it strikes a good practical balance between simplicity and mathematical rigor.

- **Choosing a smoothing constant.** This example uses 30%, or 0.3, as the smoothing constant. It's up to you to select a value for the smoothing constant, but values between 10% and 30% are often regarded as conventional. The higher the value, the more quickly the forecasts respond to changes in the baseline values — in this example, that's the cash receipts leading up to the period to be forecast. If you adjust the smoothing constant, you should also adjust the damping factor, the factor with the value 0.7 in the equation shown in Step 7, earlier. The smoothing constant and the damping factor should sum to 1.0.

> **NOTE** If you're familiar with Excel's Solver add-in, you can use it to find the value for the smoothing constant that minimizes the sum of the squared errors between the forecasts and the actual values. The Excel function SUMXMY2 is useful for calculating that criterion.

- **Detrending a series.** If your cash receipts are trending up or down consistently during the past few weeks (say, two to four months) you should consider detrending the series by working with the differences from one week to the next. For more on this issue consult an intermediate text on forecasting or econometrics.

Forecasting with regression

Another useful method of forecasting using Excel is based on regression techniques. These approaches differ from smoothing as to assumptions they make about the history of, for example, the cash receipts that you provide. If you use standard linear regression, you get what's called a *regression line*, a straight one, that minimizes the squared errors between forecasts and actual values (thus the term *least-squares regression*).

If you're new to regression, this might sound complicated. But Excel makes it easy to get regression forecasts, and for now there's no need to worry about violating assumptions. (If you were going to make a mission-critical decision based on regression analysis then there'd be much more to say about assumptions, but here you're still concerned mainly with whether you can expect to have enough cash to meet your bills for the next six weeks.)

Creating a regression forecast

The first two steps involved in creating a regression forecast are identical to those used in creating a forecast by smoothing:

1. Click the Export button, and choose to export to a new Excel workbook.

2. When you click OK, Excel opens a new workbook with an active worksheet whose final two columns look similar to columns BK and BL in Figure 8.19.

3. In cell D5, enter the date shown in cell D1, but enter it without a text label. For example, if the value "Week of Oct 17, 10" is in D1, enter in D5 **10/17/2010**.

4. In cell E5, enter
    =D5+7
    This formula puts a date in E5 that's exactly one week later than the date you entered in D5.

5. Copy and paste the formula in E5 into the range F5 through the end of the data exported from QuickBooks — that is, column BL in this example — and into an additional six columns, through column BR. You now have weekly date values in the range starting with D5 and extending six cells — that is, six weeks — into the future.

6. Enter this formula into cell D6:
    =D4-C4

This formula was used in the smoothing example. It converts weekly balances to weekly increases.

7. Copy the formula in D6 and paste it into the range E6:BL6, the end of the data exported from QuickBooks. Do not extend the formula past the final column from QuickBooks.

8. Select the range D7:BL7. Then type this formula, but don't yet press Enter:
   =TREND(D6:BL6,D5:BL5)
   assuming, again, that the balances from QuickBooks went through column BL and no farther.

9. Instead of simply pressing Enter, hold down the Ctrl and Shift keys simultaneously and then press Enter. This keyboard sequence is termed an *array entry* in Excel. When you have entered an array formula such as this one correctly, Excel surrounds it in the formula box with curly braces.

10. Select the range BM7:BR7 and array-enter this formula by pressing Ctrl+Shift+Enter:
    =TREND(D6:BL6,D5:BL5,BM5:BR5)

The result of the steps appears in Figure 8.21.

The forecasts are now in BM7:BR7 and you can copy them (in addition to the current week's value in cell BL6) into the Adjustments boxes on the Cash Receipts step of the Cash Flow Projector.

Figure 8.22 shows a chart of the actual receipts and the regression forecasts over time.

Considerations in regression forecasting

Entire books have been written about the topics in this section. The coverage here is briefer:

- **What a baseline is.** In forecasting jargon, a *baseline* is a set of observations that appear in the order of date (or even time) each observation was made; the term *time series* is also used. The baselines in this chapter are the actually recorded cash receipts that are exported from QuickBooks into an analysis package such as Excel.

FIGURE 8.21

Notice the braces (curly brackets) around the array formula shown in the formula box.

BR7		*fx* {=TREND(D6:BL6,D5:BL5,BM5:BR5)}									
	A	B	BJ	BK	BL	BM	BN	BO	BP	BQ	BR
1			Week of Nov 27, 11	Week of Dec 4, 11	Dec 11 - 15, 11						
2		10100 · Checking	28,963.61	34,066.26	55,259.93						
3		12000 · Undeposited Funds	508,616.78	509,616.78	521,692.90						
4	TOTAL		537,580.39	543,683.04	576,952.83	576,952.83	576,952.83	576,952.83	576,952.83	576,952.83	576,952.83
5			11/27/2011	12/4/2011	12/11/2011	12/18/2011	12/25/2011	1/1/2012	1/8/2012	1/15/2012	1/22/2012
6			13,191.51	6,102.65	33,269.79						
7			11,873.98	12,064.19	12,254.40	12,444.61	12,634.82	12,825.03	13,015.23	13,205.44	13,395.65

FIGURE 8.22

Linear regression forecasts to not track actuals in the way that smoothed forecasts do.

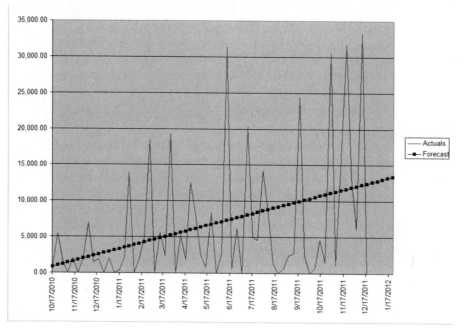

- **Evaluating a baseline's length.** Up to a point, the longer the baseline the better. The more data the equations have to work with, the more precisely they can estimate the factors that define the regression. There's no hard-and-fast rule here — much depends on various diagnostics that Excel can calculate but that are meaningless unless you've read one of those books about regression. But you're likely to be on pretty solid ground if your baseline contains roughly 50 weeks of data. So, if your company has been generating receipts for about a year, you should be well placed to forecast the next few weeks using regression.

- **Pushing the forecast too far.** The math behind the regression equations allows you to push the forecasts out well beyond the relatively brief six weeks that this chapter has covered. In the section concerning creating the regression forecasts, you saw that you can extend the forecast to six subsequent weeks just by supplying another six dates, and extending the TREND equation to include them. There's nothing to stop you from extending the forecast another six, or even 66 weeks. But the reliability of forecasts drops rapidly the farther you get from the final actual observation. Keep your forecast as short as possible, given your purpose for making it.

Monitoring Budget Variances

I f you've ever come across a numeric analysis technique called *statistical process control* you probably associate it with the notion of quality management. That's a logical association, because the technique came about as a method of monitoring manufacturing operations, of getting an early warning that a manufacturing process was going out of control. Suppose that tool wear is causing your factory to turn out o-rings with inside diameters that don't conform to specifications. You want to find out about that as soon as possible so you can take corrective action. Statistical process control (or SPC) can help you diagnose the problem early on.

Like many statistical techniques, though, SPC has applications that go well beyond those that it was originally developed for. For example, the statistical methods and experimental designs that are now used to test pharmaceuticals were originally developed to determine the best ways to brew beer and to plant crops. Similarly, you find SPC methods, originally designed for manufacturing environments, being used in the service, financial, and medical industries.

A few years ago a mid-size hospital contacted me to inquire about arranging for an Excel-based utility that would do SPC for it. The idea was to measure how well the hospital conformed to various standards such as number of accidental needle sticks, the use of restraints on patients, and arterial blood oxygen saturation levels.

But the person who bought my time, and who was responsible for putting the utility into the hospital in the first place, was the hospital's chief operating officer. And he used it to monitor budget variances.

I had never seen SPC used on budgets before and admit that I had no idea that it made sense. But it does. When the budget doesn't conform to the actual results, something's gone wrong. It could be in the planning process, or in the management of sales, or the control of expenses. SPC can help you identify that sort of problem, as well as when it started to occur, and that knowledge puts you well on the way to a solution.

In this chapter I'll try to convince you of that — and, incidentally, show you how you can use QuickBooks' budgeting and reporting tools to give you more insight on how well a company manages to its budgets.

Of course, if you're to benefit from the analysis of actual results compared to budgeted amounts, you need to have set up a budget in your company file. That process isn't explained in any detail in this book — it's more a topic for a book on how to use QuickBooks than a book on analyzing the business data found in QuickBooks. Briefly, though, if you choose Company ▶ Planning & Budgeting ▶ Set Up Budgets, you start a wizard that walks you through preliminary steps and then turns matters over to you. It can be a tedious process but it will take less time if you have a year's worth of actuals on which to base a new year's budget.

Budget variances aren't the only financial indicator that you can profitably analyze using SPC. It can be useful to monitor the ratios explored in Chapter 7, particularly the ratios that tend to vary frequently (and perhaps unpredictably) such as inventory turns ratios and average collection periods. Keeping your eye on these indicators using SPC will help you stop a minor problem from getting entirely out of hand.

Understanding Process Control Charts

The notion of charting a process is built on two basic characteristics:

- A process has a central tendency, most typically a long-term average. The long-term average of your company's variance in its budget for monthly subcontractors expenses might be $0. Some months you spend more than budgeted, some months less, and the long-term average is near $0 if your budgets make sense and your actual expenditures are rational.

- A process has spread, or variability. One month, a budget variance might be $500. Another month it might be –$750. One measure of this sort of variability is the range, and in this example the range, or the maximum minus the minimum, is $1,250.

A process control chart shows these two characteristics, along with the individual measurements, in a format that helps you visualize the quantitative nature of the process. Figure 9.1 has a simple example of a process control chart.

There are three main elements in the chart in Figure 9.1:

- Center line. It represents the process's measure of central tendency, sometimes called the long-term average. It could be either the arithmetic average or the median. In the figure, it is the horizontal line representing an average budget variance of about $5,000.

FIGURE 9.1

The horizontal axis on an SPC chart is always a measure of time: quarters, months, days, or even time of day.

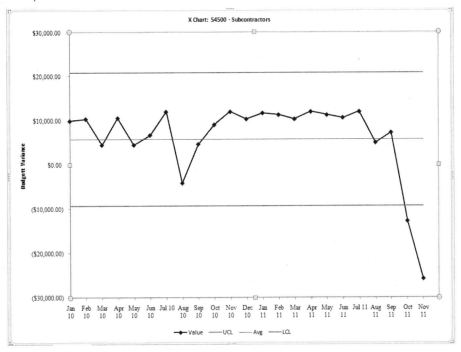

- Control limits. These are the two horizontal lines above and below the center line. The area that lies between these limits shows where you expect all, or nearly all, the individual data points to fall.

- Individual observations. Each data point represents an observation on a particular date or range of dates such as a week.

An individual observation might itself be an average. In some processes, such as budget variances, there's only one possible observation at a particular time. You can have only one monthly budget variance for a particular account as of a particular month. In a case such as this, the data point on the control chart is that single observation. But if you're applying SPC to the inside diameters of o-rings, you might chart the average diameter of 100 o-rings on a given day.

The chart you see in Figure 9.1 is usually called an *X chart*. In SPC jargon, you refer generically to any given observation as "X" (just as you originally did in Algebra I). When you're charting averages (unlike here), the chart is usually called an *X-bar chart*. That's because the usual statistical symbol for the average of a sample is an X with a horizontal line, or bar, atop the X. As you'll see in this chapter's section on "Understanding the moving range charts," there is an *MR* (moving range) *chart* to accompany the X chart.

Control limits

The control limits you see in Figure 9.1 are critically important in SPC analysis. They are always built on some measure of the variability in the process — that is, by how great an amount the individual observations differ from one another. The math that underlies SPC charts uses that measure of variability to calculate and locate the upper and lower control limits. As a result, in the normal course of events they capture over 99% of individual observations.

Therefore, if you see an individual observation that is outside the control limits, either you're looking at one of the roughly 1 in 400 that occur simply by chance, or something has gone wrong with the process.

Depending on the situation, control limits are calculated using ranges, standard deviations, or moving ranges. This section explains each approach, but not in any mind-numbing detail.

Standard deviations

If you're new to the concept of a standard deviation, you can think of it as the average amount by which the observations in a set of data differ from the simple average of the full data set. At least, that's not a bad place to start. The properties of the standard deviation have been extensively studied and are well understood, and it has some aspects that make it a particularly useful measure of the amount of variability in a data set.

In particular, the standard deviation uses every item in a data set to calculate the variability in the data set. By contrast, the range — explained next — uses only two data points.

Ranges

The range is the simplest way to estimate the variability in a series of data points. You just take the largest value and subtract the smallest value. At the time that SPC techniques were being developed, in the mid-20th century, it was important that a person be able to estimate the amount of variability in a data set simply and quickly. The calculations were usually done with paper and pencil, frequently right on the factory floor. The need for a quick and easy calculation, in a noisy and distracting environment, was a powerful argument for using the range to estimate variability.

But the range uses only two data points. Suppose you had 10 observations, as follows: 1, 8, 8, 8, 9, 9, 9, 10, 10, 10.

The range is 9. As it happens, the standard deviation is 2.66. With nine of the observations clustering at the top end of the range, within two points of one another, you can successfully argue that the standard deviation is a better expression of the amount of variability in the data set than is the range.

Nevertheless, some traditionalists prefer to use the range as a measure of variability in SPC applications.

Moving ranges

The third way to estimate variability in a data set — at least, for SPC purposes — is by way of the moving range, and it's the method used in this chapter's examples. Its use is more or less forced on you; it's not a matter of choice or of theoretical issues, as it would be if you were deciding between using the standard deviation or the range.

As I noted earlier in the chapter, the kind of data covered here tends to have only one observation per time period. Returning to the o-ring example, you might have many o-rings to check each day. You would measure their diameters and record that information, and then calculate the standard deviation of the o-ring diameters for that day. After quite a few days of recording the data, you could take the average of all those standard deviations and the result would be the basis for the control limits on your SPC chart.

That's not feasible if you're monitoring budget variances or inventory turns. For the month of February, say, there's only one monthly budget variance for the Job Materials account, and it is not possible to calculate a measure of variability for February when there's only one observation available from February — there's nothing else for it to differ from.

It would be mathematically possible to gather all the monthly budget variances for the Job Materials account, from 1/1/1995 through 12/31/2011, and calculate their standard deviation. But that approach addresses the wrong sort of variability. You would get a standard deviation, but it would address how much the individual variances deviate from the overall average of all budget variances in the particular account.

That's not the sort of variability you're interested in here. You'd like to know as soon as you get an outlier — that is, a budget variance that's unusually large, whether positive or negative — and therefore the kind of variability you're interested in is based on the differences between each period and the next.

That difference is called the *moving range*. The difference in the variances for January and for February is one moving range. The difference in the variances for February and for March is another moving range — and so on. In effect, you take the average of all those moving ranges, do a little statistical hand-waving, and the result is an estimate of the process variability. (The software you use usually does the statistical hand-waving on your behalf.)

Establishing the limits

Regardless of how you calculate the process variability, via standard deviations, ranges, or moving ranges, you wind up with a value called *sigma*. The term "sigma" is used to mean "standard deviation," but it's employed regardless of which calculation you have used.

Suppose the calculations result in a finding that the sigma value for your budget variance process is $400. SPC charts call for a *three-sigma* upper control limit and a *three-sigma* lower control limit. That is, you multiply the value of sigma — $400 in this example — by 3, and add the result to (and subtract the result from) the long-term process average. If that average is $0, your upper and lower control limits are $1,200 and –$1,200, respectively.

The value of three sigmas is chosen because going three sigmas up and three sigmas down from the long-term average captures, as noted earlier, more than 99% of the variances for the account that supplied the variances. If you see next month's budget variance fall above the upper limit or below the lower limit, you see that either something very unusual has occurred (and after all, that does happen every few hundred time periods) or something has happened to the process of managing to the budget.

Maybe the people who work in the Job Materials department already know that they are well over budget for the month, just because they were in the room when the purchases occurred. But if you are analyzing the budget variance figures you get from QuickBooks, you can view that variance in a historical context. When you have your next meeting with that department — a meeting that might well be a testy one — you'll arrive armed with the knowledge that a budget variance of this size is a once-in-10-years event.

Tighter control limits

You often see SPC charts with more than just the three-sigma upper and lower control limits. These charts include one- and two-sigma limits in addition to the three-sigma limits. Figure 9.2 has an example.

The actual expectancies are as follows:

- Between the center line and a one-sigma limit: 34.1%
- Between the one- and the two-sigma limits: 13.6%
- Between the two- and the three-sigma limits: 2.1%
- Beyond the three-sigma limit: 0.1%

The figures just given are for one side of the chart only; that is, either above or below the center line. You double the percentages to determine the amount of observations that are expected to exist on either side of the center line. For example, 34.1% of the observations are expected to fall between the center line and one sigma *above* it; another 34.1% of the observations are expected to fall between the center line and one sigma *below* it. So, 68.2% of the observations are expected to fall between one sigma above and one sigma below the center line.

Using the rules

The one- and two-sigma limits are typically used with something called the Western Electric Rules. These so-called rules are simply guidelines developed in the 1950s by the Western Electric Company to help its managers make more informed decisions about their manufacturing processes.

The idea is that there are telltale signs that a process is going out of control, other than a single data point that's outside the three-sigma limits. Briefly, those telltales, or "rules," are as follows:

1. One observation outside the three-sigma limits.

FIGURE 9.2

The one- and two-sigma limits help you react more quickly to a process that is going out of control.

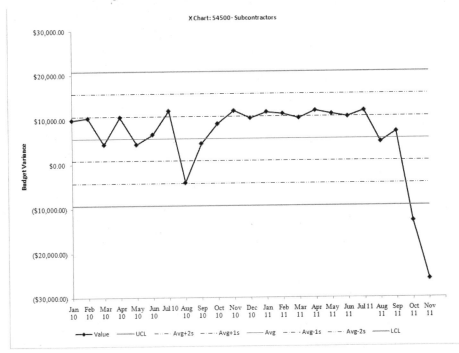

2. Two of three consecutive observations outside a two-sigma limit.

3. Four of five consecutive observations outside a one-sigma limit.

4. Eight consecutive observations on the same side of the center line.

The rules become a little more stringent the closer you get to the center line. The reason is that more observations occur, just by distributional probability, between the center line and a one-sigma limit than occur beyond that one-sigma limit; similarly, more observations occur between one sigma and the two-sigma limit than beyond the two-sigma limit, Because we expect to find more observations closer to the center line, the rules get more stringent about the number of consecutive observations needed to signal a possible out-of-control situation.

A Rule 2 violation

Figure 9.3 shows a process made up of monthly budget variances that is going out of control.

Notice the final three data points at the rightmost end of the chart. Beside each point is the numeral 2, to indicate that the second of the four rules has been violated. Two of the three consecutive data points are beyond the two-sigma limit (see the legends at the bottom of the chart for the correspondence between a line pattern and which limit it represents).

FIGURE 9.3

The labels by the data points, in this case at the right end of the chart, indicate which rule has been violated.

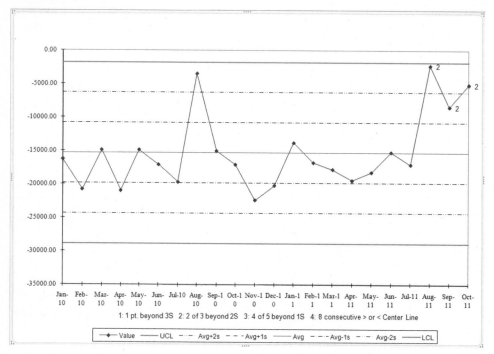

If you buy into the Western Electric rules, the violation indicated by those three data points indicates that the process has begun to go out of control. If you don't buy into them, they are nevertheless a handy way to tell that something unusual has occurred. The actual likelihood that two of these three points would be found beyond the two-sigma limit (and the third, in this case, beyond the one-sigma limit) is less than one in a thousand, unless something in the process has changed.

Usually, a change in the nature of a process is undesirable. In the normal course of events, the processes that your company runs — from manufacturing processes to financial activities — occur the way you want them to. Perhaps not optimally, but well enough that you've stayed in business. So when a process goes out of control that's probably bad enough to get your close attention.

Not always, though. So far we're dealing with budget variances. If you glance back at Figure 9.3 you'll notice that the actual values of the variances, the plotted data points, are all negative. They were calculated by subtracting the budget from the actual, so a negative value means that less was spent than was budgeted.

That's not a good situation, of course — it doesn't speak well for the budgeting process, or how well the company is managing to its budgets, or possibly both. But it's probably not as bad as spending *more* money than budgeted, month after month after month.

Because two variables are involved, the budgeted amounts and the actual expenditures, it would make sense to look at the budgeted amounts and actuals for the first 19 months and try to understand why the actuals were all less than the budget. And then check the final three months to determine why the variances suddenly got so much smaller. Did the budget amounts suddenly change? Did prices you pay suddenly spike?

Again, it's not necessary to think of the Western Electric guidelines as hard–and-fast rules, although many users of SPC techniques think of them in exactly that way. You can think of them as leading indicators warning you that something unusual may be going on that needs management's attention.

Two rule violations in one chart

Figure 9.4 shows another example of budget variances. The data come from the Rock Castle Construction sample file, and the account used is Subcontractors (part of the Cost of Goods Sold accounts).

It's not uncommon for a single chart to have more than one rule violation. In Figure 9.4, you see a Rule 1 violation for August 2010, and a Rule 4 violation extending from October 2010 through May 2011. A Rule 1 violation, as explained earlier, is one extreme data point that lies outside the upper control limit. (You can think of the upper control limit as a three-sigma limit if you want, but *upper control limit*, or UCL, is the more common term.)

A Rule 4 violation is eight consecutive observations on one side or another of the center line. In Figure 9.4, budget variances stay consistently below the center line for eight straight months. Without knowing anything about Rock Castle Construction beyond its financials (it is an imaginary company, after all), you might sensibly guess that management saw that one spike in August 2010 when the subcontractors account actually went $5,000 over budget. The COO was sufficiently unhappy that whoever was responsible for subcontractors kept the actual expenditures down for the next three quarters.

Interpreting the Rule 1 violation

I'm generally more comfortable evaluating Rule 2, 3, and 4 violations than I am Rule 1 violations. When you're looking at two of three consecutive points beyond two sigmas, or four of five consecutive points beyond one sigma, there's some confirmation built into the assessment. Those violations consist of more than just one point sticking out beyond a three-sigma limit.

After all, you're going to encounter an outlier like the one for August 2010 in Figure 9.4 every 300 or 400 observations, due to nothing more insidious than simple random chance. Apart from chance, there's always the possibility that someone made a data-entry error. But it is much less likely that several data-entry errors — consecutive errors at that — could cause a violation of Rules 2, 3, or 4. So when you do see a Rule 1 violation, you should always consider the pos-

FIGURE 9.4

A Rule 1 violation is followed by a Rule 4 violation.

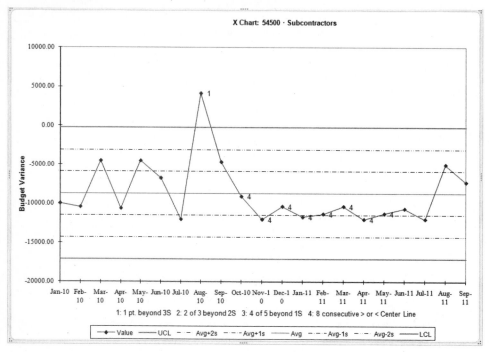

sibility that it's benign — the result of a typographical error or the inevitable, random anomaly — and not a process that's going out of control.

If the Rule 1 violation is confirmed by other rule violations, whether earlier or later, that's a different story, and you need not be quite so blasé about the Rule 1 violation.

Getting Budget Variances

The process of creating control charts based on budget variances takes two main steps: calling for and exporting the QuickBooks report, and running an Excel utility based on the exported report. This section walks you through the process.

This book's Web page — you'll find the URL on the back cover — has a link to a site where you can download an Excel workbook that does statistical process control. It is stripped down and tailored specifically to the QuickBooks budget report. It's also free. Before you can use it, though, you need to get the data out of QuickBooks and into Excel. The next section shows you how to do that.

FIGURE 9.5

Notice that the report's columns alternate between actual amounts and budgeted amounts.

Rock Castle Construction
Profit & Loss Budget vs. Actual
January 1 through December 15, 2011

Accrual Basis

	Jan 11	Budget	Feb 11	Budget	Mar 11	Budget
Ordinary Income/Expense						
Income						
40100 · Construction Income						
40110 · Design Income	3,000.00		3,150.00		3,300.00	
40120 · Equipment Rental Income	0.00		0.00		0.00	
40130 · Labor Income	17,229.00	8,500.00	12,420.00	8,500.00	15,116.50	8,500.00
40140 · Materials Income	4,118.84	12,000.00	6,539.00	12,000.00	5,369.80	12,000.00
40150 · Subcontracted Labor Income	600.00	17,500.00	2,738.00	17,500.00	1,754.95	17,500.00
40199 · Less Discounts given	0.00	100.00	0.00	100.00	0.00	100.00
40100 · Construction Income - Other	0.00		0.00		0.00	
Total 40100 · Construction Income	24,947.84	38,100.00	24,847.00	38,100.00	25,541.25	38,100.00
40500 · Reimbursement Income						
40510 · Mileage Income	0.00		0.00		0.00	
40520 · Permit Reimbursement Income	0.00		311.75		0.00	
40530 · Reimbursed Freight & Delivery	0.00		0.00		0.00	
40500 · Reimbursement Income - Other	0.00		0.00		0.00	
Total 40500 · Reimbursement Income	0.00		311.75		0.00	
Total Income	24,947.84	38,100.00	25,158.75	38,100.00	25,541.25	38,100.00

Laying out the data

QuickBooks has a report, Profit & Loss Budget vs. Actual, that shows you in one place the budgeted and actual figures for income statement accounts over time. Figure 9.5 shows that report as run on the Rock Castle Construction sample file. This report forms the basis for the control charts that Excel will produce for you.

There are just two columns for each month: a column that shows the actuals, headed by a label that shows the month and year, and an adjacent column that shows the budgeted amounts.

Establishing the report

Of course you need to have entered a budget in the company file before QuickBooks will even run this report. Assuming you've done that, the following steps will create the report shown in Figure 9.5.

1. Choose Reports ▶ Budgets & Forecasts ▶ Budget vs. Actual.

2. Budgets are created in QuickBooks on an annual basis. If you have created more than one budget, you'll have to select the budget year you want from a dropdown. Make your selection and click Next.

3. Select the Account by Month layout and click Next. In the final dialog box, click Finish.

The report initially appears as shown in Figure 9.6.

FIGURE 9.6

The percent and actual variances appear by default.

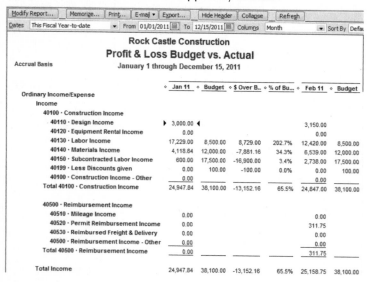

FIGURE 9.7

Leave the Show Actuals checkbox selected, but clear the $ Difference and % of Budget checkboxes.

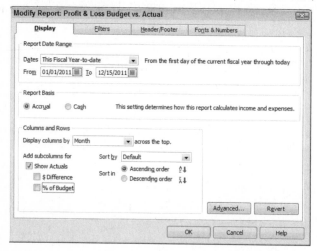

As you'll see, for the purpose of running this data through an SPC routine, you'll need to adjust the report layout because the percent and dollar variances should not be displayed. Click Modify Report, and in the Modify Report dialog box clear the $ Difference and % of Budget checkboxes. Then click OK to return to the report. The Modify Report dialog box is shown in Figure 9.7.

Normally you want to compare actuals with budgets on an annual basis, which is the reason QuickBooks asks you to select a budget year in Step 2. But there's no special reason to restrict the process control analysis to a 12-month period. And generally the more data, the longer the baseline — and the more precise and the more informative the analysis.

So it makes sense to adjust the From date at the top of the report to the earliest date that the company had both a budget and actuals. The same is true of the To date: Set it to the latest date for which there are budgeted amounts and actual results. After you have changed these two dates, click the Refresh button to force QuickBooks to update the report according to the new date range you have established.

It won't do any particular harm, but if you choose a From date that precedes the month in which you first had both a budget and actual values, the control chart will display nothing of value before it reaches a date that has a true variance. For example, if you had neither a budget nor actuals for an account before January 2009, including 2008 in the report will cause 12 months' worth of $0 variances to appear in the chart. And all those zeros are used in calculating the moving ranges used to establish the location of the control limits, so including too early a start date can result in control limits that are based in part on meaningless data.

Unless you know beforehand when both budgeted and actual amounts were recorded in QuickBooks, the best approach is to specify a fairly early From date and the final complete month as the To date. Examine the resulting report so that you can locate the date where you want the control chart to begin, and adjust the From date accordingly. (Don't forget to click Refresh.)

Exporting the report

Now the report is in shape to export. Click Export and choose to export to a new Excel workbook. When the export is complete, switch to Excel, which will show you a worksheet that looks like the one shown in Figure 9.8.

If you don't see the header information on the worksheet, it is sent instead to Excel's Page Setup options. Don't worry about it: The SPC software allows for the header's presence or absence on the worksheet.

It often happens that when you export a report from QuickBooks to Excel, you need to rearrange the data before you can do further analysis. The reason is that many QuickBooks reports show dates left to right; that is, a column for January is followed by a column for February, then one for March, and so on. The rows in the report typically represent accounts or transactions, depending on whether you have chosen a summary or a detail report.

FIGURE 9.8

Notice the active cell: Your choice of account here determines which account is analyzed.

		Jul 10	Budget	Aug 10	Budget	Sep 10	Budget
	Rock Castle Construction						
	Profit & Loss Budget vs. Actual						
	January 1, 2009 through December 15, 2011						
22	Total 40500 · Reimbursement Income	225.00		0.00		0.00	
23	Total Income	5,354.56	38,100.00	36,575.00	38,100.00	16,115.00	38,100.00
24	Cost of Goods Sold						
25	50100 · Cost of Goods Sold	0.00	3,000.00	0.00	3,000.00	0.00	3,000.00
26	54000 · Job Expenses						
27	54100 · Bond Expense	0.00		0.00		0.00	
28	54200 · Equipment Rental	0.00	150.00	0.00	150.00	0.00	150.00
29	54300 · Job Materials	2,458.75	10,000.00	2,769.87	10,000.00	0.00	10,000.00
30	54400 · Permits and Licenses	225.00	150.00	0.00	150.00	0.00	150.00
31	54500 · Subcontractors	0.00	12,000.00	16,125.00	12,000.00	7,325.00	12,000.00
32	54520 · Freight & Delivery	0.00	50.00	0.00	50.00	0.00	50.00
33	54599 · Less Discounts Taken	0.00		0.00		0.00	
34	54000 · Job Expenses - Other	0.00		0.00		0.00	
35	Total 54000 · Job Expenses	2,683.75	22,350.00	18,894.87	22,350.00	7,325.00	22,350.00
36	Total COGS	2,683.75	25,350.00	18,894.87	25,350.00	7,325.00	25,350.00
37	Gross Profit	2,670.81	12,750.00	17,680.13	12,750.00	8,790.00	12,750.00

But Excel analyses in general, and charts in particular, prefer that the data be turned 90 degrees from the QuickBooks orientation. For example, Excel considers a COGS account as a field, and the dollar amounts for COGS from month to month as records in that field. Most of Excel's analysis tools work best, and some work *only*, if the data is laid out with a field occupying a column and individual observations for that field occupying different rows in the column. Because a QuickBooks report has a field — in this example, the COGS account — occupy a row, and has individual monthly actuals for that account occupy different columns, it's just the reverse of what you need in Excel.

So you often have to use the Excel interface to transpose the data in a QuickBooks report. The SPC utility that you can obtain via the Wiley Web page for this book takes care of all that for you. Just export the report to Excel and click the SPC Charts item, as described next.

Plotting budget variances

With the report ready for analysis, you need to open the SPC workbook you obtained from this book's Web site. That workbook contains code written in Visual Basic for Applications (VBA, for short). The code puts the data that you exported from QuickBooks through some preliminary routines, calculating the budget variances and the moving ranges, testing for violations of the Western Electric Rules, and so on. Then it creates the process control charts shown earlier in this chapter.

The code just mentioned is what Microsoft Office applications terms a *macro*. It's not a particularly accurate term, but it's a legacy of the earliest versions of Excel when there really was an

Excel 4 macro language. It was arcane and comparatively weak, and when Microsoft replaced it with support for the Visual Basic programming language, the term "macro" was retained.

Visual Basic is much more powerful than the old Excel 4 macro language, and brings with it the possibility of doing genuine harm to someone's data, if the person supplying the code is so motivated. Therefore Excel warns you if you're opening a workbook that contains macros, and if you see that warning message you should not finish opening the workbook unless you trust its source.

Enabling the macros

When you open a workbook that contains macros, you should see a warning to that effect.

I say *should* because it's possible that Excel's security level has been set so low that you see no warning. That's a bad idea, and if you see no warning when you open the SPC workbook you should stop and do nothing else with Excel (and possibly other Microsoft Office applications) until you have your arms around the macro security issue.

If you're using Excel 2003 or earlier, the macro warning comes in the form of a message box and it's hard to miss. You can choose to disable macros, enable macros, or request more information. In the case of the SPC workbook, you can safely enable the macros.

If you're using Excel 2007, under most circumstances the warning is a good bit more subtle. Between the Ribbon and the worksheet grid you'll see the message bar informing you that the workbook's macros have been disabled. Click the message bar's Options button, choose Enable this Content, and click OK.

After enabling the macros, select the cell with the name of the account you want to analyze. Because of the way QuickBooks justifies the account names in the cells of an exported report, you might want to double check that you have the right selection by looking at the formula box at the top of the worksheet — that box always shows the contents of the active cell.

Your next action again depends on the version of Excel that you're running:

- If you are running Excel 2003 or earlier, choose Data ▶ SPC Charts.
- If you are running Excel 2007, click Add-Ins on the Ribbon. (The Add-Ins tab appears when you open a workbook that contains macros, and choose to enable them.) The Add-Ins tab has a group labeled Menu Commands, where you'll find SPC Charts. Click it.

After you've clicked the SPC Charts menu item, Excel takes over, and the first thing it does is check to see whether your exported report is laid out properly with actual dollar amounts alternating in columns with budgeted amounts. If it finds that the columns are not laid out as it wants, Excel displays a message about the layout and the macro stops running. You'll have to switch back to QuickBooks and re-create the report, this time with the percent and dollar difference checkboxes cleared.

FIGURE 9.9

Select the options you want Excel to use for control chart processing.

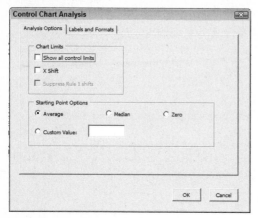

FIGURE 9.10

The main process control chart is often called an *X chart,* and the practice of allowing the center line to shift is called an *X shift.*

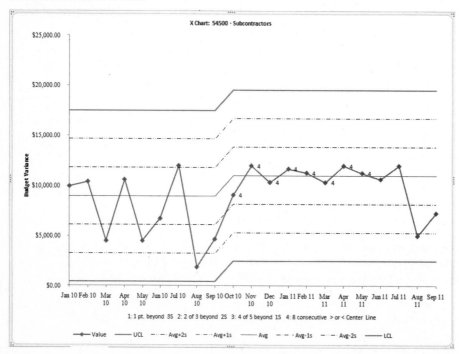

Selecting analysis options

After Excel completes its check of the report data layout, it displays the dialog box shown in Figure 9.9.

Figure 9.9 shows the Analysis Options tab only (see Figure 9.11 for the Labels and Formats tab). The three checkboxes under Chart Limits are not mutually exclusive. Their effects are described shortly.

Show All Control Limits checkbox

The first checkbox, Show All Control Limits, determines whether all six control limits are shown in the chart. If you select the checkbox, all six limits (lower control limit, −2 sigma, −1 sigma, +1 sigma, +2 sigma, and the upper control limit) appear in the chart. Seeing all the limits in the chart is particularly helpful if you're using the Western Electric Rules as guidelines to what's happening with the budget variance process.

X Shift checkbox

This checkbox controls the placement of the center line and control limits when one of the Western Electric Rules has been violated. The idea is that when that occurs, the average level of the process has shifted, either up or down. In that case, subsequent observations should be evaluated according to the location of the process's new measure of central tendency.

The center line is shifted to a level that is the average of the data points that caused the rule violation, and the control limits are also relocated. Figure 9.10 shows an example of how this effect can appear in a control chart.

In Figure 9.10, notice that the eight points that are labeled as Rule 4 violations are all above the center line *where it was located prior to the X shift* — and it's those points that cause the shift. The center line's new location is the average value of those eight points.

Before adopting a shift in level such as the one shown in Figure 9.10, there are various statistical tests that should be run. Because the SPC workbook that is made available to you works only with budget variances, and not high precision machining tolerances or measures of pharmaceutical product quality, those tests are not so critical. You might find it useful to allow the process to shift level in response to a rule violation.

Suppressing Rule 1 Violations checkbox

This checkbox is implied by a previous section, "Interpreting the Rule 1 violation."

The option is disabled unless you choose to implement X shift analysis. If you select the Suppress Rule 1 option, and therefore if you have chosen to implement X shift analysis, any Rule 1 violations found will not cause a shift in the location of the center line and the control limits.

I have had enough clients complain about typographical errors causing Rule 1 violations in their SPC charts that I've provided this option. The point in question gets charted, of course, as does the data label 1 next to the data point. But while the other rule violations shift the locations of the center line and control limits, the Rule 1 violation does not.

You are reminded of this setting in the legend at the bottom of the chart. Instead of a brief reminder of the meaning of a Rule 1 violation, you see the message, in red and boldface, that the rule has been suppressed.

Starting point options

The starting point options pertain to where the X chart's center line is initially placed; that is, the center line's value as of the first date that's charted. Your choice here can have a profound effect on the charted results. Whichever option you choose will determine the value of the first point of the center line, and, unless you choose X shift analysis, it will determine *all* values of the center line.

In turn, that determines the locations of the various control limits. They are always offset by a constant amount from the center line, so your choice affects the location of all control limits in the chart. Because process control charts evaluate individual data points in terms of the Western Electric Rules, and those rules are based on the location of the control limits, your choice will affect whether the individual budget variances are regarded as rule violations.

The good news is that if you don't like how a chart behaves as a result of one choice of a starting point, you can close the workbook that contains the chart and create another. You don't need to start over with a new QuickBooks export. Just select the exported report in Excel and click SPC Charts again, choosing a different starting point option.

Starting point: Average

The term "average" here means the usual arithmetic mean; that is, the total of all the budget variances in the chart divided by the number of variances. This option is often the most useful starting point. Unless your data is highly skewed from the theoretical normal distribution, you wind up with fewer rule violations if you select the Average as the starting point.

Starting point: Median

If you find that you get more rule violations than you would have expected from using Average as the starting point, and if those violations are found mostly on the same side of the center line (either above it or below it), consider using the Median instead. A skewed distribution of budget variances causes a center line based on the Average to occupy a position in the chart that isn't really in the center. The median, the value of the budget variance that is the 50th percentile among the charted budget variances, could bring better balance to your control chart.

Starting point: Zero

In an ideal world you would have a set of budget variances that were all zero. The people who manage the various accounts would either take in or expend money exactly in accord with the budget. This isn't an ideal world, but you're probably still shooting for budget variances that are as small as possible — certainly on the expense side of the equation.

Setting Zero as the starting point in the chart tends to emphasize it as a goal for the process. Variances that cling closely to the center line when you select Average as the starting point might appear as rule violations when you start with Zero.

This option has greater usefulness in manufacturing applications, when you're trying to measure conformance to particular process specifications and zero has meaning as a physical measure of departure from a specification.

Starting point: Custom value

The intent of this option is similar to that of the Zero option. If you have identified a goal, perhaps not as ambitious as zero, for budget variances, select this option and enter the value of that goal in the associated edit box. Now when you continue with construction of the chart, the individual data points — the budget variances — are located within control limits based on the location of the custom value you entered, and which appears as the value of the center line.

Selecting Labels and Formats options

Figure 9.11 shows the Labels and Formats tab of the Control Chart Analysis dialog box.

The specific options are as follows.

Chart Labels: Chart

Use this edit box to enter any label you want to appear at the top of the control chart. It defaults to the name of the account that you selected just before calling SPC Charts. If you want to use some other label, just drag across the default value with your mouse pointer and type the verbiage you prefer.

Chart Labels: Y-axis

Anything you type into this edit box is used as a label for the vertical, Y-axis at the left of the chart. There is no default label as there is for the Chart label. If you leave the edit box blank, the label "Value" appears to the left of the Y-axis.

You can select only one of the format options for Y-axis labels in the edit box. These labels help you determine where the center line and control limits, as well as the individual data points, are located on a numeric scale. When you see the chart, if you don't like the appearance of the labels, you can always change their format using the Excel user interface. The quickest way is to right-click the Y-axis and choose Format Axis from the contextual menu.

Y-axis Labels Format: Currency

Select this option if you want to show labels in the chart's vertical, Y-axis with dollar signs and thousands separators. Neither decimal points nor cents appear.

FIGURE 9.11

These options have no effect on the analysis. They control only the appearance of the results.

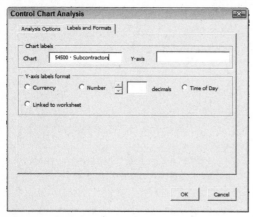

FIGURE 9.12

Compare with Figure 9.11. This chart does not call for an X shift, and you can see the Rule 4 violations above the original center line location.

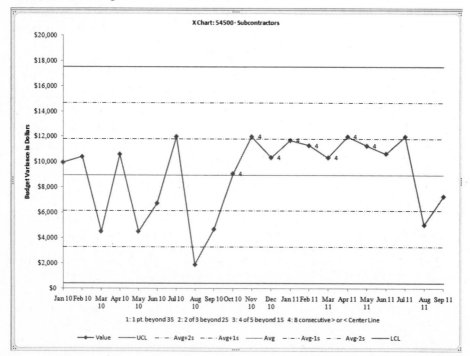

Y-axis Labels: Number

Select the Number option if you want to omit the dollar sign from the Y-axis labels. You can also use the spinner to control the number of decimals displayed in the labels. (The spinner is disabled until you select the Number option.) Click the ▲ button to increase the number of decimals, and the ▼ button to decrease it.

Y-axis Labels: Linked to Worksheet

This option causes Excel to use the same format for the axis labels as is used in the worksheet. In turn, that is determined by options you choose in QuickBooks when you create the report.

Figure 9.12 shows a control chart with the account name in the chart label, the phrase "Budget Variance in Dollars" as the Y-axis label, and currency as the Y-axis label format.

Understanding the moving range chart

When you run the SPC Charts utility, you see the X chart that has been covered extensively in this chapter. That chart, of course, plots individual budget variances over time, and shows where they fall in the context of the various control limits that Excel calculates.

Rationale for moving range charts

If you recall from the "Control limits" section early in this chapter, the moving range creates a measure of the variability in the process you've presented to Excel. Because there is one measure only per time period, the only way of quantifying the right kind of variability is through the moving range. With only one measurement possible on a given date, there is no within-date variability.

The situation is different when there are many possible measures available at any time, and that's the typical situation in manufacturing. A random sample of 10 or 20 items from a job lot provides those measures, and the analyst can apply either the standard deviation or the range to those same-date measures.

That sort of situation makes it important to look not only at the X-bar chart, which shows each average, but also the S chart, which shows each standard deviation. It is possible for compensating defects on a given day to cancel one another out in the average measurement, and the only way you'd recognize that had occurred is by way of the S chart.

Suppose that on a normal day, people on the factory floor sample 10 o-rings from the production line and measure their inside diameter; they typically find that the diameter is anywhere from 1.7 cm to 1.8 cm. They report the summary statistics to you, and on most days you note that the average is about 1.75 cm and the standard deviation is about 0.03 cm.

Today, though, you see that the quality report shows the usual average of 1.75 but the standard deviation is 0.1, more than three times normal. Looking more closely at the data, you see that of the 10 o-rings, one had an interior diameter of 1.9 while another had 1.5. These measures are outside the process specifications, and it's possible that 20% of today's entire run might be out of spec.

This MR chart does not suggest that the moving ranges jump around much until the final three dates.

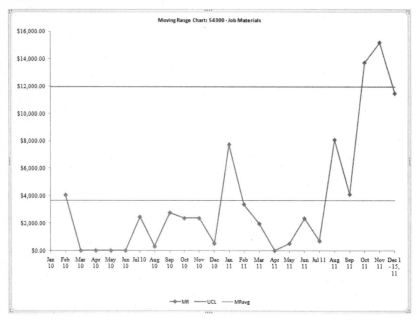

You wouldn't have caught the problem if you'd been looking only at the average measure, the amount that plotted on the X-bar chart. But it would appear in the S chart, where you would see a long line of standard deviations close to 0.03 and then one from today's run of 0.1 — a sore thumb.

In principle you can draw the same sort of conclusion from a moving range (MR) chart when you have one observation only for each date. Nevertheless, the MR chart cannot tell you much more than you have already learned from the X chart. When two consecutive observations are relatively far apart, you know that the associated moving range value is relatively large. When the observations are relatively close, the associated MR is fairly small.

Still, it's a good idea to keep an eye on the moving ranges, and they are found on a chart sheet adjacent to the X chart. (See Figure 9.13.)

In this particular MR chart, the final three observations are wildly discrepant, and a sample manager at this sample company should have a close look at what's going on with the budgets and actuals to create such large swings during the most recent three months. (If you open the Rock Castle Construction sample file and run the Budget vs. Actual report, you'll see that the issue appears to be the budgeted amounts.)

Special aspects of moving range charts

You should keep in mind these three aspects of moving range charts:

Absolute values

The moving range is always a positive number because it is defined as the absolute value of the difference between two consecutive observations. The reason for using absolute value is that the average of the moving ranges themselves tends to approach zero unless the data series is trended; that is, the level of the series is continuously increasing, or continuously decreasing. The result of using raw moving ranges would be a gross underestimate of the amount of sequential variability in the data series.

This rationale is similar to the use of squared deviations when calculating a standard deviation. If you totaled, and averaged, the raw deviations of each observation from the mean of the observations, the result would always be zero. Therefore, the deviations are squared before summing them and the result is always a positive number. (The standard deviation is the square root of the average squared deviation.)

Minimum value of zero

Because the moving ranges are always positive, due to the use of the absolute value of the difference, there is no real lower control limit in an MR chart (or a range chart or a standard deviation chart, for that matter). The lowest possible value is 0, and it is used as a floor value for the chart.

Upper control limit only

Notice in Figure 9.13 that the only control limit shown is the upper control limit; there is no one- or two-sigma control limit. The reason is that moving ranges tend to be autocorrelated; there tends to be a nonzero correlation between, say, moving ranges number 1 through 10 and moving ranges 2 through 11. This fact has implications for probability statements about the distribution of the moving ranges, and it's those statements that form the basis for locating the control limits. To attempt to distinguish reliably between one-, two-, and three-sigma limits on a moving range chart, in the way that is done on an X chart, is asking more of a handy diagnostic tool than it can deliver.

Viewing the underlying data

Every Excel chart must have data behind it to form the plotted data points and to help structure the chart's axes. The SPC Charts utility makes that data available to you in a worksheet named Data for Charts. The worksheet that is the basis for the X chart and the MR chart shown in Figures 9.12 and 9.13 appears in Figure 9.14.

The data in the worksheet is always laid out in this fashion:

- Column A: The date on which the measurement occurred.
- Column B: The measurement itself. This would occupy several columns in an X-bar and S chart context, with multiple observations per period.

FIGURE 9.14

You can refer to these numbers if something on the chart doesn't look right to you.

	A	B	C	D	E	F	G	H	I	J	K	L	M	N	O
1				Values	MR	XUCL	+2S	+1S	MRUCL	MRCL	MRLCL	XCL	-1S	-2S	XLCL
2	Jan 10	$5,949		5949		14841	11601	8361	11941	3655	0	5121	1880	-1360	-4600
3	Feb 10	$10,000		10000	4051	14841	11601	8361	11941	3655	0	5121	1880	-1360	-4600
4	Mar 10	$10,000		10000	0	14841	11601	8361	11941	3655	0	5121	1880	-1360	-4600
5	Apr 10	$10,000		10000	0	14841	11601	8361	11941	3655	0	5121	1880	-1360	-4600
6	May 10	$10,000		10000	0	14841	11601	8361	11941	3655	0	5121	1880	-1360	-4600
7	Jun 10	$10,000		10000	0	14841	11601	8361	11941	3655	0	5121	1880	-1360	-4600
8	Jul 10	$7,541		7541	2459	14841	11601	8361	11941	3655	0	5121	1880	-1360	-4600
9	Aug 10	$7,230		7230	311	14841	11601	8361	11941	3655	0	5121	1880	-1360	-4600
10	Sep 10	$10,000		10000	2770	14841	11601	8361	11941	3655	0	5121	1880	-1360	-4600
11	Oct 10	$7,638		7638	2362	14841	11601	8361	11941	3655	0	5121	1880	-1360	-4600
12	Nov 10	$10,000		10000	2362	14841	11601	8361	11941	3655	0	5121	1880	-1360	-4600
13	Dec 10	$9,470		9470	530	14841	11601	8361	11941	3655	0	5121	1880	-1360	-4600
14	Jan 11	$1,730		1730	7740	14841	11601	8361	11941	3655	0	5121	1880	-1360	-4600
15	Feb 11	$5,108		5108	3378	14841	11601	8361	11941	3655	0	5121	1880	-1360	-4600
16	Mar 11	$7,068		7068	1960	14841	11601	8361	11941	3655	0	5121	1880	-1360	-4600
17	Apr 11	$7,073		7073	5	14841	11601	8361	11941	3655	0	5121	1880	-1360	-4600
18	May 11	$6,561		6561	512	14841	11601	8361	11941	3655	0	5121	1880	-1360	-4600
19	Jun 11	$4,216		4216	2345	14841	11601	8361	11941	3655	0	5121	1880	-1360	-4600
20	Jul 11	$4,920		4920	704	14841	11601	8361	11941	3655	0	5121	1880	-1360	-4600
21	Aug 11	($3,171)		-3171	8091	14841	11601	8361	11941	3655	0	5121	1880	-1360	-4600
22	Sep 11	$948		948	4119	14841	11601	8361	11941	3655	0	5121	1880	-1360	-4600
23	Oct 11	($12,764)		-12764	13711	14841	11601	8361	11941	3655	0	5121	1880	-1360	-4600
24	Nov 11	$2,421		2421	15185	14841	11601	8361	11941	3655	0	5121	1880	-1360	-4600

- Column C: Always blank.
- Column D: The individual data points plotted in the chart. In an X-bar chart, these values would be the average of the multiple observations.
- Column E: The moving ranges calculated from the actual observations (the budget variances). The first moving range occurs at the same period as the second data point because it's not until then that a moving range can be calculated.

NOTE The calculations for all the control limits in the X chart and the MR chart are made using the average moving range. If you're interested, you can find the details in most textbooks on the topic of quality control.

- Column F: The upper control limit for the X chart.
- Column G: The upper 2-sigma control limit for the X chart.
- Column H: The upper 1-sigma control limit for the X chart.
- Column I: The upper control limit for the MR chart.
- Column J: The center line for the MR chart.
- Column K: The lower control limit for the MR chart, always set to zero.
- Column L: The center line for the X chart.
- Column M: The lower 1-sigma limit for the X chart.
- Column N: The lower 2-sigma limit for the X chart.
- Column O: The lower control limit for the X chart.

Extending SPC techniques to other QuickBooks data

As mentioned at the beginning of this chapter, there are other sorts of QuickBooks data that can profitably be analyzed using the techniques explained here. You will need two basic tools not covered here:

A utility similar to the one you can download via Wiley's Web site. The utility should not be tailored to the particular layout of the Budget vs. Actual report, as is the SPC Charts utility. There are many such utilities available on the Web, some free and some not. If you investigate this matter, bear in mind that price is not necessarily an indictor of quality. The R application, a suite of extremely sophisticated statistical analysis procedures, is free. (It's also unusually difficult to use.)

You will also need a method of converting the data in a QuickBooks report to a layout that the SPC routine you acquire can deal with. The utility detailed in this chapter manages that conversion using Visual Basic for Applications to place the data properly in Excel worksheets. Another very workable approach is to use Intuit's Software Development Kit, explained in detail in Chapters 11 and 12.

If there's an indicator that's of particular interest to you, though, you don't need to get all tied up with programming anything at all. Just start collecting that indicator on a regular basis in an Excel workbook. Update the history as needed — daily, monthly, quarterly, whatever — by running the appropriate QuickBooks report and transferring the latest indictor value to your Excel workbook. Then run an SPC utility against that data. *I am not oversimplifying this process* — it really is that straightforward.

Possible indicators that you might consider putting through an SPC routine and that are easily available from QuickBooks reports include:

- Total asset value of an inventory item at the end of each week, or month.
- Average collection period for Accounts Receivable
- Total sales per month
- Sales by item per month
- Total discounts for early payment of vendor bills
- Accounts payable by month
- Current ratio by month

The possibilities are limited only by what reports QuickBooks offers — and it's really a pretty broad set of reports — and by the directions that your inquisitiveness leads you.

Contribution and Margin Analysis

The relationships among the cost of producing or acquiring products for sale, the fixed costs that a company incurs to simply stay in business, the revenues it creates from selling its goods, and the volume of goods it sells all come together to produce net income. The ways these variables interact are predictable, but they can get complicated.

IN THIS CHAPTER

Break-even Analysis

Looking into the Sales Mix

In the course of conducting your business, you are constantly working to manage your fixed and variable costs, to control them in ways that you believe will maximize your company's profitability.

Somewhat less often, on the earnings side, your decisions make a difference to the number of units you sell, and to the prices your competition and the marketplace allow you to charge. The presence of different product lines, each with its own cost and price structure, complicates the relationships even further.

There is a standard way of dealing with these numbers, variously called contribution margin analysis, price-volume analysis, and break-even analysis. Given the complexity of the relationships between different costs and sources of income, the basics of this sort of analysis are perhaps oversimplified.

But it's usually possible to tailor the analysis to accommodate the specifics of different situations.

Although QuickBooks does not offer a predesigned chart that shows the behavior of the various costs and revenues across different levels of sales volume, it's easy enough to get your hands on the building blocks for that type of chart. This chapter shows you how to do so, and what to do with them once you have your hands on them.

Break-even Analysis

Break-even analysis and its close cousin profit-volume analysis are methods that help you understand how a company's cost and pricing structures affect its profit (or its loss) over a range of sales quantities. This sort of analysis helps you highlight two types of cost, variable and fixed, and see how a product's ability to generate profit depends on how its contribution margin behaves in different circumstances.

From time to time, as a decision maker for the company, you want to examine how the company's full product line acts as its unit sales increase, and how the company moves along that sales continuum beyond losing money, to breaking even, into areas in which it's making a profit.

At other times you want to examine the products' characteristics in isolation from those of other products. The more detailed analysis helps you decide whether the mix of products in the production and sales channels needs to change. You might decide to devote additional resources to a more profitable product, or even to retire another, ineffective product entirely.

QuickBooks does not directly support break-even analysis, but it does a good job of providing the raw numbers from which you can create your own.

Understanding types of product costs

Not all types of costs are created equal. You can try to manage all your company's costs, but some are just more stubborn than others. Some are fixed and don't change over time. Some are variable, in the sense that when you sell more products, there are more costs due to production and sales activities. And some costs are a hybrid, behaving like fixed costs in some circumstances and like variable costs in others.

It will help to get a basis for understanding the behavior of different costs, and this section focuses on that topic. Bear in mind that not all costs are pertinent, just the costs that have a fairly direct effect on your company's normal behavior in producing and selling products. For example, if a manufacturer sells a plot of land it no longer uses, the broker's fee incurred in the sale of that land is not a normal operating cost for the manufacturer.

Fixed operating costs

A fixed operating cost is one that rises or falls as a result of something other than production or sales — usually, the passage of time — and that contributes in some way to the creation of operating income. Typical examples of fixed operating costs are office rental, salaries, utilities, insurance, and so on. Notice that each of the latter cost categories tends to be fixed for a given time period and is generally unrelated to levels of production or sales.

The aspect that differentiates fixed operating costs from their complement, variable costs of production, is that fixed costs tend to remain stable as production and sales rise and fall. Within normal operating limits, whether you produce and sell 100 units or 500 units, your office rental, salaries, utilities, and so on are unlikely to change in response.

Of course, outside those normal limits, you would expect the so-called fixed costs to change. If your company has been moving along, comfortably producing and selling 100 units each month, and then some upheaval in the market causes you to start making 1,000 units each month, you might need more office space, more employees, and more insurance. It's normal for events such as the renewal of a lease to affect fixed costs, but it's abnormal for fixed costs to respond to shifts in levels of production and sales.

Variable costs

In contrast to fixed costs, variable costs are those that rise and fall as a consequence of the number of units produced and sold. The links between the sources of variable costs and their end results, the products, are usually clearer and more direct than is the case with fixed costs.

For example, an acoustic guitar manufacturer would regard supplies of rosewood as a variable cost: The more guitars it manufactures, the more wood it needs to construct its products' bodies. But it would take a major shift in the manufacturer's market for an increase or decrease in the number of guitars it produces to bring about a change in its annual vehicle insurance premiums.

In general, all the components of the costs of goods sold, from raw materials to factory overhead to the payments made to temporary workers, are regarded as variable costs. In some cases, the periodic wages of workers who participate in production only are regarded as part of COGS (cost of goods sold), thus as variable costs. Costs such as sales commissions are also regarded as variable.

Semi-variable costs

Costs don't separate themselves neatly into a fixed category and a variable category, and, as noted in the prior section on fixed costs, a cost that is normally fairly stable can from time to time become wildly variable as a function of changes in production levels.

Compounding the difficulty of classifying costs as fixed or variable is a category called *semi-variable costs*, which have both a fixed and a variable component even in normal circumstances. The classic example is the factory worker who is paid a salary and earns overtime bonuses when production accelerates. The fixed portion of that cost is the salary, and the bonuses, which vary with production levels, constitute the variable portion.

Calculating the product costs

There's not much point in defining terms such as fixed and variable costs without a reason to use them. The terms are both useful and important when you start to look for break-even points: the study of price, sales volume, variable and fixed costs, and their relationship to profit. This work is sometimes called *break-even analysis* and sometimes *profit-volume* analysis.

There's a fairly straightforward relationship between a product's variable costs, the business's fixed costs, the quantities of a product that are sold, and the company's net income. One management function in any business is to analyze that relationship. That analysis can help management determine what's necessary so that the business will, at a minimum, break even on a product.

Break-even quantified

In its simplest form, the relationship of revenues, costs, and income is:

```
Revenues - Variable Costs - Fixed Costs = Net Income
```

Variable costs are those that increase as the quantity you sell increases. Probably the most familiar type of variable cost is COGS. Suppose that you buy 100 DVDs from a wholesaler at $5 per DVD. You retail them at $20 per DVD. If you sell 10 DVDs, your COGS is 10 × $5, or $50. If you sell 20 DVDs, your COGS is 20 × $5, or $100. Your COGS is a variable cost, one that varies, often directly, with the quantity of a product you sell.

Clearly, then, if you want to make a profit you have to sell each DVD for a greater amount of money than you paid for it. That markup has to cover a variety of other costs: your salary, the cost of owning or renting your place of business, utilities such as electricity, and so on. These costs remain the same regardless of whether you sell zero or 100 DVDs, and so are termed *fixed costs*. Although they may change from time to time, they don't go up with each additional DVD you sell.

Your markup over COGS must cover the fixed costs. If you can successfully charge an even higher markup, you will be able to make a profit on your sales. At a minimum, though, you need to at least break even: You seek to generate enough revenue that you can meet both your variable costs and your fixed operating costs.

Revenue is the product of the sales price times the quantity sold. It usually helps to break those two factors apart, because it often happens that although you can do something about quantity sold, the marketplace has more control than you do over sales price. Figure 10.1 is a graphic example of the relationships between quantity sold, revenues, variable, and fixed costs.

The break-even point comes where the company makes just enough revenue to cover both its fixed and variable costs. The break-even analysis shows how, in a given company, the costs, sales prices, and volumes combine to produce its financial results.

Using the results of the analysis

If there's a problem with the company's profit picture, it's easier to understand, and possibly solve, by isolating the factors: that is, differentiating variable costs from fixed costs, and sales price from quantity sold. In the situation shown in Figure 10.1, the break-even point is at 450 units sold. If you sell more than 450, you can meet both your fixed and variable costs, and make a profit as well. If you sell fewer than 450, some of your costs won't be met and there's no profit, only loss.

So if you are trying to move out of the loss area and into the profit, or if you are trying to move farther into the profit area, you would ask yourself a few basic questions, these among them:

FIGURE 10.1

Four factors combine to determine break-even: quantity, sales price, variable costs, and fixed costs.

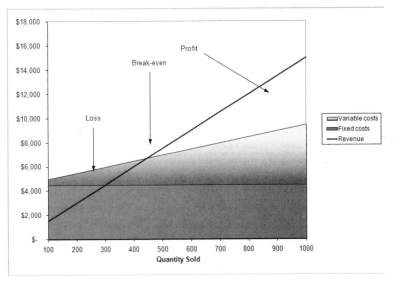

FIGURE 10.2

Raising the sales price moves the break-even point down by steepening the revenue line. The costs are unaffected.

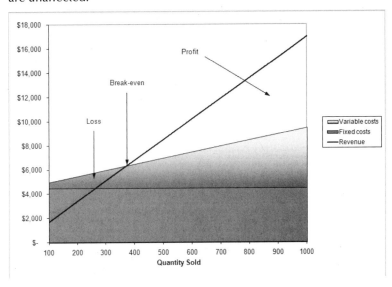

- Can I charge more per unit or has the competition established a lower pricing limit?
- Can I get my variable costs down, perhaps by buying in greater quantities from my supplier?
- Can I get my fixed costs down by reducing my G&A expenses?

Suppose you decided that you could boost your unit sales price from $15 to $17, while your variable and fixed costs remained unchanged; you would continue to pay your supplier, your landlord, the utilities company, and your staff the same amount of money. Figure 10.2 shows the result.

By charging $17 per DVD instead of $15, you break even at 375 units instead of 450. Of course, Adam Smith's invisible hand involves itself: There's no guarantee that you won't sell fewer units at the higher price. The break-even point might drop by 75 units from 450 to 375, but you might have a harder time getting there.

Terms used in break-even analysis

There are a couple of terms used in break-even analysis that will make the subsequent coverage easier to follow.

Contribution margin

The contribution margin is the difference between the sales price and the variable costs. It's helpful to think of contribution margin in terms of both individual units and a product line. Continuing the previous example, a DVD that cost you $5 and that you sold for $17 has a contribution margin of $12. If you sell 500 DVDs, that product line has a contribution margin of $6,000.

The contribution margin is always stated in currency units like dollars. It has limited applicability until you start comparing products in the course of analyzing your sales mix. But also it's a necessary step in getting to the more useful figure of the contribution margin ratio.

Contribution margin ratio

The contribution margin ratio is the result of dividing the contribution margin by the revenue. So, extending the example, each DVD (and therefore the entire product line) has a contribution margin of ($17 – $5) ÷ $17, or 0.706. The contribution margin ratio is often expressed as a percent, so in this case it is 70.6%.

Notice that although the number of units sold helps determine the contribution margin, it has no effect on the contribution margin ratio. By definition, the ratio is always relative to the revenue, and as long as the variable costs increase in proportion to the increase in the revenue, the ratio remains constant. (But see the comments regarding volume discounts in the "Simplifying assumptions" section.)

The contribution margin ratio tells you what fraction of the sales price is available to cover fixed costs and create net income. It is also a quick way to estimate break-even in revenues if you know the fixed costs: fixed costs divided by the contribution margin ratio equals break-even revenue.

For example, if the contribution margin ratio is 0.25, the fixed costs are $1,000, and you sell 40 units at $100 each, then the fixed costs divided by the contribution margin ratio is:

```
Break-even revenue = 1000 / .25
Break-even revenue = 4000
```

To check, subtract the fixed costs from the break-even revenue:

```
4000 - 1000 = 3000
```

which leaves $3,000 as the total variable cost.

If the unit sales price is $100 and you sold 40 units, then the unit variable cost is $3,000 ÷ 40, or 75, which gets us back where we began with a contribution margin ratio of 0.25.

More generally, you can use the relationship between the contribution margin ratio and fixed costs to determine any target revenue figure. Suppose that you wanted to make $500 in net income, with a contribution margin ratio of 0.25 and fixed costs of $1,000.

```
Target revenue = (1000 + 500) / .25
Target revenue = 6000
```

At the unit sales price of $100 and unit variable costs of $75, you would need to sell 60 units to get net income to $500. As a check, subtract the fixed costs and the variable costs from the revenue:

```
6000 - 1000 - (60 * 75) = 500
```

In this formulation, the break-even revenue is calculated simply by adding $0 in net income to the fixed costs:

```
Target revenue = (1000 + 0) / .25
```

About contribution margins and gross margins

You find in QuickBooks reports, including some of the reports explained in this chapter, the labels Gross Margin and Gross Margin % as column headers. There is a technical difference between a gross margin and a contribution margin, but in the current context the difference is negligible.

The gross margin (or *gross profit*) is usually defined as sales revenues, less allowances and returns, less the cost of goods sold. The contribution margin, as just defined, is the sales revenues, less allowances and returns, less the variable costs. So the difference between gross margin and contribution margin rests on the difference between COGS and variable costs.

Many companies have variable costs of production and/or sales that are not formally included in their accounting for COGS. A small company in particular might find it more trouble than it's worth to allocate a portion of its utility bill to a COGS account: For that company, the possible increase in accuracy from allocating utility costs to products does not justify the additional planning and accounting required.

Other companies, including one of the fictional sample companies whose company file accompanies the QuickBooks software, treat both labor and the cost of utilities as current assets, and include them along with inventory in a product's COGS.

So, for some cases, variable costs that would ordinarily be found in general and administrative accounts are counted in COGS. In that case, the gross margin (and the gross margin percent) found in QuickBooks reports is equivalent to the contribution margin, because the COGS is equivalent to the variable costs of production and sales.

Calculating the contribution margin

If you regard a particular product as a product line that you offer in addition to other complementary lines, it helps to know the contribution margin, and the contribution margin ratio, on both a unit basis and for all units sold in each line during an accounting period. QuickBooks makes it easy to get the margin for all units sold, often termed the *total contribution margin*. But you have to jump through a few hoops to get the unit contribution margin; that is, the contribution created by the individual unit.

Getting the total contribution margin from QuickBooks

You can calculate the total contribution margin for one or more product lines from QuickBooks' Sales by Item Summary report. The report in Figure 10.3 uses the QuickBooks sample manufacturing file.

For reasons of space, the report shown in Figure 10.3 omits two available sub-columns: Avg COGS and Gross Margin %. They appear in Figure 10.4.

To get the report as shown in Figure 10.3, including all four subcolumns, take these steps:

1. Choose Reports ▯ Sales ▯ Sales by Item Summary.
2. Choose All from the Dates dropdown.
3. Click Modify Report. In the Display tab, make sure that all four subcolumn checkboxes are filled: COGS, Avg. COGS, Gross Margin, and Gross Margin %.
4. Click the Filters tab. Select Item in the Current Filter Choices list box. The available items will now appear in a dropdown labeled Item.
5. Select the 2000-PT product from the Item dropdown.
6. Click OK in the Modify Report dialog box to return to the report.

FIGURE 10.3

The Sales by Item Summary report can be more helpful than the Item Profitability report because it shows the quantity sold.

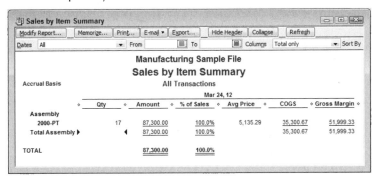

The report now appears as in Figure 10.3, except that it contains one column for the average COGS and another for the gross margin percent. You'll see how to use that information later in this chapter. For the moment, simply notice that the report displays revenue and cost information on all sales of the product the company calls 2000-PT, during the time frame in the QuickBooks file. The total contribution margin for the product is in the report, labeled Gross Margin. (See the earlier section, "About contribution margins and gross margins.")

Figure 10.4 shows the report in Figure 10.3, exported to a new Excel workbook and with the average COGS and the gross margin percent columns included. Chapter 2 goes into detail about the issues involved in exporting a QuickBooks report to Excel; all that's necessary here is to click the Export button at the top of the report and choose to export the report to a new Excel workbook.

TIP It's often easier to deal with an exported report in Excel if you suppress the separator columns, as is shown in Figure 10.4. Normally, QuickBooks puts a blank column as a separator between, in the Sales by Item Summary report, the column for Qty and the column for Amount, between the column for Amount and the column for % of Sales, and so on. You can suppress the separator columns in QuickBooks' Export Report window by clicking the Advanced tab and clearing the Space Between Columns checkbox. Then continue with your export.

Charting the break-even line

The Sales by Item Summary report gives you good information about product performance. A profit-volume or break-even analysis tells you even more about how well this company does in producing and selling its products. To keep the presentation simple, this section will assume the company produces and sells only the assembly shown in Figures 10.3 and 10.4, and the current analysis will use its sales data only. Subsequent sales mix analysis in this chapter compare the contributions made by each of four product lines this company sells.

Figure 10.5 shows the expense portion of the company's income statement, which totals its fixed costs in the Total Expense value. Notice that the expenses that compose Total Expense are incurred in support of the company's normal line of business and do not vary as a function of the quantity of the items produced and sold.

To prepare the units, revenue, and cost data for visual analysis in an Excel chart, arrange it as shown in Figure 10.6.

You can assemble the data in Figure 10.6 by taking these steps:

1. Enter the labels shown in cells A1:E1. These labels aren't strictly necessary for the chart but they're helpful, and they appear in the chart's legend.

2. In Column A, rows 2 through 11, enter the revenue for the item the company calls the 2000-PT. Notice that it is the same value as in Figure 10.4, cell G4. The sales price may not have been $5,135.29 in all sales, but the average value across those 17 sales (see Figure 10.4, cell D4) is the best estimate that's available.

3. The Quantity Sold values in column B of Figure 10.6 are there only to establish an X-axis on the chart, and have nothing to do with the quantity actually sold. Enter the value 10 in cell B2 and the value 20 in cell B3.

4. Select B2:B3 and position your mouse pointer over the fill handle (the small black square in the lower-right corner of an active cell), and drag down through B11. This action *autofills* a sequence of numbers through a range of cells. In this case you have established a sequence in Step 3: Consecutive cells are incremented by 10.

5. Enter this formula in cell C2 to establish Revenue as the product of Sales price times Quantity sold:
   =B2*A2

6. Re-select cell C2 if necessary and autofill through C3:C11, or copy and paste if you prefer. (It will not be necessary to reselect C2 if you have used Excel options to keep a cell active when you press Enter.)

7. Enter the fixed costs of $106,516, obtained from the income statement shown in Figure 10.5, into the range D2:D11.

8. The variable costs are obtained from the Sales by Item Summary (see Figure 10.4), cell I4. In this case, that value is $2,076.51. (Bear in mind that the company folds utilities and labor associated with production directly into its COGS, as explained earlier in the "About contribution margins and gross margins" section.) Enter this formula into cell E2 on your worksheet as shown in Figure 10.6 and autofill it down through E11:
   =B2*2077

9. The formula multiplies the quantity times the average variable cost, and it returns the total variable costs for a given quantity sold.

FIGURE 10.4

This report collapses across individual sales and shows you the aggregated item information.

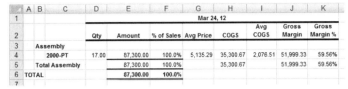

		Qty	Amount	% of Sales	Avg Price	COGS	Avg COGS	Gross Margin	Gross Margin %
				Mar 24, 12					
Assembly									
	2000-PT	17.00	87,300.00	100.0%	5,135.29	35,300.67	2,076.51	51,999.33	59.56%
	Total Assembly		87,300.00	100.0%		35,300.67		51,999.33	59.56%
TOTAL			87,300.00	100.0%					

FIGURE 10.5

This report shows the fixed expenses needed for the break-even analysis. The date range should be the same as is used in the Sales by Item report in Figure 10.3.

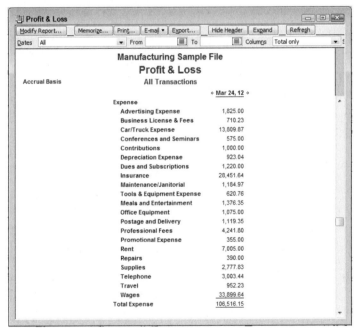

FIGURE 10.6

The data in Figure 10.4 and Figure 10.5, laid out for the purpose of creating an Excel chart.

	A	B	C	D	E
1	Sales price	Quantity sold	Revenue	Fixed costs	Variable costs
2	$ 5,135.29	10	$ 51,352.90	106,516.15	$ 20,770.00
3	$ 5,135.29	20	$ 102,705.80	106,516.15	$ 41,540.00
4	$ 5,135.29	30	$ 154,058.70	106,516.15	$ 62,310.00
5	$ 5,135.29	40	$ 205,411.60	106,516.15	$ 83,080.00
6	$ 5,135.29	50	$ 256,764.50	106,516.15	$ 103,850.00
7	$ 5,135.29	60	$ 308,117.40	106,516.15	$ 124,620.00
8	$ 5,135.29	70	$ 359,470.30	106,516.15	$ 145,390.00
9	$ 5,135.29	80	$ 410,823.20	106,516.15	$ 166,160.00
10	$ 5,135.29	90	$ 462,176.10	106,516.15	$ 186,930.00
11	$ 5,135.29	100	$ 513,529.00	106,516.15	$ 207,700.00

With the data laid out as in Figure 10.6 you're ready to create the break-even chart. Take these steps in Excel 2007:

1. Select the range C1:E11.

2. Click the Ribbon's Insert tab and then click the Area button in the Chart group to display the available Area chart types. Click Stacked Area, the second chart type shown in the first row. A new chart, embedded in the active worksheet, appears.

3. With the chart active, click the Design tab and then click the Select Data button in the Data area.

4. The Select Data Source dialog box appears. In its Horizontal (Category) Axis Labels area, click the Edit button.

5. The Axis Labels dialog box appears. Drag through the range B2:B11 in the worksheet to establish its values as the axis scale. Click OK twice to return to the chart.

6. Click to select the data series in the chart that represents Revenue (the chart legend identifies the data series' color for you). Choose Change Chart Type in the Design tab's Type area.

7. Choose a line chart without markers. The first of the line chart types is a good choice. Click OK to return to the chart. (When you begin by choosing a single data series, changing the chart type affects the selected data series only.)

8. Right-click the Variable Costs data series and choose Format Series from the contextual menu. Use the Fill option to set the data series' color and pattern to the appearance that you want. Select a midrange or higher transparency value, or the costs area in the chart will obscure the revenue line.

9. Repeat Step 8 for the Fixed Costs data series.

10. Click a gridline to select all the gridlines. Press the Delete key to remove them.

11. If you want the chart to appear in its own sheet, right-click the chart and choose Move Chart from the contextual menu. Select New Sheet from the Move Chart dialog box and click OK.

The break-even chart now appears, as shown in Figure 10.7.

FIGURE 10.7

The sale of approximately 35 assembly units allows the company to break even.

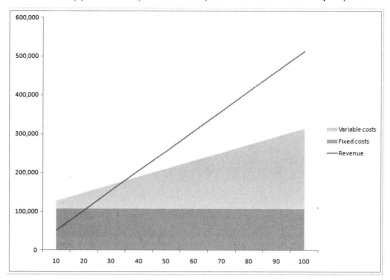

The process of creating the chart is somewhat different and considerably more straightforward using Excel 2003 or earlier. Here are the steps:

1. Select the range C1:E11 as it appears in Figure 10.6.

2. Click the Chart Wizard button on the Standard toolbar, or choose Insert ▯ Chart.

3. Step 1 of the Chart Wizard appears. Choose Area in the Chart Type list box, and select Stacked Area, the second chart type shown in the first row of the Chart Sub-type area. Click Next.

4. In the Chart Wizard's second step, click the Series tab and then click in the Category (X) Axis Labels edit box.

5. Drag through the range B2:B11 in the worksheet to establish its values as the horizontal axis scale. When you release the mouse button you are returned to the Chart Wizard. Click Next.

6. In Step 3 of the Chart Wizard, select the Gridlines tab. Make sure that the checkboxes for the various gridline options are cleared. Click Next.

7. In Step 4 of the Chart Wizard, select the As New Sheet option button. Click Finish to complete the Chart Wizard. A new chart sheet appears with a stacked area chart containing three data series.

8. Right-click the data series in the chart that represents Revenue (the chart legend identifies the data series' color for you). Choose Chart Type in the contextual menu.

FIGURE 10.8

The distance between revenues and the top of the variable costs area shows the contribution margin.

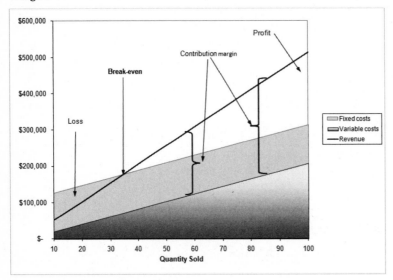

9. Choose Line from the Chart Type list box. Then choose a Line chart without markers in the Chart Sub-type area. The first of the Line chart types is a good choice. Click OK to return to the chart. (When you begin by choosing a single data series, changing the chart SM affects the selected data series only.)

10. Right-click the Variable Costs data series and choose Format Series from the contextual menu. Click the Fill Effects button to set the data series' color and pattern to the appearance that you want.

11. Repeat Step 10 for the Fixed Costs data series.

Focusing on the contribution margin

A slightly different layout for the chart helps illuminate the relationship between revenues and variable costs across the full range of units sold. Figure 10.8 shows the chart from Figure 10.7, formatted with the patterns used in Figures 10.1 and 10.2, but with the positions of variable costs and fixed costs swapped.

The view shown in Figure 10.8 underscores the importance and meaning of the contribution margin, and shows how it widens at higher levels of sales activity.

The charts in Figures 10.1, 10.2, 10.7, and 10.8 all plot three data series: revenue as a line, and variable and total costs as areas. Regardless of the version of Excel in use, it's easy to switch the positions of the data series — here, the variable cost area and the total cost area. If you click on the Variable Cost series in Figure 10.7, this formula appears in the formula box:

```
=SERIES(SheetName!$E$1,SheetName!$B$2:$B$11,SheetName!$E$2:$E$11,3)
```

where SheetName is the name of the worksheet containing the charted data. Note the numeral 3 at the end of the formula, just prior to the closing parenthesis. That value determines the order in which the series is plotted on the chart. By clicking in the formula box and altering the 3 to a 2, you can move the Variable Costs area below the Fixed Costs area, as shown in Figure 10.8.

Interpreting the break-even chart

The layout of the chart in Figure 10.8 is not traditional — it's usual to place the fixed costs at the bottom, whereas Figure 10.8 shows the variable costs at the bottom of the chart. But as noted in the previous section, this layout helps keep the focus on the contribution margin, its size, and its purpose.

Recall that the contribution margin is the difference between revenue and variable cost, at any level of sales activity. After the variable costs of production and sales — raw materials, labor costs, factory overhead, sales commissions, and so on — have been paid for, it's still necessary to cover the company's ongoing fixed costs.

The break-even chart emphasizes that the fixed costs must be paid for from the contribution margin, and that it's only when a product reaches its break-even point that the fixed and variable costs have been met, and the product begins to contribute to positive net income.

The chart usually does a better job than do the raw numbers of communicating the relative amounts of revenue, variable and fixed costs, and therefore can be helpful in suggesting ways that the break-even point can be reached more quickly. Obviously, increasing the sales price while holding the line on fixed and variable costs will only steepen the revenue line. In the chart, a steeper revenue line crosses over the fixed costs earlier, causing an earlier break-even point and enabling net income to turn positive sooner.

Of course, merely raising the sales price may make it more difficult to reach the break-even point, so reducing costs often represents the lower hanging fruit. Reducing variable costs, perhaps by changing suppliers or renegotiating purchase arrangements, has its greatest impact at the higher sales levels. Reducing fixed costs tends to increase profitability across the sales continuum, but reducing fixed costs is usually much more difficult than reducing variable costs.

Simplifying assumptions

It's best to think of break-even analysis as a useful tool that assists you in your planning and decision-making, rather than as a formalized analytic procedure that's conducted with great precision. You want to use the analysis to help guide your everyday decisions about product mix, sales volumes, and commissions and pricing, not as an empirical methodology to guide operations research.

So you make some simplifying assumptions about the state of nature. They're reasonable assumptions, even though you're aware they're a bit unrealistic. And you know that if the reality of the situation violates the assumptions, either it won't be by much, or you'll see that you have to somehow account for the violation. (For example, you assume that fixed costs will stay within certain limits. If you see that they're not staying put as time passes — for example, your rental costs for office space doubles and the contribution margin is no longer enough to cover your fixed costs — you adjust your numbers accordingly.)

Here, very briefly, are the assumptions you normally make when you undertake a break-even analysis.

- **You do not offer customers volume discounts.** Over the range of sales volume you're concerned with, you charge Mertz & Ricardo as much per unit for the 100 units it buys as you do Unger & Madison for its five units. Sure, this is unrealistic, but remember that this sort of analysis must take several different variables into account, and if you allow for a nonlinear price-volume trendline, you're doing operations research, not everyday business planning. Keep your model simple, at least at first, and tinker with it later.

- **The sales mix stays put over the revenue range.** Suppose you offer three product lines, and in a month when you make revenues of $20,000, the three lines account for 60, 25, and 15%, respectively, of the revenues. You assume those shares remain constant in months when your sales are not $20,000 but $50,000.

- **Fixed costs stay within a manageable range.** Again, across the normal sales range, you assume fixed costs do not vary substantially. If fixed costs total between $9,000 and $10,000 in a month when you produce and sell 200 units, then you won't have fixed costs of $20,000 in a month when you move 400 units.

- **Proportionate variable costs stay fixed.** By definition, variable costs vary as production and sales vary. However, you assume that the percent of revenue that goes to pay variable costs remains the same across the normal range of revenue. If your variable costs are $1,000 when you produce 100 units, you assume that they will be roughly $2,500 when you produce 250 units.

- **You sell everything you produce or acquire.** For more basic planning purposes, you don't want to calculate variable costs based on one number of units produced or purchased, and then have to calculate revenues based on a different number of units sold. That's too complex for a rough-and-ready take on how your business operates. You can always build carrying costs into the model later.

Looking into the Sales Mix

The analysis in the prior section is simplified. It deals with just one product, whereas the sample company produces and sells four assemblies and other products as well. That's normally the case with real companies, of course, and this section explains how to extend the single product analysis to multiple product situations.

With that broader picture in place, you're in a position to look farther into the performance of individual products. In so doing, you look at the mix of your products and how well each contributes to the company's profitability.

The approach you use to obtain the required numbers for a multiple product analysis is just an extension of the approach already used in this chapter for the single-product case. Here's how to extend it for more than one product.

Adjusting the QuickBooks report

To begin the analysis using QuickBooks' sample manufacturing file, follow the steps outlined to create the Sales by Item Summary report shown in Figure 10.3, with one exception: In Step 5, where you specify which item or items to select, choose All Assembly Items. When you complete the report in QuickBooks it should look much like it does in Figure 10.9.

After you have created the report shown in Figure 10.9, export it to a new Excel workbook (you may want to display the Avg. COGS and Gross Margin % columns as well as those shown in Figure 10.9). The Excel version of the report will appear as in Figure 10.10.

At this point it's best to combine selected information from the Sales by Item Summary report and the Profit & Loss report shown in Figure 10.5. Figure 10.11 has the pertinent data.

To reconcile the data in Figure 10.10 with that in Figure 10.11, bear in mind that the QuickBooks report calculates gross margin on the basis of units sold: that is, the total of the difference between sales price and variable costs, for all sales of an item. That is what appears in Figure 10.10. To make comparisons between products clearer, Figure 10.11 reports contribution margin for one unit only.

> **NOTE** Recall that this sample company (as well as many actual companies) posts labor and factory overhead costs such as utilities directly to COGS. Therefore the gross margin (revenue less COGS) is equivalent to contribution margin (revenue less variable costs).

Look at the contribution margin ratios in row 5 of Figure 10.9. They vary fairly widely, from 31 to 60%. Recall that the contribution margin ratio is calculated with this formula:

```
Contribution margin ratio = (Sales price - Variable costs) / Sales price
```

The contribution margin ratio can be interpreted as a percentage of sales dollars: what's left over after paying to make or acquire an item, available to cover fixed costs and apply to net income. As a percentage of sales dollars, the contribution margin ratio does not change as the number of units sold changes, assuming that both the sales price and the variable costs remain constant.

FIGURE 10.9

Contribution and cost data are the starting point for an analysis of sales mix.

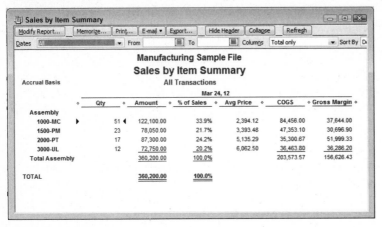

FIGURE 10.10

The exported worksheet contains the Avg. COGS and the Gross Margin % columns.

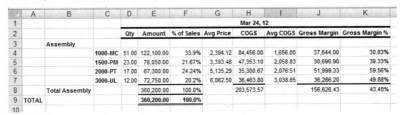

FIGURE 10.11

The contribution margin is per unit. The contribution margin ratio (or gross margin percent) is constant across different numbers of units.

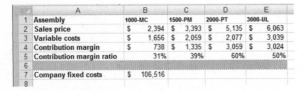

NOTE **That last assumption is a major assumption. It's typical for a company to offer volume discounts to its customers, and to accept volume discounts from its suppliers. If either discount applies to a meaningful degree within the company's normal range of purchases and sales, it should be accounted for in the analysis by recalculating the contribution ratio at different levels of sales and production volume. Although that's potentially an important correction, it is beyond the scope of this chapter. You can find information on procedures by doing a Web search for *nonlinear cost-volume-profit models*.**

So, given a constant contribution margin ratio across the normal range of sales volume, a larger ratio provides more revenue for fixed costs and net income. That makes for efficient sale. Resources you invest in a product with a relatively large contribution margin ratio result in a greater return. The analysis explained in this chapter not only enables you to quantify contribution margin ratios and break-even points, but also positions you to compare products using those indicators as standard candles.

Calculating each product's break-even in units

Figure 10.12 builds on Figure 10.10 to calculate the break-even point for each of the four assemblies.

The first step in finding the break-even points is to determine the sales mix as measured by units sold. Following the layout in Figure 10.12, begin by entering this formula in cell B8:

```
=SUM(B4:B7)
```

You can now easily use the total quantity sold in cell B8 to determine the percent of all sales attributable to each of the four products. Enter this formula in cell B13:

```
=B4/$B$8
```

FIGURE 10.12

The figures for the sales mix by units are calculated: The QuickBooks report does not show these ratios.

	A	B	C	D	E	F	G	H	I
1		Mar 24, 12							
2	Product	Qty	Amount	% of Sales	Avg Price	COGS	Avg COGS	Gross Margin	Gross Margin %
3									
4	1000-MC	51	122,100	33.9%	2,394	84,456	1,656	37,644	30.83%
5	1500-PM	23	78,050	21.67%	3,393	47,353	2,059	30,697	39.33%
6	2000-PT	17	87,300	24.24%	5,135	35,301	2,077	51,999	59.56%
7	3000-UL	12	72,750	20.2%	6,063	36,464	3,039	36,286	49.88%
8	Total	103	360,200	100.0%		203,574		156,626	43.48%
9			360,200	100.0%					
10									
11	Product	Sales mix by units							
12									
13	1000-MC	50%							
14	1500-PM	22%							
15	2000-PT	17%							
16	3000-UL	12%							
17	Total	100%							

This formula gives you the percent of the 103 sales that corresponds to the number of sales of the 1000-MC product, 50%.

Notice the dollar signs in the denominator of the formula. They anchor the denominator to that cell, the eighth row in the second column. Because of the dollar signs, you can copy and paste the formula to any other cell and the denominator's address remains the same.

Excel's autofill capability is one way to copy and paste. After you have entered the formula in cell B13, and with B13 as the active cell, move your mouse pointer over the cell's fill handle, the small black square in the cell's lower-right corner. Your cursor turns to a crosshairs, and when it does so, press the mouse button and drag down to cell B17. When you release the mouse button, you'll find that the formula in B13 has been copied into the next four cells, each with a different numerator and the same denominator:

```
=B5/$B$8
=B6/$B$8
=B7/$B$8
=B8/$B$8
```

The cell address of the numerator changes because it contains no dollar sign. In Excel terms, the numerator contains a *relative address*, and the denominator contains an *absolute address*.

> **TIP** If you're doing all this on a laptop in seat 25-B while the plane is bouncing through heavy weather over Tulsa, you'll find that it's hard to put the insertion point between the B and the 8 in B8. The easy way is to drag across the B8 in the formula box and, while it's highlighted, press F4. Then press Enter to establish the formula. You'll find that Excel has inserted the dollar signs in the right places.

Next, calculate the contribution margin supplied by each unit. This is simply the average sales price for each product less its average COGS. The Sales by Item Summary provides the average sales price and the average COGS, but not the difference between them. Enter this formula in cell C13, shown in Figure 10.13:

```
=E4-G4
```

Using the same autofill procedure as was just described for the sales percentages, copy that formula from C13 into C14:C16. There is no cell reference to make absolute this time, so there are no dollar signs in the cell addresses.

Then multiply each product's unit contribution margin by its sales mix. This will weight the share of the unit contribution margin by its share of the total units sold. Figure 10.14, for example, shows that the average contribution margin for the 1000-MC product is $738. The product's share of the overall sales mix, in terms of units sold, is 50%. So its portion of the combined unit contribution margin is 50% of $738, or 365. (I am ignoring fractions of dollars in this analysis, which results in small apparent math errors.)

FIGURE 10.13

The unit contribution margin does not always vary directly with the average sales price.

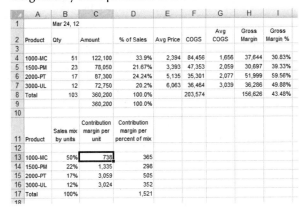

C13				fx	=E4-G4			
	A	B	C	D	E	F	G	H	I
1		Mar 24, 12							
2	Product	Qty	Amount	% of Sales	Avg Price	COGS	Avg COGS	Gross Margin	Gross Margin %
3									
4	1000-MC	51	122,100	33.9%	2,394	84,456	1,656	37,644	30.83%
5	1500-PM	23	78,050	21.67%	3,393	47,353	2,059	30,697	39.33%
6	2000-PT	17	87,300	24.24%	5,135	35,301	2,077	51,999	59.56%
7	3000-UL	12	72,750	20.2%	6,063	36,464	3,039	36,286	49.88%
8	Total	103	360,200	100.0%		203,574		156,626	43.48%
9			360,200	100.0%					
10									
11	Product	Sales mix by units	Contribution margin per unit						
12									
13	1000-MC	50%	738						
14	1500-PM	22%	1,335						
15	2000-PT	17%	3,059						
16	3000-UL	12%	3,024						
17	Total	100%							

FIGURE 10.14

The combined contribution margin is not the simple average of four contribution margins, but is weighted by each product's share of the unit sales mix.

	A	B	C	D	E	F	G	H	I
1		Mar 24, 12							
2	Product	Qty	Amount	% of Sales	Avg Price	COGS	Avg COGS	Gross Margin	Gross Margin %
3									
4	1000-MC	51	122,100	33.9%	2,394	84,456	1,656	37,644	30.83%
5	1500-PM	23	78,050	21.67%	3,393	47,353	2,059	30,697	39.33%
6	2000-PT	17	87,300	24.24%	5,135	35,301	2,077	51,999	59.56%
7	3000-UL	12	72,750	20.2%	6,063	36,464	3,039	36,286	49.88%
8	Total	103	360,200	100.0%		203,574		156,626	43.48%
9			360,200	100.0%					
10									
11	Product	Sales mix by units	Contribution margin per unit	Contribution margin per percent of mix					
12									
13	1000-MC	50%	738	365					
14	1500-PM	22%	1,335	298					
15	2000-PT	17%	3,059	505					
16	3000-UL	12%	3,024	352					
17	Total	100%		1,521					
18									

We're almost there. The final task is to obtain the overall break-even point in units, and then prorate that across the existing sales mix. Recall that the break-even point in dollars is calculated by dividing the total fixed costs by the *contribution margin ratio*. Similarly, the break-even point in units is calculated by dividing the total fixed costs by the *Contribution margin*. So, enter the total fixed costs from the Profit & Loss into the worksheet, perhaps in cell D19. Then, enter this formula in cell E17 (see Figure 10.15):

```
=D19/D17
```

FIGURE 10.15

Notice that the break-even points in units follow the pattern of actual unit sales in B4:B7.

					E13		f_x	=$E$17*B13	
	A	B	C	D	E	F	G	H	I
1		Mar 24, 12							
2	Product	Qty	Amount	% of Sales	Avg Price	COGS	Avg COGS	Gross Margin	Gross Margin %
3									
4	1000-MC	51	122,100	33.9%	2,394	84,456	1,656	37,644	30.83%
5	1500-PM	23	78,050	21.67%	3,393	47,353	2,059	30,697	39.33%
6	2000-PT	17	87,300	24.24%	5,135	35,301	2,077	51,999	59.56%
7	3000-UL	12	72,750	20.2%	6,063	36,464	3,039	36,286	49.88%
8	Total	103	360,200	100.0%		203,574		156,626	43.48%
9			360,200	100.0%					
10									
11	Product	Sales mix by units	Contribution margin per unit	Contribution margin per percent of mix	Break-even in units				
12									
13	1000-MC	50%	738	365	35				
14	1500-PM	22%	1,335	298	16				
15	2000-PT	17%	3,059	505	12				
16	3000-UL	12%	3,024	352	8				
17	Total	100%		1,521	70				
18									
19			Company fixed costs	106,516					

You now have the break-even point, in units, for the combination of all four products. To get the prorated number of units to sell, in order to reach that combined break-even, enter this formula in cell E13:

```
=$E$17*B13
```

As before, autofill that formula through cells E14:E16. Notice how the absolute reference to $E$17 behaves in those cells.

To review: If you have followed the steps outlined in this section, you have started with the Sales by Item Summary report and the Profit & Loss report, each covering the same period of time. You have used the Sales by Item Summary report to obtain the breakdown of units sold across product lines, and you have used the resulting mix to calculate the pattern of unit contribution margins for the product lines.

In turn, those contribution margins total to the unit contribution margin for a combined unit contribution. Dividing that into the total fixed costs returns the total break-even point in units. That total break-even point is multiplied by the sales mix to get the break-even point for each specific product.

There's nothing magic about those specific product break-even points. They do tell you how many of each product you need to sell to break even, given that your customers buy your products in the same mix they did while QuickBooks was recording the company's sales history.

Calculating each product's break-even in dollars

In part because of how QuickBooks reports sales data in the Sales by Item Summary report, it's quicker and easier to get each product's break-even point in dollars than it is in sales units. Figure 10.16 shows the necessary information.

With the percent of sales for each product, and the total percent, in B13:B17, calculate the break-even for the full product line in cell C17 by dividing the total fixed costs in D19 by the combined gross margin percent (again, this is just another term for the contribution margin ratio) in cell I8. Enter this formula in cell C17:

```
=D19/I8
```

Now you can quickly get the sales dollars for each product that results in the combined break-even point, assuming that the pattern of sales in the past continues. Enter this formula in cell C13:

```
=B13*$C$17
```

and autofill it into C14:C16. The dollar signs anchor the denominator to the cell containing the total break-even figure of $244,960.

Evaluating product contributions

The analysis so far has fleshed out the contribution margin and sales mix characteristics from QuickBooks Sales by Item Summary report. It's often useful to compare the break-even charts

---

FIGURE 10.16

The percent of sales in B13:B17 is copied-and-pasted from D4:D8, and represents the sales mix of dollars rather than the sales mix of units.

	A	B	C	D	E	F	G	H	I
	C17			f_x =D19/I8					
1		Mar 24, 12							
2	Product	Qty	Amount	% of Sales	Avg Price	COGS	Avg COGS	Gross Margin	Gross Margin %
3									
4	1000-MC	51	122,100	33.9%	2,394	84,456	1,656	37,644	30.83%
5	1500-PM	23	78,050	21.67%	3,393	47,353	2,059	30,697	39.33%
6	2000-PT	17	87,300	24.24%	5,135	35,301	2,077	51,999	59.56%
7	3000-UL	12	72,750	20.2%	6,063	36,464	3,039	36,286	49.88%
8	Total	103	360,200	100.0%		203,574		156,626	43.48%
9			360,200	100.0%					
10									
11	Product	% of Sales	Break-even in dollars						
12									
13	1000-MC	33.9%	83,037						
14	1500-PM	21.67%	53,080						
15	2000-PT	24.24%	59,371						
16	3000-UL	20.2%	49,475						
17	Total	100%	244,960						
18									
19		Company fixed costs		106,516					
20									

FIGURE 10.17

The profit potential for the combined product line is less promising.

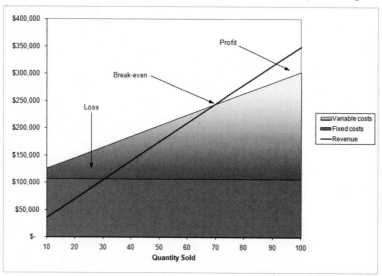

for a given product with the break-even chart for the combined product line. Figure 10.7 and Figure 10.8 show the break-even chart for the sample company's 2000-PT product. Figure 10.17 shows the break-even chart for all four products combined.

The break-even point in units for product 2000-PT, as shown in Figure 10.8, is about 35. Compare that to the break-even point for all four products taken together, in Figures 10.15 and Figure 10.17, which is about 70. There's nothing particularly magical about this result. When you sell a product with a larger contribution margin ratio, you're going to make more money more quickly.

In the current comparison, the average contribution margin ratio for all products (see, for example, cell I8 in Figure 10.16) is 43.48%. For the 2000-PT, the contribution margin ratio is 59.56% (again, see Figure 10.16). If the company could manage to sell 35 2000-PT assemblies instead of the 17 cited in Figure 10.16, it wouldn't have to sell anything else to break even on the variable and fixed costs.

The situation is different for the assembly named 1000-MC. If you calculate its contribution margin ratio from the numbers shown in Figure 10.18, you see that at 31% it's about half the margin for the 2000-PT assembly.

The contribution margin ratio for this product is 31%. The margin is relatively low, in comparison with the other three assemblies in the company's product line, and at the current level of fixed costs the company would need to sell nearly 150 units to break even. The chart is shown in Figure 10.19.

FIGURE 10.18

You can see in row 11 that the revenues have not yet caught up with the combined variable and fixed costs.

	A	B	C	D	E
	C13		f_x =(C2-E2)/C2		
1	Sales price	Quantity sold	Revenue	Fixed costs	Variable costs
2	$ 2,394	10	$ 23,941	$ 106,516	$ 16,560
3	$ 2,394	20	$ 47,882	$ 106,516	$ 33,120
4	$ 2,394	30	$ 71,824	$ 106,516	$ 49,680
5	$ 2,394	40	$ 95,765	$ 106,516	$ 66,240
6	$ 2,394	50	$ 119,706	$ 106,516	$ 82,800
7	$ 2,394	60	$ 143,647	$ 106,516	$ 99,360
8	$ 2,394	70	$ 167,588	$ 106,516	$ 115,920
9	$ 2,394	80	$ 191,530	$ 106,516	$ 132,480
10	$ 2,394	90	$ 215,471	$ 106,516	$ 149,040
11	$ 2,394	100	$ 239,412	$ 106,516	$ 165,600
12					
13	Contribution margin ratio:		31%		

FIGURE 10.19

This assembly does not show a profit within the sales quantity range analyzed for its product line.

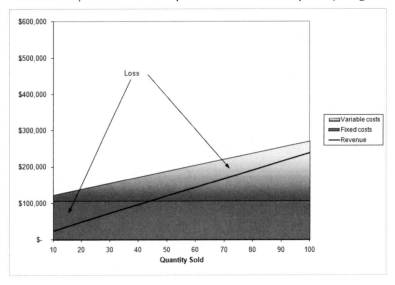

Viewed solely from the profit-volume perspective, the 1000-MC product analyzed in Figures 10.18 and 10.19 should be discontinued and any resources freed up should go to the 2000-PT product depicted in Figures 10.6 and 10.8. But the considerations are usually broader than that. For example, the less profitable product might be regarded as a loss leader that will channel buyers into later purchases of the more profitable products.

FIGURE 10.20

Reducing the sales price only without reducing costs requires a higher sales volume to break even.

				Mar 24, 12					
	Qty	Amount	% of Sales	Avg Price	COGS	Avg COGS	Gross Margin	Gross Margin %
Assembly								
1000-MC	51.00	122,100.00	33.9%	2,394.12	84,456.00	1,656.00	37,644.00	30.83%
1500-PM	23.00	78,050.00	21.67%	3,393.48	47,353.10	2,058.83	30,696.90	39.33%
2000-PT	17.00	87,299.93	24.24%	5,135.29	35,300.67	2,076.51	51,999.26	59.56%
3000-UL	12.00	72,750.00	20.2%	6,062.50	36,463.80	3,038.65	36,286.20	49.88%
Total Assembly		360,199.93	100.0%		203,573.57		156,626.36	43.48%
TOTAL		360,199.93	100.0%					
Average revenue		$ 3,497		Breakeven revenue	$ 244,960			
Fixed costs		$106,516		Breakeven units	70			

				Mar 24, 12					
	Qty	Amount	% of Sales	Avg Price	COGS	Avg COGS	Gross Margin	Gross Margin %
Assembly								
1000-MC	51.00	122,100.00	34.95%	2,394.12	84,456.00	1,656.00	37,644.00	30.83%
1500-PM	23.00	78,050.00	22.34%	3,393.48	47,353.10	2,058.83	30,696.90	39.33%
2000-PT	17.00	76,500.00	21.9%	4,500.00	35,300.67	2,076.51	41,199.33	53.86%
3000-UL	12.00	72,750.00	20.82%	6,062.50	36,463.80	3,038.65	36,286.20	49.88%
Total Assembly		349,400.00	100.0%		203,573.57		145,826.43	41.74%
TOTAL		349,400.00	100.0%					
Average revenue		$ 3,392		Breakeven revenue	$ 255,214			
Fixed costs		$106,516		Breakeven units	75			

Even apart from these considerations, it's obvious that reducing the sales price on any product will require selling more units to stay at or above the current level of net income. Unless you also reduce the variable or the fixed costs, lowering the selling price will reduce the contribution margin of the product.

But there may be reasons, ranging from the competition to an aging product line, that cause the company to consider reducing the selling price on a product. By applying the methods explained in this chapter, the company can quantify the effect of that decision.

Lowering the sales price

Suppose you own the company examined in the examples in this chapter. You might consider tinkering with the sales price of the 2000-PT, exchanging some of the profit for a greater sales volume. It's possible that might increase the product's overall profitability, if you can sell enough of them.

For example, you might reduce the sales price of the 2000-PT from $5,135 to $4,500. What effect would that have on the break-even analysis? The data for the full product line would change as shown in Figure 10.20, which repeats the QuickBooks analysis for both sales price values for the 2000-PT.

Figure 10.20 shows the relevant comparison. As the company accounts for its costs, the COGS captures all the variable costs of production, so the Gross Margin and the Gross Margin % numbers in the Sales by Item Summary report for this company are equivalent to contribution margins and contribution margin ratios. The overall contribution margin ratio for the product line is 43.48%.

Just a little math is needed to get comparative break-even points. As has been noted earlier in this chapter, the break-even point, measured in revenue, is the fixed costs divided by the contribution margin ratio.

With the original pricing for the 2000-PT, the break-even point in revenue is $106,516.15 in fixed costs divided by the contribution margin ratio of 43.48%, or $244,960. That break-even revenue divided by the average sale's revenue of $3,497 results in break-even sales units of 70 (compare to the chart shown in Figure 10.17).

With the contemplated price reduction, the contribution margin ratio drops to 41.74% (see cell K21 in Figure 10.20). The effect is to raise the break-even revenue to $255,214, which when divided by the average sale revenue of $3,392, results in a break-even point of 75, measured in units sold.

A reduction in the sales price of the 2000-PT assembly from $5,135 to $4,500 is a reduction of $635, or 12%. As a result, the break-even point increases by 7% from 70 to 75 for all assemblies. If the reduction in sales price brings about a 7% increase in units sold — assuming the same distribution of sales across the four assemblies — then no harm will be done. If the change in sales price brings about greater than the 7% increase, then the company's profitability improves as a result.

Notice that the analysis does not address the issue of whether an increase in sales volume will occur — it speaks only to the financial implications of changing the product's price. Still, the analysis gives the decision maker more information with which to make the decision.

Reducing fixed costs

As another example of using the price-volume and break-even analyses to help guide decisions, consider what might happen if the company were to reduce its staffing. Its fixed costs would decrease if it eliminated the position of office manager. The variable costs would not change, because the installers' and assemblers' wages are handled as variable costs.

Eliminating the office manager would save $28,125 during the period represented by the QuickBooks data used in these examples. Along with the savings in fixed costs would come a probable decrease in sales activity of about 10% per year, due to a reduced level of customer service and management of the ordering process. Would the savings be worth it as measured by profitability?

Figure 10.21 shows the relevant data. The upper portion of the worksheet, the range A1:K12, is as in Figure 10.20. The lower portion reduces the fixed costs from $106,516 in cell E12 to $78,391, a difference of $28,125 in savings from eliminating the office manager salary.

The range H27:H29 shows the result in net income. There are, as expected, $28,125 in savings from eliminating the fixed cost salary of the office manager. But because there would be no one

FIGURE 10.21

The focus shifts here from break-even analysis to net income.

		Qty	Amount	% of Sales	Avg Price	COGS	Avg COGS	Gross Margin	Gross Margin %
					Mar 24, 12				
Assembly									
1000-MC		51.00	122,100.00	33.9%	2,394.12	84,456.00	1,656.00	37,644.00	30.83%
1500-PM		23.00	78,050.00	21.67%	3,393.48	47,353.10	2,058.83	30,696.90	39.33%
2000-PT		17.00	87,299.93	24.24%	5,135.29	35,300.67	2,076.51	51,999.26	59.56%
3000-UL		12.00	72,750.00	20.2%	6,062.50	36,463.80	3,038.65	36,286.20	49.88%
Total Assembly			360,199.93	100.0%		203,573.57		156,626.36	43.48%
TOTAL			360,199.93	100.0%					
Average revenue		$ 3,497			Breakeven revenue		$ 244,960		
Fixed costs		$106,516			Breakeven units		70		

		Qty	Amount	% of Sales	Avg Price	COGS	Avg COGS	Gross Margin	Gross Margin %
					Mar 24, 12				
Assembly									
1000-MC		46.00	110,129.52	33.88%	2,394.12	76,010.00	1,652.39	34,119.52	30.98%
1500-PM		21.00	71,263.08	21.92%	3,393.48	42,618.00	2,029.43	28,645.08	40.2%
2000-PT		15.00	77,029.35	23.69%	5,135.29	31,771.00	2,118.07	45,258.35	58.75%
3000-UL		11.00	66,687.50	20.51%	6,062.50	32,817.00	2,983.36	33,870.50	50.79%
Total Assembly			325,109.45	100.0%		183,216.00		141,893.45	43.65%
TOTAL			325,109.45	100.0%					
Average revenue		$ 3,496			Breakeven revenue		$ 179,611		
Fixed costs		$ 78,391			Breakeven units		51		
				Savings in fixed salary cost	$	28,125			
				Reduced contribution margin	$	14,733			
				Projected increase in net income	$	13,392			

routinely available to answer the phone, respond to prospects' questions, schedule deliveries, and so forth, the sales fall by 10% across the board.

The drop off in sales causes a decrease in revenues of $35,090. But the variable costs also decrease, by $20,357, because there are fewer units sold. The contribution margin therefore decreases less than the revenues, by $14,733 (see cell H28 in Figure 10.21).

So $28,125 in savings is available from eliminating the office manager (more, actually, because of other costs such as the employer's portion of FICA and health insurance premiums, but we wanted to keep the analysis simple). Offsetting the savings is an estimated $14,733 in lost margin. The result is still a gain of $13,392 in net income.

Viewed solely from the perspective of the company's profitability, it makes sense to let the office manager go. There are usually other considerations, of course. And it would make good sense to do a sensitivity analysis to see what the effect is if the projected loss of sales is, say, 15% instead of the 10% used in this example. A decision maker would want to know how far sales have to fall before it stops making financial sense to eliminate the office manager's position.

Part IV

Designing Your Own Analysis

11

Using the QuickBooks Software Development Kit

A software development kit, whether it's for QuickBooks, Microsoft Office, Adobe Acrobat, or any of a long list of popular applications, is a set of tools you can use to extend the application's reach. The software development kit (SDK) for QuickBooks is comparatively easy to use, but *learning* how to use it is another matter. I'll try to improve that situation in this chapter.

In the previous paragraph, I said that an SDK can help extend an application's reach. That's an ambiguous statement, but the ambiguity is deliberate: It's very difficult to define crisply just what the SDK can do for you. The best I can do is to cite some examples of how I've used it:

- To calculate inventory valuation and the cost of goods sold according to FIFO (first-in, first-out) order, and to automate the use of a different method of calculating average cost than QuickBooks uses.

- To create donor acknowledgment letters for nonprofits (which Intuit wrongly implies that its QuickBooks nonprofit edition can do).

- To enable the batch entry of sales receipts, so the user need not fill out a separate sales receipt for each sales transaction.

- To create bills of materials and where-used lists for assemblies.

I use the SDK for various other purposes. The point is that if you want to do something with the information that's in QuickBooks, and if it's difficult to get the data out using reports, then the SDK is usually a good alternative. Even if exporting a report is a feasible solution, using the SDK can work better than exporting reports.

There are downsides to using the SDK, and I'll explain those as well. When you have finished reading this chapter you will have a basic grounding in how to use the SDK and you'll be better placed to decide whether using it can help you get more out of QuickBooks.

An Example QuickBooks SDK Application

Here's an example of the sort of thing you can do with the SDK. It's conceptually straightforward and solves a problem that quite a few new users encounter. Even though the solution is straightforward, I'll make some simplifying assumptions — it's an example, after all.

Suppose that when you were just starting out with QuickBooks, you entered the names of several hundred customers in the Customer Center. Instead of entering a value in the First Name edit box and another in the Last Name edit box, you entered each customer's full name in the Full Name edit box. Now, several months later, you'd like to send out some letters using only the customer's first name in the salutation; for example, *Dear Judy* instead of *Dear Judy Reed*.

Therefore, you'd like to parse the customer name and put the first name into QuickBooks' First Name field and the last name into the Last Name field. You'd like to automate the process, not because you expect to have to do it again in the future, but because you have hundreds of customer names to parse.

The QuickBooks SDK provides generic programming code that you can easily adapt to meet your particular requirement. The next section steps you through one possible solution.

> **NOTE** I structured this example as I did to keep things simple. Here's a similar scenario, just slightly more complicated: Suppose you wanted customers to appear in the Customer Center and in reports in alphabetical order by last name. If so, you would want the customer name to appear as "Last Name, First Name." The QuickBooks user interface won't let you manage that by typing the first and last name into their respective edit boxes. The most efficient solution is to use a minor variation on the approach outlined here: Type the customer name as you want it to appear, and then use the SDK to tease out the first name and last name and put them into their respective fields.

Retrieving the data

Before you can edit QuickBooks data using the SDK you have to get at the data. There are two phases to extracting data from QuickBooks via the SDK: establishing a connection to QuickBooks and then presenting a query to QuickBooks through that connection.

After presenting the query and acquiring its results, you need to do the required editing and write the edited data back to QuickBooks. The next section explains the connection and query processes; then I cover the editing and write-back processes.

Establishing the connection and query

You don't need to be a programmer to use the SDK, but you do need to be able to modify the existing program code to get it to solve your particular problem. You'll see how to do that here. You'll also see how the code supplied by the SDK manages your connection to QuickBooks.

To edit any QuickBooks record using the SDK, you need at a minimum the record's values in three fields, and the code presented in this section shows you how to go about retrieving that data. The three fields are as follows:

The record's ID

Each record in QuickBooks has a unique ID that unequivocally identifies the record. You cannot access the ID through QuickBooks' user interface; for example, the Customer Center does not display customer IDs, and neither does any report. If you want to modify Judy Reed's record in the Customer Center, you can easily do so by selecting her record. But if you want to use the SDK's code to edit many records at once, you need access to the customers' IDs.

The record's edit sequence value

Every time you alter a customer record, QuickBooks supplies the record with a new edit sequence number, similar to an ID number. (QuickBooks does so regardless of whether you carry out the edit via the user interface or via the SDK.) The customer ID identifies the particular customer, and the edit sequence number identifies the current version of the customer's record.

QuickBooks is a multi-user application, so it's possible, if unlikely, that someone else might want to edit Judy Reed's customer record at nearly the same time you do. So, to keep things straight, QuickBooks requires that you supply the edit sequence number that it assigned her record the *last* time the record was edited. To supply that edit sequence number, you need first to have retrieved it.

If you supply the correct edit sequence number along with the new values for Judy Reed, QuickBooks knows that you're editing the most recently saved version of her record. If you supply the wrong number, that could be because someone else edited the record between the time that you retrieved it and the time that you try your update. It's important that you work with the most recent version of the customer's data, so QuickBooks won't accept your update if you don't supply the current edit sequence number. Once you have the customer IDs and edit sequence numbers, QuickBooks lets you modify the other information in the customer record via the SDK.

The fields to edit in the record

In this case, you want to access the Customer Name. You need it so that you can split it into a first name and a last name. Later, when you're ready to write your data back to QuickBooks, you want the code to write those values into the customer record's FirstName and the LastName fields.

Establishing the code

The code described in this section is in the Basic programming language. You can run it in any application that supports the use of Basic, including Microsoft Excel and Microsoft Word.

It's important to recognize that the code presented here is taken directly from the QuickBooks SDK. I have modified it so that it focuses on the essentials, as follows:

■ The code as supplied by the SDK contains certain tests. For example, it checks to see whether a query that you submit successfully returns any records from the QuickBooks company file. Such tests are helpful, even essential, in a production environment, but in an example they get in the way of the main points and so I have deleted them here.

■ The code as supplied by the SDK does not use certain helpful features that may be available in the application running the code. I have added a couple of such statements to the code: The statements put the data from QuickBooks into an Excel worksheet, just to make the results clearer. I'll identify those statements for you.

Again, the important thing to remember is that of the 32 statements in this section, I supplied only three, and made minor modifications to four more. The remaining statements all come directly from the SDK. In many cases you can do the same thing I've done: Copy the code that's supplied by the SDK and then tweak it a little to suit your own purposes.

Before running the code you should be sure you have QuickBooks running, with the company file you're interested in open. You should also make sure that QuickBooks is not displaying a dialog box that is waiting for input from you.

NOTE It never hurts to back up your QuickBooks company files, and using the SDK's code provides you another opportunity to do so. I have never experienced a situation in which running the SDK code corrupted or otherwise damaged the data in a company file; in fact, I have used the SDK to correct damage that was caused by misusing the user interface. Nevertheless, you should consider backing up your company file before running code that you develop via the SDK, and I strongly recommend that you do so before running any code that's intended to modify data in your company file.

The first six statements in this little program establish a subroutine and declare that four variables exist. The subroutine is identified by the keyword Sub and the variable declarations begin with the keyword Dim (short for *Dimension*, a legacy term that's been around at least since the earliest days of Fortran).

```
Sub DoCustomerQueryRq()

Dim sessionManager As New QBSessionManager
Dim requestMsgSet As ImsgSetRequest
Dim customerQuery As ICustomerQuery
Dim responseMsgSet As ImsgSetResponse
```

The four Dim statements declare that four variables exist. The keyword As indicates that each variable is of the type that follows the As: ImsgSetRequest, ICustomerQuery, and so on. These types are defined in QuickBooks. You don't need to know what they are, what they represent, or what properties they have. It doesn't hurt to know, of course, and if you're curious you can find out more about them by consulting the SDK's on-screen documentation — more about that in later sections of this chapter.

The next two statements establish a message for QuickBooks that will request some data; the first statement includes information about the country version of QuickBooks that the code assumes is in use, as well as the release version information. The second statement defines the request message as one that asks for information about customers.

```
Set requestMsgSet = sessionManager.CreateMsgSetRequest("US",6,0)
Set customerQuery = requestMsgSet.AppendCustomerQueryRq
```

Then the session is opened so that the request for data can be passed to QuickBooks.

```
sessionManager.OpenConnection "BAQB", "Parse Customer Name"
```

You have plenty of discretion in specifying the arguments in this statement. The first argument is an application identifier, and in this example it's specified as "BAQB" but could be your name, or initials, or even an empty pair of quotation marks (" "). You do need to provide some text value for the second argument, which here is "Parse Customer Name" and is saved as a Company Preference in QuickBooks; Choose Edit ▶ Preferences ▶ Integrated Applications, and click the Company Preferences tab.

When the SessionManager.OpenConnection statement is executed, QuickBooks responds by displaying the QuickBooks – Application Certificate dialog box shown in Figure 11.1.

Select one of the four options in the Application Certification dialog box. It's probably most convenient to select Yes, Whenever this QuickBooks Company File Is Open. Even if you needed to run this particular example on your company files, you would need to use it only once. But you might want to periodically run other analysis applications that you develop, and you don't want to deal with the dialog box shown in Figure 11.1 every time. Subsequently, you can always modify your choice in QuickBooks' Integrated Applications preferences.

The next statement actually starts the session that extracts data from QuickBooks. The empty quotation marks are where you could place the company file's path and name if one weren't already open in QuickBooks. The omDontCare argument specifies that you don't care whether QuickBooks is open in single-user mode or multi-user mode.

```
sessionManager.BeginSession "", omDontCare
```

Now the variable responseMsgSet is identified as the place to put the request's results (in this example, the results of performing a customer query). The DoRequests action directs the requestMsgSet to QuickBooks, which responds by putting the requested data into the response message set.

```
Set responseMsgSet = sessionManager.DoRequests(requestMsgSet)
```

When QuickBooks has responded to the query (which for this example is usually a matter of seconds at most), the code ends its session with QuickBooks and closes the connection.

```
sessionManager.EndSession
sessionManager.CloseConnection
```

FIGURE 11.1

You'll have a chance to confirm your choices after you click Continue in the Application Certificate dialog box.

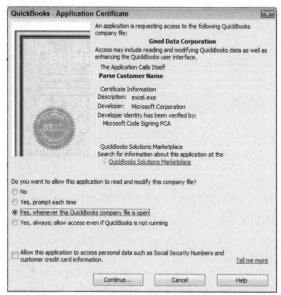

Last, the response from QuickBooks (contained in the `responseMsgSet` variable) is sent to another subroutine that actually separates a customer's first and last names. That subroutine is shown in the next section. Then, the current subroutine ends.

```
ParseCustomerQueryRs responseMsgSet
End Sub
```

Look back to the seventh statement in this subroutine, where the customer query is set to `AppendCustomerQueryRq`. The latter is an existing query available to you via the SDK and its connection to QuickBooks. As it stands, it makes reference to all customers and to all customer fields — name, billing address, shipping address, credit card information, and so on. (For purposes other than dealing with customer records, you use different messages; there are several for items, for accounts, for vendors, for transactions, and so on.)

When you start writing your own applications for use with the SDK, you can often trim down the volume of data that's returned from QuickBooks, both the number of fields and, via filters, the number of records. For now, the important point to recognize is that you don't need to assemble a query from scratch. You just need to know that one exists and what its name is — and you can get that from the SDK's Onscreen Reference.

Bringing the data into Excel

I have adapted, slightly, the SDK code shown in this section — and I'll show you where I've done so — to put the query results into an Excel worksheet where you can see them. So doing isn't the most efficient way of accomplishing the task, but it helps to see intermediate results as you're getting comfortable with what's going on.

The subroutine covered in this section, `ParseCustomerQueryRs`, is also available from the SDK. As was the case in the previous section, the code has been modified to focus on the actual work; I have removed tests that are included in the SDK-supplied code and that I'd want to use in a production situation. I have also removed a `For ... Next` loop that would execute once for each request the code sends to QuickBooks. In this example there's only one request, so I removed the loop.

The `Sub` statement establishes the subroutine and specifies `responseMsgSet` as the subroutine's only argument:

```
Public Sub ParseCustomerQueryRs(responseMsgSet As IMsgSetResponse)
```

The sequence of events, starting with the code shown in the previous section, has been:

1. Submit a query to QuickBooks.

2. Accept a response from QuickBooks. The response in this example contains customer records with each customer's data in the various customer fields.

3. The subroutine named `ParseCustomerQueryRs` has been called, and the response from QuickBooks, named `responseMsgSet`, has been passed to the subroutine as part of the call.

Now the `ParseCustomerQueryRs` subroutine writes the customer records and three of the fields in the response to an Excel worksheet.

Six variables are declared. The code you get from the QuickBooks SDK declares all but one, RowNum. I have declared RowNum so that the code will know which row in the worksheet to use when it writes a particular customer's data.

```
Dim RowNum As Integer, j As Integer
Dim responseList As IResponseList
Dim response As IResponse
Dim customerRetList As ICustomerRetList
Dim customerRet As IcustomerRet
```

Three variables that are needed to obtain customer-by-customer data are set, and the first row that will contain customer data is assigned the value 2:

```
Set responseList = responseMsgSet.responseList
Set response = responseList.GetAt(i)
Set customerRetList = response.Detail
RowNum = 2
```

The SDK supplies the three Set statements; I supplied the statement that assigns 2 as RowNum's starting value.

A loop is started. It runs once for every record returned by the query to the customerRetList variable. Notice that the index to the records starts at zero: lists such as the returned customer data are zero-based in the SDK.

```
For j = 0 To customerRetList.Count - 1
```

The elements in the customerRet variable are set equal to all the field values for the current, jth customer in customerRetList. The customerRet variable represents a specific customer, whereas customerRetList contains all customers returned from QuickBooks.

```
Set customerRet = customerRetList.GetAt(j)
```

Now the three fields needed to complete the task — the customer ID, the record's edit sequence value, and the customer name — are written to the active worksheet. The ID goes in the first column, the edit sequence in the second column, and the customer name in the third column. All three values are written to the row specified by the current value of RowNum:

```
ActiveSheet.Cells(RowNum, 1) = customerRet.ListID.GetValue
ActiveSheet.Cells(RowNum, 2) = customerRet.EditSequence.GetValue
ActiveSheet.Cells(RowNum, 3) = customerRet.Name.GetValue
```

After the three values are written to the worksheet, the value of RowNum is incremented and the loop proceeds to the next customer. When the final customer record has been processed, the subroutine ends.

```
        RowNum = RowNum + 1
    Next j
    End Sub
```

The result of running these two subroutines appears in Figure 11.2, where only four customers are shown.

All that's needed now is to separate the first from the last names, and write them back to QuickBooks. That process is explained in the next section.

Modifying the QuickBooks data

As you'll see in the section "Using the Onscreen Reference," you get the necessary code to accomplish a task such as modifying customer data by finding the appropriate message in a dropdown supplied by the SDK. You have to know what you're looking for, and that knowledge comes only with experience using the SDK. Even the first time through, though, you'd probably find the one covered here, because it's called CustomerMod.

FIGURE 11.2

The `RowNum` variable in the subroutine was initialized to 2 to leave room for the column headers.

	A	B	C
1	Customer ID	Edit Sequence Number	Customer Name
2	80000001-1250100403	1250384419	Alan Ambrose
3	80000002-1250100420	1250448635	Bev Bivens
4	80000003-1250100433	1250448649	Conrad Carlberg
5	80000004-1250100495	1250448655	David d'Artagnan

Understanding the customer modification code

To edit the customer data — in this case, to supply each customer record with a value for the First Name and the Last Name fields — you don't use the `CustomerQuery` message that you used to retrieve the existing data from QuickBooks. You've already retrieved the data, and now it's time to edit it, so you use a different message, the `CustomerMod` message. By asking for that message you get the code shown in this section. As before, I've done some editing to what the SDK provides, and I'll point out any code that I've changed or added.

As before, the subroutine begins with several declarations, each provided by the SDK:

```
Public Sub DoCustomerModRq()

Dim sessionManager As New QBSessionManager
Dim requestMsgSet As IMsgSetRequest
Dim responseMsgSet As IMsgSetResponse
Dim customerMod As IcustomerMod
```

I have omitted the arguments `Country`, `MajorVersion`, and `MinorVersion` from the `Sub` statement. It's not good programming practice, but for current purposes I supply them later as constants.

I have declared four variables in addition to those declared by the SDK. Three are declared as string (that is, pure text) variables; they are for use in parsing the customer name. The fourth is used to keep track of the code's progress through the data in the worksheet shown in Figure 11.2.

```
Dim FirstName As String, LastName As String, FullName As String
Dim RowNum As Integer
```

A message set that will contain the edits to the customer records is created. The version of this statement that's provided by the SDK uses the variables `Country`, `MajorVersion`, and `MinorVersion` instead of the constants US, 6, and 0. Solely for this example, it's more efficient to use the constants and so I've done so in the next statement.

```
Set requestMsgSet = sessionManager.CreateMsgSetRequest("US", 6, 0)
```

Then the code is instructed to continue processing requests even if an error is found in any one of them. (The alternative to `roeContinue` is `roeStop`, which causes processing of requests to stop if and when an error is found.)

```
requestMsgSet.Attributes.OnError = roeContinue
```

Now a loop is run, in this case four times, from 2 to 5. (I have supplied this loop to show how you can modify many records in QuickBooks by executing a single procedure; the SDK's example code shows you how to modify one record only.) The loop works its way through the four rows in the worksheet that contain customer data; again, refer to Figure 11.2. Each time the loop executes, another modification request is appended to the message set that will later be passed to QuickBooks.

```
For RowNum = 2 To 5
    Set customerMod = requestMsgSet.AppendCustomerModRq
```

The customer ID and the edit sequence number are picked up from the active worksheet. These values are found in the row identified by the current value of RowNum, and in the first and second columns respectively. I supplied the worksheet locations in the code.

```
customerMod.ListID.SetValue ActiveSheet.Cells(RowNum, 1)
customerMod.EditSequence.SetValue ActiveSheet.Cells(RowNum, 2)
```

I have supplied the next three statements, which take care of the actual parsing of the customer's full name into separate first and last names. The customer name, consisting of the customer's first name followed by the customer's last name, is read from the active worksheet into the string variable FullName.

```
FullName = ActiveSheet.Cells(RowNum, 3)
```

Next, use Visual Basic's InStr function to locate the space between the first name and the last name in FullName. Use the Left function to get the character string that comes before the blank space:

```
FirstName = Left(FullName, InStr(FullName, " ") - 1)
```

That is, if FullName were "Judy Reed" then the variable FirstName would resolve to the expression Left("Judy Reed", 5 - 1) or simply "Judy."

Now Use the length of the FirstName to locate the LastName:

```
LastName= Right(FullName, Len(FullName) - Len(FirstName) - 1)
```

Use the Len function to get the length of FullName and subtract from that the length of FirstName. Subtract 1 to account for the blank space. The result is the number of characters at the right end of the FullName string that make up the customer's LastName.

Then assign the values in FirstName and LastName to the corresponding fields in the customer modification message set, and go back to the start of the loop to pick up the next customer. Or, if it's the final time through the loop, exit the loop and execute the next statement following the loop.

```
customerMod.FirstName.SetValue FirstName
```

```
           customerMod.LastName.SetValue LastName
    Next RowNum
```

The `CustomerMod` message now has the first and last names of each customer, parsed out of the customer's full name. Next, establish a connection to QuickBooks and begin a data exchange session. Send the message set with the customer modifications to QuickBooks. Then end the session, close the connection, and end the subroutine.

> **NOTE** What follows has occurred earlier when the Customer Query connected with QuickBooks to retrieve the customer IDs, edit sequence values, and customer names. The difference here is that the code submits values to QuickBooks instead of retrieving them.

```
    sessionManager.OpenConnection "BAQB", "Parse Customer Name"
    sessionManager.BeginSession "", omDontCare

    Set responseMsgSet = sessionManager.DoRequests(requestMsgSet)

    sessionManager.EndSession
    sessionManager.CloseConnection

    End Sub
```

If you actually run this code on your own company file, you'll find that everything prior to the first space in a customer's full name is used as the First Name field for that customer record. Everything following the first blank space is used as the Last Name field for that record.

Assumptions in the code

Because the code as given so far in this chapter is intended solely as an introductory example, it makes a variety of assumptions about the customer data in the company file. This section identifies those assumptions and provides some suggestions as to how you might handle them. Although they are specific to the customer name example, you should be able to generalize them to other, more complex situations.

Four records only

The code as written assumes that there are only four customers whose names need to be parsed. The retrieval code does not make this assumption; it returns as many records to the worksheet as there are customers in the company file. But the code that parses the names and sends modifications to QuickBooks assumes that the records are in rows 2 through 5 of the worksheet. The code in question looks like this:

```
    For RowNum = 2 To 5
    [Code that parses the names and passes the values to the message set]
    Next RowNum
```

Here is a more general approach, one that depends only on the data starting in row 2:

```
    Dim LastRow As Integer
```

```
LastRow = ActiveSheet.Cells(2, 1).End(xlDown).Row
For RowNum = 2 To LastRow
[Code that parses the names and passes the values to the message set]
Next RowNum
```

The major difference is that the loop terminates, not after RowNum passes 5, but after RowNum passes the value stored in the variable named LastRow. Here's how LastRow gets its value:

Suppose that your worksheet has some unknown number of records starting in row 2 and that every record has a value in column A. This is the situation in the current example: Every customer record has an ID value in column A, as the retrieval code is written. A moderately experienced Excel user knows that to find the final used row, you select cell A2, press Ctrl+↓. Excel responds by selecting the bottommost of the contiguous cells in column A that contain values. In this example, if cells A1:A100 contain values and cell A101 is empty, Excel responds by selecting cell A100.

This fragment does the same thing programmatically:

```
ActiveSheet.Cells(2, 1).End(xlDown)
```

And when you add .Row to it, as follows:

```
LastRow = ActiveSheet.Cells(2, 1).End(xlDown).Row
```

the statement returns the row number of that last contiguous cell. By assigning that number to the variable LastRow, you can run the loop knowing that it will stop after it processes the last customer record, and not before.

One first name, one last name

The code as written assumes that the customer's full name consists of a first name, followed by a blank space, followed by a last name. There are many types of customer names that do not follow this pattern; for example, the presence of a middle name, an honorific such as *Dr.* or a suffix such as *Sr.* throws off the code's logic. If you ran the code on a full name such as "Dr. Benjamin Spock," it would return "Dr." as the first name and "Benjamin Spock" as the last name. James T. Kirk's first name would be "James" and his last name would be "T. Kirk."

There are various ways to handle something like this. One is to ignore the problem. If you had, say, 800 customer names in your company file and estimated that perhaps eight of them would pose this sort of problem, it's easier to run the code and do the corrections by hand after the fact, in the QuickBooks Customer Center.

A different approach is to write code that counts the number of blank spaces in the full name. If there is one blank space only, run the code as given. If there are two blank spaces, put everything to the right of the second blank in the LastName variable, and everything between the blanks in a MiddleName variable. Unfortunately, this approach fails when full names include prefixes such as *Ms.* and suffixes such as *Jr.*

A third approach, similar to the first given in this section, is to move the statements that parse the name into the subroutine that writes the full name to the worksheet, and parses it into as many sections as the full name contains. Before you run the customer modification code, examine the results of the parsing in the worksheet and correct any errors there. You might allocate one column each for a prefix (which the SDK terms a *salutation*), first name, middle name, last name, and a suffix. Edit the modification code accordingly, so that you have a section such as this:

```
For RowNum = 2 To 5
    Set customerMod = requestMsgSet.AppendCustomerModRq
    customerMod.ListID.SetValue ActiveSheet.Cells(RowNum, 1)
    customerMod.EditSequence.SetValue ActiveSheet.Cells(RowNum, 2)
    customerMod.Salutation.SetValue ActiveSheet.Cells(RowNum, 3)
    customerMod.FirstName.SetValue ActiveSheet.Cells(RowNum, 4)
    customerMod.MiddleName.SetValue ActiveSheet.Cells(RowNum, 5)
    customerMod.LastName.SetValue ActiveSheet.Cells(RowNum, 6)
    customerMod.Suffix.SetValue ActiveSheet.Cells(RowNum, 7)
Next RowNum
```

The advantage to this approach is that you can visually scan all the results in a worksheet and make any necessary corrections by hand before you run the modification code. Otherwise you have to find errors and make corrections one by one in QuickBooks' Edit Customer dialog box.

This specific advantage is just a single instance of a much more general benefit to using the SDK, as follows:

 It can be much more efficient to add or edit QuickBooks records in the aggregate in an Excel worksheet than one by one in a QuickBooks dialog box.

It can be more efficient to edit In a worksheet for various reasons. For example:

- In a worksheet you have access to many editing functions, such as copy and paste, search and replace, and sorting records, that can make the process of adding or modifying information much faster. In a QuickBooks dialog box, you can edit only one record at a time.

- It often happens that you want to edit a subset of records. You normally cannot pick a subset of records, whether by means of a filter or a sort, to edit using the QuickBooks interface. That means you have to step through the records one by one, looking for records that you want to edit. By contrast, Excel has two general types of filters, AutoFilter and Advanced Filter, that ease the selection of records that you want to edit *en masse*.

- There are some types of summaries and details that you simply cannot get from reports, whether designed by QuickBooks or customized by the user. An example is the relationship between an invoice and the payment of the invoice. The QuickBooks user interface doesn't enable you to view them together, which you often want to do in the event of, for example, partial payments. Linking the invoices and payments in a worksheet is a good solution.

No runtime errors

To keep the focus on the main task of parsing customer names and updating QuickBooks with the result, the example code given so far has omitted certain tests and recovery paths. While Intuit does not represent the code that accompanies the SDK as the most efficient, or as exemplary of best practices, it does include some useful protections. I cover a few of them here so that you'll recognize them when you use the SDK code to create your solutions based on what the SDK provides.

One sequence that you'll find in virtually all the Visual Basic code that comes with the SDK concerns arranging for an orderly exit if something unexpected happens. By "unexpected" I mean something such as a runtime error — a situation that prevents the code from continuing to run to a normal completion. Such a situation might be, for example, a customer with only one name. Here's a typical setup:

```
Public Sub DoCustomerQueryRq(country As String, majorVersion As _
    Integer, minorVersion As Integer)
```

You should tell the code what to do next if an error occurs, and you can do so with an On Error statement. In this case, the code will branch to a statement labeled Errs.

```
On Error GoTo Errs
```

Declare and initialize two Boolean variables: bSessionBegun, which stores information about whether a QuickBooks session has begun, and bConnctionOpen, which stores information about whether a connection to QuickBooks is open. (*Boolean* refers to logical constructs; in this case, True and False.) At the outset these variables are set to False.

```
Dim bSessionBegun As Boolean
bSessionBegun = False
Dim bConnectionOpen As Boolean
bConnectionOpen = False
```

When the connection is opened, and when the session is begun, set the two Boolean variables to True.

```
sessionManager.OpenConnection "BAQB", "Parse Customer Name"
bConnectionOpen = True
sessionManager.BeginSession "", omDontCare
bSessionBegun = True

[Code that manages the exchange of information with QuickBooks]
```

When all goes as expected, the information is exchanged with QuickBooks and program control flows normally, the session is ended and the connection is closed. The Boolean variables are set to False, and the subroutine is exited. Exiting the subroutine stops the processing, or, if another subroutine called this one, control returns to the calling subroutine.

```
sessionManager.EndSession
    bSessionBegun = False
    sessionManager.CloseConnection
    bConnectionOpen = False

    Exit Sub
```

However, suppose that an error occurred during the exchange of information with QuickBooks or during the processing of the data. According to the On Error statement at the start of this subroutine, control comes here when an error occurs:

```
    Errs:
```

The statements following the Errs label execute next. Notice that if no error occurred, the Exit Sub statement would divert control away from these statements; the subroutine is exited before control comes to Errs. Otherwise, the first statement after the Errs label displays a message box with information about the error:

```
    MsgBox "HRESULT = " & Err.Number & " (" & Hex(Err.Number) & ") " _
        & vbCrLf & vbCrLf & Err.Description, vbOKOnly, "Error"
```

Then, following the Errs label in the code that you get from the SDK, there is a statement that normally causes *its own* runtime error:

```
    SampleCodeForm.ErrorMsg.Text = Err.Description
```

Unless you happen to have a user form named SampleCodeForm in your Excel workbook, the code will stop with a runtime error. Even if you have a form with that name, nothing will happen because the code does not cause the form to be shown. Because I don't want to show a user form in the event of an error, I routinely delete this statement from code that I obtain from the SDK.

With that statement out of the way, an orderly termination can take place. The QuickBooks session is terminated and the connection is closed. Notice that the EndSession command executes only if a session has begun, and the CloseConnection command executes only if a connection is open.

```
    If (bSessionBegun) Then
        sessionManager.EndSession
    End If
    If (bConnectionOpen) Then
        sessionManager.CloseConnection
    End If

    End Sub
```

Arranging for the Dynamic Link Library

There's one particular tool that you absolutely must have if you're to use the sort of programming explained in the previous section. That tool is a *dynamic link library*, or DLL, which is provided for free by Intuit. This section explains the rationale for the DLL and how you can obtain it along with the rest of the SDK.

Accessing QuickBooks objects

Although this section is about a file called a dynamic link library, or DLL, it helps to start with a brief history lesson. The Basic programming language was developed in the 1960s. It was originally intended as an introductory language but its comparative simplicity brought it wide popularity, and support for it was included with the early PC operating systems.

Extensions to Basic

Microsoft extended the Basic language in the 1990s by adding support for graphic elements such as dialog boxes and controls such as command buttons and tab strips. Because programmers could now incorporate these elements and display them on a computer screen, the language was known as Visual Basic.

Versions of Visual Basic, called Visual Basic for Applications, or VBA, were included in Microsoft Office applications such as Excel and Word beginning in the mid-1990s. These versions are "for Applications" because they include direct support for objects that exist in the application. For example, in Excel VBA you can make reference to a particular worksheet and cell with syntax like this:

```
Workbooks("Financials").Worksheets("Balance Sheet").Cells(1,1)="2010"
```

Pure Visual Basic has no idea what a workbook is, or a worksheet or a cell, but VBA for Excel knows exactly what they are. The reason is that the Excel object model — a sort of library that defines objects like worksheets, rows, columns, and other characteristics of Excel workbooks — is "exposed" to VBA. With the definitions of those objects available, VBA can manipulate them. So Visual Basic for Applications is a distinct version of Visual Basic that knows about objects in a Microsoft Office application.

You don't have to do anything special to make the library of Excel objects available to code written in Excel VBA. That's taken care of for you. But Microsoft did not also expose the QuickBooks object model to VBA.

Suppose you want to use Excel VBA to manipulate QuickBooks objects. That's often an effective technique because Excel isn't a great accounting package any more than QuickBooks is a great financial analysis package. You need to arrange to expose the QuickBooks object model to Visual Basic for Applications. And the QuickBooks SDK has a way for you to do that. The steps are somewhat tedious, but once through them is enough for any given computer.

An overview of the DLL

The DLL is one of several files in the SDK that might be installed on your computer; the particular one that gets installed depends primarily on the operating system you're running. Once the DLL has been installed, all you need to do is ensure that any code based on the SDK knows that the DLL is available. So, there are three basic steps to making these arrangements: Downloading and running the installer, becoming familiar with the Onscreen Reference guide, and referencing the DLL. These steps may sound intimidating, but they're really not, as the next sections show.

Getting the SDK

The SDK is available from Intuit for free. The license agreement is not unusually restrictive, and it tells you that you're not permitted to take the actions that most SDKs forbid: reverse-engineering the product, for example.

I recommend that you get Version 6 of the SDK. At the time this book was written, both Version 7 and Version 8 were available, but I do not recommend them. These versions do have some bells and whistles that are not available in Version 6, such as sample code written in C# and support for multiple currencies in QuickBooks 2009.

However, the Basic code samples in Versions 7 and 8 are written per VB.Net conventions, and many statements are not recognized by VBA. I have been using Versions 5 and 6 of the SDK since 2006 and cannot say that I have missed any of the enhancements in Versions 7 and 8. (Although I personally prefer C# to Basic, it's not directly available in Excel.) If you regard the Version 7 or 8 enhancements as essential to implementing whatever you might have in mind, and if you want to run your application in VBA, be aware that you'll have to program your way around the example code provided in Versions 7 and 8.

To download the SDK, point your Web browser to `www.developer.intuit.com`. Before you can download an SDK, you need to join the Intuit Developer Network. Membership is free, and although I've been enrolled for several years I have never received an unsolicited e-mail from them — or if I did, I've forgotten it and they complied with my opt-out request.

Once you've joined the Intuit Developer Network, navigate to the site's QuickBooks SDK download page. Don't be misled by references to Version 8 (or even later); earlier versions of the SDK are available on the same page. Towards the bottom of the QuickBooks SDK download page you'll see several links to Version 6, Version 5, and so on. Click on Version 6 and follow the instructions to download the installer to your computer.

Once the installer has downloaded, double-click it to execute the installation. You may be required to close certain applications, or to accept a reboot after the installation has concluded. There's no special reason to retain the downloaded installer after it's finished its work, so you can delete it.

The installation process puts a new item in your Start menu: QuickBooks SDK 6.0. If you select that item, you will find that it subsumes a number of documents and folders. Beyond all question the most useful is the Onscreen Reference; later sections of this chapter explore what you can find there.

Other than the Onscreen Reference, the other critically important file is named qbfc6.dll. You'll never open it directly, but you will need to make an application such as Microsoft Excel aware of its existence. A Windows search is the surest way to locate it, but after installing the SDK you should find it in `C:\Program Files\Common\Intuit\QuickBooks`.

One other document of interest, also available from QuickBooks SDK 6.0 in the Start menu, is found in the Documentation – PDF folder, and is named QBSDK Programmer's Guide. You'll need the free Adobe Reader to open it (if you don't have it already, you can get it at `www.adobe.com/reader`). The Programmer's Guide is about 600 pages long, and I find it helpful from time to time as a detailed reference when I need fuller documentation than is available in the Onscreen Reference.

Using the Onscreen Reference

The Onscreen Reference (which the SDK refers to as the OSR; the world of alphabet soup is too much with us) is an HTML document, found under QuickBooks SDK 6.0 in your Start menu. I've bookmarked it in my browser so I can get to it quickly. It has its drawbacks, but I have found it an excellent resource for learning about the SDK and also for getting help when I get stuck.

Selecting messages

You use the Onscreen Reference when you want to know what kinds of queries you can direct at QuickBooks, what fields are involved with those queries, and how to put together code that carries out a query. When you open the Onscreen Reference for Version 6 of the SDK, you see the screen shown in Figure 11.3. (Of course, you won't see the contents of the Select Message dropdown until you click it.)

The Select Message dropdown contains a list of roughly 200 messages to select from. Suppose you choose CustomerQuery, which is one of the two queries explained in this chapter (the other is CustomerMod; the OSR generally uses the term *query* for code that returns data to you, and the term *mod* for code that modifies data in QuickBooks). Choosing CustomerQuery displays the window shown in Figure 11.4 in your browser.

Types of messages

The term "message" is a generic one and it subsumes different types of communications with QuickBooks. These types include the following.

Queries

As the SDK uses the term *query*, it means a message that retrieves data from QuickBooks. So the CustomerQuery message retrieves information about customers, the InvoiceQuery message retrieves information about invoices, and the ItemQuery retrieves information about items. A

FIGURE 11.3

The Select Message dropdown gives you access to all the available queries.

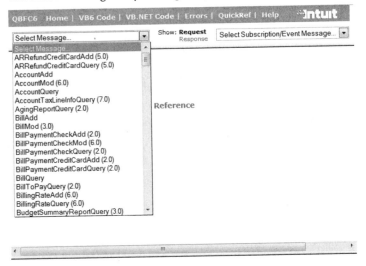

FIGURE 11.4

The window shown is specific to a request. Different elements appear for a response, which is shown in Figure 11.7.

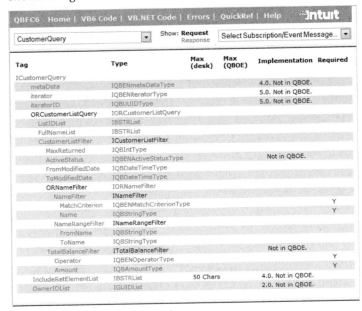

query message does not add or modify information in the QuickBooks company file, but it may be necessary to run a query to prepare for modifying data in the file.

Reports

Report messages duplicate information that you can get from built-in QuickBooks reports. For example, the AgingReportQuery returns information that duplicates one of the aging reports. By setting a value in the message, you can arrange for an aging report on accounts receivable (either summary or detail), accounts payable (either summary or detail), and collections.

Most QuickBooks reports either categorize individual transactions (detail reports) or roll transactions into categories (summary reports). You could run a query message that provides the transaction information that you could subsequently process; the result might duplicate information that you get from a report. It might therefore seem as though it's not necessary to deal with report messages.

However, there are at least two general benefits to running a report message:

■ You don't have to do the processing that categorizes transactions, or that totals their dollar amounts.

■ You avoid errors in processing that lead to inconsistencies between your application and the output of the built-in report.

Add messages

An add message, as you might expect, adds records to the QuickBooks company file. You could use the CustomerAdd message to add new customer records to the company file. When you do so, you can simultaneously specify the values that belong to a customer record: the phone number, the street address, the contact name, and so on.

Add messages can be particularly useful when you are establishing a new company file using data from another application. If you can sweep members of a list such as customers, or transactions such as invoices, into the company file in one batch, you can save a huge amount of time and avoid typographical errors, compared to entering the data manually in the QuickBooks user interface.

Modification messages

You use a modification message to edit information in a QuickBooks record (a customer, item, vendor, transaction, etc.) that already exists in the file. Suppose the phone company added an overlay area code in your city. You would probably have to change the area code that you now have assigned to many of your customers. It might well be much more efficient to change all those area codes in an Excel worksheet and then update your company file all at once using a CustomerMod message.

Requests and responses

Requests and responses are not different types of messages, but rather two parts of a message. Figure 11.4 shows that in the OSR you can switch back and forth between information in the

Request part and the Response part by clicking on the part you want to see. Different elements are shown depending on which part, request or response, you've selected. When it comes time to view the associated sample code, the code that's returned depends on whether a request or a response is currently selected.

The request portion functions to define a query, such as which customers to return, a range of dates for invoices, or a total balance filter to return the names of vendors for whom the balance is larger or smaller than a given amount. If the message is an Add or a Modification, the request portion supplies the values for a record's fields, such as a customer's billing address, an inventory item's description, or the active status of an account. For a report message, the request portion roughly corresponds to the options you set when you modify a report in the QuickBooks user interface.

A query's response carries the values of the fields that the request specified, for the records it specified. You'll almost always need to modify the code associated with a query response so that your application knows what to do with the data that's been retrieved. The same is true of reports, but it can be much trickier to modify a report's response code: You'll find that you're dealing with indeterminate rows and columns instead of defined field names.

The response portion of an Add or Modify request is almost exclusively a duplication of the information supplied in the request. As such, you can use the response as an audit trail, to verify that the changes or additions you called for in the request actually took effect. Among the additional information are fields that report the date and time the edit took place, the date and time the record (the customer, the item, the vendor, and so on) was originally created in the company file, and the current edit sequence value (see the "Establishing the connection and query" section near the beginning of this chapter).

Information about elements

The Tag column label in the OSR is due to the SDK's support for XML, which uses the term *tag* to mean a type of identifier. In the context of the OSR, the Tag column calls out the elements whose values you can set to control the type and the volume of the information in your request. This section provides a brief overview of each element. Later in this chapter you'll find examples of the way you use each element in your code.

In Figure 11.4, the columns to the right of the Tag column provide information on each element listed, as follows:

Type

This column shows the type of data used by the element. The types are almost all specific to QuickBooks (as opposed to, for example, Integer). I have found little use for this information.

Max (desk) and Max (QBOE)

These columns show the maximum number of characters a string element can contain, or the permissible range of a numeric value, when you're addressing either the desktop or online edition of QuickBooks. I have found little use for this information.

Implementation

This column shows QuickBooks editions in which the element is not implemented. For example, Figure 11.4 shows that using the SDK you cannot use the `metaData` element with the Online Edition of QuickBooks (QBOE). The Implementation column may also show which version of the SDK introduced the element. So `metaData` was introduced in version 4.0 and `iterator` was introduced in version 5.0.

Required

A Y in this column indicates that the element is required, *subject to the context*. For example, Figure 11.4 shows that `MatchCriterion`, the 14th element, is required: there's a Y in the Required column. But it's required only if you choose to set the `NameFilter`, and that's not required. If you do set the `NameFilter`, to return only a particular Name from QuickBooks, you must set the `MatchCriterion` so that the Name starts with, contains, or ends with a particular string. Otherwise, if you're not using the `NameFilter`, `MatchCriterion` is not required.

Elements in the CustomerQuery message

Some elements listed in the OSR appear in many messages. For example, Figure 11.4 shows `metaData` as an element. That element, `metaData`, can be useful in various queries and appears in the request section of most of them. Other elements are specific to a particular message. This section provides an overview of the `CustomerQuery` elements. Elements such as `metaData` function identically in other messages. Elements that are specific to `CustomerQuery` are often analogous to similar elements in other messages (record filters, for example), You can often infer their function in other messages from their function in the `CustomerQuery` message.

 TIP A convenient feature of the OSR is that you can click on the name of an element and find brief explanatory information in the window's bottom frame.

metaData

`metaData` returns information about the number of records a query's response contains. I sometimes use it to display a progress indicator when I expect there are many records to retrieve. The default value, `mdNoMetaData`, returns no count of records. Unless you want to get a record count, you can leave the statement in place or delete it entirely. The code as it appears in the queries looks like this in the `CustomerQuery` message:

```
customerQuery.metaData.SetValue mdNoMetaData
```

and like this in the `TransactionQuery` message:

```
transactionQuery.metaData.SetValue mdNoMetaData
```

Notice that the code as written, which conforms to the SDK's syntax, does not use simple assignment statements of this sort for QuickBooks objects:

```
transactionQuery.metaData = mdNoMetaData
```

(You can still use this sort of assignment for simple variables that you declare). Instead of =, the code uses the `SetValue` syntax. Similarly, here's a statement that obtains a value from QuickBooks, which appeared earlier in this chapter, in the section "Establishing the code":

```
ActiveSheet.Cells(RowNum, 3) = customerRet.Name.GetValue
```

Here the = is used as an assignment operator, but you need to use the `GetValue` action to actually access the value of the Name; then the assignment to the worksheet cell can occur. Just be aware of this and don't worry about it: If you omit a `SetValue` or a `GetValue` from a line of code that needs it, the compiler will complain and (unhelpfully) tell you that the property or method isn't supported. Most often, code that you get from the OSR will have any statements you need and will provide special syntax like `SetValue` or `GetValue`.

iterator and iteratorID

The SDK has a special variable called `iterator`. It is a way of breaking records returned from QuickBooks into chunks, so if you have 100 records to retrieve from QuickBooks, you could obtain them in 10 chunks of 10 records each. The `iteratorID` tells you which chunk you're working on. I have found little opportunity to use `iterator`s in the context of quantitative analysis.

The ORCustomerListQuery

The `ORCustomerListQuery` works as a record filter. Although it is specific to customers and used only in the `CustomerQuery` message, it works largely in the same way as filters in other messages; for example, the `InvoiceQuery` message uses an `ORInvoiceQuery` filter, and the `VendorQuery` message uses an `ORVendorListQuery`. Some query messages use a more generic name for their filters; for example, both the `ItemInventoryQuery` message and the `ClassQuery` message use the name `ORListQuery` for their filters.

Regardless of the name, these filter elements subsume several sub-elements that act as filtering criteria. Your code specifies a criterion and assigns a value to it; when QuickBooks processes the request message, it returns only those records that meet the filter's criterion. In the case of the `ORCustomerListQuery`, for example, you can specify any one of the following sub-elements and criteria:

ListIDList

Using this criterion, you include one or more IDs in your request. Each member of the list (in this example, each of the customers in the company file) has a unique ID. If you have access to those ID values — perhaps because you have already run a query that has returned the IDs to you — then you can specify the IDs to restrict the records to those IDs.

FullNameList

Each record in a list has a unique ID, but it also has a unique full name. You can use the `FullNameList` to specify full names for your query to return. In the case of the

CustomerQuery message, the full name follows the familiar *Customer:Job* pattern, such as "Abercrombie, Kristy:Family Room."

CustomerListFilter

If you specify this criterion, there are several subelements that you can set. These subelements are not mutually exclusive.

- Use the MaxReturned element to limit the number of records returned to a value that you specify.

- The ActiveStatus element allows you to specify active records only (the default), inactive records only, or either.

- Use the FromModifiedDate and the ToModifiedDate criteria to establish a range of dates during which records might have been modified; only records that have been modified within that range are returned.

- The TotalBalanceFilter returns records with an open balance that you specify. You call for QuickBooks to return records with an open balance that is less than, equal to or less than, equal to, greater than, or equal to or greater than the amount you specify. Obviously, this is useful for locating customers who owe you a certain amount of money, or more.

- You can also specify an ORNameFilter filter, explained in more detail later.

It's important to note that there are some mildly complex rules about which elements can be used to create filters. Don't worry about memorizing the rules, because they are embedded in the sample code you can get from the SDK. But you should know that these rules exist to understand what the code is doing with them.

More specifically, in the CustomerQuery message, you can set either an ID list, a full name list, or a customer list as the filter. But if you choose the CustomerListFilter, you can mix and match the MaxReturned element, the ActiveStatus element, the FromModifiedDate and the ToModifiedDate, and the Name list as you prefer: use MaxReturned and omit ActiveStatus, or use only the date criteria, or use ActiveStatus and NameList, and so on as you see fit.

Using the ORNameFilter

The ORNameFilter has both a name-by-name filter, the NameFilter, and a range filter, the NameRangeFilter. Use the former to specify a name or names, and the latter to specify two names and all names between them.

The NameFilter

Before you decide to use the NameFilter it's useful to understand how it may return different results from the FullNameList filter, explained earlier in this section. When a hierarchy exists in a list, using the FullNameList filter returns only the records for which you supply the criteria. In the CustomerQuery message, for example, if you specify that the

`FullNameList` criterion is "Abercrombie, Kristy:Family Room," you will get only the record for that particular customer and job.

If you use "Alexander, Kristy" as the criterion for the `FullNameList` filter, QuickBooks returns "Alexander, Kristy" as both the customer name and the customer full name.

Things are different with the `NameList` filter, which pays attention not to the combination of customer name and job, but just to the customer name. In the Rock Castle Construction sample file, these four records exist for the customer named "Alexander, Kristy":

- "Alexander, Kristy"
- "Alexander, Kristy:Family Room"
- "Alexander, Kristy:Kitchen"
- "Alexander, Kristy:Remodel Bathroom"

In contrast to the `FullNameList` filter, if you use the filter `ORNameFilter` and call for the name to equal "Alexander, Kristy" then QuickBooks returns all four records, because the customer name associated with each of them is "Alexander, Kristy."

The NameRangeFilter

Using the `NameRangeFilter` enables you to specify a "from" name and a "to" name. QuickBooks returns those two names, and all names between them. If you omit the From name, QuickBooks starts at the beginning of the list; if you omit the To name, QuickBooks returns records through the end of the list.

Be sure the "from" name comes alphabetically earlier than the "to" name. Specifying "from" as "Smith, Bill" and "to" as "Babbitt, George" results in an error.

The IncludeRetElementList element

Normally, all available fields are returned from QuickBooks for each record that meets any filter criteria you have set. In the case of the `CustomerQuery` message, more than 90 fields would be returned.

For most business analysis applications, that's not a serious issue. You request the data set once and analyze it. That's usually the end of the road, at least for the current accounting period. On the other hand, if you're constantly retrieving data for customer service reps, it might put a strain on your network to return 90 fields to the service rep when only three or four fields are needed.

And if you have tens of thousands of records to retrieve from QuickBooks, those 90 extra, unneeded fields could easily make a difference in the time it takes to process your request. Even if you only send off the request once a month, why wait so long for the data to come back?

You can trim down the list of fields that QuickBooks sends back to you by using the `IncludeRetElementList`. Just name the fields you want returned; only they will traverse your network, assuming you're using one. You do need to be sure that you don't later try to do something with a field that you didn't call for; that would cause a runtime error in your code.

The OwnerIDList element

In QuickBooks, you can create custom fields in a company file. (This book isn't a QuickBooks user's guide, but if you're unfamiliar with the process, one place to start is to open the Customer Center, click the Edit Customer button in the Customer Information pane, and then click Define Fields.) You can retrieve custom fields in a message such as CustomerQuery. But you have to tell QuickBooks who you are.

Custom fields are public; that is, they're visible to anyone who's allowed to view data in the company file. So, although you have to supply what's called an *owner ID* to view custom fields, everyone has the same ID. It's 0 (that's *zero*).

You can also create fields that are called *private data extensions*. You create them, and access them, only via the SDK. You cannot use the QuickBooks user interface to view or edit a private data extension. Even through the SDK, you need to supply a lengthy ID value. If you are retrieving a private data extension in your message, you submit that ID here.

In sum, if you want to obtain data from a custom field, you (and everyone else) have an owner ID of 0. If you created a private data extension (and thereby obtained a lengthy, nonzero owner ID), use that ID in the OwnerIDList element.

Exploring the CustomerQuery Request Code

You've already seen a highly abbreviated version of the CustomerQuery request code earlier in this chapter, in the section "Establishing the code." Subsequently, in the section "Elements in the CustomerQuery message," you saw coverage of all the elements that can be called out in a CustomerQuery request. This section puts the two together, in the form of code for the request as it comes directly from Version 6 of the SDK.

The code is commented in the SDK, but the comments are mostly tautological, and there are no examples of exactly how you supply, for example, a filter criterion. In this section, I hope to spare you the hours of trial and error I spent playing hide and seek with the SDK documentation. (I'm no SDK newbie, but it still took me hours to get the code to run to completion the first time out.)

Laying the groundwork

Before you can run any code supplied by the SDK, there are a couple of quick steps you need to take. You need to establish a place to put the code and to tell the code where to find the DLL (see this chapter's earlier section, "Accessing QuickBooks objects.")

I'll assume that you want to run the code from the Excel platform, but that's not a requirement. You could just as easily run it from any application that can interpret Visual Basic. In Excel, you would take these steps.

1. Open a new Excel workbook. Press Alt+F11 to open the Visual Basic Editor.

2. Choose Insert ▶ Module to put a new module sheet in your project.

3. Switch to the Onscreen Reference. Reminder; after you have installed the SDK, you'll find the OSR in your Start menu, under QuickBooks SDK 6.0.

4. Select CustomerQuery from the Select Message dropdown (refer to Figure 11.3). The window shown in Figure 11.4 appears.

5. Click the VB6 Code link. The code window shown in Figure 11.5 appears.

6. Right-click in the code window and choose Select All from the contextual menu.

7. Press Ctrl+C to copy the selected code. Switch back to the Visual Basic Editor.

8. Press Ctrl+V to paste the selected code into the new module sheet.

As mentioned earlier in the section "Extensions to Basic," you need to make the QuickBooks object model available to your code using these steps:

1. With the Visual Basic Editor active, choose Tools ▶ References. The References – VBA Project window opens, as shown in Figure 11.6. (You will almost certainly see different items appear in the list box.)

2. Scroll down the Available References list box until you find the reference to the qbFC6 1.0 Type Library (that's the DLL file). Fill its checkbox and click OK.

3. Switch back to the Excel workbook window and save your workbook. So doing saves the code that you have pasted from the SDK into the module, and also saves the reference you set to the qbFC6 library.

 You do not need to establish a reference to the qbFC6 library more than once in a given Excel workbook, no matter how many modules and subroutines it contains.

Using Option Explicit

After I have pasted code from the OSR into a VBA module, I find it valuable to insert two option statements at the very top of the module, before any lines of code. The first is:

```
Option Explicit
```

This option requires that all variables be declared before they can be used. Most of the variables I use when I code analysis procedures for QuickBooks data are supplied by the SDK, and the SDK always declares the variables that it uses.

FIGURE 11.5

The statements that begin with an apostrophe are comments. You can replace or delete them if you want.

```
Public Sub DoCustomerQueryRq(country As String, majorVersion As Integer, minorVersion As Integer)

On Error GoTo Errs

   'We want to know if we've begun a session so we can end it if an
   'error sends us to the exception handler.
   Dim bSessionBegun As Boolean
   bSessionBegun = False
   Dim bConnectionOpen As Boolean
   bConnectionOpen = False

   ' Create the session manager object.
   Dim sessionManager As New QBSessionManager

   ' Create the message set request object for the specific version messages.
   Dim requestMsgSet As IMsgSetRequest
   Set requestMsgSet = sessionManager.CreateMsgSetRequest(country, majorVersion, minorVersion)
   requestMsgSet.Attributes.OnError = roeContinue

   BuildCustomerQueryRq requestMsgSet, country

   ' Connect to QuickBooks and begin a session.
   sessionManager.OpenConnection "IDN", "Sample QBFC Code"
   bConnectionOpen = True
   sessionManager.BeginSession "", omDontCare
   bSessionBegun = True

   ' Perform the request and obtain a response from QuickBooks.
   Dim responseMsgSet As IMsgSetResponse
   Set responseMsgSet = sessionManager.DoRequests(requestMsgSet)
```

FIGURE 11.6

Be sure you fill the qbFC6 1.0 Type Library checkbox. It's easy to just click on the reference but forget to fill its checkbox.

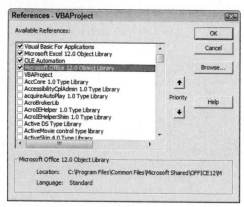

But somewhere between occasionally and frequently, I want to use variables other than those in the SDK's code. For example, I might want to use a variable named `ScratchSheet` that contains the name of an Excel worksheet where I'm doing some intermediate calculations on data that I've brought back from QuickBooks. If I have put `Option Explicit` at the top of the module, I am forced to declare and use the `ScratchSheet` variable using something like this:

```
Dim ScratchSheet As String
ScratchSheet = "Sheet1"
```

Then if I later try to use the `ScratchSheet` variable but erroneously type "ScrathSheet" as follows:

```
ScrathSheet = "Sheet2"
```

Visual Basic will complain that I'm trying to use a variable that has not been declared. My attention is drawn to the statement and I see that I inadvertently left out a "c" in the variable's name. I make the correction and move on.

But the default is to allow you to declare variables on the fly, simply by using them. If I had not used `Option Explicit`, Visual Basic would not complain when it encountered a name that I had not previously declared. I would not be alerted to the fact that I had mistyped a variable name. The result might be entirely benign, but on the other hand I might wind up with a problem when I didn't find what I expected to find on Sheet2. And it could take me a while to figure out what went wrong.

There's an option you can set in the Visual Basic Editor for any Microsoft Office application. With the Visual Basic Editor window active, choose Tools ▶ Options. On the Edit tab, fill the Require Variable Declaration checkbox, and click OK. Now whenever you insert a new module into a workbook, the `Option Explicit` statement will automatically be entered at the top of the module.

Using Option Base 1

I use memory arrays in much of my code for QuickBooks. I like to store data that comes back from QuickBooks in arrays rather than in worksheets or database tables when it's feasible to do so. (There are various reasons for that, beyond both the scope of this book and the limits of your patience.) And I like my arrays to start with element number 1. That is, I prefer the first element in an array to have the index 1, the second element to have the index 2, and so on.

Unfortunately for me, the default in VBA is for the first element in an array to be indexed as 0, the second element to be indexed as 1, and so on. Again, there are some fairly slick reasons for that arrangement to be the default, but I don't need any of those reasons. It saves wear and tear on my neurons for the first element in an array named `CustArray` to be `CustArray(1)`, the second to be `CustArray(2)`, and so on.

I can arrange for this by placing `Option Base 1` at the top of the module, right below `Option Explicit`. There is no automatic option that you can set to arrange for this and it's just something that I remember to do.

You might prefer not to use `Option Base 1` in code that you prepare for the analysis of QuickBooks data. QuickBooks lists that come back in result messages do not conform to the `Option Base 1` specification; they start at element number 0 no matter what you do. You might find it annoying to use one indexing system for your own arrays but be forced to accept a different indexing system for QuickBooks lists.

Fine-tuning the code

Now it's time to make adjustments to the code you obtain from the SDK, so that it will do what you want it to. I'll step you through the four subroutines — two from a request message and two from a response message — that you can paste into modules in your Excel workbook. By following the comments that I put in the code, and simultaneously examining the code itself, you will be able to adapt the SDK's code so that it retrieves the data you're after and puts it where you want it. The request and the response are both from the `CustomerQuery` message.

> **NOTE**   Although this lengthy example pertains specifically to a query about the customers in a QuickBooks company file, other sorts of queries follow the structure you see here very closely. You'll find after a little study that you can use the same techniques with other QuickBooks objects, such as items, accounts, reports, transactions, and so on.

Request messages that you find in the SDK all follow the same basic structure. They begin with a main subroutine (in the `CustomerQuery` message, it's named `DoCustomerQueryRq`) that establishes some variables and prepares to initiate a QuickBooks session. Then another subroutine (named `BuildCustomerQueryRq`) is called, which actually structures the query: Options are set and filters are specified. Control returns to the main subroutine, which passes the message to QuickBooks.

After QuickBooks has finished processing the request, it returns a response to your code. The main subroutine passes the response along to a third subroutine, which checks the validity of the response. That third subroutine is named `ParseCustomerQueryRs` in this example, and is one of two that form the response part of the `CustomerQuery` message. `ParseCustomerQueryRs` passes a valid response along to `ParseCustomerRet`, which handles the task of getting values from the response and putting them where you can use them: in variables or, if you arrange things properly, in worksheet cells.

> **TIP**   Again, the names of these subroutines are easily generalized to other queries. For example, if you were establishing an inventory item query, the subroutines as named by the SDK would be `DoItemInventoryQueryRq`, `BuildItemInventoryQueryRq`, `ParseItemInventoryQueryRs`, and `ParseItemInventoryRet`. All that changes is the name of the query, from `Customer` to `ItemInventory`.

NOTE Sometimes a line of code needs to wrap to the next available line, whether that's in a code module or on a page in this book. (The next statement is an example: it's too long to fit on one line.) In that case, you need to indicate that the statement continues on the next line, and in Visual Basic for Applications you do that by means of a space and an underscore (_). So, in the next statement shown here, there's a space and an underscore after the second **As** keyword. This indicates that the statement has not concluded but is continued on the next line.

Here's the code:

```
Public Sub DoCustomerQueryRq(country As String, majorVersion As _
    Integer, minorVersion As Integer)
```

Right off the bat, there's an issue. The variables `country`, `majorVersion`, and `minorVersion` in the parentheses are called *arguments*. At the moment the subroutine begins, those arguments are supposed to contain values. So I like to add a short subroutine, usually at the very top of the module, that supplies values to the arguments and simultaneously calls the main routine. It usually looks something like this:

```
Sub RunQuery()
DoCustomerQueryRq("US", 6, 0)
End Sub
```

With that subroutine in place, I can put my mouse pointer on its Sub statement, and press F5 to run it because it has no arguments in its Sub statement: The F5 key has no idea what an argument is. The next statement calls the SDK's `DoCustomerQueryRq` and supplies values for the arguments it uses.

Now back to the code from the SDK:

```
On Error GoTo Errs
```

As you'll see later, there's a segment of the code identified by the label `Errs`. The `On Error` statement says that in case of an error (for example, the code refers to a field name that does not exist in QuickBooks customer records), control flows to the `Errs` label and the code that immediately follows it. That code arranges for orderly termination of the subroutine in case of an error; if no error occurs, that code is not run.

The following four statements declare and assign values to two Boolean variables. The statements are explained earlier in the section "No runtime errors," but, briefly, they set two flags that prove useful in case the error recovery code needs to be run.

Note that the SDK code declares variables, by means of `Dim` statements, just before the point where they are first used. Many people, myself included, who cut their coding teeth on the Pascal language much prefer to declare variables at the beginning of the subroutine that uses them. If you're among the enlightened, feel free to move all the `Dim` statements to the top of the subroutine. If you do so, you might find in an almost vanishingly small number of cases that you need to reinitialize the variable at the point that the SDK had declared it.

```
Dim bSessionBegun As Boolean
bSessionBegun = False
Dim bConnectionOpen As Boolean
bConnectionOpen = False
```

An object called `sessionManager` is declared and, using the `New` keyword, created. The aptly named session manager has various useful actions associated with it, such as the ability to open and close a connection to QuickBooks, to establish a request message that is passed to QuickBooks and a response message that is received from QuickBooks, and so on.

```
Dim sessionManager As New QBSessionManager
```

Then the message itself is declared. The session manager assigns the message certain attributes that are determined by the country, major version, and minor version. (The country refers to the QuickBooks edition; for the U.S., for Canada, and so on. The versions refer not to QuickBooks but to the version of the SDK that's in use.)

```
Dim requestMsgSet As IMsgSetRequest
Set requestMsgSet = sessionManager.CreateMsgSetRequest(country, _
    majorVersion, minorVersion)
```

The Visual Basic Editor in Microsoft Office applications has an option that lets you determine what happens in the event of an error; for example, break on all errors, break on errors that you haven't allowed for, and break on errors in a special kind of module called a *class module*. You can also specify in the request message what should happen in the event of an error. The following statement calls for QuickBooks to continue processing requests even if it encounters a request with an error in it. You can use `roeStop` instead of `roeContinue` if you want QuickBooks to stop processing requests when it finds one with an error.

```
requestMsgSet.Attributes.OnError = roeContinue
```

With the request message set established, it's time to tailor it to your requirements — in particular, any record filters that you want to include. The main subroutine calls the `BuildCustomerQueryRq` subroutine, with the request message set and the country version of QuickBooks as its arguments. The `BuildCustomerQueryRq` subroutine is explained later, after the conclusion of the main `DoCustomerQueryRq` subroutine.

```
BuildCustomerQueryRq requestMsgSet, country
```

After the characteristics of the request message set have been determined, the connection to QuickBooks can be opened and the session begun. Note that the two Boolean variables declared earlier are now set to `True`, as soon as the connection is opened and the session begun.

```
sessionManager.OpenConnection "IDN", "Sample QBFC Code"
bConnectionOpen = True
sessionManager.BeginSession "", omDontCare
bSessionBegun = True
```

Now declare a response message set: The request message set has been prepared, and will tell QuickBooks what you want it to do. QuickBooks also needs a response message set into which it will place the results of performing the request.

```
Dim responseMsgSet As IMsgSetResponse
```

Pass the request message set to QuickBooks by attaching it as an argument to the session manager's DoRequests action. In effect, the next statement says this: "Session manager, take the request message set that we've built and have QuickBooks comply with the request. Put the results in the response message set that I just declared."

```
Set responseMsgSet = sessionManager.DoRequests(requestMsgSet)
```

Now that the request has been processed, end the session and close the connection. Set the corresponding Boolean variables to False.

```
sessionManager.EndSession
bSessionBegun = False
sessionManager.CloseConnection
bConnectionOpen = False
```

The response from QuickBooks is in hand, but you can't see its results. Call the subroutine ParseCustomerQueryRs with the response message as one argument and the country as the other. The ParseCustomerQueryRs subroutine prepares the response data for placement, in this case to an Excel worksheet.

The reason that the country argument originated in the main subroutine and is passed to other subroutines is that some of the code in those subroutines might be executed, or skipped, depending on which country is represented in QuickBooks itself. As it happens, the BuildCustomerQueryRq subroutine does not adjust its request according to the value of country; the argument is there only because it's there in many other SDK subroutines that build message requests. But, as you'll see, the response makes use of the country argument; for example, if the country is something other than "US" then a value for the country's sales tax is returned in the response.

```
ParseCustomerQueryRs responseMsgSet, country
```

After the data has been parsed by the ParseCustomerQueryRs subroutine, the next statement terminates the main subroutine DoCustomerQueryRq. If some other procedure called the subroutine (for example, the simple three-line subroutine RunQuery shown near the beginning of this section) then control returns to it. Otherwise, the subroutine ends and execution is halted.

```
Exit Sub
```

However, suppose an error has occurred in the execution of the code (as distinct from during the processing of the request; an error there is handled by the message set's OnError attribute, explained earlier). Then the flow of control comes to the section of the subroutine headed by the label `Errs` — also explained earlier in this section.

```
Errs:
```

The code as supplied by the SDK first displays a message box with the identifying number of the error that occurred, along with its description. I tend to leave this statement in my code as long as I have it under development. When I believe that my product is ready to be used in a production setting, I remove it — it's unlikely to help any end user — and replace it with a message that urges the user to contact my company if the message appears.

```
MsgBox "HRESULT = " & Err.Number & " (" & Hex(Err.Number) & ") " _
    & vbCrLf & vbCrLf & Err.Description, vbOKOnly, "Error"
```

I always remove the next statement, which assumes the presence of a control — actually, a user form — named SampleCodeForm with a text edit box. I never have such a form in my VBA projects, and so I remove the statement, which merely duplicates some of the functionality of the prior `MsgBox` statement, to prevent the code from trying to find a form that isn't there.

```
SampleCodeForm.ErrorMsg.Text = Err.Description
```

Finally, in the event an error has occurred, some cleanup work is required. The code is about to stop running and in that case you don't want to keep a QuickBooks session going or a connection open. So, test whether the session has begun and has not ended; if so, end the session. Test whether the connection is open; if so, close the connection. Then end the subroutine.

```
If (bSessionBegun) Then
    sessionManager.EndSession
End If

If (bConnectionOpen) Then
    sessionManager.CloseConnection
End If
End Sub
```

The next section looks at the subroutine that actually builds the request for data.

Building the request message

The `BuildCustomerQueryRq` subroutine needs much more editing than the `DoCustomerQueryRq` subroutine. The reason is that `DoCustomerQueryRq` sets up some standard processes, such as establishing a session and a connection with QuickBooks. But building the query requires you to tailor it to your own needs: how the available filters should work if you want to use them, whether you want to restrict the fields that are returned, and whether you want access to any custom fields or private data.

There are times that I don't want to do any tailoring at all. Then, I might simply take the two absolutely necessary statements from the `BuildCustomerQueryRq` subroutine and put them in the DoCustomerQueryRq subroutine, removing the call to BuildCustomerQueryRq. Those two statements declare and set the customerQuery variable, and are the fifth and sixth statements shown later, in the BuildCustomerQueryRq subroutine.

Notice that BuildCustomerQueryRq takes two arguments, both passed to it by DoCustomerQueryRq.

```
Public Sub BuildCustomerQueryRq(requestMsgSet As IMsgSetRequest, _
    country As String)
```

I have never seen the following If test evaluate to True; given that the code gets this far, the requestMsgSet must have been declared correctly. However, there's almost no cost to leaving the test in place. If for some reason the If test evaluates to True, then control returns to DoCustomerQueryRq and the error handler in that subroutine will take over.

```
If (requestMsgSet Is Nothing) Then
    Exit Sub
End If
```

Here are the two statements you absolutely must provide. You need to tell QuickBooks which query to execute, and you do that by appending the customer query request to the request message set:

```
Dim customerQuery As ICustomerQuery
Set customerQuery = requestMsgSet.AppendCustomerQueryRq
```

If you don't want metadata (which in QuickBooks queries tells you approximately how many records your query can return) you can omit the next statement, because the default is, as shown, no metadata. If you want metadata only, instead of mdNoMetaData use mdMetaDataOnly. If you want both metadata and the actual records, use mdMetaDataAndResponseData.

```
customerQuery.metaData.SetValue mdNoMetaData
```

When you set the reference to the qbFC6 object library (see the section "Laying the groundwork" earlier in this chapter) you get a side benefit. Suppose that you have edited the metadata statement so that it looks like this:

```
customerQuery.metaData.SetValue
```

When you type a space after SetValue, the Visual Basic Editor responds by displaying a contextual menu that contains all the possible values the metaData element can take on. You don't need to remember them or look them up in a document. But you do need to know what each of the possible values means, so that you can select the one you want.

The way to get the number of records from metadata is described shortly, in the section "Understanding the ParseCustomerQueryRs subroutine." It takes only one statement.

I seldom have needed to retrieve data in chunks, so I usually omit the next two statements. The iterator is explained earlier in this chapter, in the section "iterator and iteratorID."

The code as supplied by the SDK often supplies "val" as a sort of placeholder, where a value is needed and there are too many possible values to display in a contextual menu. In those cases, you must either supply the value you want or omit the statement. If you just leave "val" in place, it will normally result in a runtime error. (The exception occurs when "val" is a syntactically permissible value. But syntactically permissible is not the same thing as meaningful.)

```
customerQuery.iterator.SetValue itStart
customerQuery.iteratorID.SetValue "val"
```

At this point in the BuildCustomerQueryRq code, the process of structuring the filters begins. If you do not want to use filters at this point (and if you want all fields except custom fields), you can omit everything from here to the End Sub statement.

I often omit the remaining code. I prefer to bring all the data for a particular type of query back from QuickBooks and do any necessary filtering later. An exception occurs when I am requesting transaction data; then, it usually turns out that I want to filter for transactions that take place between a given start date and end date. Ordinarily there are many more transactions than there are customers, so I want to trim down the volume. But when I'm dealing with a list of at most a few hundred customers, I prefer to keep the code to a minimum and omit the filters. That makes the code a lot easier to maintain.

Assuming that you want to use the filters for the CustomerQuery message — or at least understand how they work — they are repeated here as the SDK provides them.

First a simple string variable is declared. It contains the name of the filter you want to use. At this point the filters are mutually exclusive, so setting the string variable to a particular value is tantamount to selecting which filter you want to use.

```
Dim orCustomerListQueryORElement1 As String
orCustomerListQueryORElement1 = "ListID"
```

The code that the SDK provides assumes that you want to use ListID as a filter. As the code is supplied, you could instead choose FullName or CustomerListFilter. You would do that by using one of these statements instead of the one supplied by the SDK:

```
orCustomerListQueryORElement1 = "FullName"
```

or

```
orCustomerListQueryORElement1 = "CustomerListFilter"
```

At this point the SDK code sets the filtering criteria according to your choice of filter:

```
If ( orCustomerListQueryORElement1 = "ListID" ) Then
    customerQuery.ORCustomerListQuery.ListIDList.Add "val"
```

Assuming you want to use the `ListID` filter, there are some points that you should keep in mind:

- The value `"val"` is not and never will be a QuickBooks customer ID. If you want to filter using `ListID`, replace `"val"` with a legitimate ID value.

- A customer ID in QuickBooks is a lengthy string, something such as 80000001–1250100403. It would be crazy to try to actually type a value like that into your code. It becomes more rational if you already have those ID values stored in, say, an Excel worksheet or a database table. Then you could arrange to loop through the ID values and add them to the request message.

- The `ListIDs` used in the `CustomerQuery` identify full names; they correspond to fully qualified records of the Customer:Job sort.

- If for some reason you find it necessary to filter for a few customers using their `ListIDs`, you can use a structure like this:

```
If ( orCustomerListQueryORElement1 = "ListID" ) Then
    customerQuery.ORCustomerListQuery.ListIDList.Add _
        "70000001-1250100403"
    customerQuery.ORCustomerListQuery.ListIDList.Add _
        "80000001-1250100403"
    customerQuery.ORCustomerListQuery.ListIDList.Add _
        "90000001-1250100403"
```

The SDK code continues by checking to see if you want to use a full name instead of a `ListID`.

```
ElseIf ( orCustomerListQueryORElement1 = "FullName" ) Then

    customerQuery.ORCustomerListQuery.FullNameList.Add "val"
```

Again, don't leave `"val"` where it is. Replace it with "Abercrombie, Kristy:Remodel Kitchen" or some other full name from your company file. A full name in the case of a `CustomerQuery` message consists of the customer name and a job name, separated by a colon. It's not quite as crazy to use a `FullNameList` in code as it is to use `ListIDs` in code, but it's not a good idea. Unless there's a compelling reason to do so, it's seldom wise to hard-code values such as these into your code. There are usually better ways, such as loops that pick up values from elsewhere, or arguments passed from calling procedures.

As is the case with the `ListID`, if you have more than one full name to use you can stack several `Add` statements.

Last, you might choose to use the `CustomerListFilter` rather than the `ListID` or the `FullName`.

```
ElseIf (orCustomerListQueryORElement1 = "CustomerListFilter") Then
```

If you use `CustomerListFilter`, you have access to several filters that can be used in combination. I don't use the `MaxReturned` setting unless I'm in the early stages of debugging my code, when a careless mistake is likely to cause a problem whether I'm getting 10 records or 1,000.

```
customerQuery.ORCustomerListQuery.CustomerListFilter.MaxReturned. _
    SetValue 10
```

Change the value 10 to some other value if you want. You can omit the statement entirely if you don't want to put an arbitrary cap on the number of records to return from QuickBooks.

To get only customers who are currently defined as active, use this statement or omit it entirely:

```
customerQuery.ORCustomerListQuery.CustomerListFilter.ActiveStatus. _
    SetValue asActiveOnly
```

The default is asActiveOnly, as given by the SDK. You could also use asInactiveOnly or asAll.

To return only customer records that have been modified during a particular range of dates, specify both a "from" date and a "to" date, as follows:

```
customerQuery.ORCustomerListQuery.CustomerListFilter _
    .FromModifiedDate.SetValue #2003/12/31 09:35#, False
customerQuery.ORCustomerListQuery.CustomerListFilter _
    .ToModifiedDate.SetValue #2003/12/31 09:35#, False
```

Notice that the two dates given earlier are identical. This is merely a quirk of the code as supplied by the SDK. Normally you'll want to set the "from" date earlier than the "to" date. You can omit the time of day if you want. Note the use of # to delimit the date/time values — that's how you distinguish the date/time data type from other types.

You could also pass a "from" and a "to" date to the subroutine from a calling subroutine. In that case, you would assign the dates of interest to variables and pass the variables as arguments. Don't use #s if you use this method; instead, declare the variables that you pass as the Date type.

You can use MaxReturned, ActiveStatus, and modification dates with one another, and you can put the next filter, orNameFilterORElement2, into the mix as well. However, there are two filters that can be specified by orNameFilterORElement2, and you can use only one. You can specify a particular customer name or you can specify a range of names, but not both. So the SDK code uses another If structure. First, the variable that holds your choice is declared, and then it's assigned a value; the SDK's choice is to give it the value NameFilter:

```
Dim orNameFilterORElement2 As String
orNameFilterORElement2 = "NameFilter"
```

If you're using the NameFilter, you must begin by deciding what sort of match you want for your criterion. Suppose you supply the criterion value "Arp." Then, if the criterion type is StartsWith, QuickBooks will return customer names such as Arpel and Arpent. If the criterion type is `Contains`, QuickBooks returns customer names such as Carpenter. And if the criterion type is `EndsWith`, you get customer records with names such as Garp.

Although any or all of the filters explained here can be completely omitted from your code, you must supply specific information if you decide to use the `NameFilter`. You can't just supply a name or part of a name. Your request must include the type of match you want: `mcStartsWith`, `mcEndsWith`, or `mcContains`.

```
If ( orNameFilterORElement2 = "NameFilter" ) Then
    customerQuery.ORCustomerListQuery.CustomerListFilter _
        .ORNameFilter.NameFilter.MatchCriterion.SetValue mcStartsWith
    customerQuery.ORCustomerListQuery.CustomerListFilter _
        .ORNameFilter.NameFilter.Name.SetValue "val"
```

Don't forget to change the `"val"` supplied by the SDK to an actual customer name or name fragment. In this case, because the customer name is a string variable of indeterminate length, you could get Valjean, Corvallis, or Stoval, depending on the criterion type you choose.

You can specify an alphabetical range of names instead of a specific name. The range's "from" name must precede the "to" name alphabetically. If you're going to filter in this fashion, adapt the following statements by replacing the two instances of `"val"` with the two name values that frame the range of names you're after:

```
ElseIf ( orNameFilterORElement2 = "NameRangeFilter" ) Then

    customerQuery.ORCustomerListQuery.CustomerListFilter _
        .ORNameFilter.NameRangeFilter.FromName.SetValue "val"
    customerQuery.ORCustomerListQuery.CustomerListFilter _
        .ORNameFilter.NameRangeFilter.ToName.SetValue "val"
End If
```

Just to keep perspective, it helps to back up and review where we are. At this point, the code is building a request message that will be submitted to QuickBooks. The request pertains to customer information in QuickBooks' active company file. The request can have record filters that determine which customer records are returned from QuickBooks, as follows; only one of the three options can be used:

- You can choose to filter on customers' `ListIDs`, which are lengthy values assigned by QuickBooks, and which you'll have to retrieve from QuickBooks before you can use them as filter criteria.
- You can choose to filter on customers' full names, using the Customer:Job pattern.
- Or you can choose to filter according to what the SDK terms the `CustomerListFilter`. In that case, you can specify one or more ways to limit the records that are returned: `MaxReturned`, `ActiveStatus`, a range of modification dates, and either a customer name filter or a range of customer names.

There is one more filter you can apply, the customer's total open balance. As is the case with the `NameFilter`, you have to select the type of criterion you want to use. The code supplied by the SDK assumes that you'll want to retrieve customers whose open balance is less than your criterion value, and so it supplies the criterion type oLessThan:

```
customerQuery.ORCustomerListQuery.CustomerListFilter _
    .TotalBalanceFilter.Operator.SetValue oLessThan
```

More often, you're going to be interested in customers whose open balance is equal to or greater than some figure, so you'd use oGreaterThanEqual instead of oLessThan.

Then you need to specify the value of the criterion itself:

```
customerQuery.ORCustomerListQuery.CustomerListFilter _
    .TotalBalanceFilter.Amount.SetValue 2.00
```

Obviously, you should change the sample value of 2.00 to whatever criterion you want to use for the customer's open balance.

The final End If closes the lengthy If ... Then ... Else structure that characterizes the BuildCustomerQueryRq subroutine. (It was initiated at the outset by testing whether you set orCustomerListQueryORElement1 to "ListID".)

```
End If
```

The section of the code that pertains to filtering records has now concluded. You can at this point provide or omit one or more statements that specify the particular fields you want QuickBooks to return. Simply name the fields in statements like this one:

```
customerQuery.IncludeRetElementList.Add "val"
```

Replace "val" by the name of a field you want to return. Add one or more similar statements to specify additional fields.

You do need to know the names of the fields, and there are two reasonably convenient places to find the relevant field names. One is in the subroutine named ParseCustomerRet, which is covered in the next section. It names all the available fields in expressions like customerRet.FirstName.GetValue. In that expression, customerRet identifies the source and type of data, FirstName is the name of the field, and GetValue actually returns the FirstName value in the current customer record.

Another and perhaps more convenient place to see a list of the available field names is in the OSR itself. Refer to Figure 11.4. In the window displayed there, if you click Response, the elements that pertain to the response message appear, as shown in Figure 11.7. Those elements are the available field names.

The list shown in Figure 11.7 is much more compact than the code in the ParseCustomerRet subroutine, but you have to switch to the OSR to access it.

Finally, the last specification in the BuildCustomerQueryRq subroutine is:

FIGURE 11.7

The first few fields of almost 90 that you can retrieve from QuickBooks customer records.

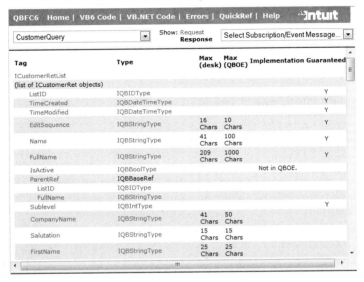

```
customerQuery.OwnerIDList.Add _
    "{22E8C9DC-320B-450d-962A-87CF7246D080}"
```

The statement specifies an owner ID, a random one in the SDK's sample code, which is the ID assigned to the user who created a private data field. As explained earlier in this chapter, in the section "The OwnerIDList element," you can use the SDK to create private data, a sort of custom field that can be accessed only through the SDK. But you can access the private data only if you supply the owner ID that belongs to the creator of the private data field.

If there is private data in the company file, you need to supply the owner ID (or the owner IDs, if there are more private data fields), and the previous code statement is where you do that. If no private data exists in the company file, or if you're not interested in it, do not supply the ID.

However, the company file might contain custom fields, which you can create using the QuickBooks user interface. Those fields are not considered private, but you still need to supply an owner ID to access them via the SDK. Anyone can use the generic owner ID of 0, to get at custom data, as follows:

```
customerQuery.OwnerIDList.Add "0"
```

Note that the specific owner ID for private data is enclosed within curly brackets and quotation marks, but the generic owner ID is enclosed by quotation marks only.

The subroutine ends here:

```
End Sub
```

At this point, control returns to the subroutine that called `BuildCustomerQueryRq`. Using the structure offered by the SDK, that calling subroutine is `DoCustomerQueryRq`. If you refer back to that subroutine, in the section "Fine-tuning the code," you'll see that it next submits the request message set, as built in this section, to QuickBooks. After the `DoRequests` action is complete, a response message set is received from QuickBooks. It remains to do something with the response, and that process is the topic of the next section.

Exploring the CustomerQuery Response Code

The `CustomerQuery` request code, as supplied by the SDK, consists of two subroutines. `DoCustomerQueryRq` performs housekeeping tasks such as declaring variables, establishing communications with QuickBooks, calling the subroutine that actually builds the query, accepting the response from QuickBooks, and forwarding the response. The `BuildCustomerQueryRq` subroutine actually assembles the elements of the query that define which records QuickBooks is to send back and which fields are to be included in the response.

Similarly, the response code comprises two subroutines: `ParseCustomerQueryRq` and `ParseCustomerRet`. The former subroutine performs some initial tests to verify that it's receiving the right kind of response and that the response is valid. If those tests are passed, the subroutine loops through the individual members of the response.

For each member in the response, the subroutine calls `ParseCustomerRet`, which actually gets the value on each field for each customer record. At that point it's up to you what to do with the data. The following section explains the `ParseCustomerQueryRq` subroutine, and the subsequent section explains the `ParseCustomerRet` subroutine.

Understanding the ParseCustomerQueryRs subroutine

In keeping with the approach I've taken in this chapter, I won't modify the code as supplied by the SDK. But I'll include information here and there to suggest how you might manage the data and the code. The assumption is that you are running the code from the Excel VBA platform, and you'll see how to save the QuickBooks data to an Excel worksheet. But the same concepts apply if you prefer to store the records and fields in a true database table or even some other location.

Much of the code in the `ParseCustomerQueryRs` subroutine will probably seem arbitrary or unnecessary. But keep in mind that it doesn't hurt and it might conceivably help; and also that it's been written for you, so that you don't have to modify or maintain it. Just copy it from the OSR into your code module.

Bear in mind that you can move all the `Dim` statements, which declare the names and types of variables, up to the start of the subroutine, immediately following the `Public Sub` statement. Also bear in mind that you can omit from the `ParseCustomerRet` subroutine any field you're not interested in. If you omit a field, your code will run a tiny bit faster and will be a little easier to maintain, but you'll have more work to do if you change your mind and decide you want it after all.

The processing of the response from QuickBooks begins with a statement that initiates the `ParseCustomerQueryRs` subroutine:

```
Public Sub ParseCustomerQueryRs(responseMsgSet As IMsgSetResponse, _
country As String)
```

As noted earlier in the section "Fine-tuning the code," the version of QuickBooks as deter-mined by the country (`"US"`, `"CA"`, and so on) is passed to this subroutine because certain fields are available in some versions but not in others.

```
If (responseMsgSet Is Nothing) Then
    Exit Sub
End If
```

As is the case with `requestMsgSet` in `DoCustomerQueryRq`, it doesn't hurt to include the earlier test, although you would have had to run `ParseCustomerQueryRs` without provid-ing a response from QuickBooks to get any noticeable result from the test.

Declare and set a variable to hold the responses found in the response message set that was passed to this subroutine. Test that an actual list of responses (which might well contain one response only) has been assigned to the response list from the response message set. If that test fails, exit the subroutine; control will be returned to DoCustomerQueryRq's error-handling routine.

```
Dim responseList As IResponseList
Set responseList = responseMsgSet.responseList
If (responseList Is Nothing) Then
    Exit Sub
End If
```

Now loop through the list of responses (again, there may be only one response). Use the vari-able `i` as the loop counter. Notice that the response list begins with response number 0. If there's only one response, then `responseList.Count` equals 1, and the loop will start at response number 0 and also end there. The `GetAt` action is used to access a full response, not merely a single value (then, the `GetValue` action would be used).

```
Dim i As Integer
For i = 0 To responseList.Count - 1
    Dim response As IResponse
    Set response = responseList.GetAt(i)
```

I use the next statement, or a version it, to help me figure out what I've done wrong. The response message has a status code of 0 if all has gone well so far. In that case, the code contin-ues and returns the data that's been requested.

However, if the status code is a value other than 0, there's something wrong with the way I've structured my request. I can use that status code to help determine what the problem is.

As the SDK supplies the test for the response's status code, it looks like this:

```
If (response.StatusCode = 0) Then
```

I prefer to structure it like this:

```
If (response.StatusCode <> 0) Then
    MsgBox response.StatusMessage
Else
```

And then continue with the code as given by the SDK. The benefit I derive is that if I've somehow arranged for an error in my request, I'll see a message on my screen that gives me the information about the error. The message might tell me that a particular value is not allowed as a criterion for a filter.

If, instead of displaying response.StatusMessage, you display response.StatusCode, you must return to the OSR and click Errors at the top of the window. Doing so displays the window shown in Figure 11.8.

For example, if you see that message box and it tells you that the error code was 1, you know that you've done something wrong in setting up your filters: You've made their combined effect so restrictive that QuickBooks couldn't find a single customer that met all their criteria. However, displaying response.StatusMessage in preference to response.StatusCode often gives you better, more specific information than you can get from the OSR's error listing.

It is at this point in the code that you can obtain the metadata that tells you how many records have been retrieved. That statistic is stored in response.retCount, so you could store the result in a worksheet, perhaps in the 100th column of the first row, with something like this:

```
ActiveSheet.Cells(1,100) = response.retCount
```

Or give yourself a real time message with this:

```
MsgBox response.retCount & " records have been retrieved."
```

To continue with the code as given by the SDK:

```
If (Not response.Detail Is Nothing) Then
    Dim responseType As Integer
    responseType = response.Type.GetValue
    Dim j As Integer
    If (responseType = rtCustomerQueryRs) Then
```

FIGURE 11.8

The error numbers are accompanied by a clue to what you might have done wrong building the request.

All StatusCode Values

Code	Meaning	Explanation
0	The QuickBooks server processed the request successfully.	Status OK
1	No match.	The filters used in the query request did not return any matching objects from QuickBooks.
500	One or more objects cannot be found	The query request has not been fully completed. There was a required element ("fieldValue") that could not be found in QuickBooks.
501	Object not in this qbXML specification	Unable to represent objectName "fieldValue" in this version of the SDK.
510	Object cannot be returned	Unable to return object.
530	Unsupported field	The field "fieldName" is not supported by this implementation.
531	Unsupported enum value	The enum value "fieldValue" in the field "fieldName" is not supported by this implementation.
540	QBOE max returned warning	The number of matching elements in query exceed the absolute upper limit (1000). (QBOE only.)
550	Cannot save notes	The objectName object was saved successfully, but its corresponding Notes record could not be saved.
560	Deprecated field used	This field will not always be supported.
600	No cleared state to return	(For error recovery; no message is returned.)
1000	Internal error	There has been an internal error when processing the request.
1010	System not available	System not available.
1030	Unsupported message	This request is not supported by this implementation.
1060	Invalid request ID	The request ID "fieldValue" is invalid, possibly too long. (The maximum is 50 characters.)

The response detail contains customer-by-customer information; there's a record in the detail for each customer that has been returned from QuickBooks. The variable `customerRetList` is declared and the detail records are assigned to it.

Then the code loops through each customer record and hands it off to the final subroutine involved in this process, `ParseCustomerRet`. In that call, notice that the current member of the customer list is passed by means of the `GetAt` action. The value for `country` is also passed along so that the code can decide whether to look for specific fields in the response detail.

```
Dim customerRetList As ICustomerRetList
Set customerRetList = response.Detail
For j = 0 To customerRetList.Count - 1
    ParseCustomerRet customerRetList.GetAt(j), country
Next j
End If
            End If
        End If
    Next i
End Sub
```

At the completion of the `ParseCustomerQueryRs` subroutine, control returns to `DoCustomerQueryRq` to make sure of an orderly completion of the process.

Managing the ParseCustomerRet subroutine

Here's the subroutine that actually gets hold of the customer's values for you to store as you think best:

```
Private Sub ParseCustomerRet(customerRet As ICustomerRet, country _
    As String)
```

Test to make sure that there's actually something in the current customer record. If not, exit this subroutine and go back into the loop to get the next customer record:

```
If (customerRet Is Nothing) Then
    Exit Sub
End If
```

The following two statements are typical of how the SDK's code accesses a field and makes it available to you. The first statement declares a variable of the proper type for each field. The second statement assigns the value that was returned from QuickBooks to that newly declared variable. Here's the code that corresponds to the customer's ID:

```
Dim listID1 As String
listID1 = customerRet.ListID.GetValue
```

If you do nothing else with this code, the data eventually just goes to byte heaven. The SDK offers no code that you can use to save or otherwise process the value of the customer's ListID. When the subroutine has finished acquiring data from the response, control returns to the loop that called the subroutine. The subroutine is called for the next customer, the variable listID1 is declared again, and whatever value it held before has been lost.

Therefore, it's in this subroutine that you must make arrangements to save or process the data that comes back from QuickBooks.

Notice that the listID1 variable has the numeral 1 appended to its name. The next variable is declared as timeCreated2, the next is timeModified3, and so on. This approach helps avoid declaring the same variable twice, because each variable has a unique number appended to its name: declaring a variable twice in the same procedure causes a compile error. (In a few cases, a field's listID and the associated fullName share the same number; for example, the SDK's code for the CustomerQuery includes listID8 and fullName8.)

If you glance back at this chapter's section "Bringing the data into Excel," you'll see that I suggest assigning each value to a row that belongs to the current customer, in a column that belongs to a particular field. I pass a variable that I declare, named RowNum, from the loop in ParseCustomerQueryRs to the current subroutine, ParseCustomerRet. I increment RowNum by 1 each time the loop executes, and I write the current value to that row and to the column I have assigned to the current field.

Therefore in my adaptation of the SDK code, the loop in ParseCustomerQueryRs looks like this:

```
RowNum = 2
For j = 0 To customerRetList.Count - 1
    ParseCustomerRet customerRetList.GetAt(j), country, RowNum
    RowNum = RowNum + 1
Next j
```

My version of the statement that initiates the `ParseCustomerRet` subroutine is:

```
Private Sub ParseCustomerRet(customerRet As ICustomerRet, country _
    As String, RowNum As Integer)
```

Notice that RowNum has been added as an argument to the `ParseCustomerRet` subroutine. In this way, I can get the current row number from `ParseCustomerQueryRs` and into `ParseCustomerRet` for use in keeping track of where the data should be written.

With those arrangements made, here's what I do with the `ListID` field. You can use the same approach for any field returned from QuickBooks:

```
ActiveSheet.Cells (RowNum, 1) = customerRet.ListID.GetValue
```

Notice that with this approach you don't need to declare a variable such as `ListID1`, as the SDK's code does, and assign the current value to it. You simply write the value directly to a worksheet cell, where it's available later. But if you have some other or additional use for the value, you'll probably want to assign it to a variable as suggested by the SDK.

For example, when I'm bringing inventory data back from QuickBooks, I sometimes want to keep a running total of the quantity of a particular item that was bought or sold in a given transaction. I also want to write the current transaction's inventory quantity to a worksheet. To keep the number of accesses to the customer record to a minimum, I might use code such as this:

```
TxnQuantity = colData.Value.GetValue
RunningTotal = RunningTotal + TxnQuantity
ActiveSheet.Cells (RowNum, 5) = TxnQuantity
```

NOTE The `ListID` value, for an object such as a customer or an item, and the `TxnID`, for any transactions such as a sales receipt or a purchase, are necessary values if you want to delete either a member of a list or a transaction. I seldom delete a member of a list, by means either of the QuickBooks user interface or the SDK, but I sometimes find it necessary to delete inventory adjustment transactions. Use the `TxnDel` message to delete transactions and the `ListDel` message to delete members of lists. (You still can't delete a customer who's associated with a transaction or job, however.) If you want to use `TxnDel` or `ListDel`, you'll need to supply the object's ID, and to get that you need to run the appropriate query, such as the `CustomerQuery` I'm explaining in this chapter.

Continuing with the code as supplied by the SDK:

```
Dim timeCreated2 As Date
timeCreated2 = customerRet.TimeCreated.GetValue
```

```
Dim timeModified3 As Date
timeModified3 = customerRet.TimeModified.GetValue

Dim editSequence4 As String
editSequence4 = customerRet.EditSequence.GetValue

Dim name5 As String
name5 = customerRet.Name.GetValue

Dim fullName6 As String
fullName6 = customerRet.FullName.GetValue
```

You see the pattern. Declare a variable with the `Dim` statement, and then assign the appropriate field from the response to that variable. Again, you can add a statement that writes the value to an Excel worksheet or a database table if you want — and there's not much point to running the code in the first place if you're not going to do anything with the data.

At this point the SDK code introduces a wrinkle:

```
If (Not customerRet.IsActive Is Nothing) Then
    Dim isActive7 As Boolean
    isActive7 = customerRet.IsActive.GetValue
End If
```

Refer back to Figure 11.7, and notice that the final column on the right, labeled Guaranteed, contains some Y entries. The Y, standing for Yes, means that the associated element is guaranteed to be returned in the response from QuickBooks.

Given that a response passes the tests administered in the `ParseCustomerQueryRs` subroutine, the response is guaranteed to include a value for `ListID`, `TimeCreated`, `TimeModified`, and so on, through `FullName`. A little farther down the list, `Sublevel` is also guaranteed. (`Sublevel` indicates how far down the hierarchy the record exists: The customer is at the top, and the customer:job is one level down from the customer.)

However, the presence of values in the remaining fields is not guaranteed by the SDK. The first such field is the `IsActive` field. Suppose there is nothing in `customerRet.IsActive` for a particular customer. In that case, the statement

```
isActive7 = customerRet.IsActive.GetValue
```

will fail, and cause the code to stop with a runtime error. Therefore, the SDK code surrounds the variable declaration and assignment statement with an `If` test; if there's nothing in `IsActive` for the current customer, no attempt is made to declare and make an assignment to the `IsActive7` variable — and an error is avoided.

From this point to almost the end of the subroutine, the fields are not guaranteed to contain values, and so all the declarations and assignments use this structure:

```
If (Not customerRet.fieldname Is Nothing) Then
    [Assignment Statement]
End If
```

Here's an alternative. An earlier section in this chapter, "No runtime errors," briefly covered the On Error GoTo Errs statement in the SDK code. A similar statement

```
On Error Resume Next
```

has a similar effect. If a runtime error occurs, the execution of the code is not interrupted, but instead continues at the next statement. In effect the error is ignored.

In this long subroutine, that's exactly what we want to happen. If a value is missing for IsActive, or ParentRef, or CompanyName, or any of about 80 other fields that are not guaranteed, then an error will occur when the code tries to assign a missing value to a variable such as IsActive7, or to a worksheet cell such as ActiveSheet.Cells (RowNum, 7). No harm is done when On Error Resume Next is in effect; the code merely progresses to the next field.

In consequence, once I've set On Error Resume Next, I can trim down the code for any given field to one statement. Instead of this:

```
If (Not customerRet.ParentRef Is Nothing) Then

    Dim fullName8 As String
    fullName8 = customerRet.ParentRef.FullName.GetValue

    Dim listID8 As String
    listID8 = customerRet.ParentRef.ListID.GetValue

End If
```

I can trim it to this:

```
ActiveSheet.Cells (RowNum, 8)=customerRet.ParentRef.FullName.GetValue
ActiveSheet.Cells (RowNum, 9)=customerRet.ParentRef.ListID.GetValue
```

There is little point in repeating the remainder of the SDK code for the ParseCustomerRet subroutine, except for custom fields and private data, which are explained at the end of this section. As the code is provided by the SDK, all the remaining fields are dealt with by testing whether they contain legitimate values; if they do, a variable is declared and the corresponding value is assigned to that variable.

As an alternative, if you're interested in those fields, assign their values to the current RowNum in a worksheet, to a column that remains constant for that field. For example, the two statements immediately prior write the customer's parent full name to column 8 — that's column H — in the worksheet, and the customer's parent's ListID to column 9. (There's nothing special about those columns; you can put the data from the fields in any column you find convenient or useful.)

If you're not interested in a field, you can delete the code that deals with it. However, I suggest that you consider merely commenting out the statement; you do this by inserting an apostrophe at the start of the statement. That changes it to a comment, which is non-executable. Such a statement will be skipped during the execution.

I suggest that you consider commenting out the code pertaining to those fields instead of deleting them because you might change your mind later. It's a lot easier to remove an apostrophe, and thus re-establish an executable statement, than it is to find it again in the SDK code and copy and paste it back into your module. Once you have your code working the way you want, and have run it several times without any problems, then it's more likely that you can safely delete the code.

Here is the code for the final standard field returned by the CustomerQuery. I include it so that you can orient yourself with the code as shown in the OSR:

```
If (Not customerRet.PriceLevelRef Is Nothing) Then

    Dim fullName82 As String
    fullName82 = customerRet.PriceLevelRef.FullName.GetValue

    Dim listID82 As String
    listID82 = customerRet.PriceLevelRef.ListID.GetValue

End If
```

That If block ends the retrieval of the standard fields in the CustomerQuery. The remaining code deals with the retrieval of any custom fields or private data that might be in the company file. If there are no custom fields or private data, or if you're not interested in them, you can simply omit the following If block. Otherwise, include the code just as supplied by the SDK, but make the usual arrangements for saving the results:

```
If (Not customerRet.DataExtRetList Is Nothing) Then
    Dim j As Integer
    For j = 0 To customerRet.DataExtRetList.Count - 1
```

More than one custom field can be defined, so the SDK code for CustomerQuery loops through as many such fields as exist in the company file's customer records.

```
Dim dataExtRet83 As IDataExtRet
Set dataExtRet83 = customerRet.DataExtRetList.GetAt(j)
If (Not dataExtRet83.owner ID Is Nothing) Then
    Dim ownerID84 As String
    ownerID84 = dataExtRet83.owner ID.GetValue
End If
```

You had to supply owner ID in `BuildCustomerQueryRq` to get the custom fields or private data, so there's no special reason to capture it here.

```
Dim dataExtName85 As String
dataExtName85 = dataExtRet83.DataExtName.GetValue
```

`DataExtName` is the name of the custom field or private data. For example, in the Rock Castle Construction file, there's a custom field named B-Day associated with the Customer record.

```
Dim dataExtType86 As ENDataExtType
dataExtType86 = dataExtRet83.DataExtType.GetValue
```

You're unlikely ever to need access to the data type, so even if you're returning a custom field you can omit the `DataExtType` code.

```
Dim dataExtValue87 As String
dataExtValue87 = dataExtRet83.DataExtValue.GetValue
```

The value stored in a custom field or private data is returned by `DataExtValue.GetValue`.

```
        Next j
    End If
End Sub
```

The loop terminates, the If test for custom data ends, and so does the subroutine. Control passes back to `ParseCustomerQueryRq` and from there back to the original subroutine, `DoCustomerQueryRq`.

If you have worked your way through this presentation, you're well placed to generalize it to other SDK queries: for example, queries for lists such as accounts and items, and transactions such as bills and invoices. The basic structure is the same: two request subroutines (one to direct the communications and one to build the query specifics), and two response subroutines (one to test the response's validity and one to put the field values into variables). The names of the subroutines change, as do the names of the fields, but the concepts and structures are largely the same from query to query.

Reports via the SDK are a different matter, and are among the topics to be taken up in Chapter 12.

Managing Reports Using the QuickBooks Software Development Kit

Chapter 11 explains in some detail the construction of queries that you can submit to QuickBooks via the Software Development Kit, or SDK. Sometimes you request the information from QuickBooks because it's intrinsically interesting; perhaps it forms the basis for an analysis that you want to run but that you can't coax out of QuickBooks directly.

And sometimes you want the information because it's necessary to accomplish some other objective. A good example is the edit sequence number, which you have to submit to QuickBooks as part of a request to edit existing information. Without first querying QuickBooks for that edit sequence number, you would not know the value to send to QuickBooks along with the modification you have in mind.

These messages, as the SDK calls them, have to do with queries for information, and with the modification, addition, and deletion of records from QuickBooks. There is another kind of message termed a *report*, and you're right, it has to do with QuickBooks reports.

In the QuickBooks user interface, when you click the Reports menu, you see a list of between 15 and 20 (depending on your QuickBooks version) classifications of reports you can run. Most of these reports are what QuickBooks refers to as *preset reports*. That is, their characteristics have already been prepared by Intuit; you can tinker with them some, but the basic structure of what you're going to get is prearranged. And "preset" just sounds better than "canned."

Deciding to Run Reports through the SDK

You can also run those reports via the SDK. As described in Chapter 11, you might choose to run a request message and its corresponding response message to access the customer or item or account information from a QuickBooks company file. Similarly, as described in this chapter, you might choose to run a report request message and corresponding response to get a P&L report, or a balance sheet, or an inventory valuation summary report.

If you've worked your way through Chapter 11, you know that, regardless of the message type, a request consists of a main subroutine that handles the communications with QuickBooks and another subroutine that builds the query to your specifications. The message response consists of a subroutine that checks the validity of the response, and another subroutine that actually converts the response to usable data.

It's similar with a report. The request includes a subroutine that manages the communications with QuickBooks and one where you set the reports attributes — much like you do in a preset report's Modify Report dialog box. One of the response subroutines checks the validity of the data, and the other subroutine delivers the values that normally appear in the report.

Are you asking yourself why you'd want to bother with all that? Good. That's a question you should be asking. I have three answers for you. If you don't find any of them satisfactory, this chapter isn't for you.

Answer 1: Running reports periodically

It may be that you want to get a P&L and a balance sheet once a month, along with a few other status reports like an inventory valuation summary, a payroll summary, and an aging report. If so, you probably have made some modifications to those reports, so that they include information that you find valuable and omit data that you don't. It might be, for example, that you are very interested in seeing income and expenses both as dollars and as a percent of sales, but you could not care less about a comparison with the same accounting period last year.

So you probably make the changes to the preset reports that fit your own business needs and save, or "memorize," the report so that you don't have to make the same modifications again when the next accounting period rolls around.

But you still have to open the reports manually before you can review them on your computer screen or send them to the printer. Agreed: It doesn't take much to do that, but you still have to do it. And if you have ten reports or so that you want to consult regularly, it becomes somewhat more tedious to get them all opened, reviewed, and printed.

If you arrange to have the reports generated through the SDK, you can do it all by running just one utility. Built the right way, you can arrange for a driver routine to first run a P&L, then a balance sheet, then an inventory report, and so on in a matter of seconds. That's the thing about a computer: It may be stupid as a chair, but it's wonderfully fast.

And you can save all those preferences for subcolumns, for cash versus accrual, for years or quarters or months across the top, and various other options in the code that you assemble, so they'll be there next accounting period.

Is there a downside? Sure. You have to decide where to put the data. But the code that's supplied by the SDK does a reasonable job of helping you out with that, by telling you what the current row and column numbers are. When you know those, and the values to store, you're well placed to create automatically all the reports you want.

Answer 2: Analyzing the report's data

Several other chapters in this book explain how to generate quantitative analyses of your QuickBooks data in a platform such as Microsoft Excel, and — as you surely know — QuickBooks supports the export of reports directly to Excel worksheets in a variety of ways.

But QuickBooks' export capabilities are rudimentary. You cannot, for example, orient a summary report so that it's turned 90 degrees from its orientation in the QuickBooks user interface, and run dates down the left border and accounts across the top. That orientation can be useful for reasons ranging from fitting properly on an overhead slide to submitting the data to Excel's analysis tool pack. (The tool pack offers powerful functions, but it's also extremely persnickety about how you hand data off to it.)

If you create the report by adapting the SDK's code, you can orient it any way you want. For example, to achieve a 90-degree transposition of the report, use the row numbers that the code gives you as column numbers, and vice versa.

Answer 3: Combining reports

Way back in Chapter 1, I pointed out that many QuickBooks Pro Advisors start with a client's reports when they need to track down the source of unexpected results. For example, they can make inferences about what might have gone wrong if two reports disagree, when they normally should report the same total figures.

They have memorized reports that they want to run, of course, but it's often the case that they need only a few numbers from a given report to compare with, or provide context for, numbers in a different report.

Rather than running a series of memorized reports to get just a few significant numbers, it can work much more efficiently to run the reports via a stack of SDK requests and responses, keeping only the data that's of interest and ignoring the rest. At the end of the run, all the important numbers can be placed along with the appropriate identifiers on a single page or worksheet. (My thanks for this idea to this book's technical editor, Bill Murphy.)

An Overview of a Report Message

If you're still here, then I've convinced you at least provisionally that there can be good reasons to create reports using the SDK. You can still change your mind, of course, and the next question you should be asking yourself is whether there's enough bang for the buck. In this case, the buck consists mostly of becoming familiar with the code so that you can modify it to suit your purposes.

This section steps you through a request and response in much the same way that Chapter 11 did for a query and a modification message. You'll see where in the code you can make the

TABLE 12.1

Report Messages and Preset Reports

GeneralSummaryReportQuery	GeneralDetailReportQuery
Balance Sheet Previous Year Comparison	1099 Detail
Balance Sheet Standard	Audit Trail
Balance Sheet Summary	Balance Sheet Detail
Customer Balance Summary	Check Detail
Expense by Vendor Summary	Customer Balance Detail
Income by Customer Summary	Deposit Detail
Income Tax Summary	Estimates by Job
Inventory Stock Status by Item	Expense by Vendor Detail
Inventory Stock Status by Vendor	General Ledger
Inventory Valuation Summary	Income by Customer Detail
Physical Inventory Worksheet	Income Tax Detail
Profit and Loss by Class	Inventory Valuation Detail
Profit and Loss by Job	Job Progress Invoices vs. Estimates
Profit and Loss Previous Year Comparison	Journal
Profit and Loss Standard	Missing Checks
Profit and Loss YTD Comparison	Open Invoices
Purchase by Item Summary	Open POs
Purchase by Vendor Summary	Open POs by Job
Sales by Customer Summary	Open Sales Order By Customer
Sales by Item Summary	Open Sales Order By Items
Sales by Rep Summary	Pending Sales
Sales Tax Liability	Profit and Loss Detail
Sales Tax Revenue Summary	Purchase by Item Detail
Trial Balance	Purchase by Vendor Detail
Vendor Balance Summary	Sales by Customer Detail
	Sales by Item Detail
	Sales by Rep Detail
	Transaction Detail by Account

minor modifications needed to tailor a report so that it directly addresses your requirements. You'll also see where you need to insert a line of code to write the results directly to an Excel worksheet.

Report categories

The QuickBooks SDK places different reports into different categories (very different from the categories you see in the QuickBooks user interface). This book touches on the topic of report categories in Chapter 1, in the section "Understanding QuickBooks reports," which explains the differences between summary and detail reports. It's important to flesh out the topic here,

TABLE 12.1

Report Messages and Preset Reports (continued)

GeneralSummaryReportQuery	GeneralDetailReportQuery
	Transaction List by Customer
	Transaction List by Date
	Transaction List by Vendor
	Unbilled Costs by Job
	Unpaid Bills Detail
	Vendor Balance Detail
PayrollSummaryReportQuery	**PayrollDetailReportQuery**
Employee Earnings Summary	Employee State Taxes Detail
Payroll Liability Balances	Payroll Item Detail
Payroll Summary	Payroll Review Detail
	Payroll Transaction Detail
	Payroll Transactions by Payee
JobReportQuery	**TimeReportQuery**
Item Estimates vs. Actual	Time by Item
Item Profitability	Time by Job Detail
Job Estimates vs. Actuals Details	Time by Job Summary
Job Estimates vs. Actuals Summary	Time by Name
Job Profitability Detail	
Job Profitability Summary	
AgingReportQuery	**BudgetSummaryReportQuery**
AP Aging Detail	Balance Sheet Budget Overview
AP Aging Summary	Balance Sheet Budget vs. Actual
AR Aging Detail	Profit and Loss Budget Overview
AR Aging Summary	Profit and Loss Budget vs. Actual
Collections Report	Profit and Loss Budget Performance

because you choose a message — which is tantamount to an SDK report category — from the Onscreen Reference (OSR) depending on which report you want to generate.

Table 12.1 presents the correspondence between preset reports and the report message you need to use to obtain each one. The name of the report message is shown under the category heading. See the section "Examining a Report Message's Code," later in this chapter, for the steps involved in getting the code that's supplied by the SDK for a given report.

Specifying the report

Each report message, shown in boldface in the table, has a setting in the request portion of the message where you can specify the particular report that you're after. For example, if you wanted your basic report to be a Balance Sheet Standard report, you would choose the GeneralSummaryReportQuery message, because that's where the Balance Sheet Standard report is located in the table. Then, in the code for the request, you would find where the SDK has put this statement:

```
generalSummaryReportQuery.GeneralSummaryReportType.SetValue _
    gsrtBalanceSheetPrevYearComp
```

(The SDK uses the Balance Sheet Prev Year Comparison report as an example in its sample code for the General Summary Report message.) Replace this

```
gsrtBalanceSheetPrevYearComp
```

with this

```
gsrtBalanceSheetSummary
```

As explained in Chapter 11, when you paste code from the SDK into a Visual Basic for Applications (VBA) module and set a reference to the qbFC6 type library, selecting a different argument is easy. In the module, just delete the reference to the existing argument (here, gsrtBalanceSheetPrevYearComp), including the blank space immediately before the argument. Now, when you re-enter that blank space, you get a contextual menu that lists all the report types found in the message you chose.

Scroll down that list to gsrtBalanceSheetSummary, or some other report that you want to create, and press the Tab key. The entry for that report automatically appears in the code.

Custom summary and detail reports

If you want to replicate a preset report, you find the report you're after in Table 12.1. Then, using the OSR, you select the report message belonging to that the report.

As shown in Chapter 11, you obtain the request and the response code for the message, paste it into VBA modules, and edit the code in order to tailor the report as you see fit. The advantage to using a message that returns a preset report is that many aspects of the report are easily available to you.

For example, you can choose to set the report's date range to Last Fiscal Quarter or This Month to Date. In a summary report, you can call for subcolumns that show the prior period's results as well as the current period's. In a detail report, you can call for columns such as Account, Class, and Memo that might not be available unless you specify them as options.

So a preset report offers plenty of options for you to select from. But nothing's free, and the cost here is that you have to accept some limitations to a report's design if you want to take advantage of its conveniences. Both summary and detail reports contain subtotals and totals interspersed among the other lines in the report: the Sales by Item Detail and the Sales by Item Summary reports include a subtotal for each item. You might not want those subtotals to be in the report because if you want to total the figures, the subtotals result in inflated sums unless you first go to the trouble of removing them.

That's one reason that queries such as the `ItemQuery` are useful. The information returns from QuickBooks without niceties such as subtotals, totals, and blank lines that separate groups in a report. A query's results are less organized than a report's, but from the standpoint of preparing an analysis they're cleaner.

Custom summary and detail reports occupy a middle ground between preset report messages and query messages in the SDK. They place fewer restrictions, such as mixing different data sources, in your way than do preset reports (but they offer fewer options). They offer more ways to organize the data as it's returned from QuickBooks than do query messages (but there's less flexibility as to where to put the results).

For example, suppose you wanted to create a report laid out as a table to show which customers spent how much money on each item you sell. One possibility would be to structure a Custom Summary report that put customer types (such as commercial and residential) in columns and items in rows. There's no preset summary report that provides that data, largely because customer type does not appear in the lists of fields available for most preset reports.

You could create a query message that would return individual transactions, including the customer type, the item sold, and the sales revenue. But you would have to filter at some point for sales transactions, and the data would come back from QuickBooks in list format, not organized as a report.

So this is the sort of problem for which you might want to consider using a Custom Summary or Custom Detail report: You want some of the conveniences associated with a QuickBooks report, but you also want to exercise more control over the contents than a preset report offers.

You can create a Custom Summary or Custom Detail report either from the QuickBooks user interface or by means of the SDK. However, because a custom report has many fewer restrictions on its data source and basic layout than does a preset report, you won't find the custom report messages in the categories shown in Table 12.1. They constitute their own messages, `CustomSummaryReportQuery` and `CustomDetailReportQuery`.

Examining a Report Message's Code

With the preceding material as an introduction, it's useful to look at the report message code as supplied by the QuickBooks SDK. If you have not yet looked through the material in Chapter 11, you should consider reading or reviewing it before you dig into the present material on report messages. The query messages in Chapter 11 share many concepts with the report messages in this chapter.

Acquiring the code

As usual, to get to the message code, take these steps:

1. Start Excel or open a new workbook. Press Alt+F11 to switch to the Visual Basic Editor.

2. Choose Insert ▶ Module twice to establish two new modules.

3. Open the Onscreen Reference (OSR), found in the Start menu under QuickBooks SDK 6.0.

4. Use the Select Message dropdown to locate and select the GeneralSummaryReportQuery message.

5. The OSR window changes to display the fields and settings available in the selected report query; see Figure 12.1. Make sure that Request is selected at the top of the window and click the VB6 Code link.

6. A new window appears that contains the code for the request portion of the message. Choose Select All from your browser's Edit menu, or right-click anywhere in the code and choose Select All from the contextual menu.

7. Choose Edit ▶ Copy.

8. Switch to Excel's Visual Basic Editor and choose Edit ▶ Paste to paste the request code into the module. See Figure 12.2.

9. In the Visual Basic Editor's Project pane, double-click the second module you established in Step 2, to display it on your screen. It should be empty (or nearly so, if you call for Option Explicit to be supplied automatically in new modules).

10. Switch back to the OSR and close the window with the request code.

11. In the window that displays the GeneralSummaryReportQuery message, click the Response link. The fields and settings that apply to the response appear. Click VB6 Code.

12. Repeat Steps 6 through 8 to establish the response message code in the second module.

13. Choose Tools ▶ References and scroll down the Available References list box to find the qbFC6 1.0 Type Library; see Figure 12.3. Fill its checkbox and click OK.

14. Switch back to the main Excel window and save the workbook.

FIGURE 12.1

Click a tag to see some of its specifications at the bottom of the window.

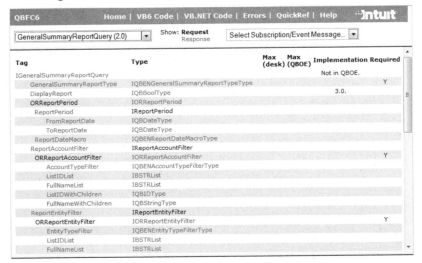

You now have an Excel workbook with the unaltered SDK code that retrieves the data for a general summary report from QuickBooks. I find it helpful to use the Visual Basic Editor's Properties window to name the modules, in this case something like `GeneralSummaryRequest` and `GeneralSummaryResponse`. (Embedded spaces are not allowed in module names.)

NOTE The next section covers Visual Basic code that you can run to create a report, and provides guidance about causing the code to execute. Running code that generates a report involves no modification to data in your company file. Nevertheless, it's often a good idea to back up a company file before you open it by means of code. Particularly when I'm still developing my code, I either back up an important company file first, or I use an unimportant company file that I've built as a test bed.

The summary report request message

The code for the report request will look familiar if you have worked through Chapter 11. It starts by establishing a driver subroutine that takes as its arguments the country that your version of QuickBooks assumes, plus the major and minor versions of the SDK that you're using.

```
Public Sub DoGeneralSummaryReportQueryRq(country As String, _
    majorVersion As Integer, minorVersion As Integer)
```

The latter statement is the one that initiates the processing of the report. It takes three arguments, and that's inconvenient. As explained in Chapter 11, I usually supply another short subroutine such as the following three-statement procedure:

The VB Editor usually shows three windows: the Project Explorer window in the upper left, the Properties window in the lower left, and the Code window on the right.

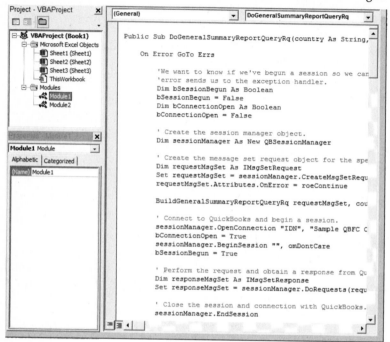

You should not have to browse to find qbFC6 1.0 Type Library; after successful installation it should automatically appear in the References list.

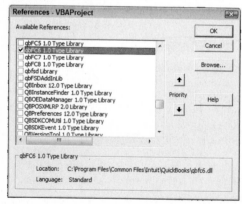

```
Sub GetReport()
DoGeneralSummaryReportQueryRq "US",6,0
End Sub
```

With the `GetReport` subroutine established, I can click on the `Sub GetReport()` statement, which includes no arguments, and press F5 to start the processing. If I click on a `Sub` statement that includes arguments and press F5, I get prompted to supply the name of a macro. In other words, the Visual Basic interface gets confused if I try to run a subroutine with arguments by pressing F5. Therefore I arrange things so that I begin with a subroutine that has no arguments; that subroutine calls the one that I really want to run.

Bear in mind as you review this material that in the code, the underscore at the end of a line is a continuation character, meaning that the statement has been split into at least two separate lines and is continued on the line following the underscore. This convention is part of Visual Basic. However, it is not used in the code samples from the OSR; there, lengthy statements are simply allowed to trail off the right side of the screen. So when you examine code in the OSR and see a statement that appears truncated, try scrolling right to see if there's more to the statement than is initially in view.

A label, `Errs`, is found later in this subroutine. In the event that an error occurs in this code, control flows to the first executable statement following the `Errs` label. (Errors can occur in the assembled request, but those are identified in QuickBooks, and you use the response's status code to diagnose the error.) You'll find more about that in the section "The summary report response message."

```
On Error GoTo Errs
```

Two Boolean variables are declared and set to `False`; they will be useful in the event that error processing is needed.

```
Dim bSessionBegun As Boolean
bSessionBegun = False
Dim bConnectionOpen As Boolean
bConnectionOpen = False
```

A variable named `sessionManager` is declared and set equal to the object that has all the actions and objects needed to manage a QuickBooks session.

```
Dim sessionManager As New QBSessionManager
```

A request message set is declared. This message set will contain all the specifications you select in the subroutine named `BuildGeneralSummaryReportQueryRq`, covered in its own section in this chapter. The request message set will be submitted to QuickBooks for processing, and the responses — in this case, the responses are data values to populate the report — will be returned from QuickBooks in a response message.

```
Dim requestMsgSet As IMsgSetRequest
Set requestMsgSet = sessionManager.CreateMsgSetRequest _
(country, majorVersion, minorVersion)
```

As noted, it's possible to create errors in the request message set; for example, you might decide to ask for accounts to occupy columns in the report, but not all report types support that option. The code supplied by the SDK does not check for that sort of error: It is caught only after QuickBooks has tried to interpret the request.

So, the code needs to tell QuickBooks what to do if it encounters that sort of error in the request. The principal choices are to continue processing any other requests that are in the message (roeContinue), or to stop processing and pass the response back to your code (roeStop).

```
requestMsgSet.Attributes.OnError = roeContinue
```

Now control is handed off to the BuildGeneralSummaryReportQueryRq subroutine, explained in the next section. The request message set is passed to the subroutine because its attributes (which specific report is wanted, the desired range of dates, and so on) must be set. In the case of a general summary report, the country argument is superfluous because the subroutine does not use it.

```
BuildGeneralSummaryReportQueryRq requestMsgSet, country
```

NOTE You could delete the `country` argument here, in the call to the subroutine, but if you do so then you need to delete it from the list of arguments in the called subroutine's first statement.

After the BuildGeneralSummaryReportQueryRq subroutine has completed successfully, control returns here. With the request built, it's time to open the connection to QuickBooks and begin a session, setting the associated Boolean variables to True. The omDontCare argument used to begin the session indicates that it doesn't matter whether QuickBooks is in single- or multiuser mode.

```
sessionManager.OpenConnection "IDN", "Sample QBFC Code"
bConnectionOpen = True
sessionManager.BeginSession "", omDontCare
bSessionBegun = True
```

Now the response message set, which will hold the returned report data, is declared. Then the session manager delivers the request message set to QuickBooks by means of its DoRequests method, which also assigns the results to the newly declared response message set.

```
Dim responseMsgSet As IMsgSetResponse
Set responseMsgSet = sessionManager.DoRequests(requestMsgSet)
```

Once the response message set has been populated with report data and other information (such as row and column counts, and error codes), the session can be terminated and the connection closed. The Boolean variables are updated accordingly.

```
sessionManager.EndSession
bSessionBegun = False
sessionManager.CloseConnection
bConnectionOpen = False
```

Finally, the response message set is sent to the subroutines that validate the response and parse out the report data from the message set, into a form that you can use directly. The `country` argument is included by the SDK's code in an excess of caution, because the receiving subroutines do not make use of it.

```
ParseGeneralSummaryReportQueryRs responseMsgSet, country
```

In the normal course of events, no errors have occurred and when the code encounters the `Exit Sub` statement, processing ceases, or if the subroutine was called by another, control returns to the calling procedure.

```
Exit Sub
```

On the other hand, if an error occurs, control comes to the first executable statement following the `Errs` label, which is the following `MsgBox` statement.

```
Errs:
MsgBox "HRESULT = " & Err.Number & " (" & Hex(Err.Number) & ") " &
    vbCrLf & vbCrLf & Err.Description, vbOKOnly, "Error"
```

The message box displays some information about the error, which you may or may not find helpful in diagnosing it.

TIP Early in development, I usually leave the `MsgBox` statement in place, because it sometimes gives me a useful hint to the source of the problem. If an error occurs, though, I then tell my code to break on all errors. In the Visual Basic Editor, I choose Tools ▶ Options and click the General tab. I choose the Break On All Errors option in the Error Trapping area. Now when an error occurs, the code stops at the statement that causes the error and displays the statement, highlighted in yellow. This is often a much more efficient way of locating the source of an error than relying on the sketchy information in the message box. Once I have the error located and fixed, I change back the error trapping on the General tab, usually to Break On Unhandled Errors.

Unless you have created a user form in your Visual Basic project named SampleCodeForm, you should delete the next statement. It adds no useful functionality to your code.

```
SampleCodeForm.ErrorMsg.Text = Err.Description
```

Finally, if an error occurred, you want to make sure that the session is ended and the connection is closed. The `End Sub` either stops the processing or passes control back to any calling subroutine that might have been used.

```
If (bSessionBegun) Then
    sessionManager.EndSession
End If
If (bConnectionOpen) Then
    sessionManager.CloseConnection
End If

End Sub
```

This section has described the main, top-level subroutine involved in creating and processing a general summary report message. It is in many ways similar to the corresponding subroutine used for a direct query, as explained in Chapter 11. But the next section, which shows how you adapt the SDK's code to tailor your report request message, differs substantially from what's found in Chapter 11.

Building the report request

For the typical query, such as those explained in Chapter 11, most of the subroutine that builds the request specifications pertains to record filters: perhaps most often a range of dates for the query to use in selecting records to return. That sort of filter is also used in building a report request, but in addition you specify attributes such as the specific type of summary report you want. You also specify choices such as column contents that you might make for the report in the QuickBooks user interface.

As always, the subroutine begins with a statement that names it and its arguments.

```
Public Sub BuildGeneralSummaryReportQueryRq(requestMsgSet As _
    IMsgSetRequest, country As String)
```

Notice that the list of arguments corresponds to the arguments in the statement that calls this subroutine, both as to their order and their type. There's no requirement that the names of the arguments be the same as in the calling statement, but it can be convenient to use the same names and that's the approach that the SDK takes.

```
If (requestMsgSet Is Nothing) Then
    Exit Sub
End If
```

A variable is declared that will hold the summary report query, and the query is appended to the request message set passed here from the main subroutine.

```
Dim generalSummaryReportQuery As IGeneralSummaryReportQuery
Set generalSummaryReportQuery = _
    requestMsgSet.AppendGeneralSummaryReportQueryRq
```

The next statement specifies *which* summary report you want. The SDK code uses the Balance Sheet Prev Year Comparison report as an example. There are 25 preset summary reports that you can choose from. As noted earlier in the section "Specifying the report," it's easy to select another report type. Using the Delete or the Backspace key, remove the report type that's presently specified. As part of that removal, delete the blank space between SetValue and

FIGURE 12.4

The dropdown does not appear if you have not arranged a reference to the type library; see Figure 12.3.

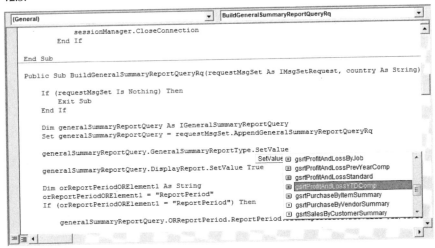

the name of the report type. Then retype that blank space; when you do, a contextual menu appears with a list of the preset report types that are available from the General Summary Report Query. (See Figure 12.4.)

You will need to interpret the names of those report types in order to choose the one you want. For example, you'll need to infer that `gsrtProfitAndLossYTDComp` means Profit & Loss Year To Date Comparison, but you shouldn't have any trouble with that or any of the other reports.

```
generalSummaryReportQuery.GeneralSummaryReportType.SetValue _
    gsrtBalanceSheetPrevYearComp
```

Particularly during development, I find the next statement of great value. I can use `True` to display in QuickBooks the preset report I have chosen. That often helps me figure out errors I might have made in structuring the report in the code. But you'll want to remember to re-set the value to `False` after the code's been debugged: If it's left `True`, the report is re-created in the QuickBooks user interface every time the code is run. You can wind up with seventeen instances of the same report open in QuickBooks. Then you'll have to close them.

```
generalSummaryReportQuery.DisplayReport.SetValue True
```

The remainder of the subroutine concerns setting filters for the report data. In most cases, you must choose between alternatives — for example, a range of specific dates versus a *type* of date range, such as the current fiscal year or the previous fiscal year. Those choices are managed by If … Else If … End If blocks of code. Then you need to specify some layout preferences, such as how report columns should be defined (Customer? Vendor? Item? Account? and so on).

Filtering by date

The first choice for the report filters concerns the date range:

```
Dim orReportPeriodORElement1 As String
orReportPeriodORElement1 = "ReportPeriod"
```

A normal string variable, orReportPeriodORElement1, is declared and set equal to "ReportPeriod" for specific dates; if you want instead to use a calculated range of dates such as Last Fiscal Quarter you would set the string variable equal to "ReportDateMacro".

The values assigned to the string variable are arbitrary. Whereas an attribute such as FromReportDate is a name that has meaning to QuickBooks, the values "ReportPeriod" and "ReportDateMacro" do not. You could instead use values that have more meaning to you, such as "Specific Dates" and "Accounting Period". Or "Bonnie" and "Clyde". It really doesn't matter, so long as you have a way to say that you want a range of specific dates instead of an accounting period, or vice versa.

```
If (orReportPeriodORElement1 = "ReportPeriod") Then
    generalSummaryReportQuery.ORReportPeriod.ReportPeriod. _
        FromReportDate.SetValue #12/31/2003#
```

Reset the "from" and the "to" date values as given in the SDK to the date values you want, assuming that you want to use a range of specific dates. Enclose them between # characters to show that you're supplying date values.

```
generalSummaryReportQuery.ORReportPeriod.ReportPeriod. _
    ToReportDate.SetValue #12/31/2003#
```

But if you want to restrict the report to an accounting period that's relative to the current date, you use what the SDK calls a *date macro*. Your choice of period is set in the next two statements. The first statement simply indicates that you have chosen the accounting period option rather than the specific dates option:

```
ElseIf (orReportPeriodORElement1 = "ReportDateMacro") Then
```

The second of the two statements specifies the accounting period. As the SDK presents the code, the default value of All as used in the QuickBooks user interface is used, although "All" is translated to "rdmAll". Other choices you have include rdmLastMonth, rdmLastQuarter, rdmThisQuarterToDate, and all the other options you're familiar with from designing your reports in the QuickBooks report window.

```
generalSummaryReportQuery.ORReportPeriod.ReportDateMacro. _
    SetValue rdmAll
```

Terminate the report date If block and move on to the account filter If block:

```
End If
```

Filtering by account

A string variable that holds your choice as to type of account filter is declared and given the value `AccountTypeFilter`. Using this value you can restrict the report results to information regarding different types of accounts, such as Income, Asset, Expense, and Liability.

```
Dim orReportAccountFilterORElement2 As String
orReportAccountFilterORElement2 = "AccountTypeFilter"

If (orReportAccountFilterORElement2 = "AccountTypeFilter") Then
```

The next statement is where you specify the type of account you want. The value supplied by the SDK is `atfAccountsPayable`, but your many other choices include `atfARAndAP`, `atfCostOfSales`, and `atfEquity`.

```
generalSummaryReportQuery.ReportAccountFilter. _
    ORReportAccountFilter.AccountTypeFilter.SetValue _
        atfAccountsPayable
```

If you don't want to specify a type of account, you might still want to specify a particular account. In that case, you have more choices: whether to identify an account with its `ListID` or with its full name, and whether to include an account's subaccounts.

Either a `ListID` or a full name uniquely identifies a particular object — here, an account. Certainly it's a lot easier to use the full name, because it's easy to find out what the full name is: Just examine the chart of accounts in the QuickBooks user interface. It's more difficult to get the account's `ListID`: you have to run a query as outlined in Chapter 11, because that ID never appears in the user interface.

On the other hand, the SDK documentation suggests that using the `ListID` is a surer method because an account name can be changed. The only way to change an account's `ListID` is to delete the account and then create a new one to take its place. But that also requires the deletion of any transactions and items used with that account.

Whichever method you select, full name or `ListID`, and assuming that you want to filter by account at all, you can specify that you want the account along with its child records (in this case, a child record is a subaccount). The code you use to make your selection, full name or `ListID`, with or without child records, is self-explanatory. Of course you will want to replace the placeholder `"val"` with an actual `ListID` or full name.

```
ElseIf (orReportAccountFilterORElement2 = "ListID") Then

    generalSummaryReportQuery.ReportAccountFilter. _
        ORReportAccountFilter.ListIDList.Add "val"

ElseIf (orReportAccountFilterORElement2 = "FullName") Then

    generalSummaryReportQuery.ReportAccountFilter. _
        ORReportAccountFilter.FullNameList.Add "val"
```

```
        ElseIf (orReportAccountFilterORElement2 = "ListIDWithChildren") Then

            generalSummaryReportQuery.ReportAccountFilter. _
                ORReportAccountFilter.ListIDWithChildren.SetValue "val"

        ElseIf (orReportAccountFilterORElement2 ="FullNameWithChildren") Then

            generalSummaryReportQuery.ReportAccountFilter. _
                ORReportAccountFilter.FullNameWithChildren.SetValue "val"

        End If
```

Filtering by entity: customer, vendor, employee, or other name

If you want to filter for a particular customer, vendor, or employee in your summary report, use the entity filter. As with the account filter, you can use the `ListID` or the full name, and you can specify whether child records should be returned. For example, specifying full name with children as the filter and supplying a customer name as the criterion would return the jobs associated with that customer.

```
        Dim orReportEntityFilterORElement3 As String
        orReportEntityFilterORElement3 = "EntityTypeFilter"
        If (orReportEntityFilterORElement3 = "EntityTypeFilter") Then
```

Your first choice in the entity filter indicates whether you want to filter for all customers, for all vendors, or all employees. You can also filter for another type of entity, a member of the Other Names list.

```
        generalSummaryReportQuery.ReportEntityFilter. _
            ORReportEntityFilter.EntityTypeFilter.SetValue etfCustomer
```

If instead you want to filter for a particular customer, vendor, employee, or name on the Other Names list, use the `ListID` or the full name, without or with child records, as follows:

```
        ElseIf (orReportEntityFilterORElement3 = "ListID") Then

            generalSummaryReportQuery.ReportEntityFilter. _
                ORReportEntityFilter.ListIDList.Add "val"

        ElseIf (orReportEntityFilterORElement3 = "FullName") Then

            generalSummaryReportQuery.ReportEntityFilter. _
                ORReportEntityFilter.FullNameList.Add "val"

        ElseIf (orReportEntityFilterORElement3 = "ListIDWithChildren") Then

            generalSummaryReportQuery.ReportEntityFilter. _
                ORReportEntityFilter.ListIDWithChildren.SetValue "val"
```

```
ElseIf (orReportEntityFilterORElement3 = "FullNameWithChildren") Then

    generalSummaryReportQuery.ReportEntityFilter. _
        ORReportEntityFilter.FullNameWithChildren.SetValue "val"

End If
```

Again, be sure to replace the SDK's `"val"` placeholder with a legitimate value for any type of entity that you intend to use as a filter.

Note that if an object has no children, specifying full name with children is equivalent to specifying the full name only.

Filtering by item

Filtering on the basis of one or more Items follows the same basic pattern as is used for accounts and entities (customers, vendors, employees, and other names). You can choose to filter on an item type by setting the `ItemTypeFilter`, and the SDK's code shows that possibility by supplying the `itfAllExceptFixedAsset` item type. Other item type choices are as you would select them on the Filters tab of the Modify Report dialog box: Inventory, Assembly, Service, and so on. You need to take a little care in mapping the items available in the SDK code to those available in the user interface — for example, what the Filter tab refers to as All Parts is referred to in the SDK code as `itfNonInventory`.

On the other hand, if you prefer to select a specific item, with or without subitems, you supply either the `ListID` or the item's full name. Remember that the `"val"` the SDK code supplies is intended as just a placeholder, but because an item name is a string, `"val"` will not cause a debug error. It will not return any records, though, unless you have defined an item whose full name is `"val"`.

```
Dim orReportItemFilterORElement4 As String
orReportItemFilterORElement4 = "ItemTypeFilter"

If (orReportItemFilterORElement4 = "ItemTypeFilter") Then
    generalSummaryReportQuery.ReportItemFilter. _
        ORReportItemFilter.ItemTypeFilter.SetValue itfAllExceptFixedAsset

ElseIf (orReportItemFilterORElement4 = "ListID") Then

    generalSummaryReportQuery.ReportItemFilter. _
        ORReportItemFilter.ListIDList.Add "val"

ElseIf (orReportItemFilterORElement4 = "FullName") Then

    generalSummaryReportQuery.ReportItemFilter. _
        ORReportItemFilter.FullNameList.Add "val"

ElseIf (orReportItemFilterORElement4 = "ListIDWithChildren") Then

    generalSummaryReportQuery.ReportItemFilter. _
        ORReportItemFilter.ListIDWithChildren.SetValue "val"
```

```
    ElseIf (orReportItemFilterORElement4 = "FullNameWithChildren") Then

        generalSummaryReportQuery.ReportItemFilter. _
            ORReportItemFilter.FullNameWithChildren.SetValue "val"

    End If
```

Filtering by class

The final set of filters for you to choose among pertains to Class. If you have set up different values of Class in the company file, you can filter on Class by means of ListID or FullName, with or without children (for subclasses, if you have set them up). There is no type within Class, as there is with Items and Entities, so that filter option does not exist in the Class filter.

```
Dim orReportClassFilterORElement5 As String
orReportClassFilterORElement5 = "ListID"
If (orReportClassFilterORElement5 = "ListID") Then
    generalSummaryReportQuery.ReportClassFilter. _
        ORReportClassFilter.ListIDList.Add "val"

ElseIf (orReportClassFilterORElement5 = "FullName") Then

    generalSummaryReportQuery.ReportClassFilter. _
        ORReportClassFilter.FullNameList.Add "val"

ElseIf (orReportClassFilterORElement5 = "ListIDWithChildren") Then

    generalSummaryReportQuery.ReportClassFilter. _
        ORReportClassFilter.ListIDWithChildren.SetValue "val"

ElseIf (orReportClassFilterORElement5 = "FullNameWithChildren") Then

    generalSummaryReportQuery.ReportClassFilter. _
        ORReportClassFilter.FullNameWithChildren.SetValue "val"

End If
```

Additional report request specifications

The date, account, entity, item, and class filters explained earlier can be used in combination, but the individual choices within each are mutually exclusive — note the use of Else If statements in each If block. There is only one other filter in the general summary report message that is handled in that fashion, the date modified filter. For analysis purposes, this filter's applicability is quite limited and it is displayed later without comment.

There are some additional filters and specifications that you can use, and you can use them in combination with the filters explained so far:

```
generalSummaryReportQuery.ReportTxnTypeFilter. _
    TxnTypeFilterList.Add ttfAll
```

If you want to restrict the report to a particular type of transaction, use `ttfBill`, `ttfCharge`, `ttfDeposit`, or any of the other transaction types supported in QuickBooks, instead of `ttfAll`. You will want to take care that a transaction type filter does not conflict with any account filter that you've specified. No harm will befall you if you call for `ttfCheck` as the transaction type and have already specified `atfAccountsPayable` as the account type to select, but you won't get back any useful information.

The modification date filter works like the date filter explained earlier, but it attends to the date on which transactions were last modified rather than the date on which they were created.

```
Dim orReportModifiedDateORElement6 As String
orReportModifiedDateORElement6 = "ReportModifiedDateRangeFilter"
If (orReportModifiedDateORElement6 = _
    "ReportModifiedDateRangeFilter") Then

    generalSummaryReportQuery.ORReportModifiedDate. _
        ReportModifiedDateRangeFilter.FromReportModifiedDate. _
        SetValue #12/31/2003#

    generalSummaryReportQuery.ORReportModifiedDate. _
        ReportModifiedDateRangeFilter.ToReportModifiedDate. _
        SetValue #12/31/2003#

ElseIf (orReportModifiedDateORElement6 = _
    "ReportModifiedDateRangeMacro") Then

    generalSummaryReportQuery.ORReportModifiedDate. _
        ReportModifiedDateRangeMacro.SetValue rmdrmAll

End If
```

Use the next two filters just as you would in the QuickBooks user interface using the Detail Level and Posting Status filters on the Filters tab of the Modify Report dialog box.

```
generalSummaryReportQuery.ReportDetailLevelFilter.SetValue rdlfAll

generalSummaryReportQuery.ReportPostingStatusFilter.SetValue _
    rpsfEither
```

At this point in the SDK code you specify layout options in addition to filters. To put a different account in each report column, set `SummarizeColumnsBy` to `scbAccount`; use `scbMonth` to have columns represent months; `scbVendor` puts a different Vendor's data in each column. There are of course other choices, and each corresponds to an entry in the Columns dropdown in a summary report.

You do need to exercise some common sense when you select a method for summarizing the report's columns. Suppose you have already specified `gsrtProfitAndLossStandard` as the general summary report type. If you also select `scbAccount` as the basis to summarize columns, QuickBooks declines to complete the request. The response status message, which you can obtain when you parse the response from QuickBooks (see the next section), states that "The enumerated value 'Account' may not be used in the element 'SummarizeColumnsBy' in this request." The situation is analogous to the report options in the QuickBooks user interface, which do not enable you to put Account in the columns of a Profit & Loss report.

```
generalSummaryReportQuery.SummarizeColumnsBy.SetValue scbAccount
```

The SDK enables you to call for subcolumns, as does the QuickBooks user interface, but it does not enable you to control which subcolumns are returned. Call for subcolumns by setting the `IncludeSubcolumns` value to `True`; suppress them by setting it to `False`. In the user interface, you can specify subcolumns for prior period, year to date, prior year, percent of row and percent of column; there are other choices to show dollar and percent changes.

By contrast, the SDK setting is either `True` or `False` — either return subcolumns or don't. If you do call for subcolumns, you will get prior period, prior year, percent of row, and percent of column. (The OSR is incorrect in this respect: Despite what the OSR states, the SDK *does* return the percent of row subcolumn.)

Similarly, some summary reports (for example, the Inventory Valuation Summary) do not support the use of subcolumns. In fact, your code cannot call for that report and also use the `IncludeSubcolumns` in any fashion, even to set its value to `False`. Doing so causes a status error in a response message from QuickBooks.

It's often a good idea to check the user interface to see what options a given report supports before you specify them in your adaptation of the SDK code. For example, if you open the Inventory Valuation Summary report, you'll see that you do not have access to the usual Columns dropdown at the top of the report; if you then click the Modify Report button, you'll see that you have no options on the Display tab other than the report dates. There's no Advanced button, so you can't specify Active or All for Rows or Columns, and you can't specify a fiscal year, calendar year, or income tax year for the reporting calendar.

Therefore, if your code specifies `gsrtInventoryValuationSummary` as the report type, you cannot also specify a value for any of the following in the SDK code:

- `SummarizeColumnsBy`
- `IncludeSubcolumns`
- `ReportCalendar`
- `ReturnRows`
- `ReturnColumns`
- `ReportBasis`

Continuing the code as supplied by the SDK:

```
generalSummaryReportQuery.IncludeSubcolumns.SetValue True
generalSummaryReportQuery.ReportCalendar.SetValue rcCalendarYear
generalSummaryReportQuery.ReturnRows.SetValue rrActiveOnly
generalSummaryReportQuery.ReturnColumns.SetValue rcActiveOnly
generalSummaryReportQuery.ReportBasis.SetValue rbAccrual
```

Most QuickBooks users will probably want to alter at least some of the earlier five settings:

- Subcolumns can be useful when you really need information about, for example, a prior period or prior year; if you don't need that data, they just clutter up the report and make it harder to interpret the important data.

- Single proprietorships, partnerships, and many small businesses tend to want their reports on a calendar year, but on a cash basis rather than an accrual basis.

- To make sure that reports are laid out in the same way from one period to the next, I usually prefer to specify `rrAll` and `rcAll` for `ReturnRows` and `ReturnColumns`.

```
End Sub
```

The End Sub statement terminates the `BuildGeneralSummaryReportQueryRq` subroutine. Control returns to `DoGeneralSummaryReportfQueryRq`, which passes on the request message that was just built to the subroutine named `ParseGeneralSummaryReportQueryRs`. That subroutine is covered next.

The summary report response message

As with the standard SDK query messages explained in Chapter 11, report response messages have two subroutines that parse the request: one to check aspects of the response such as its status code, and one to actually extract the report data from the response and put it into local variables, into worksheet cells, or into a database table. For the General Summary Report, the subroutines are named `ParseGeneralSummaryReportQueryRs` and `ParseReportRet`.

The `ParseGeneralSummaryReportQueryRs` subroutine is very nearly identical to the corresponding subroutine for the standard query response message explained in Chapter 11, so the textual comments here are very limited. The `ParseReportRet` subroutine is quite different from the version covered in Chapter 11 and there are many more comments on that subroutine in the next section.

```
Public Sub ParseGeneralSummaryReportQueryRs(responseMsgSet As _
    IMsgSetResponse, country As String)

If (responseMsgSet Is Nothing) Then
   Exit Sub
End If

Dim responseList As IResponseList
Set responseList = responseMsgSet.responseList
If (responseList Is Nothing) Then
   Exit Sub
End If
```

Using the SDK code it's possible to "stack" several report requests in a given message. You could, for example, request a P&L standard report, a balance sheet summary report, and a sales by customer summary report in one run. If you do, then the response list has not just one but three responses to handle, and it steps through them using this `For` loop, controlled by a loop counter, the integer variable `i`.

In the main subroutine `DoGeneralSummaryReportQueryRq`, explored earlier in this chapter, you might have used this statement:

```
requestMsgSet.Attributes.OnError = roeContinue
```

Specifying `roeContinue` means that if, in the process of looping through the requests, QuickBooks finds an error, it continues with the next remaining request. If instead you used `roeStop`, QuickBooks stops processing the requests at the one that caused the error and returns control to `ParseGeneralSummaryReportQueryRs`.

```
Dim i As Integer
For i = 0 To responseList.Count - 1
    Dim response As IResponse
    Set response = responseList.GetAt(i)

    If (response.statusCode = 0) Then
```

Dealing effectively with the response status code is particularly important in report response messages. Because you have considerable latitude as to the report's layout in the `BuildGeneralSummaryReportQueryRq` subroutine, there are many more ways to go wrong — at least during the development phase — and therefore you want an effective means of determining the source of the problem.

The SDK's code merely checks to see whether the response status code is 0 (zero). If it is, then the code considers that the data has been obtained properly and it can be extracted by the `ParseReportRet` subroutine.

Early on during the process of developing a new utility based on QuickBooks data, though I make more mistakes than not, and it helps to know as much about them as possible, I use this structure in place of the prior `If` statement:

```
If (response.statusCode <> 0) Then
    MsgBox response.StatusMessage
Else
```

Using this approach, I get an explanatory message if there's an error that QuickBooks identified in the response. The message tells me which statement caused the error, so that I can locate it more quickly. For example: "Cannot use the element 'Return Rows' in this response." When I see this message, I know that either I've picked the wrong summary report, one that doesn't allow me to specify whether or not rows must have activity during the report period, or that I forgot to comment out the `ReturnRows` statement in `BuildGeneralSummaryReportQueryRq`.

On the other hand, if the response status code does equal 0, processing continues without interruption.

To continue with the code as supplied by the SDK, the response type is tested to ensure that it contains the expected detail data. If so, the response type is picked up for subsequent use:

```
If (Not response.Detail Is Nothing) Then
    Dim responseType As Integer
    responseType = response.Type.GetValue
```

The next declaration, provided by the SDK code, is superfluous. An integer variable j is not used in this procedure. I point this out not to carp at the Intuit programmers, but to urge you to bring some skepticism to the table when you work with the SDK's code. It's not guaranteed to be bulletproof. (The declaration of the variable is harmless in the context.)

```
    Dim j As Integer
```

If the type of response is as expected, declare the variable reportRet to contain the detail information in the report response, and pass it to the ParseReportRet subroutine, where the data is actually extracted.

```
        If (responseType = rtGeneralSummaryReportQueryRs) Then
            Dim reportRet As IReportRet
            Set reportRet = response.Detail
            ParseReportRet reportRet, country
            End If
        End If
    End If
    Next i
End Sub
```

The End Sub statement terminates the ParseGeneralSummaryReportQueryRs subroutine. By the time it is reached, the ParseReportRet subroutine will have executed once for each report request. It is explained next.

Finding data in the report

We arrive now at the hard part of processing a report message in QuickBooks: finding the data you're looking for. Here's the problem:

Intuit chose to put its preset reports into categories, as explained at the start of this chapter. The general summary report category consists of 25 reports, the general detail report category has 34 reports.

For many reports, all you have to do is change the report identifier in the subroutine that builds the request message. For example, you could use this specification:

```
generalSummaryReportQuery.GeneralSummaryReportType.SetValue _
    gsrtBalanceSheetStandard
```

Or this one:

```
generalSummaryReportQuery.GeneralSummaryReportType.SetValue _
    gsrtSalesByItemSummary
```

And without changing anything else in the code, you would wind up with a report of the type you specified. The reason is that the code that plucks the values that appear in the report is generalized, and is not specific to the contents of a particular report. To continue the previous example, there's nothing in the code that looks for a Total Current Assets value if you chose to get the standard balance sheet report. Nor is there anything that looks for the average cost of the widgets you sold last quarter, assuming you chose to get a sales by item summary report.

The report parsing code doesn't work by looking for variables that have specific names, as does code that parses a query. Instead, the code obtains information from QuickBooks about each value in a report; for current purposes, it's enough to know that the information includes a row number, a column number, and a value to place in the intersection of each row and column. That value could be an item's average cost or it could be a company's total current assets. It could be a row label that identifies a particular customer's job. The code neither knows nor cares.

That's a blessing and a curse. The blessing part is that in many cases all you have to do is change the report type and run the code again in order to get a different report. That means less coding, both for you, and for the Intuit programmers.

The curse part is that if you're a user rather than a QuickBooks programmer, it can be difficult to find particular values that you're looking for. I don't mean that it's difficult to find them visually. You can always print or display the report on your screen and then you can find the value by looking for it. What I mean by finding particular values is locating them programmatically, using code, so that you can subject them to further processing.

Suppose you determine that a company's total banking assets value is found in row 10, column 2 of the balance sheet summary run at the end of the third quarter. There's no reason that it won't be found in row 15, column 2 of the same report run at the end of the fourth quarter. Other accounts sneak in from period to period, pushing the row with their total amount further down the report. There isn't always an answer to this sort of problem, but sometimes there is.

A moving target

For example, if you always run reports for the same company, or on a small number of company files, as a practical matter you know what account numbers and names are used. If you need to find a value, you can have your code scan the report as it comes back from QuickBooks for an account number, and then do something with the associated dollar amount. You might assign it to a different variable that you hold onto until your code is ready to put it, along with other selected account figures, in a custom report that you've designed.

A static target

Another possibility is that you want to deal with figures that are associated with static labels. For example, it doesn't matter what company file you're working with if you're looking for a dollar figure for total current assets. QuickBooks *always* supplies a row in balance sheets that has the label Total Current Assets. You needn't have any special information about a company's account names or numbers. You just have your code look for Total Current Assets and when it's found you have the row number. Look in a column to the right for the associated value.

The code that is presented next for `ParseReportRet` is exactly as it's supplied by the SDK (more precisely, by the SDK's OSR), with two types of exception (I draw your attention to each as it occurs in the code):

- In some places I move code up from where the SDK places it. This is always to make sure that I have access to the current report row number when I need it to write a report value.

- Whenever I need to supply a statement, not provided by the SDK, to write a value, I insert that statement.

Again, I'll note both exceptions as they arise. There are very few.

With all that as preliminary stage-setting, here's the parsing code itself:

```
Private Sub ParseReportRet(reportRet As IReportRet, country As _
    String)

If (reportRet Is Nothing) Then
    Exit Sub
End If
```

After checking that the complicated `reportRet` variable does contain something, the code continues by getting the information normally placed at the top of the report, including the subtitle, and basis (accrual or cost) report title. I do not use this information and, because it can interfere with subsequent row locations, I do not save it to a worksheet.

Dealing with the report's header area

The first few lines of code are concerned with getting report header information, including the report title, subtitle, and basis.

```
Dim reportTitle1 As String
reportTitle1 = reportRet.ReportTitle.GetValue

Dim reportSubtitle2 As String
reportSubtitle2 = reportRet.ReportSubtitle.GetValue

If (Not reportRet.ReportBasis Is Nothing) Then
    Dim reportBasis3 As ENReportBasis
    reportBasis3 = reportRet.ReportBasis.GetValue
End If
```

Information on the number of rows and columns that the report will occupy is available, but it's not data that I have use for:

```
Dim numRows4 As Long
numRows4 = reportRet.NumRows.GetValue

Dim numColumns5 As Long
numColumns5 = reportRet.NumColumns.GetValue
```

I do have a use for the numColTitleRows6 variable, which is declared and used next. It contains the number of rows that are occupied by the column titles. In most instances, column titles contain values such as dates or account names that occupy one row only. There are some cases in which the column titles require two rows. For example, you might choose a Profit & Loss Standard report and want to display a different column for each customer:job pair. Then, the job name occupies the first of two rows used by the column title and the customer name appears in the second row.

As you'll see, it's important to know how many rows are used by the column titles in order to properly locate most of the subsequent report values, such as dollar amounts.

Picking up and writing the column titles

```
Dim numColTitleRows6 As Long
numColTitleRows6 = reportRet.NumColTitleRows.GetValue
```

A nested loop begins, with the outer loop, indexed by the integer j, executing once for each column in the report while column titles are being processed.

```
Dim j As Integer
For j = 0 To reportRet.ColDescList.Count - 1
    Dim colDesc7 As IColDesc
    Set colDesc7 = reportRet.ColDescList.GetAt(j)
```

The inner loop, indexed by the integer k, executes once for each row occupied by the column title — although as noted, most column titles occupy one row only. On the way through the loop the code picks up the row which is to contain the column title.

```
Dim k As Integer
For k = 0 To colDesc7.ColTitleList.Count - 1
    Dim colTitle8 As IColTitle
    Set colTitle8 = colDesc7.ColTitleList.GetAt(k)
```

The variable named titleRow9 contains the row number to be used.

```
Dim titleRow9 As Long
titleRow9 = colTitle8.titleRow.GetValue

If (Not colTitle8.Value Is Nothing) Then
    Dim value10 As String
    value10 = colTitle8.Value.GetValue
```

The variable `value10` contains the column labels themselves. As the code loops through the report's column titles, it assigns the title for the current column to `value10`.

Here are three statements that I insert into the code as supplied by the SDK, immediately after the current column title has been placed in `value10` by the prior statement:

```
Dim colID12 As Long
colID12 = colDesc7.colID.GetValue
ActiveSheet.Cells(titleRow9, colID12) = value10
```

The first two statements are actually from the SDK code but initially they appear farther down, so I simply move them up. I supply the third statement, beginning with `ActiveSheet`, which writes the value to the worksheet.

The SDK's code captures the columns that are to contain the column titles, but it does so a little too late if there is a two-part title such as customer:job. I move the declaration and assignment statements for `ColID12` up so that they come immediately after `value10` has been assigned its value. (I would declare `ColID12` at the top of the procedure as a matter of programming style, but here I'm complying with the SDK's approach.) With the column known, as well as the row and the value, I can write the title to the worksheet and then complete the loop, if necessary, picking up and writing any other values that form the column title.

```
        End If
    Next k

    Dim colType11 As ENColType
    colType11 = colDesc7.ColType.GetValue
```

The reference to `ColType` fails with some reports, such as the Inventory Valuation Summary. This is a more serious problem with the SDK code than is the superfluous variable declaration mentioned in the previous section.

`ColType` returns information about the type of data in the column: currency values such as debits and credits, date values such as due dates and delivery dates, and so on. I never need to learn what sort of data is in a column — other than by looking at it — so I comment out the next two statements by putting an apostrophe (') at the start of each one. Of course if you want to format the results programmatically, you need this information to decide what number format to apply to the column.

Another way to deal with the problem is to use `On Error Resume Next`. Because doing so means that I don't find out about all errors, I prefer not to use it unless there's an excellent reason. In this case, I prefer to simply comment out the `colDesc7.ColType.GetValue` statement; I just don't need it.

```
    Dim dataType13 As ENdataType
    dataType13 = colDesc7.DataType.GetValue

    Next j
```

The data type is another way to determine the cell format if you want to assign it in code. It applies to the column title, though, not to the type of report data that will follow the title.

Obtaining and writing the report's detail data

The code now starts to process the report's quantitative data. For each row category (for example, Current Assets) the code writes the values for the individual members of that category (for example, specific current asset accounts). When the code has finished writing the detail information, it writes information about the current category's subtotals before it moves on to the next category. The final task is to write total information, if the report has any.

```
If (Not reportRet.ReportData Is Nothing) Then
```

The code enters a loop that executes once for each row of detail information in the report. The loop is indexed by the integer variable m. Several tests are run at the outset to make sure that data exists in each data row.

```
Dim m As Integer
For m = 0 To reportRet.ReportData.ORReportDataList.Count - 1
    Dim orReportData14 As IORReportData
    Set orReportData14 = reportRet.ReportData.ORReportDataList.GetAt(m)

If (Not orReportData14.DataRow Is Nothing) Then
    If (Not orReportData14.DataRow.RowData Is Nothing) Then
        If (Not orReportData14.DataRow.RowData.rowType Is Nothing) Then
```

The row type identifies the category of data in each row. For example, the row type in a Profit & Loss or Balance Sheet report is *account*. In a Customer Balance summary the row type is *name*. You're unlikely to have use for this information.

```
Dim rowType15 As ENrowType
    rowType15 = orReportData14.DataRow.RowData.rowType.GetValue
End If

If (Not orReportData14.DataRow.RowData.Value Is Nothing) Then
```

The next variable to be declared and assigned a value, value16, is the full name of the current row's label. It does not normally appear in the report itself. For example, if you're running a Profit & Loss summary, value16 might equal *40100 · Construction Income:40130 · Labor Income*. In the report itself, you would see only *40130 · Labor Income* on the line, indented to the right of its parent account, *40100 · Construction Income*, which would appear in an earlier row. Because it does not appear in the report, I ignore value16.

```
Dim value16 As String
    value16 = orReportData14.DataRow.RowData.Value.GetValue
End If

End If
```

The code begins a loop to process each column within the current, *m*th report row; the loop is indexed by the integer n.

```
If (Not orReportData14.DataRow.ColDataList Is Nothing) Then
    Dim n As Integer
    For n = 0 To orReportData14.DataRow.ColDataList.Count - 1
        Dim colData17 As IColData
        Set colData17 = orReportData14.DataRow.ColDataList.GetAt(n)

        Dim colID18 As Long
        colID18 = colData17.colID.GetValue
```

ColID18 contains the column number that the loop through columns is currently processing.

```
        If (Not colData17.Value Is Nothing) Then
```

The code at last arrives at the variable that sequentially holds the bulk of the data in the report. Depending on the current location of the inner loop through a row's columns, value19 might contain either a row label or the actual numeric data, such as an account balance or an inventory quantity on hand. If it contains a row label, that label is the child element in a parent:child relationship. That is, if a report's rows are based on customer:jobs, value19 contains the name of the job. A different variable, value23, contains the parent element (see later).

```
            Dim value19 As String
            value19 = colData17.Value.GetValue
        End If
```

Again, you will have little use for the current column's data type:

```
        If (Not colData17.DataType Is Nothing) Then
            Dim dataType20 As ENdataType
            dataType20 = colData17.DataType.GetValue
        End If
```

I move the following two statements up from where the SDK code provides them, so that at the point I acquire a value to write to the worksheet I know which row to write it into.

```
        Dim rowNumber21 As Long
        rowNumber21 = orReportData14.DataRow.rowNumber.GetValue
```

I insert the following statement to write the current value of value19 in a worksheet cell. The statement uses ColID18, obtained 11 statements back, to locate value19 in a column. It uses the current data row's row number, rowNumber21, *adjusted* for the number of rows in the column title (see earlier in this section), to locate value19 in a row:

```
ActiveSheet.Cells(rowNumber21 + numColTitleRows6, colID18) = value19
```

Returning to the code as supplied by the SDK:

```
        Next n
        End If
    End If
    If (Not orReportData14.TextRow Is Nothing) Then
        Dim rowNumber22 As Long
        rowNumber22 = orReportData14.TextRow.rowNumber.GetValue
```

The variable `rowNumber22` contains the row number for the next value variable, `value23`.

```
    If (Not orReportData14.TextRow.Value Is Nothing) Then
        Dim value23 As String
        value23 = orReportData14.TextRow.Value.GetValue
```

I noted earlier that the variable `value19` can contain either a row label or a numeric value. If `value19` contains a row label, it is a child element such as a job name or a subaccount. The parent element is contained in `value23`, and I write it to the worksheet with this inserted statement:

```
    ActiveSheet.Cells(rowNumber22 + numColTitleRows6, 1) = value23
```

Because this label always is put in the first column, I take the unusual step of hard-coding the column number to the constant `1`.

```
    End If
    End If
```

Getting the subtotals

Now the code processes the report's subtotal rows. The structure is very much the same as for the report's detail rows:

```
    If (Not orReportData14.SubtotalRow Is Nothing) Then
    If (Not orReportData14.SubtotalRow.RowData Is Nothing) Then
```

The subtotal row type functions in the same way as the data row type, explained earlier with the variable `rowType15`. You're unlikely to need it.

```
        If (Not orReportData14.SubtotalRow.RowData.rowType Is Nothing) Then
            Dim rowType24 As ENrowType
            rowType24 = orReportData14.SubtotalRow.RowData.rowType.GetValue
        End If
```

I ignore `value25` because it is almost immediately overwritten by `value28`.

```
        If (Not orReportData14.SubtotalRow.RowData.Value Is Nothing) Then
            Dim value25 As String
            value25 = orReportData14.SubtotalRow.RowData.Value.GetValue
        End If
    End If
```

The code enters a loop similar to the loop shown earlier that is indexed by the integer variable n. That loop executed once for each column in the current data row. The next loop, indexed by the integer variable p, loops through the columns in the current subtotal row.

```
If (Not orReportData14.SubtotalRow.ColDataList Is Nothing) Then
```

I move the next two statements up to precede the loop. The variable rowNumber30 contains the row number in which the subtotals are to be written, and I write the actual subtotal figures into that row.

```
Dim rowNumber30 As Long
rowNumber30 = orReportData14.SubtotalRow.rowNumber.GetValue

    Dim p As Integer
    For p = 0 To orReportData14.SubtotalRow.ColDataList.Count - 1
        Dim colData26 As IColData
        Set colData26 = orReportData14.SubtotalRow.ColDataList.GetAt(p)
```

The variable colID27 contains the column number for the current subtotal value.

```
        Dim colID27 As Long
        colID27 = colData26.colID.GetValue

    If (Not colData26.Value Is Nothing) Then
        Dim value28 As String
        value28 = colData26.Value.GetValue
```

I insert the following statement into the code; it writes the current subtotal value to the worksheet, in the subtotal row and current column.

```
    ActiveSheet.Cells(rowNumber30 + numColTitleRows6, colID27) = value28
```

The code from the SDK continues:

```
        End If
            If (Not colData26.DataType Is Nothing) Then
                Dim dataType29 As ENdataType
                dataType29 = colData26.DataType.GetValue
            End If
            Next p
        End If
End If
```

Writing the total values

Finally, the code writes the totals for the report, if the report has totals. Totals in this context are not necessarily grand totals. A balance sheet report, for example, has a total row for assets and a total row for liabilities and equity.

```
If (Not orReportData14.TotalRow Is Nothing) Then
If (Not orReportData14.TotalRow.RowData Is Nothing) Then
If (Not orReportData14.TotalRow.RowData.rowType Is Nothing) Then
   Dim rowType31 As ENrowType
   rowType31 = orReportData14.TotalRow.RowData.rowType.GetValue
End If
```

I ignore value32. It is undocumented and I have never seen the code that assigns it execute.

```
If (Not orReportData14.TotalRow.RowData.Value Is Nothing) Then
   Dim value32 As String
   value32 = orReportData14.TotalRow.RowData.Value.GetValue
End If
End If
If (Not orReportData14.TotalRow.ColDataList Is Nothing) Then
```

I move the next two statements from below the next loop to above it. As the loop moves through the reports columns, I want to write the total values to the worksheet, and that requires that I know which row to write them to.

```
Dim rowNumber37 As Long
rowNumber37 = orReportData14.TotalRow.rowNumber.GetValue
```

This final loop, indexed by the integer variable q, again cycles through the report columns and writes total values into those columns.

```
Dim q As Integer
For q = 0 To orReportData14.TotalRow.ColDataList.Count - 1
   Dim colData33 As IColData
   Set colData33 = orReportData14.TotalRow.ColDataList.GetAt(q)
```

The variable colID34 identifies the column number where the total value should be written.

```
Dim colID34 As Long
colID34 = colData33.colID.GetValue
```

The variable value35 contains first the label for the total row, and on subsequent iterations through the loop it contains the totals themselves.

```
If (Not colData33.Value Is Nothing) Then
   Dim value35 As String
   value35 = colData33.Value.GetValue
```

I insert the following statement to write each total value to the worksheet:

```
ActiveSheet.Cells(rowNumber37 + numColTitleRows6, _
   colID34) = value35
End If
```

```
        If (Not colData33.DataType Is Nothing) Then
            Dim dataType36 As ENdataType
            dataType36 = colData33.DataType.GetValue
        End If
    Next q
    End If
    End If
    Next m
```

When the final instance of the index variable m is completed, the final row of the report has been written.

```
    End If
    End Sub
```

The end of the subroutine passes control back to the calling subroutine, ParseGeneralSummaryReportQueryRs. In turn, that subroutine passes control back to the main subroutine, DoGeneralSummaryReportfQueryRq, and the code ends.

Examining the output of the message

When the code has finished running, you will find that the active Excel worksheet looks something like the one shown in Figure 12.5. The actual appearance of course depends on the filters you set and the layout options you chose.

The report shown in Figure 12.5 was created using the version of the Rock Castle Construction sample file that accompanies QuickBooks 2008. The code used the following settings in the BuildGeneralSummaryReportQueryRq subroutine:

```
Set generalSummaryReportQuery = _
    requestMsgSet.AppendGeneralSummaryReportQueryRq
generalSummaryReportQuery.GeneralSummaryReportType.SetValue _
    gsrtProfitAndLossStandard
generalSummaryReportQuery.ORReportPeriod.ReportPeriod. _
    FromReportDate.SetValue #1/1/2010#
generalSummaryReportQuery.ORReportPeriod.ReportPeriod. _
    ToReportDate.SetValue #12/31/2011#
generalSummaryReportQuery.ReportDetailLevelFilter.SetValue rdlfAll
generalSummaryReportQuery.ReportPostingStatusFilter. _
    SetValue rpsfEither
generalSummaryReportQuery.SummarizeColumnsBy.SetValue scbYear
generalSummaryReportQuery.ReturnRows.SetValue rrAll
generalSummaryReportQuery.ReturnColumns.SetValue rcAll
generalSummaryReportQuery.ReportBasis.SetValue rbAccrual
```

Note that the report, as created in Excel by the SDK's report query code, lacks two of the drawbacks of a report exported to Excel from the QuickBooks user interface:

The result still needs some work if you intend to use it as a report document; the currency values should be formatted, for example.

	A	B	C	D
1		Jan - Dec 10	Jan - Dec 11	TOTAL
2	Ordinary Income/Expense			
3	Income			
4	40100 · Construction Income			
5	40110 · Design Income	3400	36729.25	40129.25
6	40120 · Equipment Rental Income	0	0	0
7	40130 · Labor Income	24820	238352.37	263172.37
8	40140 · Materials Income	43672.23	176180.55	219852.78
9	40150 · Subcontracted Labor Income	119321.5	133858.81	253180.31
10	40199 · Less Discounts given	0	-48.35	-48.35
11	40100 · Construction Income - Other	0	0	0
12	Total 40100 · Construction Income	191213.73	585072.63	776286.36
13	40500 · Reimbursement Income			
14	40510 · Mileage Income	0	0	0
15	40520 · Permit Reimbursement Income	1388	2348.75	3736.75
16	40530 · Reimbursed Freight & Delivery	0	896.05	896.05
17	40500 · Reimbursement Income - Other	0	0	0
18	Total 40500 · Reimbursement Income	1388	3244.8	4632.8
19	Total Income	192601.73	588317.43	780919.16
20	Cost of Goods Sold			
21	50100 · Cost of Goods Sold	5620.85	19446.14	25066.99
22	54000 · Job Expenses			
23	54100 · Bond Expense	0	0	0
24	54200 · Equipment Rental	0	1850	1850
25	54300 · Job Materials	14630.35	157988.97	172619.32
26	54400 · Permits and Licenses	225	700	925
27	54500 · Subcontractors	53350	74367.95	127717.95
28	54520 · Freight & Delivery	0	797.1	797.1
29	54599 · Less Discounts Taken	0	-201.81	-201.81
30	54000 · Job Expenses - Other	0	0	0
31	Total 54000 · Job Expenses	68205.35	235502.21	303707.56
32	Total COGS	73826.2	254948.35	328774.55
33	Gross Profit	118775.53	333369.08	452144.61

No exported formulas

Exported reports have formulas in their subtotals and subtotals. If you cut and paste cells from the exported report to a different worksheet, the formulas usually won't address the correct precedent cells when they're pasted. The report as created using code has values only. This means that you can move values around in the worksheet in any way you wish, without worrying that you're disturbing the results of subtotal and total formulas.

No text formatting

A report exported to Excel has formatted cells, and many of them are formatted as Text. You cannot successfully enter a formula in a cell with the Text format; you first have to reformat it to General, or Currency, or Number, or some other format that processes formulas correctly. The report as created by the use of code does not alter the format that exists in the target worksheet, which will be General for all cells unless you have changed it before running the code.

Index

Index

Index